The Path of the Law and Its Influence
The Legacy of Oliver Wendell Holmes, Jr.

Oliver Wendell Holmes, Jr. (1841–1935), is arguably the most important American jurist of the twentieth century. His essay *The Path of the Law,* first published in 1898, is the seminal work in modern American legal theory. In it, Holmes detailed his radical break with legal formalism and created the foundation for the leading contemporary schools of American legal thought. He was the dominant source of inspiration for the school of legal realism, and his insistence on a practical approach to law and legal analysis laid the basis for the realists' later concentration upon the pragmatic and empirical aspects of law and legal procedures.

This volume brings together some of the most distinguished legal scholars from the United States and Canada to examine competing understandings of *The Path of the Law* and its implications for contemporary American jurisprudence. For the reader's convenience, the essay is reprinted in the Appendix.

The book will be of interest to professionals and students in law and the philosophy, history, economics, and sociology of law.

Steven J. Burton is William G. Hammond Professor of Law at the University of Iowa.

Cambridge Studies in Philosophy and Law

GENERAL EDITOR: Gerald Postema (University of North Carolina, Chapel Hill)

AVISORY BOARD

Jules Coleman (Yale Law School)
Antony Duff (University of Stirling)
David Lyons (Boston University)
Neil MacCormick (University of Edinburgh)
Stephen Munzer (U.C.L.A. Law School)
Philip Pettit (Australian National University)
Joseph Raz (University of Oxford)
Jeremy Waldron (Columbia Law School)

Other books in the series:

Jeffrie G. Murphy and Jean Hampton: *Forgiveness and Mercy*
Stephen R. Munzer: *A Theory of Property*
R. G. Frey and Christopher W. Morris (eds.): *Liability and Responsibility: Essays in Law and Morals*
Robert F. Schopp: *Automatism, Insanity, and the Psychology of Criminal Responsibility*
Steven J. Burton: *Judging in Good Faith*
Jules Coleman: *Risks and Wrongs*
Suzanne Uniacke: *Permissible Killing: The Self-Defense Justification of Homicide*
Jules Coleman and Allen Buchanan (eds.): *In Harm's Way: Essays in Honor of Joel Feinberg*
Warren F. Schwartz (ed.): *Justice in Immigration*
John Fischer and Mark Ravizza: *Responsibility and Control*
R. A. Duff (ed.): *Philosophy and the Criminal Law*
Larry Alexander (ed.): *Constitutionalism*
Robert F. Schopp: *Legal Positivism in American Jurisprudence*
William Edmundson: *Three Anarchical Fallacies: An Essay on Political Authority*
Arthur Ripstein: *Equality, Responsibility, and the Law*
Heidi M. Hurd: *Moral Combat*

The Path of the Law and Its Influence

The Legacy of Oliver Wendell Holmes, Jr.

Edited by

Steven J. Burton

University of Iowa

PUBLISHED BY THE PRESS SYNDICATE OF THE UNIVERSITY OF CAMBRIDGE
The Pitt Building, Trumpington Street, Cambridge, United Kingdom

CAMBRIDGE UNIVERSITY PRESS
The Edinburgh Building, Cambridge CB2 2RU, UK   http://www.cup.cam.ac.uk
40 West 20th Street, New York, NY 10011-4211, USA   http://www.cup.org
10 Stamford Road, Oakleigh, Melbourne 3166, Australia
Ruiz de Alarcón 13, 28014 Madrid, Spain

© Cambridge University Press 2000

This book is in copyright. Subject to statutory exception
and to the provisions of relevant collective licensing agreements,
no reproduction of any part may take place without
the written permission of Cambridge University Press.

First published 2000

Printed in the United States of America

Typeface Times Roman 10/12 pt.   *System* QuarkXPress 4.04   [AG]

A catalog record for this book is available from the British Library

Library of Congress Cataloging in Publication Data
The path of the law and its influence : the legacy of Oliver Wendell Holmes, Jr. /
edited by Steven J. Burton.
p. cm. – (Cambridge studies in philosophy and law)
Includes index.
ISBN 0-521-63006-1 (hb)
1. Law – Philosophy.   2. Holmes, Oliver Wendell, Jr., 1841–1935 – Contributions in
philosophy of law.   I. Burton, Steven J.   II. Series.
K230.H632 .A37 2000
340′.1 – dc21   99-054696

ISBN 0 521 63006 1   hardback

Contents

Acknowledgments		*page* ix
List of Contributors		xi
	Introduction STEVEN J. BURTON	1
1	Law as a Vocation: Holmes and the Lawyer's Path ROBERT W. GORDON	7
2	The Bad Man and the Good Lawyer DAVID LUBAN	33
3	Why Practice Needs Ethical Theory: Particularism, Principle, and Bad Behavior MARTHA C. NUSSBAUM	50
4	Theories, Anti-Theories, and Norms: Comment on Nussbaum DAN M. KAHAN	87
5	Traversing Holmes's Path toward a Jurisprudence of Logical Form SCOTT BREWER	94
6	Holmes on the Logic of the Law THOMAS C. GREY	133
7	Holmes versus Hart: The Bad Man in Legal Theory STEPHEN R. PERRY	158
8	The Bad Man and the Internal Point of View SCOTT J. SHAPIRO	197
9	Oliver Wendell Holmes, Jr., and William James: The Bad Man and the Moral Life CATHARINE PEIRCE WELLS	211

10	Emerson and Holmes: Serene Skeptics SANFORD LEVINSON	231
11	The Path Dependence of the Law CLAYTON P. GILLETTE	245
12	Changing the Path of the Law GILLIAN K. HADFIELD	278
13	Holmes, Economics, and Classical Realism BRIAN LEITER	285
14	Comment on Brian Leiter's "Holmes, Economics, and Classical Realism" JODY S. KRAUS	326

Appendix: The Path of the Law (Oliver Wendell Holmes, Jr.)   333
Index   351

Acknowledgments

Most of the essays in this volume are based on papers given at a Centennial Symposium entitled "The Path of the Law in the Twentieth Century," held at the University of Iowa College of Law on 24–25 January 1997. That conference inaugurated and was funded by the Richard S. Levitt Distinguished Lectureship. We are grateful to Mr. Levitt, whose generosity has the magnitude of a Holmesian enterprise. Gratitude also goes to Dean N. William Hines of the College of Law and Professor Mark Osiel and Ken Kress, all of whom with me were coorganizers of the event. I also thank the research assistants who helped prepare the manuscript for publication, notably Jesse Weiss and David Rojza. Finally, but not least, I thank my assistant, Stephen Rhodes, who kept track of the details and made a smooth-running conference and editorial process possible.

Steven J. Burton
Iowa City, Iowa

Contributors

Scott Brewer is Professor of Law at Harvard University.

Steven J. Burton is William G. Hammond Professor of Law at the University of Iowa.

Clayton P. Gillette is Perre Bowen Professor of Law at the University of Virginia.

Robert W. Gordon is Johnston Professor of Law at Yale University.

Thomas C. Grey is Nelson Bowman Sweitzer and Marie B. Sweitzer Professor of Law at Stanford University.

Gillian K. Hadfield is Associate Professor of Law at the University of Toronto.

Dan M. Kahan is Professor of Law at the University of Chicago.

Jody S. Kraus is Professor and E. James Kelly, Jr. Research Professor of Law at the University of Virginia.

Brian Leiter is Loe A. Worsham Centennial Professor in Law and Professor of Philosophy at the University of Texas at Austin.

Sanford Levinson is W. St. John Garwood and W. St. John Garwood, Jr., Regents Chair in Law at the University of Texas.

David Luban is Frederick J. Haas Professor of Law and Ethics at Georgetown University.

Martha C. Nussbaum is Ernst Freund Professor of Law and Ethics at the Law School, Philosophy Department, and Divinity School of the University of Chicago.

Stephen R. Perry is John J. O'Brien Professor of Law and Professor of Philosophy at the University of Pennsylvania.

Scott J. Shapiro is Assistant Professor of Law at the Benjamin N. Cardozo School of Law of Yeshiva University.

Catharine Peirce Wells is Professor of Law at Boston College Law School.

The Path of the Law and Its Influence

Introduction

STEVEN J. BURTON

Oliver Wendell Holmes, Jr., is, as Thomas Grey put it, "[t]he great oracle of American legal thought."[1] More than any other figure, he lived greatly in the law.

- As a justice of the U.S. Supreme Court for thirty years, he was the "Great Dissenter," whose opinions in *Lochner, Schenk,* and other important cases became and remain the law.
- Some call his 1881 book, *The Common Law,* "[t]he best book on law ever written by an American."[2]
- *The Common Law* opens with the most famous American legal quotation: "The life of the law has not been logic, it has been experience."[3]
- Holmes later developed this theme theoretically in his 1897 essay, *The Path of the Law*.[4] Some call this essay "[t]he best article-length work on law ever written."[5] Others disagree but do not doubt its importance in shaping American legal thought in the twentieth century.

This volume focuses on *The Path of the Law* and its legacy, with due attention to both its context in history and the contemporary relevance of its themes. Thus, some of our contributors place this essay in the intellectual climate of its time; some trace its influence; others discuss one or another of its themes in the light of current thinking.

This volume does not dwell on biography, interesting as Holmes's life was. (Three biographies of him, including an acclaimed one by G. Edward White,[6] have been published in recent years.) Nor do we focus on Holmes's product on the bench or his fascinating correspondence. Our main concern is with the ideas in *The Path of the Law* and their current relevance: to what extent are we, and should we continue to be, Holmesians?

Holmes used an epigrammatic style in *The Path of the Law,* and it is through his epigrams that we can preview the richness of the essay. In many ways it elaborates on the opening passage in his earlier work, *The Common Law,* which contains the most famous Holmes quotation of all:

The life of the law has not been logic: it has been experience. The felt necessities of the time, the prevalent moral and political theories, intuitions of public policy, avowed or unconscious, even the prejudices which judges share with their fellow-men, have had a good deal more to do than the syllogism in determining the rules by which men should be governed.[7]

Holmes's foil here is Christopher Columbus Langdell's then-dominant legal formalism, with its devotion to logic and the syllogism.[8] John M. Zane later described this legal approach in a much-quoted passage:

The judicial power can only adjudicate. It can render a judgment upon a particular concrete set of facts. Every judicial act resulting in a judgment consists of a pure deduction. The figure of its reasoning is the stating of a rule applicable to certain facts, a finding that the facts of the particular case are those certain facts and the application of the rule is a logical necessity. The old syllogism, "All men are mortal, Socrates is a man, therefore he is mortal," states the exact form of a judicial judgment.[9]

In opposition to legal formalism, Holmes (by the most common, though controversial readings) offered both critical and constructive thoughts.

On the critical side, *The Path of the Law* may be most notable for its attack on logic:

[T]he logical method and form flatter that longing for certainty and repose which is in every human mind. But certainty generally is illusion, and repose is not the destiny of man. (466)

To the extent that we too reject formalism, we dwell in Holmes's intellectual shadow. The legal realists did. The critical legal studies movement did. The law-and-economics movement does. To a large extent, then, we are Holmesians.

Holmes's critique, however, sweeps far more broadly than legal formalism. He grounds his attack on a general philosophical claim. Logic, which is necessary to legal formalism, itself cannot be "the life of the law." It cannot determine the law's evolution. He said:

[Logic] is outside the law of cause and effect, and as such transcends our power of thought, or at least is something to or from which we cannot reason. (465)

Here, I think, Holmes expects logic to do something no one should expect it to do.[10] Logic is not something "to or from which" we reason; it is something *with* which we reason, and without which we do not. Perhaps I am drawing too fine a line. But, I think, partly because of Holmes's eloquence on the subject, many of us today suspect logic as such. If so, we are Holmesians.

Holmes deploys a similar skepticism about law's conduct-guiding (normative) content and function:

For my own part, I often doubt whether it would not be a gain if every word of moral significance could be banished from the law altogether. (464)

We should, in his words, "wash [our moral notions] with cynical acid" (462).[11] To a considerable extent, today, we doubt moral claims as such; we think they are relative to culture, or expressions of taste or convention, or situational – and nothing more.[12] To the extent that moral skepticism infuses our thinking about law, again, we are Holmesian.

Consequently, Holmes advanced his famous "bad man" theory:

> If you want to know the law and nothing else, you must look at it as a bad man, who cares only for the material consequences which such knowledge enables him to predict, not as a good one, who finds his reasons for conduct . . . in the vaguer sanctions of inner conscience. (459)

For example,

> The duty to keep a contract at common law means a prediction that you must pay damages if you do not keep it – and nothing else. (462)

So even a promise – a central paradigm of moral obligation – creates no rights or duties. To the extent that today we respect "efficient" contract breaches and the like, we are Holmesian.

To generalize, in Holmes's legal world

> a legal duty so called is nothing but a prediction that if a man does or omits certain things he will be made to suffer in this or that way by judgment of the court, and so [too] of a legal right. (458)

Holmes's denial of law's normativity – of law as a provider of legal or moral rights and duties, of legal or moral reasons for acting one way or another (whether "goodly" or badly) – appears to have been thorough.[13] How many of us, today, deprivilege a judicial opinion's statements and applications of legal rules or principles, its talk of rights and duties? How many of us look to them only as bases for predicting future legal events? I do not know. But, to the extent that we do, we are Holmesian.

Holmes's critiques of legal formalism and law's normativity, without more, could easily be dismissed as nihilistic. Holmes, however, was too much the Establishment Yankee for that. He offers constructive thoughts toward the end of his essay, suggesting that law should be a study of causes and effects, and that legislators should pursue that study in order to formulate effective policies.

Holmes's commitment to theories of cause and effect was philosophical – not a proposal for one perspective on law to accompany other perspectives. He wrote, again philosophically,

> The postulate on which we think about the universe is that there is a fixed quantitative relation between every phenomenon [including law] and its antecedents and consequents. (465)

Recall Holmes's reason for rejecting logic – that it lies outside the laws of cause and effect and therefore transcends our power of thought. Can he really mean that thought directed to any end but causal explanation is not rational?

Here is a related thought, couched in sexist language:

> For the rational study of the law, the black-letter man may be the man of the present, but the man of the future is the man of statistics and the master of economics.[14] (469)

For many of the legal realists (surely not solely because of Holmes), the law is a social phenomenon. We observe it. We describe it and identify the causes of legal events. We are scientists. Thus, realists advocated empirical methods for the study of law. Such methods are now employed, often to great advantage, by the interdisciplinary fields of law-and-society, law-and-history, law-and-psychology, law-and-anthropology, law-and-economics. Chief Judge Richard Posner is the grand man of economic analysis. Holmes's portrait hangs in his office.

There are normative ways of doing economics – and other things, too. Perhaps Holmes would not approve. He seemed to think that we should explain the evolution of the law – the path of the law – through history. We should observe "the life of the law" from experience. Marked from our day, Holmes's prediction about statistics and economics looks prophetic. Such interdisciplinary studies greatly enhance our understanding of legal events.

Holmes, may have thought, however, that actors, like judges and legislators, should see their acts solely as causes of consequences:

> [A] body of law is more rational and more civilized when every rule it contains is referred articulately and definitely to an end which it subserves, and when the grounds for desiring that end are stated. (469)

Empirical studies can help judges, for example, more effectively implement the goals they have adopted. But what would Holmes consider the grounds for endorsing a goal? His skepticism about justice and morals seems to disqualify any notion of better or worse grounds. Rather, "a decision can do no more than embody the preference of a given body in a given time and place" (466). For Holmes, such preferences or desires ground legal policy that, acting on a stage set by tradition, moves the law out from under the dead hand of the past.

Law here seems deeply political – political in the sense of exercising power. To what extent, then, are today's adherents of "critical legal studies," "feminist legal theory," and "critical race theory" – perhaps all of us – in this way Holmesian?

Of course, Holmes was a conservative, whose politics might well have led him to the right, not the left. More important, however, can Holmesians of any political stripe argue in good faith that their views are better or more just than their rivals'? For Holmes, questions like these call for answers based on "our" desires, our clients' desires, or the community's desires, and nothing else.

If so, to return to the beginning of *The Path of the Law*, perhaps law must be a matter of prediction. Accordingly, he wrote what may be the main thesis of the essay:

The prophecies of what courts will do, and nothing more pretentious, are what I mean by the law. (461)

If law is a matter of cause and effect, one would think that predictions are possible. If logic and morals are irrational or irrelevant, because they do not bear on "the life of the law," what else can we do but predict the course? Note that, again, Holmes's grounds are philosophical.

As Robert Gordon reminds us in Chapter 1 of this volume, *The Path of the Law* was delivered as a vocational address at the dedication of Boston University's then-new law-school building. Perhaps Holmes was describing legal practice for future lawyers, who were certain to make lots of predictions. But, ironically, the essay gives no arguments based on experience. It offers, instead, an apparently general and exclusive definition of law. Moreover, of the pages contained in the law books, Holmes wrote: "In these sibylline leaves are gathered prophecies of the past upon the cases in which the axe will fall" (457). Here, it seems, legal rules and principles, in statutes and cases, are not justifications for official action, nor do they prescribe conduct, inside or outside the courthouse. Rather, they are guides to help hired guns shoot straighter, whatever their clients' desires. Nothing else. If this seems implausible, consider these words:

It is to make the prophecies easier to be remembered and to be understood that the teachings of the decisions of the past are put into general propositions and gathered into textbooks, or that statutes are passed in a general form. (458)

For many today, for example, judges' opinions do not even contain prophecies of what later courts will do. Opinions are epiphenomena, rationalizations, just rhetoric or ritual – safe to ignore. To the extent that we believe this, yet again we are Holmesian.

Curiously, *The Path of the Law* ends with inspiring, even mystical, passages. Chief among these, for me, are those expressing suspicion about tradition. Consider:

It is revolting to have no better reason for a rule of law than that, "so it was laid down in the time of Henry IV." It is still more revolting if the grounds upon which it was laid down have vanished long since, and the rule simply persists from blind imitation of the past. (469)

Moreover, Holmes's advice to the law students at Boston University has stood the test of a century well.

The way to gain a [sound] view of your subject is . . . to get to the bottom of the subject itself. The means of doing that are, in the first place, to follow the existing body of dogma into its highest generalizations by the help of jurisprudence; next, to discover from history how it has come to be what it is; and, finally, so far as you can, to consider the ends which the several rules seek to accomplish, the reasons why those ends are desired, and what is given up to gain them, and whether they are worth the price. (476)

Read liberally, this is a grand view of legal study, the vision of a great mind, realized in Holmes's long lifetime as in no other American's. He advises students of the law – including professors, practitioners, judges, and observers – to aim high, knowing we will fall short of perfection.

For some of us, the fun and satisfaction of learning suffice to motivate. For others, however, Holmes concludes his essay with more Holmesian advice: "To an imagination of any scope, the most far-reaching form of power is not money, it is the command of ideas" (478). No American's legal ideas have been more far-reaching than Holmes's. This volume pays tribute to him in his most coveted currency.

Notes

1. Thomas C. Grey, "Holmes and Legal Pragmatism," *Stanford Law Review* 41 (1989):787, 787.
2. Richard A. Posner, "Introduction," in *The Essential Holmes: Selections from the Letters, Speeches, Judicial Opinions, and Other Writings of Oliver Wendell Holmes, Jr.,* ed. Richard A. Posner (Chicago: University of Chicago Press, 1992), x.
3. O. W. Holmes, Jr., *The Common Law,* ed. M. Howe (Boston: Little, Brown, [1881] 1963), 5.
4. Oliver Wendell Holmes, Jr., "The Path of the Law," *Harvard Law Review* 10 (1897):457–78 (cited hereafter parenthetically in the text by page number). The text of the essay is reprinted in the Appendix with star paging to the original article and two modern editions.
5. Posner, "Introduction."
6. G. Edward White, *Justice Oliver Wendell Holmes: Law and the Inner Self* (New York: Oxford University Press, 1993).
7. Holmes, *Common Law.*
8. See Thomas C. Grey, "Langdell's Orthodoxy," *University of Pittsburgh Law Review* 45 (1983):1.
9. M. Zane, "German Legal Philosophy," *Michigan Law Review* 16 (1918): 288, 337–38.
10. For an intense analysis of this issue, see Scott Brewer's essay, Chapter 5 of this volume.
11. Brian Leiter explores Holmesian "realism" in Chapter 13 of this volume.
12. Martha C. Nussbaum responds to this Holmesian concern in her essay, Chapter 3 of this volume.
13. See H. L. A. Hart, *The Concept of Law* (Oxford: Clarendon Press, 1961), and the essays by Stephen Perry (Chapter 7) and Catharine Peirce Wells (Chapter 9) in this volume.
14. Clayton P. Gillette's essay (Chapter 11 of this volume), lies in this Holmesian tradition.

1

Law as a Vocation: Holmes and the Lawyer's Path

ROBERT W. GORDON*

In Louisa May Alcott's *Eight Cousins,* first published in 1875, a young woman called Rose is being given a conventional girl's upbringing by her aunts, in a dark and stuffy old mausoleum of a house. Then Uncle Alec becomes Rose's new guardian. He strides into the house, throws open the curtains and the windows, and hustles his ward into the outdoors. He throws out her old confining clothes and buys her new ones, changes her diet, and, with his vigorous scientific intellect, begins helping her to clear her mind of received opinions. With the very first sentence of *The Path of the Law* – "When we study law we are not studying a mystery but a well-known profession" – we know Uncle Alec has arrived and that the old Victorian mansion will never be the same again.

I. The Nineteenth-Century Vocational Address

Holmes's speech is all the more visibly iconoclastic because it fits into a familiar nineteenth-century form. The lawyers of Victorian America cherished the vocational address. At law school commencements, gatherings of the bar, or memorial services for colleagues, the lions of bench and bar improved the occasion with speeches on the lawyer's calling and his duty to that calling. Alien though these hundreds of orations are to the modern ear, repellent at times in their self-importance and hypocrisy, they reveal something admirable, too: a profession struggling to span the abyss between its high-sounding ideals and what so often seem its dull, trivial, and even sordid quotidian practices, to express an idea of law as a calling that could lead a man to honor, social usefulness, and self-respect.

---

* I am grateful for the comments of Thomas Grey, David Luban, Mark Osiel, Tanina Rostain, and Richard Thornburgh on earlier versions of this essay, for Martha Nussbaum's advice on Stoic ideas in the formation of nineteenth-century professional identity, for Wendie Schneider's help in unearthing vocational speeches, and for the criticism and encouragement of participants in the conference "The Path of the Law in the Twentieth Century" at the University of Iowa College of Law in January 1997.

The standard address points the novice toward a high road of practice and warns him off a low road. Law, as ideally practiced, was a science of principles. Principles were generated by induction from particulars, decided cases, which vaguely partook – by proximity as it were – of the traditional authority of top–down natural law principles, as well as of the authority of modern science. Cases also drew their authority from the common law, that slow, organic growth that gradually adapts to changing social needs and circumstances. Science was to be enhanced by liberal learning: the ideal lawyer was educated both in broader legal fields, for comparative and historical perspective – the civil law, the Roman law, and the law of nations – and in liberal studies outside the law: classics, literature, the history of ancient and modern republics.

Besides learning, the upright lawyer possessed character acquired by experience, especially the experience of being entrusted with his clients' money and secrets, and the responsibility of counseling people in trouble and perplexity. "He sees domestic tragedies and domestic comedies – the effects of prosperity and adversity – the home countenance and the mask of society – the open and closed chambers in men's bosoms."[1] These personal attainments translate into social virtues. By training and experience, the lawyer is peculiarly fitted to assume the role of trustee of the basic framework of society – the system of rules that protects individual rights, and the system of legal relations and duties that protects organic social bonds. As an advocate, the lawyer helps clients to vindicate their legal rights. But the lawyer also represents the law, the system of principles, rules, rights, and obligations that holds the social order together. "This leadership of the lawyer is not accidental nor enforced, but natural and resulting from his relations to society. That which binds society together, and makes possible its successes and its blessings, is the mystic force which we call 'law.'"[2] He educates and guides clients in the performance of their legal obligations. He is an expert adviser to the judiciary in the interpretation of the laws and (through law reform movements and institutions) to the legislature. Through judicial review the private lawyer is connected with the highest functions of statesmanship, even the bringing of majority will before the altar of Constitutional principle.[3]

The lawyer might well crown his career by becoming a judge himself and was of all professionals most likely, as well as most fitted, to become a legislator; but even as a private lawyer, he was a statesman. "[W]hile lawyers, and because we are lawyers, we are statesmen."[4] In his key social roles – vindicator of rights and upholder of social order – the ideal lawyer is a mediator between extremes of ideology and faction. As a private lawyer, he protects the rights of individual property and liberty from the overbearing forces of the state and other private interests. As a statesman – judge, legislator, official adviser to courts, legislatures and officials, civic activist, and counselor to clients – his job is to ward off the twin dangers of populism (leveling and redistributive impulses) and special interests (demands by the powerful on the state for monopolies, privileges, subsidies and exemptions, and corruption of courts and officials to obtain them) that threaten those rights.[5] He is a conservator of legal institutions and principles, but not a reactionary; a reformer equipped to adapt law to keep pace with changing social needs and views, but not a radical. Above all – by virtue of his ability to see matters from all sides but remain independent from all partisan factions and interests – the lawyer may serve as a peacemaker and compromiser, a calmer of personal and social passions, who counsels overexcited clients to avoid litigation and overheated social movements to refrain from destroying the organic social bonds of custom, reinforced by law, that hold the social fabric – and the national union – together.

These addresses admonish as well as celebrate. They point the finger at the all too prevalent departures from the ideal, the lawyers who bring the bar into deserved disrepute. The regular villains fall into three types. (1) the unscientific lawyer, incapable of statesmanship because epistemologically challenged: the mere "case lawyer" or "book lawyer, the man of forms, and cases, and black-letter lore, and of nothing else,"[6] who can argue only by close analogy and pile up citations favoring his partisan cause – unable even to perceive the broader principles at issue in his cases. (2) The lawyer who is in the profession only to make money. Lawyers' "obligations as citizens, professional dignity, personal character, the refinements of society and home – of what value are they to those whose life, whose passion, whose God, is GOLD, and the political emolument and sensual pleasures which it secures?" asked the New Jersey lawyer Joseph Jackson in 1859. "Avarice, more than all other causes combined, defeats justice, impairs the usefulness of the bar, and sinks too many of its followers almost to the level of Satan himself."[7] (For instructive contrast, the speakers pointed with lugubrious relish to lawyers who amassed fortunes but left no record of accomplishment, unlike lawyers who cared little for money and died poor but acquired honor and reputation.) (3) Finally – and perhaps most surprising, to the modern ear – the lawyer is reproached who allows himself to become the mere unthinking instrument of clients' passions and partisan ends, however senseless or unworthy. Lawyers who argued that the private bar served justice and other important public purposes by vindicating their clients' private rights had, of course, to deal with the reality that some clients seek to avoid justice or wreak injustice upon others. The dominant solution of modern lawyers to this dilemma, the doctrine of unswerving partisan loyalty, was roundly rejected. The famous admonition of Lord Brougham to the effect that the lawyer must fight for his client, heedless of any other interest in the universe,[8] was often quoted, but invariably with disapproval. Lawyers were much more likely to agree with Simon Greenleaf:

While our aid should never be withheld from the injured or the accused, let it be remembered, that [. . .] our duties are not concentrated in conducting an appeal to the law; – that we are not only lawyers, but citizens and men; – that our clients are not always the best judges of their own interests, – and that having confided these interests to our hands, it is for us to advise to that course, which will best conduce to their permanent benefit, not merely as solitary individuals, but as men connected with society by enduring ties.[9]

No one argued that lawyers were morally unaccountable for clients' conduct. On the contrary,

If his client presses [the lawyer] . . . [to] direct him as to future conduct, he must, as a moral and accountable being, point that client's feet into paths that lead to justice, not toward wrong and oppression . . . Should he [. . .] favor the unjust schemes of a bad client, he becomes equally guilty with him; as much as if they two had originally conspired in malicious scheming.[10]

The stakes, as pictured in these addresses, were extremely high, the alternatives stark. If law was not practiced as an "elevated science" and social trusteeship, it was a "pernicious and driving trade."[11] "Better than any other . . . position or business," said Rufus Choate, in one of the best-known and most-quoted speeches, the lawyer's "profession enables him to *serve the State*," and it is this and only this that

raises [law] from a mere calling by which bread, fame and social place may be earned, to a function by which the republic may be served. It raises it from a dexterous art and a subtle and flexible science – from a cunning logic, a gilded rhetoric, and an ambitious learning, wearing the purple robe of the sophists and letting itself to hire – to the dignity of almost a department of government – an instrumentality of the State for the well-being and conservation of the State.[12]

To be sure, the power of these vocational addresses to command a modern reader's sympathy has its limits. Some of them are the wails of wounded aristocrats fallen among a democratic people who are inexplicably unimpressed with polish and refinement; or of wounded intellectuals among a commercial people who want law to help them get on with business, without much caring about its theory and history; or just of elite lawyers anxious to differentiate their status from – and deflect public criticism onto – lower-order practitioners. And one often suspects that the reform effort too often begins and ends with the ceremonial speeches themselves; that is, that they are Sunday sermons for wealthy Anglicans, uplifting the worshipers by the reminder that they are vaguely connected to a higher world of thought and action but need take no action except to savor the connection.[13] More subtly still, one could see the vocational addresses as performing the function that Perry Miller attributed to Puritan jeremiads, which were

more than a hypocritical show, more than a rhetorical exercise. They were necessary releases, they played a vital part in the social evolution because they ministered to a psychological grief and a sickness of the soul that otherwise could find no relief . . . They were social purgations, enabling men to make a public expiation for sins that they could not avoid committing, freeing their energies to continue working with the forces of change. [. . .] [The people] knew inwardly that they had betrayed their fathers, or were betraying them; they paid homage to them in the ceremony of humiliation and thus regained something of their self-respect, though paradoxically they had to acquire it by confessing their iniquities.[14]

II. Holmes the Destroyer

The Path of the Law is also a vocational address, but one in which Holmes makes it clear he has come to clean house. Swinging his modernizing broom, Holmes attacks the older tradition as so many cobwebs. Law is "not a mystery but a well-known profession" – *whisk*. A profession is just a job "people will pay" others to do[15] – *whisk*. What lawyers are paid for is the "business" of showing clients how to avoid "danger" from the state – *whisk, whisk*. He is at special pains to demystify the law by de-moralizing it – to arrive at what he calls a "businesslike understanding of the matter."

A legal duty so called is nothing but a prediction that if a man does, or omits certain things he will be made to suffer in this or that way by judgment of the court – and so of a legal right . . . If you want to know the law and nothing else, you must look at it as a bad man, who cares only for the material consequences which such knowledge enables him to predict.[16]

He goes out of his way to endorse the view of "our friend, the bad man":

I am much of his mind. The prophecies of what the courts will do in fact, and nothing more pretentious, are what I mean by the law. ("Path," 393)

and to express outright hostility to the use of moral language to define legal liabilities:

If you commit a tort, you are liable to pay a compensatory sum. If you commit a contract, you are liable to pay a compensatory sum unless the promised event comes to pass, and that is all the difference. But such a mode of looking at the matter stinks in the nostrils of those who think it advantageous to get as much ethics into the law as they can. (394)

I often doubt whether it would not be a gain if every word of moral significance could be banished from the law altogether . . . We should lose the fossil records of a good deal of history and the majesty got from ethical associations, but by ridding ourselves of an unnecessary confusion we should gain very much in the clearness of our thought. (396)
Whisk, whisk, whisk.

Once the law's claim to be a moral science is out in the trash, next to go is its claim to be a logical one – "the notion that a given system, ours, for instance, can be worked out like mathematics from some general axioms of conduct," that "if [we were] doing [our] sums right," we would get right answers (396). In fact, "[m]ost of the things we do, we do for no better reason than that our fathers have done them or that our neighbors do them, and the same is true of a larger part than we suspect of what we think" (398). "Behind the logical form lies a judgment as to the relative worth and importance of competing legislative grounds, often an inarticulate and unconscious judgment, it is true, and yet the very root and nerve of the whole proceeding" (397). The main product of this delusion, that the habitual is the logical, turns out to be the most cherished object in the entire mausoleum, the fundamental law of the Constitution. What nineteenth-century judges had been elaborating as doctrines emanating from basic principles of liberty and property, Holmes contemptuously describes as the fear of "socialism" felt by "the comfortable classes of the community . . . generalized into acceptance of the economic doctrines which prevailed about fifty years ago" (398).

History and tradition are the next to go. For Holmes, the main reason to study history is that it disabuses us of our reverence for tradition, by revealing that traditional forms are often irrational "survivals" of practices rooted in the power politics and dominant assumptions of past times – perpetuated into our own by blind imitation, distortion and overgeneralization, and above all by spurious rationalization – the invention and reinvention of novel policy rationales for outdated doctrines. Holmes recommends the study of history primarily to cure the bar of its backward-looking orientation. "It is revolting to have no better reason for a rule of law than that so it was laid down in the time of Henry IV" (399). Once we are rid of blind reverence for the past, he looks forward to the time when "the part played by history in the explanation of dogma shall be very small" (402–3).

But the most dramatic contrast between *The Path of the Law* and the standard vocational speech is not in what is mocked but what is missing. Nowhere here is there any reference to the lawyer as minister of justice or trustee for his clients or for society at large – the lawyer as protector of rights, as force for conservative order or as far-seeing legal statesman, as mediator between classes or between capitalism and democracy. After everything Holmes has said of the law's empty chatter about morals and rights and duties, its purported sanctification by tradition and the teleology of progress, and its purported rational content as a deduction from conceptual axioms, this omission is hardly surprising. He would seem to have shredded all of the fancy costumes in which nineteenth-century lawyers tried to dress up their profession.

III. Holmes the Creator

But if everything musty in the old house is to go, how will the house be refurnished? When Uncle Alec has finished clearing Rose's mind of cant, what does he encourage her to learn instead? The most obvious candidates to replace the lawyer as moralist and curator of worn-out traditions, as mouther of high-sounding but imprecise generalizations, as unselfconscious retailer of outmoded prejudices and policies, were clearly these: the lawyer as neutral predictor of the output of courts, and the lawyer as policy analyst and utilitarian social engineer. Thus, at any rate, have most subsequent generations – with varying degrees of approval and horror – read the message of *The Path of the Law*.

Probably the most common reading of the speech is that it sets forth a purely positivist theory of law – a deflated, demoralized, "disenchanted" view (to use Max Weber's term) of the legal system. To those who like this view, the "bad man" is just the rational man – *homo law-and-economicus* – who treats all legal rules as prices on conduct, risks of sanctions to be discounted by the probability of enforcement, data for cost–benefit analysis. On this reading, Holmes anticipates the great shift – not completed until nearly our own time – in professional self-conceptions from exemplary character and social trusteeship to instrumental expertise.[17] To less approving eyes, Holmes recommends that the lawyer regard the legal system in a wholly alienated and instrumental fashion – not as a set of norms established for common membership in a political community, nor as an attempt to realize (however imperfectly) ideals of justice or social integration – but simply as random and arbitrary outputs of state force, which are opportunities for or obstacles to realizing his client's self-interested projects. To Holmes's fiercest critics, he seems to be arguing that state-enforced Might is Right.

A second interpretation views *The Path of the Law* as promoting a more active and constructive task than that of predicting the-law-as-it-is: the task of making conscious and articulate the social purposes that legal rules have been fashioned to serve, to assess through study of actual effects how effectively those purposes are served in actuality, and to reform the law to make it serve those purposes more efficiently. Liberal Progressives took this as encouragement to expose the reactionary and obsolete social and economic theory ("Mr. Herbert Spencer's Social Statics," in the memorable phrase of Holmes's *Lochner* dissent) lurking in Constitutional principles and as support for their program of redistributive regulation. More recently, neoclassical legal economists have taken it as prefiguring their program of restating the latent functions of law as promoting "efficiency" and reforming such law as is inefficient.

Yet although the neutral predictor and policy engineer are obviously elements of Holmes's vision, they are only pieces of a complex whole. Holmes in *The Path of the Law* is not putting forward a theory of law, but rather (to paraphrase Wallace Stevens) "thirteen ways of looking at" law – sketches of approaches to the legal system that present it in a new light.

Take the "bad man" and the "prediction theory." The latter cannot possibly be a theory that law has no moral content. "The law is the witness and external deposit of our moral life," Holmes says in the *Path of the Law* (392), and elsewhere makes clear that the law of any age is saturated with "prevalent moral and political theories" as well as "[t]he felt necessities of the time . . . intuitions of public policy, avowed or unconscious, even the prejudices which judges share with their fellow-men."[18] Nor can this plausibly be supposed to be a realist's description of law practice. The lawyer as neutral predictor is too neutral for belief. He may not be a moralist, but he is not an advocate or strategist either. As Holmes, who had practiced law for fourteen years, must have been aware, the corporate lawyer of the 1880s and 1890s was, even less than his present-day counterpart, a passive analyst of the law: he was an active shaper of it, a drafter of bills favoring his clients and a lobbyist to push them through legislatures; a bargainer with regulators, flatterer of judges, seducer of juries; a skilled artificer of law and fact, crafting narratives and arguments to influence interpretations; a strategic manipulator of procedural tactics designed to inflict costs and delays on adversaries.[19]

More fundamentally, the "bad man" may be amoral himself, but the lawyer hoping to advise him cannot, as a practical matter, ignore the fact that the legal system incorporates many moral norms and judgments and that legal decision makers may be morally outraged by the bad man's conduct – that a jury may see his case as an occasion to "send corporate America a message" or treat a deliberate and opportunistic breach of contract as more reprehensible and requiring a severer sanction than an inadvertant breach. To the extent that the legal positivist aims at an accurate description of the content of the legal system, he must ignore the positivist who wants to separate law from morals. If he tries to "understand the law and nothing else," he will never understand the law in operation.

It makes more sense to read Holmes as recommending a heuristic for a very limited purpose: when analyzing legal doctrine, which is only part of a modern lawyer's job, disregard all of the moral-sounding phrases in legal language – "malice," "fault," "intention," "right," "duty"; dig beneath those phrases to find out what for each rule is the set of circumstances that triggers the liability and what sanctions actually attach; then redescribe the rule in language that avoids the imprecision of the moralistic phrasing. The bad man turns out to be one of Uncle Alec's practical jokes – a deliberate provocation, a device to shock the audience out of a complacent and into an enquiring state of mind.

IV. *The Path of the Law* and the Profession Today

In our own day, of course, a wholly de-moralized view of the lawyer's role has achieved wide currency. In this view, which began to creep into professional rhetoric around 1900 but was not firmly established until very recently, the practice of law is almost completely privatized, shorn of all of its public functions save a thin residue of the "officer-of-the-court" duty of candor to tribunals. Law as a system of public values is no longer supposed to concern private lawyers in their ordinary work: those public aims are relegated to the specialized province of policymakers and judges. It concerns private lawyers only in their optional after-hours *pro bono* efforts. Lawyers and their work are often evaluated by a strictly commercial metric. Public boasts made by managers of great law firms, assessments of lawyers by the legal press, surveys of lawyers asking which have the highest status in the profession – all rank firms by the income they generate for partners, and rank lawyers by the status of their clients and by their wins for clients, regardless of how dubiously achieved and of damage to others and the public.

But it would be wrong to identify Holmes with the privatized and commercialized ethic of (a significant segment of) today's profession. The tough talk that opens *The Path of the Law* means to puncture the pompous balloons of a rhetorical tradition, but not for the purpose of disenchanting the lawyer's calling, of which, as we shall see, Holmes actually held a highly romantic, indeed Quixotic, view. The initial deflation is meant to bring listeners back down to reality, have them feel the hard and dirty ground beneath them for a moment – but then to raise their eyes to a farther horizon. Holmes's ultimate purpose is not to deflate, but, no less than the tradition he mocks, to exalt the lawyer's calling – to point to a mode and spirit of engagement with law that lifts it above the humdrum and sordid. This was one of his abiding preoccupations.

> How can the laborious study of a dry and technical system, the greedy watch for clients and practice of shopkeeper's arts, the mannerless conflicts over often sordid interests, make out a life? . . . They are the same questions that meet you in any form of practical life. If a man has the soul of Sancho Panza, the world to him will be Sancho Panza's world; but if he has the soul of an idealist, he will make – I do not say find – his world ideal.[20]

Holmes fought against the reduction of the goal of law practice to making money by his characteristic method of frankly acknowledging the prevalence and even the validity of commercial motives but then appealing to something beyond them:

> The object of ambition, power, generally presents itself nowadays in the form of money alone. Money is the most immediate form, and a proper object of desire. "The fortune," said Rachel, "is the measure of the intelligence." That is a good text to waken people out of a fool's paradise. But, as Hegel says, "It is in the end not the appetite, but the opinion, which has to be satisfied." To an imagination of any scope the most far-reaching form of power is not money, it is the command of ideas . . . We cannot all be Descartes or Kant, but we all want happiness. And happiness, I am sure from having known many successful men, cannot be won simply by being counsel for great corporations and having an income of fifty thousand dollars. An intellect great enough to win the prize needs other foods besides success.[21] ("Path," 405–6)

The problem for Holmes is that, as we have seen, he has placed skeptical roadblocks across all of the generally recommended paths for those who would seek meaning and value in the lawyer's work. For him, the notion that the search for universal scientific laws will ultimately reveal a cosmic moral order is a pathetic anthropomorphic conceit. "We are in the universe, not it in us." Nor can legal principles, rightly understood, be regarded as organic social bonds holding society together: rather, they express conflicting forces locked in perpetual struggle. Rights are only what significant social blocs, "the crowd," are "willing to die for." Legal tradition is not a source of experience perfected or principles maturing over time, but a mass of survivals maintained through fictions and confusions, at best worth keeping only because people have come to rely on them. There seems little scope in such a world for the lawyer-statesman.

V. The Lawyer's Vocation

Nevertheless, in *The Path of the Law* and other speeches and writings Holmes consistently advances quite a redemptive view of the lawyer's calling in a disenchanted world. He puts forward two broad ideal conceptions of the calling, envisioning the lawyer as (1) the soldier, or "jobbist," to use Holmes's own term, and (2) the "thinker," or scientist, exploring new territory. The second category must be broken down into several others: the "abstract" or "impractical" student of the law, on the one hand, and several "practical" kinds of thinker, on the other, including the legal-doctrinal theorist, the critical legal historian, and the master of social science (or the "science of legislation," to use a term then in general use). Finally, there is the superthinker, or great speculative philosopher, who, ironically, ultimately exercises the greatest practical influence of all.

A. *The Soldier or Jobbist*

The soldier, or "jobbist," is a familiar figure out of the Puritan ethic, the man who labors humbly in his calling, subordinating himself to the *techne* (specialist craft ethic) of that calling. ("Jobbist" is Holmes's own coinage, from his "imaginary society of the jobbists, who were free to be egotists or altruists in the usual Saturday half-holiday provided they were neither while at work."[22]) His is what Hegel called "the heroism of dumb service," like that of the soldier who finds a secret existential satisfaction in the meticulous performance of the most trivial details of army routine. Holmes liked to quote the Anglican poet George Herbert: "Who sweeps a room as [in] Thy [cause] / Makes that and the action fine."[23]

It seems to me ... that the rule for serving our fellow-men ... that the beginning of self-sacrifice and of holiness – is to do one's task with one's might. If we do that, I think we find that our motives take care of themselves. We find that what may have been begun as a means becomes an end in itself; that self-seeking is forgotten in labors ... ; that our personality is swallowed up in working [to] ends outside ourselves.[24]

Holmes famously made this jobbist ethic into the keystone of his conception of the judge as "the supple tool of power" whose job is to serve existing precedent "simply because it exists"; "if my fellow-citizens want to go to Hell I will help them"[25] by faithfully carrying out their foolish and self-defeating legislation.[26] The practitioner's connection to the ideal is through his participation in "the body of our jurisprudence . . . to which the least may make their contribution and inscribe it with their names. The glory of lawyers, like that of men of science, is more corporate than individual. Our labor is an endless organic process."[27]

> You argue a case in Essex. And what has the world outside to do with that, you say. Yet you have confirmed or modified or perhaps have suggested for the first time a principle which will find its way into the reports and from the reports into the text books and so into the thought of the common law, and so into its share into governing the conduct of civilized men.[28]

Of course if, like Holmes, you are convinced that the "endless organic process" is a Darwinian struggle of powers, interests, and unconscious instincts clawing at one another for dominance and survival, the value of being part of the process consists only in being a living link in the food chain, chewing or being chewed. It is one thing to aspire to be Darwin; it is another to aspire to be one of Darwin's specimens. Holmes repeatedly seems to confuse the two. While praising a well-known Boston railroad lawyer for sticking to his profession instead of seeking a wider fame in public service, he observes:

> The external and immediate result of an advocate's work is but to win or lose a case. But remotely what the lawyer does is to establish, develop or illuminate rules which are to govern the conduct of men for centuries; to set in motion principles and influences which shape the thought and action of generations which know not by whose command they move. The man of action has the present, but the thinker controls the future; his is the most subtile [subtle], the most far-reaching power. His ambition is the vastest, as it is the most ideal.[29]

B. The Thinker or Scientist

"The men whom I should be tempted to commemorate would be the originators of transforming thought. They often are half obscure, because what the world pays for is judgment, not the original mind."[30] One cannot help but suppose that this curious composite, the lawyer who works on little cases but thinks transforming thoughts about them, fits one lawyer only: Holmes himself, condemned to a state-court docket of trivial miscellaneous causes, almost unknown outside Massachusetts, save to a handful of cosmopolitan intellectuals in England and Germany who give him his due as an original legal thinker and historian.

Holmes says: "The law is the calling of thinkers."[31] But of course the ordinary lawyer is not a thinker. Holmes's own practice experience gave him a distaste for any but the most intellectual aspects of an ordinary lawyer's work. "I hate business and dislike practice, apart from arguing cases."[32] His advice on connecting law practice with the ideal rarely permitted the lawyer just to labor humbly in his calling. It required a more heroic intellectual commitment. To the extent that *The Path of the Law* is a vocational address, that higher aspiration is its major theme: the lawyer as thinker or scientist.

Holmes's strongest praise, as David Luban has stressed in his fascinating essay on Holmes and Nietzsche,[33] was always reserved for activities directed toward no practical end (an embarrassment to those who would like to portray Holmes as primarily a utilitarian policy wonk). As he says in another of his major speeches, "Law in Science and Science in Law,"

> I by no means share that morality which finds in a remoter practice the justification of philosophy and science. I do not believe that we must justify our pursuits by the motive of social well-being . . . The man of science in the law is not merely a bookworm . . . I doubt if there is any more exalted form of life than that of a great abstract thinker, wrapt in the successful study of problems to which he devotes himself, for an end which is . . . simply to feed the deepest hunger and use the greatest gifts of his soul.[34]

One way of pursuing the legal vocation in the grand manner, therefore, is as a disinterested scientist, studying the law historically, as a "great anthropological document," to "discover what ideals of society have been strong enough to reach that final form of expression . . . to study it as an exercise in the morphology and transformation of human ideas."[35] Holmes himself had spent all of his spare time in his years of practice on just such an "impractical" project, the historical sections of his book *The Common Law*. But the moment he issues this ringing scholar's manifesto, he takes some of it back – just as he resigned his post as a Harvard Law School professor a few months after taking it up, in order to accept a judgeship:

> But after all the place for a man who is complete in all his powers is in the fight. The professor, the man of letters, gives up one-half of his life that his protected talent may grow and flower in peace. But to make up your mind at your peril upon a living question, for purposes of action, calls upon your whole nature . . . [Though I appreciate the disinterested scientific study of the law,] of course I think, as other people do, that the main ends of the subject are practical.[36]

G. Edward White's fine biography of Holmes has plausibly speculated that he was impelled to describe the activity of judging – which most practicing lawyers regard as somewhat removed from the fray – as a life of action on the battlefield because he felt guilty about surviving the Civil War and quitting his term of service early, while many of his friends died.[37] Perhaps he felt impelled as well to justify quitting practice and its battlefields, the clash of adversary advocates and business rivals, for the more contemplative work of the judge. Whatever may have been his personal motives, he insisted repeatedly that most of the forms of intellection applied to law are highly practical ones.

As noted, there are (at least) three types of practical lawyer-thinker in *The*

Path of the Law: the legal-doctrinal theorist, the historian, and the scientific policy analyst, to list them in the chronological order in which they dominated Holmes's own persona in the evolution of his ideas. The job of the doctrinal theorist is to organize and rationalize the body of existing common law doctrine into as broad generalizations as can be found. "Jurisprudence, as I look at it, is simply law in its most generalized part. Every effort to reduce a case to a rule is an effort of jurisprudence . . . One mark of a great lawyer is that he sees the application of the broadest rules" ("Path," 403). The reason why the lawyer must expel moral concepts from legal analysis and must shun merely "dramatic" classifications of rules such as those for "Railroads or Telegraphs" (403) in favor of more fundamental conceptions is that the narrow categories hinder, rather than help, the lawyer to predict the consequences of legal rules. "[M]orals are imperfect social generalizations expressed in terms of feeling, and . . . to make the generalizations perfect we must wash out the emotion and get a cold head."[38] Unlike his contemporary C. C. Langdell, Holmes did not think that law was a "science" in the sense that once one has induced the general laws or principles one can then deduce from them all possible applications: for Holmes law was historically contingent and changing, shot through with conflicting and contradictory lines of precedent and principle. But he did believe in generalization as a pragmatic aid to prediction – and that both lawyers and judges would be better at their jobs (getting the law "right," in the sense of achieving consistency with other applications) if they made more and better use of the tools of theory:[39]

Theory is the most important part of the dogma of the law, as the architect is the most important man . . . in the building of a house . . . [Theory] is not to be feared as unpractical, for, to the competent, it simply means going to the bottom of the subject. ("Path," 405)

The second lawyer-thinker, the historian, is better employed at the disinterested or impractical study of the law as a "great anthropological document" – and Holmes was a great admirer of modern scientific historians of law such as Heinrich Brunner and F. W. Maitland, who were so employed. But the practical use of history is merely auxiliary, a "helpmeet" to the true masters of modern law, the social scientists. Holmes's essay "Law in Science" makes the point most effectively:

From a practical point of view . . . [history's] use is mainly negative and skeptical . . . [I]ts chief good is to burst inflated explanations. Every one instinctively recognizes that in these days the justification for a law for us cannot be found in the fact that our fathers have always followed it. It must be found in some help which the law brings toward reaching a social end which the governing power of the community has made up its mind that it wants. And when a lawyer sees a rule in force he is very apt to invent, if he does not find, some ground of policy for its base . . . Many [laws] might as well be different, and history is the means by which we measure the power which the past has had to govern the present in spite of ourselves, so to speak, by imposing traditions which no longer meet their original end. History sets us free and enables us to make up our minds dispassionately whether the survival which we are enforcing answers any new purpose when it has ceased to answer the old.[40]

The example here is an exception to the hearsay rule, admitting earlier statements of complainants in trials for rape. Although this doctrine had recently been fitted out with a policy rationale – to Holmes the very implausible one that a "virtuous" woman who has been raped will want to disclose the crime as soon as possible – historical research reveals that the exception originated in the early procedural requirement that felony victims must raise the "hue and cry."[41] The use of history here is thus negative and critical, arguing for the elimination of a rule by exposing its source in a context now archaic or irrelevant.

So – to quote one of the most famous passages in *The Path of the Law*,

> History . . . is a part of the rational study [of the law] because it is the first step toward an enlightened skepticism, that is, toward a deliberate reconsideration of the worth of those rules. When you get the dragon out of his cave on to the plain and in the daylight, you can count his teeth and claws, and see just what is in his strength. But to get him out is only the first step. The next is either to kill him, or tame him and make him a useful animal. ("Path," 399)

Holmes then introduces his deus ex machina, the most mysterious character in the entire menagerie, the practical lawyer-scientist:

> For the rational study of the law the black-letter man may be the man of the present, but the man of the future is the man of statistics and the master of economics. (399)

This is the policy analyst, who is needed because neither doctrinal theory nor history can supply an adequate rational justification for deciding cases – or for fashioning broad legal principles or legislative policies – one way instead of another. "Behind the logical form" of doctrinal reasoning "lies a judgment as to the relative worth and importance of competing legislative grounds, often an inarticulate and unconscious judgment, it is true, and yet the very root and nerve of the whole proceeding" (397). This is the voice of the antiformalist Holmes, who held that decisions in hard cases were decisions on (usually inarticulate) policy grounds, that rational judges would either make the grounds more articulate or, seeing that debatable matters of policy were at stake, refrain from "[generalizing] into [Constitutional principles] acceptance of the economic doctrines which prevailed about fifty years ago" (398). This Holmes, in his own time, was a hero to Progressive reformers and legal realists, and in ours to law-and-economics scholars, the Holmes who carried forward the project of Bentham and Mill to rationalize and reform the body of law according to utilitarian criteria.

From much excellent work on this aspect of Holmes,[42] it is clear that the Progressives' sense of kinship with Holmes was largely misplaced, for he thought most of their reform agenda twaddle, though they were clever at appropriating his authority for that agenda.⁴³ His deference as a judge to dominant community opinion, as reflected in legislation or the discretionary decisions of local officials, led him to vote more frequently even than his "conservative" brethren to sustain grossly illiberal legislative and administrative acts – practically the sole exceptions being the free-speech cases of his post-1919 U.S. Supreme Court career.⁴⁴ Holmes as utilitarian or proto-lawyer-economist has fared somewhat better than Holmes as Progressive-liberal, though here too there are some reasons for skepticism – most obviously, Holmes's scorn for the merely practical and his dream of rational utopias. "[W]ho of us could endure a world, although cut into five-acre lots and having no man upon it who was not well fed and well housed, without the divine folly of honor, without the senseless . . . knowledge out-reaching the flaming bounds of the possible, without ideals the essence of which is that they never can be achieved?"⁴⁵ That is not a question you are going to find in the *Journal of Law and Economics*. Holmes reserved his greatest enthusiasm for quests for the unattainable.⁴⁶

What does Holmes think is the role of policy analysis in the practical work of lawyers? Most often, despite the military metaphors, the policy man is rather removed from the thick of battle (on the intelligence staff, as it were), engaged in the "study" of the law. From such a vantage point the thinker may retheorize entire fields of law with a view to recommending legislative change. The example Holmes gives us is a core issue of penal policy: "Does punishment deter?" If "crime, like normal human conduct, is mainly a matter of imitation, punishment . . . may . . . keep it out of fashion." If, on the other hand, "the typical criminal is a degenerate, bound to swindle or to murder by . . . organic necessity" then deterrence is useless; he must be incapacitated or destroyed ("Path," 400). Despite Holmes's skepticism about the limits of rational understanding, he shared with most intellectuals of his time a striking confidence that "science" would be able to answer such questions.

But he also recommends policy analysis to those in the front lines of legal action – chiefly, it appears, to law reformers. He recommends it to judges – "[I]nasmuch as the real justification of a rule of law . . . is that it helps to bring about a social end which we desire, it is no less necessary that those who make and develop the law should have those ends articulately in their minds"⁴⁷ – but only to a very limited extent. Usually judges should not "undertake to renovate the law," because the stability of existing law is important. But in hard cases where principles and precedents conflict, "the judges are called on to exercise the sovereign prerogative of choice."⁴⁸ And "as a step toward the ideal" of "study of the ends sought to be attained [by law] and of the reasons for desiring them," "every lawyer ought to seek an understanding of economics. The present divorce between our schools of political economy and law seems to me an indication of how much progress in political economy needs to be made" ("Path," 408). Thus "every lawyer" ought to some extent to be involved in the public enterprise of the rational reformation of the law.

Yet the big dilemma for Holmesians is this: if you think social ideals are just strongly held preferences – or unconscious instincts – that get into the law because at a given time they have enough force behind them, how is the policy analyst supposed to weigh these values – to "determine . . . the relative worth of our different social ends"? Of course, if his historian-helper has demonstrated that a legal rule is a mere survival, expressing an obsolete policy that nobody believes in any more, the policy expert simply purges that rule. And if a policy has triumphed with such overwhelming force that it is supported by an unchallenged consensus, the only debates are technical ones about how to carry the policy out. But what of the situation that Holmes believes to be the common one, that policies are debatable because opposing forces are locked in struggle? Holmes suggests a range of approaches.

1. MYSTERIOUS QUANTIFICATION. "Law in Science" gives the fullest rendering of the problem. Science consists of the "substitution of quantitative for qualitative measure":

[In] the law we only occasionally can reach an absolutely final and quantitative determination, because the worth of the competing social ends which respectively solicit a judgment for the plaintiff or the defendant cannot be reduced to number and adequately fixed. The worth, that is, the intensity of the competing desires, varies with the varying ideals of the time, and, if the desires were constant, we could not get beyond a relative decision that one was greater and one was less. But it is of the essence of improvement that we should be as accurate as we can.[49]

What is to be our method for improving our accuracy? Translating "worth" into "intensity" does not solve the problem, because Holmes's theory of value is based on power. He cannot use something like "willingness to pay" in markets or shadow markets, because he is just as or more impressed by willingness to kill or sacrifice in blood to obtain what one wants. Liability for industrial accidents "is really the question how far it is desirable that the public should insure the safety of those whose work it uses . . . [T]he economic value even of a life to the community can be estimated, and no recovery, it may be said, ought to go beyond that amount" ("Path," 398). That is Holmes in his utilitarian mood. But the Darwinian Holmes recognizes that the value of a life to the community is a fighting issue and that the answer depends on who has the power to do the estimating.

2. ARBITRARY RULES AND LINES. The aim of turning judgments of quality into judgments of quantity therefore rarely produces a metric for resolving socially contested policy disputes. If courts cannot duck such disputes (that is, follow the policy of abstention I take up next), it is best if they simulate scientific exactness by drawing arbitrary lines, turning vague standards such as "duty of care" or "reasonable notice of dishonor" into bright-line rules.

3. ABSTENTION, OR THE PASSIVE VIRTUES. For judges, the practical result of Holmes's scientific policy–analytic approach to law is to restrain them from acting at all, if they need not:

> As law embodies beliefs that have triumphed in the battle of ideas and then have translated themselves into action, while there still is doubt, while opposite convictions still keep a battle front against each other, the time for law has not come; the notion destined to prevail is not yet entitled to the field.[50]

The applications that made him famous, of course, were his dissents in Fourteenth Amendment cases once he had reached the Supreme Court. When the policy analyst uncovers as the real basis of a doctrinal formula (e.g., "liberty of contract") a hotly contested policy debate – "the economic doctrines of fifty years ago" or "Mr. Herbert Spencer's Social Statics" versus doctrines of the present – Constitutional courts should stay out of the fight.

4. ACTIVISM, OR LEVELING THE PLAYING FIELD. On rare occasions, Holmes as policy-conscious judge took a more actively innovative role, urging courts help to level the playing field so that forces in social combat could fight on more equal terms, or at least less encumbered by arbitrary handicaps or advantages imposed by the legal system. The important occasions – all dissents – are his Massachusetts labor opinions[51] and his federal free-speech opinions. In the state cases, he thought it wrong for his court to grant injunctions against picketing workers in order to protect employers' "property," because all economic struggle harmed some people's property and much of this harm (like that inflicted by competition) was "privileged" and uncompensated. Believing that his court was deciding a policy issue on nothing stronger than prejudice, Holmes thought that it should abstain and let capital and labor fight it out in the marketplace and legislature. The more dramatic occasions are the great free-speech dissents,[52] in which Holmes believed that the government was impermissibly interfering in the struggle for dominance in the marketplace of ideas, in violation of a Constitutional norm promoting that struggle as "the best test of truth."

5. RESTRAINT IN THE PROMOTION OF CAUSES. Holmes says: "I cannot but believe that if the training of lawyers led them habitually to consider more definitely and explicitly the social advantage on which the rule they lay down must be justified, they sometimes would hesitate where now they were confident, and see they were taking sides upon debatable and often burning questions" ("Path," 398). The context indicates that Holmes is still talking about judges here ("a tribunal of lawyers"), and surely this is so, for it is the *business* of lawyers to "take sides on debatable and often burning questions."

But there are payoffs for immersion in policy science for lawyers too – chiefly, it seems, for lawyers for social-reform movements. In the 1880s and

1890s, professionals formed the vanguard of the Mugwump and Progressive movements, and lawyers were active, as never before, as agents of social improvement. Policy science, for them, was a means of mastering necessity, of understanding the structural determinants of poverty, vice, urban squalor, alcoholism, prostitution, political corruption, monopoly power, and "wasteful competition," in order to conquer them as public-health science had conquered epidemic disease. For Holmes, however, science pointed chiefly in the opposite direction, to recognition of the limits that necessity imposes. Holmes sounds no theme more often than that science teaches hard lessons of scarcity and the limits of social intervention; the implication is clear that the lawyer trained in science usually has to tell his clients, especially if they are workers fighting for minimum or higher wages or for increased accident compensation or for redistribution through progressive taxation, that they cannot get these things, except at what may be an unacceptably high price.[53]

Probably I am too skeptical as to our ability to do more than shift disagreeable burdens from the shoulders of the stronger to those of the weaker . . . To know what you want and why you think that such a measure will help it is the first but by no means the last step towards intelligent legal reform. The other and more difficult one is to realize what you must give up to get it, and to consider whether you are ready to pay the price.[54]

One can see why Holmes's views appeal to present-day conservative legal economists; even more than theirs, his was a bleak Malthusian negative-sum view of reform: *any* redistributions would impair production incentives or be eaten up by population increases or otherwise add to the burdens of those who sought to benefit.[55] But to give him credit, though he mostly thought it was labor unions and social democrats who stood in need of education, he also thought wealthy interests and their lawyers needed prudential counseling informed by consequentialist analysis to tell them when repressive tactics that had usually worked for them were likely to backfire. The scientifically trained lawyer could tell clients when their own or their group's desires were likely to be self-defeating. In that role there is at least a minimalist theory of socially responsible law practice.

Holmes's view of the policy analyst is in a way an updated version of Tocqueville's view of lawyers as ingrained conservatives, who serve as a counterforce to democratic excess by braking the momentum of popular majorities. It is a considerable irony, therefore, that Holmes's views – that private-law doctrines are saturated with policy judgments that lawyers should explicitly articulate, criticize, and rationalize – should have most inspired the practice of several generations of Progressives, who quoted those views as manifestoes for their social-reform activism.

VI. Holmes as a Public Professional

Holmes and many of his contemporaries at the Boston bar faced a common situation and responded to it in interestingly different ways. They were liberally educated gentlemen in a world that no longer valued their skills or deferred to their learning, virtue, or class position – a businessman's world, competitive, ruthless, relentlessly philistine, and, in this period, especially corrupt; and a politician's world dominated by ethnic urban machines rather than patrician elites. Many of the old elites simply made their peace with the new conditions and also made a lot of money. Many famous ones dropped out – Henry James quit after a year at Harvard Law School to live in Europe and write out his alienation from the American scene; Henry and Brooks Adams, after a fling with muckraking and reform politics, became professional Cassandras, committed to long-run deterministic theories of the degradation of society; John Jay Chapman became a political agitator and radical social critic. For my purposes, the most interesting lawyers were those who stuck with law and chose a strategy of engagement. One strategy was to convert the old elites from a class with pretensions to universal virtue into another political party; this was the strategy of the "Best Men," the Mugwump reformers who sought to reclaim politics from the corrupt business-ethnic-machine alliances. Another strategy, typified by the railroad reformer Charles Francis Adams, Jr., was to try to shift decision making out of democratic political arenas and into institutions that professional elites had a better shot at dominating – either the judiciary or (for Progressives) a professional civil service and administrative commissions.

The two most activist lawyers of Holmes's Boston provide an instructive contrast. Moorfield Storey (1845–1929), a president of the American Bar Association, was a corporate lawyer whose clients included the Union Pacific Railroad and the United Fruit Company. He was also a committed abolitionist and radical Reconstructionist, served as Charles Sumner's secretary, and later became counsel and first president of the National Association for the Advancement of Colored People. His commitment to the core beliefs of classical-liberal legalism – to the protection of a sphere of formally equal individual rights for every person – was one he applied with rigorous consistency, leading him to oppose most forms of regulation of business and legislative protection for workers and nearly all concerted labor union actions. It also led him to campaign against American imperialism (because it treated foreign subjects as lesser breeds with less than the full complement of rights), the racist and anti-Semitic admissions policies of Harvard and the American Bar Association, and, most determinedly, all forms of subordination of black persons, including segregation, restrictive covenants, employers' cheating on sharecropper contracts, disenfranchisement of voters, and lynching. His primary credo for lawyers was that they should be "independent," that is, avoid identification with clients, in order to play the role of social mediator, to "keep the community orderly and peaceful . . . and adjust the disputes which arise among its members."[56]

Louis D. Brandeis (1856–1941) was also one of Boston's leading corporate lawyers and, like Storey, active in public causes. He was a spearhead of Boston Progressive reformers' campaigns for anticorruption legislation and regulatory control of public utilities. He is best known as the progenitor of modern "public-interest" law, as the "Lawyer for the People," who argued cases on behalf of diffuse constituencies such as women and consumers, designed novel approaches to rate regulation, and served as a public intervenor and mediator in labor disputes. He carried his public perspectives into much of his activity as a private lawyer, taking a quasi-judicial perspective on his clients' problems and helping his business clients find structural solutions to systemic social problems such as workers' insecurity and seasonal unemployment. His main social project was the attempt, through antitrust policy and democratizing the governance of decentralized collectives such as companies and unions, to enable individuals to realize the republican ideals of self-development and self-government in a modern industrial polity by decentralizing the economy. Like Holmes, Brandeis thought the lawyer should be a policy analyst, armed with a knowledge of social fact and social science. Unlike Holmes, who thought social struggle was often a zero-sum game and that the best use of science was to dampen the ardor of reformers by showing them they could not get what they wanted, Brandeis believed (like other Progressives) that lawyers trained in social science could serve the cause of social improvement by recommending to warring parties and factions solutions that would improve the position of all.[57]

What would Holmes have thought about such approaches to the lawyer's vocation as Storey's and Brandeis's? One thing is clear: after the Civil War, he was no longer a man of social causes. He had no taste for any of the reform enthusiasms that swept up many lawyers in contemporary Boston. In general, the firm of Shattuck Holmes & Munroe represented the "dominant interests in its community, not the oppressed of Boston or New England," said Mark Howe, adding drily: "If any of the partners had a social conscience his practice did not reveal it."[58] Toward Storey's long crusade for the civil rights of blacks, Holmes on the bench proved indifferent or hostile. As a U.S. Supreme Court justice, he voted more regularly even than his conservative colleagues to deny petitions of blacks claiming violations of their civil rights;[59] generally he deferred to state legislatures and local authorities, with whose "political" judgments he was unwilling to interfere. In most cases involving race, the lessons of "experience" were, apparently, that if the white South, as the "de facto dominant power in the community," wanted to subordinate its black citizens under the thinnest cover of formally legal equal treatment, there was nothing the federal courts could or should do about it.[60] Though Holmes admired Brandeis personally for his intelligence and intensity, he was scathing about most projects of social improvement (except eugenics), describing them as futile or self-defeating. Holmes's tough-minded scientific naturalism led him almost to relish the brutality of quasi-natural forces – such as race domination and the expansion of large-scale corporate capitalism – and to be very skeptical about the capacity of legal controls to soften the impact of natural necessity.

Yet although he gave up on social causes, Holmes did not withdraw from the world of ordinary occupations and become a pessimistic Cassandra, like his friend Henry Adams, or an expatriate aesthete, like his contemporaries Henry James and George Santayana. Although his idea of heroic lawyering is the life of the thinker, he did not choose a scholar's life. He was impelled to worldly service by his aristocratic and Puritan sense of duty. Though most at home in English intellectual circles, he made his career among Boston practical men, lawyers and businessmen who were mostly contemptuous and distrustful of any manifestation of intellectual intensity. His soldier's or jobbist ethic exemplifies a subtle shift in the ideals of Yankee professional culture and its virtues of Emersonian self-reliance, of the masculine man and gentleman, and of independence and public service. To be sure, there are continuities – such as the Stoic disdain for grasping for money, the belief that the man who allows his life to be taken over by money getting is, like the man of unbridled sexuality, incapable of self-command. But the meaning of public service had to change, in a world where the reins had been handed over to others: it now meant neutral execution of the will of others. Holmes believed that most of the things legislatures taxed citizens for were foolish and counterproductive, but he made a ritual out of paying his own taxes, not drinking during Prohibition, and above all, as a judge, deferring with perverse relish to Progressive, idiotic, and brutal state policies alike.[61]

For Holmes, heroism lay in self-sacrificing service to the crowd, but even more in the intellectual heroism demanded to stare the facts of life in the face. "If we think of our existence not as that of a little god outside, but as that of a ganglion within, we have the infinite behind us. It gives us our only but our adequate significance."[62] The highest cause of the lawyer-hero turns out to be that of science itself – not a withdrawal from life after all, but a passionate embrace of it. Talking about law as an expression of or means of enforcing moral standards is delusive cant: understood socially, law is a resultant of power, instinct, and need; understood historically, law has for centuries been disposing of its notionally moral content in favor of "objective standards"; for the practicing lawyer with clients to serve, law is simply predictions of where and when the public ax will fall. But – like the realization that human beings are not God's specially favored creatures at the center of the universe, but an insignificant, accidental piece of the vast whole – this disillusioned, de-moralized view leads on, not to cynicism but to glory. He is a hero who not only can face the cold unfeeling universe without flinching, but who can use his intelligence to uncover its impersonal laws. Ultimately, the "abstract speculation" of great thinkers like Descartes or Kant is the most practical activity of all, because of its power of "controlling the conduct of men" for centuries to come. By the end of *The Path of the Law*, Holmes is telling us that he venerates the law as one of the vastest products of the human mind, as a calling of thinkers, who, by grasping the "remoter and more general aspects of law," may become "master[s]" of their calling, "connect [their] subject with the universe and catch an echo of the infinite, a glimpse of its unfathomable process, a hint of the universal law" (406).[63]

That is a grand ambition. Yet my reaction to it is something like Max Beerbohm's reaction to the ant: "The ant sets an example to us all; but not a good one."[64] Holmes is most inspiring and useful in his endorsement and demonstration of the disinterested intellect, the practical role of theory, the emancipating use of history, and the importance of understanding and evaluating doctrines, decisions, and legislative reforms in terms of their likely costs and consequences. Holmes also seems a much more accurate and penetrating observer of society and the legal system than the liberal reformers of his time, or ours – much more acutely aware of the pervasiveness of power relations and coercion in social life, and of the fact that people fight and oppress and rise up for ideals as often as for material interests. But as a guide to living in the law as a vocation – though certainly far superior to the promoters of the unabashedly privatized, profit-seeking ethic that emerged in Holmes's time and dominates ours – he is strangely disappointing. Though acknowledging that legal actors and decision makers have discretion to choose, more often than not he urges them to defer to power even more than their role requires, to be passive instruments of society's or their clients' ends rather than active forces to help refigure and transform those ends. His soldier's or jobbist's faith is largely one of blind obedience to disagreeable orders, rather than the intelligent and resourceful soldier's active adaptation of orders to circumstances and the demands of conscience. He discards the traditional roles for lawyers as seekers of justice, social mediators and curators of the legal framework, and although he substitutes for those functions an undoubtedly valuable role as consequentialist policy analyst, he does not expect lawyers to do much with the role except temper the ambitions of reform movements. His ultimate ethic is one of isolated acts of heroic intellectual achievement. But if there is to be spring cleaning in the Heartbreak House of the law, it will have to come from efforts both more collaborative and more engaged.

Notes

1 James V. Campbell, *Law and Lawyers in Society* (address to graduating class at Law Dept., Univ. of Michigan) (Detroit: F. A. Schober, 1866), 16.
2 David J. Brewer, "A Better Education the Great Need of the Profession," *Yale Law Journal* 5 (1895):1, 3.
3 See, e.g., Lemuel Shaw, "Profession of the Law in the United States" (address before the Suffolk Bar, 1827), *American Jurist* 7 (1832):56, 64.
4 Rufus Choate, "The Position and Functions of the American Bar, as an Element of Conservatism in the State" (address to Harvard Law School, 1845), in *Addresses and Orations of Rufus Choate,* 3d ed. (Boston: Little, Brown, 1879), 133, 154.
5 I have to take issue here with Geoffrey Hazard, who has written that until recent times the bar's primary social role in the American constitutional-democratic order was that of protector of the property rights of business from challenge by state policies driven by popular politics, a "conception of its role [that] gave the legal profession a useful place in society

and gave lawyers a sense of meaning and common identity" (Geoffrey Hazard, "The Future of Legal Ethics," *Yale Law Journal* 100 [1991]:1239, 1278). In its public ideology, and certainly in its judicial politics, the nineteenth-century bar was much more even-handed, recognizing that rent-seeking coalitions of the wealthy could pose as great a risk to republican institutions as popular majorities; and the Mugwump and urban-Progressive reform movements, dominated by elite lawyers, promoted reforms to break the power of what they saw as the dangerously corrupt alliance between business interests and popular politicians. In actual practice, of course, elite lawyers tended to do most of their work for wealthy clients, but rarely with anything like the consistent and undivided loyalty to particular business clienteles that, in the twentieth century, has come to characterize elite practice.

6 H. W. Warner, *A Discourse on Legal Science* (address to the Corporation of the New York Law Institute, 1832) (New York: G. C. & H. Carvill, 1833), 34.

7 Joseph Jackson, *The Relations of the American Lawyer to the State* (address to Harvard Law School) (Cambridge, Mass.: Welch, Bigelow, 1859), 12. It must be said that Jackson added that it is just that although lawyers should be well compensated, that most of them were underpaid.

8   An advocate [. . .] in the discharge of his duty knows but one person in the world, and that person is his client. To save that client by all means and expedients, and at all hazards and costs to other persons, and among them to himself, is his first and only duty; and in performing this duty he must regard the alarm, the torments, the destruction he may bring upon others. Separating the duty of a patriot from that of an advocate, he must go on reckless of consequences; though it should be his unhappy lot to involve his country in confusion.

Henry, Lord Brougham, trial of Queen Caroline, as quoted (with disapproval) in George Sharswood, *A Compend of Lectures on the Aims and Duties of the Profession of the Law* (Philadelphia: T. & J. W. Johnson, 1854), 29.

9 Simon Greenleaf, *A Discourse . . . at the Inauguration of the Author as Royall Professor of Law in Harvard University* (Cambridge, Mass.: J. Munroe, 1834), 17.

10 D. Bethune Duffield, *The Lawyer's Oath* (address to Univ. of Michigan Law Dept. graduating class) (Ann Arbor, Mich. Steam Printing, 1867), 10.

11 Job R. Tyson, *Discourse on the Integrity of the Legal Character* (address to Law Academy of Philadelphia) (Philadelphia: J. C. D. Clark, 1839), 10.

12 Choate, "Position and Functions of the American Bar," 135–36. By the "State" Choate does not mean the government, but society considered as an organic whole.

13 As Stephen Botein has acutely pointed out, American lawyers sacralized the judiciary and its functions because judges were effective symbols of the public-regarding professionalism that lawyers had little occasion to exhibit in private practice. See Stephen Botein, "What We Shall Meet Afterward in Heaven: Judgeship as a Symbol for American Lawyers," in *Professions and Professional Ideologies in America,* ed. Gerald Geison (Chapel Hill: University of North Carolina Press, 1983), 49, 50–54.

14 Perry Miller, "Declension in a Bible Commonwealth," in *Nature's Nation* (Cambridge, Mass.: Harvard University Press, 1967), 48–49.

15 Holmes once wrote a friend: "I don't see why we shouldn't do our job in the station in which we were born without waiting for an angel to assure us that it is the jobbest job in jobdom." Holmes to Morris R. Cohen, 27 May 1917, in *The Holmes–Cohen Correspondence,* ed. Felix S. Cohen (New York: College of the City of New York, 1948), 10.

16 Oliver Wendell Holmes, Jr., "The Path of the Law," in *The Collected Works of Justice Holmes,* ed. Sheldon Novick (Chicago: University of Chicago Press, 1995), vol. 3, 391, 392. Cited hereafter parenthetically in the text as "Path." ("The Path" is reprinted in the

Appendix with star paging.) Novick's edition of the *Collected Works* is cited hereafter in the notes as "CW."

17. On this shift, and its dating to the 1960s, see Steven Brint, *In an Age of Experts: The Changing Role of Professionals in Politics and Public Life* (Princeton: Princeton University Press, 1994), 40–43.
18. Oliver Wendell Holmes, Jr., "The Common Law" (1881), in CW, vol. 3, 109, 115.
19. Limited evidence survives of Holmes's own practice methods, other than in appellate advocacy; what there is suggests that he could be at times an aggressive advocate, quite capable of stretching a factual record and verbally savaging the other side's client to gain a point. See Mark de Wolfe Howe, *Justice Oliver Wendell Holmes: The Proving Years, 1870–1882* (Cambridge, Mass.: Harvard University Press, 1963), 125–27.
20. Oliver Wendell Holmes, Jr., "The Profession of the Law (lecture to Harvard undergraduates, 1886)," in CW, vol. 3, 471–72.
21. Who is this materialistic girl, Rachel, whom he refers to? I have been unable to discover but suspect she is the great nineteenth-century French actress (1821?–58) who took that stage name.
22. Holmes to John C. H. Wu, 26 March 1925, in *Justice Holmes to Dr. Wu: An Intimate Correspondence, 1921–1932* (New York: Central Book, 1947), 27.
23. Oliver Wendell Holmes, Jr., "Law in Science and Science in Law" (1899), in CW, vol. 3, 406, 420 (text as corrected on 456, note 10.10).
24. Oliver Wendell Holmes, Jr., "Sidney Bartlett" (1899), in CW, vol. 3, 480, 481.
25. Holmes to Harold Laski, 4 March 1920, in *Holmes–Laski Letters,* ed. Mark de Wolfe Howe (Cambridge, Mass.: Harvard University Press, 1953), vol. 1, 249.
26. For the best account of Holmes's judicial practice, see Thomas C. Grey, "Molecular Motions: The Holmesian Judge in Theory and Practice," *William and Mary Law Review* 37 (1995):19.
27. Oliver Wendell Holmes, Jr., "Daniel S. Richardson" (1890), in CW, vol. 3, 482, 482–83.
28. Oliver Wendell Holmes, Jr., "Address to the Essex Bar" (undated), in CW, vol. 3, 528.
29. Holmes, "Sidney Bartlett," 481.
30. Oliver Wendell Holmes, Jr., "John Marshall" (1901), in CW, vol. 3, 500, 501.
31. Holmes, "Profession of the Law," 472.
32. Holmes to James Bryce, 17 August 1879, quoted in *Justice Oliver Wendell Holmes: The Proving Years, 1870–1882,* ed. Mark de Wolfe Howe (Cambridge, Mass.: Harvard University Press, 1963), 280. Howe tells us, however, that the young lawyer was impressed by, though he did not personally like, powerful business clients. Holmes, says Howe, "possessed a somewhat awed respect for the qualities of mind and temperament which the more prominent clients of his office possessed. Though he often testified that business problems and business affairs were as disagreeable to him as they were mysterious, he commonly added to that testimony a word of admiration for the gifts of those men who had successfully mastered them" (111).
33. David Luban, "Justice Holmes and the Metaphysics of Judicial Restraint," *Duke Law Journal* 44 (1994):449, 478.
34. Holmes, "Law in Science and Science in Law" 406, 412.
35. Ibid., 407.
36. Ibid., 412.
37. G. Edward White, *Justice Oliver Wendell Holmes: Law and the Inner Self* (New York: Oxford University Press, 1993), 212–13.

38 Holmes to Lewis Einstein, 21 May 1914, in *The Essential Holmes,* ed. Richard A. Posner (Chicago: University of Chicago Press, 1992), 114.
39 See Thomas C. Grey, "Holmes and Legal Pragmatism," *Stanford Law Review* 41 (1989):787.
40 Holmes, "Law in Science and Science in law," 412.
41 Ibid., 413. Notwithstanding this ringing endorsement of the practical ends of critical history, Holmes, when he had the chance to eliminate this vestigial doctrine as a judge, declined to do so, doubtless consulting another of his generalized metaprinciples that judges should be "slow to innovate," on the ground that existing law, though it might well be faulty, has a claim founded in the protection of reliance interests to be followed simply because it exists. See *Commonwealth v. Cleary,* 172 Mass. 178 (1898), and the discussion in Mark Tushnet, "The Logic of Experience: Oliver Wendell Holmes on the Supreme Judicial Court," *Virginia Law Review* 63 (1977):975.
42 See, e.g., H. L. Pohlmann, *Justice Oliver Wendell Holmes and Utilitarian Jurisprudence* (Cambridge, Mass.: Harvard University Press, 1984); Patrick J. Kelley, "A Critical Analysis of Holmes's Theory of Torts," *Washington University Law Quarterly* 61 (1983–84):681.
43 See Yosal Rogat, "Mr. Justice Holmes: A Dissenting Opinion," *Stanford Law Review* 15 (1962–63):3, 254; G. Edward White, "The Rise and Fall of Justice Holmes," *University of Chicago Law Review* 39 (1971):51; David Hollinger, "The 'Tough-Minded' Justice Holmes, Jewish Intellectuals, and the Making of an American Icon," in *The Legacy of Oliver Wendell Holmes,* ed. Robert W. Gordon (Stanford: Stanford University Press, 1992):216–28.
44 See generally White, *Justice Oliver Wendell Holmes,* 333–53.
45 Oliver Wendell Holmes, Jr., "The Soldier's Faith" (1895), in CW, vol. 3, 486, 487.
46 Luban, who has carefully demonstrated the many respects in which Holmes's thought is not utilitarian (Luban, "Justice Holmes," 517–23 n. 210), argues that Holmes's interest in policy-making "ran entirely in the direction of improving the organic integrity of legal doctrine, not improving society" (511). This seems to me to go too far. Holmes had at least one longstanding and determinedly pursued utilitarian project: the rational reform of tort law into an accident-compensation system free of moral imputations of "fault" for socially valuable industrial activities, and the substitution of across-the-board rules fixing standards of care for idiosyncratic (hence unpredictable) jury estimations of negligence. Though "[m]ost of the things we do, we do for no better reason than that our fathers have done them or that our neighbors do them, . . . [i]t does not follow . . . that each of us may not try to set some corner of his world in the order of reason, or that all of us collectively should not aspire to carry reason as far as it will go throughout the whole domain" ("Path," 398–99; 1000).
47 "Law in Science," 418.
48 Ibid., 418–19.
49 Ibid., 415.
50 Oliver Wendell Holmes, Jr., "Law and the Court" (1913), in CW, vol. 3, 505, 506–7.
51 *Vegelahn v. Guntner,* 167 Mass. 92, 108 (1896); *Plant v. Woods,* 176 Mass. 492, 505 (1900).
52 Esp. *Abrams v. U.S.,* 250 U.S. 616, 627 (1919).
53 In a letter to Harold Laski, he gives this illuminating example: "If you require guards to machinery you say the detriment of increased cost to the public is less than that caused

by the loss of certain fingers &c. If you say minimum wage you say those who can't get it must starve or be supported, and in the latter case those who get the wages must do the supporting." Holmes to Laski, 28 February 1919, in *Holmes–Laski Letters,* ed. Mark de Wolfe Howe (Cambridge, Mass.: Harvard University Press, 1953), vol. 1, 187.

54 Oliver Wendell Holmes, Jr., "Ideals and Doubts" (1915), in CW, vol. 3, 442, 443, 444.
55 For the best concise account of Holmes's views on political economy, see Stephen Diamond, "Citizenship, Civilization and Coercion: Justice Holmes on the Tax Power," in Gordon, *Legacy,* 115, 143–48.
56 Storey, "A Civilian's View of the Navy" (1897), quoted in William B. Hixson, *Morefield Storey and the Abolitionist Tradition* (New York: Oxford University Press, 1972), 152–53.
57 Clyde Pillenger, "Elusive Advocate: Reconsidering Brandeis as People's Lawyer," *Yale Law Journal* 105 (1996):1445, a singularly thorough and intelligent reassessment of Brandeis's public-interest practice, comes to a more critical conclusion than mine about Brandeis's attempts to represent his clients and the public interest simultaneously.
58 Howe, *Proving Years,* 109–10.
59 See Rogat, "Mr. Justice Holmes: A Dissenting Opinion," 307–8.
60 White, *Justice Oliver Wendell Holmes,* 342–43.
61 Diamond, "Citizenship, Civilization and Coercion," 148–54.
62 Oliver Wendell Holmes, Jr., "Natural Law" (1918), in CW, vol. 3, 445, 448.
63 Holmes liked to compare the lawyer-thinker (himself, really) to the great Arctic explorers:
   One found oneself plunged in[to] a thick fog of details – in a black and frozen night, in which there were no flowers, no spring, no easy joys. Voices of authority warned that in the crush of that ice any craft might sink . . . [I]f he is a man of high ambitions he must leave even his fellow adventurers and go forth into a deeper solitude and greater trials. He must start for the pole. In plain words he must face the loneliness of original work.
   Oliver Wendell Holmes, Jr., "Address at Brown University Commencement" (1897), in CW, vol. 3, 517, 518.
64 David Cecil, *Max, A Biography* (Boston: Houghton Mifflin, 1965), 345.

2

The Bad Man and the Good Lawyer

DAVID LUBAN*

One of the great virtues of Robert Gordon's essay is to remind us that *The Path of the Law* started as a speech – and not just a speech, but a speech at a ceremonial occasion – and not just a speech at a ceremonial occasion, but a ceremonial speech belonging to a popular nineteenth-century genre, the vocational address.[1]

But what a vocational address it is! Gordon argues that Holmes "would seem to have shredded all of the fancy costumes in which nineteenth-century lawyers tried to dress up their profession," that he places "skeptical roadblocks across all of the generally recommended paths for those who would seek meaning and value in the lawyer's work." I agree; and I agree as well with Gordon's second principal point, that Holmes nevertheless held the lawyer's job in high, sometimes fantastically romantic, esteem.[2] The question is why.

One possible reason that *The Path of the Law* offers slim pickings for the lawyer's vocation could be that it is not primarily a vocational address. As readers of his speeches know, Holmes had a marvelous sense of occasion, and the occasion of its delivery was the dedication of a law-school building.[3] Perhaps, then, the speech, delivered to law students, is not about how to practice law, but how to study law. The first four words are "When we study law," and Holmes reminds us of his topic no fewer than ten times.[4] If the essay contains very little about a life in the law, surely that is in part because a life in the law is not Holmes's theme.

This cannot be the whole story, however. Holmes surely intended the double meaning of the title, alluding to the lawyer's vocation as well as to the historical development of law – although we should remember that the only path he mentions in the speech itself is "the narrow path of legal doctrine" (178), bounded by the twin pitfalls of morality and logic.[5] The emphasis on jurispru-

---

* A much-expanded version of my present essay appears as "The Bad Man and the Good Lawyer: A Centennial Essay on Holmes's 'Path of the Law,'" *New York University Law Review* 72 (1997):1547. (Reproduced by permission.)

dence unfolds organically from the opening paragraphs, which tell us that we understand the law by understanding the way lawyers advise their clients in practice. However, whatever views of the lawyer's vocation Holmes expresses here he expresses indirectly; the vision of law practice it contains has to be dug out by inference. In what follows, I want to continue the spadework that Gordon has begun.

I. The Paths Forsaken

Gordon demonstrates that unlike the standard vocational speech, *The Path of the Law* ventures not a hint of the familiar argument that the lawyer, an officer of the court, is therefore a minister of justice and a trustee for society at large. I would go farther: it seems to me that the essay contains the raw materials for an out-and-out demolition of this argument. The demolition carries contemporary resonance, moreover, because the minister of justice argument is alive and well in the late twentieth century as in the nineteenth century. It has been advanced, in somewhat differing forms, by contemporary legal ethicists, including William Simon, Gordon, and me.[6]

According to this way of thinking about legal practice, the key intellectual task facing a lawyer is to analyze the social purpose of a legal rule, the better to align a client's interests with it. According to Holmes, however, there is simply no purpose there. When we begin probing into the purpose behind a legal rule, we must work back historically from the present, carefully dissecting away each era's reformulation of the legal rule and scrutinizing them closely. What we typically discover is one of three things: a rote reiteration of an earlier rule, a flat-out misunderstanding of an earlier rule, or a bit of creative fiction as judges spin out conjectural purposes for rules that in reality are nothing more than vestigial solutions to forgotten problems.[7]

Sometimes, of course, today's legal rule has the same purpose as its predecessors, because legal practices and institutions continue to face the same problem. Even then, however, Holmes believes that it is simply a mistake to hear harmony in that purpose. Instead, Holmes explains the purposes of law through metaphors of conflict, struggle, and tension.[8] In all cases, the alleged "purpose" of the law is simply the desire of the triumphant victors rather than that of the subjugated: he is jesting in earnest when he writes: "I used to say when I was young, that truth is the majority vote of that nation that could lick all others."[9] Holmes describes the law in the most brutal terms, as "the stern monition that the club and the bayonet are at hand ready to drive you to prison or to the rope if you go beyond the established lines."[10] Why, then, would a lawyer be morally obligated to align his client's interests with legal purposes?

Could it be, then, that Holmes had a principled belief in the adversary ethic of zealous partisanship? In one way, the answer is yes, because Holmes believed in the value of combat and of the sweet science of war. But in the sense of contemporary legal ethicists' debates, the answer is clearly no. For Holmes, there is no moral rationale for partisan legal combat, except that "when war has begun any cause is good, . . . life is war, and . . . the part of man in it is to be strong."[11] Here, as elsewhere, Holmes likened lawyers to soldiers, and his credo was that "the faith is true and adorable which leads a soldier to throw away his life in obedience to a blindly accepted duty."[12]

Notice that this soldierly conception of duty bears no relation to another familiar justification for law practice, namely service to clients. In all of Holmes's writings, I have found only two sentences that come within shouting distance of this idea: in his eulogy for George Otis Shattuck, he writes: "He was a model in his bearing with clients. How often have I seen men come to him borne down by troubles which they found too great to support, and depart with light step, having left their weight upon stronger shoulders."[13] That is all. More typical is his description of law practice as "the greedy watch for clients and practice of shopkeepers' arts, the mannerless conflicts over often sordid interests."[14] Remember that the only client who appears in *The Path of the Law* is the bad man.

Gordon points out, and criticizes, another of Holmes's vocational ideas: that a lawyer can take satisfaction in making an anonymous contribution to the fabric of the social order, or at least of the common law. I have found five speeches, mostly grim eulogies, in which Holmes expatiates on this theme.[15] But, as Gordon asks, where is the satisfaction in being one of Darwin's specimens? In a memorial speech, Holmes says that "[w]hat we have done is woven forever into the great vibrating web of the world."[16] The comfort in that thought is roughly the same as the comfort in knowing that your mortal remains will enrich the topsoil and eventually belong to a cloud of interstellar gas.

To conclude this brief survey of blocked escapes, let me turn to the mystical final paragraph in *The Path of the Law*, where Holmes suggests that the law, properly studied, allows us to "catch an echo of the infinite, a glimpse of its unfathomable process, a hint of the universal law" (202). What are the insights into cosmic processes that law offers to the thinker? Here is his idea: [A]s the facts of the law are facts of the universe they are worthy of their share of the only intellectual interest there is – the interest of being seen in their universal relations."[17] In other words, law is interesting, but only because everything is – and even then only when viewed in relation to everything else.[18] And "the hint of universal law" Holmes speaks of in *The Path of the Law* turns out to be an appreciation of how savage life really is. Holmes was a Malthusian and a Darwinian, who firmly believed that legal reform can accomplish nothing much beyond shifting burdens to the losers in a zero-sum economic game. In one way Holmes was every inch a philosopher, in the mold of Spinoza and Nietzsche: all were thinkers who believed that self-command comes through thinking, and, in particular, thinking the impersonal universe through to its indifferent bottom. But, to say the least, redemption through contemplating a hostile universe is a life ideal likely to be rejected by all but a small number of lawyers.

Indeed, Holmes's notion of the lawyer-thinker, to which he returns again and again, is an idiosyncratic one, and in my view Holmes never really made up his mind how to reconcile the life of thought with the life of action. He insisted that "[t]he law is the calling of thinkers,"[19] and in one of his lawyer eulogies Holmes unfavorably compared the businessman – the man of action – with the advocate, who as a thinker controls the future.[20] Yet when he was practicing law, Holmes complained that "the men who really care more for a fruitful thought than for a practical success are few everywhere."[21] He went on to say that except for arguing cases he disliked practice and added mournfully: "I console myself by studying toward a vanishing point which is the center of perspective in my landscape – but that has to be done at night."[22]

That was his motivation for seeking an academic appointment, but within three months he quit his professorship to accept a seat on the Supreme Judicial Court of Massachusetts. Years afterward, he wrote to Felix Frankfurter (in a letter that does not make law professors stand up and cheer) that "academic life is but half life – it is withdrawal from the fight in order to utter smart things that cost you nothing except the thinking them from a cloister."[23]

In short, Holmes at various times asserted that "the place for a man who is complete in all his powers is in the fight";[24] that all that makes the fight worthwhile is the thinker's "infinite perspective" on it; and that nobody engaged in the fight has the leisure or the inclination to assume that perspective. It is hard to avoid the suspicion that judging was the only legal profession that could satisfy Holmes's inconsistent demands – and Gordon is probably right to read Holmes's views about the lawyer-thinker as largely personal and autobiographical.[25]

One final possibility: as I have argued in the past,[26] Holmes was a vitalist, who believed that salvation lies in living out any ideals whatever, provided they are demanding enough to call forth all of our powers and still remain beyond us. In connection with the title "The Path of the Law," it is interesting that he once wrote that "the true path is the line of most resistance."[27] Perhaps Holmes is right, but what is noteworthy is that he gives us no hint of what a lawyer's ideal might consist in, beyond having ideals.

Checkmate? Only if Holmes's arguments in *The Path of the Law* are right.

II. The Bad Man

The opening pages of *The Path of the Law* introduce three themes: the "bad man" thesis, the "confusion between morality and law" (169), and the prediction theory of law. By the bad man thesis I mean the claim that "[i]f you want to know the law and nothing else, you must look at it as a bad man, who cares only for the material consequences which such knowledge enables him to predict" (171).

There is a puzzle here, however, once we ask why we must adopt the bad man's point of view if we want to know the law. It will help to address a prior question: Who or what is this bad man? Is he, as former U.S. Attorney General Richard Thornburgh has suggested, simply "the client in need of legal advice"? Is he a rational calculator, what Gordon has felicitously dubbed *homo law-and-economicus?* Is he, as Catharine Peirce Wells suggests (Chapter 9), any outsider to the legal system – for example, a feminist in a patriarchal society? Is he, in Sanford Levinson's friendly amendment to Wells's idea (Chapter 10), a self-reliant, morally autonomous individual who may give way before superior force but will not let the law tell him what is right or wrong? To answer these questions, it behooves us to look closely at the role the bad man plays in Holmes's argument.

Holmes introduces the bad man, he tells us, as a thought experiment to "dispel a confusion between morality and law" (169). What is fascinating in the experiment is that Holmes aims to demonstrate an abstract jurisprudential proposition by sketching the scenario of a lawyer advising a client: this linkage is the single best proof of Gordon's claim that *The Path of the Law* is a vocational address. In effect, Holmes tells the young lawyer in his audience that if he wants to avoid confusion, he should imagine the bad man seated across the desk in his offices and think the matter through from his point of view. But what is the confusion that they will avoid thereby?

Holmes explains the confusion between morality and law by discussing three typical instances of it:

(1) the belief that if something is one of the rights of man in a moral sense, it must therefore be a legal right as well (171);
(2) the belief that law "is a system of reason, . . . a deduction from principles of ethics . . . , which may or may not coincide with the decisions" (172);
(3) the belief that legal duty is filled "with all the content which we draw from morals" (173).

The general point of both propositions (1) and (2) seems to be that moral precepts (or at least those dealing with subjects that concern the legal system) are, *a fortiori,* legal precepts: (1) emphasizes the necessary connection between law and morality, while (2) emphasizes the rational and systematic character of both law and ethics. It appears that Holmes's root reason for describing both (1) and (2) as confusions is to deny what might be termed the "morality-is-law thesis":

Morality-is-law Thesis: Every moral precept is a legal precept.

Holmes's (3), on the other hand, concerns the content of legal duties, and his general point is that even when legal language employs moral terminology, it is a confusion to interpret the law morally.

Focusing on the morality-is-law thesis makes it seem that Holmes's will be an argument on familiar legal-positivist terrain, aiming to establish that it is not morality but institutional pedigree that makes a precept law. This restates the so-called separation thesis – shorthand for the thesis of the separation of law and morality – defended most prominently in our century in H. L. A. Hart's celebrated 1958 essay "Positivism and the Separation of Law and Morals."[28] One of Hart's most important principal points in this essay is that accepting the separation thesis strengthens rather than weakens the role of morality in human life. If law is wicked, Hart says, it remains law nevertheless, but because legal duty is not the same as moral duty, there is no moral reason to obey it, and an upright person will defy wicked law. Those who think that wicked law is not really law at all are indulging in wishful thinking – wishful thinking that is immature in that it needs to fortify the autonomous conscience with the authority of law, and illiberal in that it fails to distinguish the individual from the state.

If Holmes's aim was primarily to defend the separation thesis, then I think that the intriguing suggestions of Levinson and Wells would indeed be very appealing. Holmes might well have dramatized their argument by picking some law his audience would have agreed was wicked – the Fugitive Slave Act, for example – and making the bad man into an antebellum abolitionist who (unlike John Brown) did not want to risk penalties for disobedience. Had Holmes done that, the *frisson* of outrage many of us still experience when the bad man steps onto the stage would dissipate, for we would understand that the bad man need not actually be bad – or rather, we would understand that "bad" in the legal sense need not mean "bad" in the moral sense.

Of course, Holmes did no such thing, and that is surely evidence that he was not trying to make Hart's argument. He said "bad man," and if any doubt lingers that he meant "bad man," let us recall that he contrasts the bad man with the good man, "who finds his reasons for conduct, *whether inside the law or outside of it,* in the vaguer sanctions of conscience" (171). Note the italicized phrase, which makes it clear that Holmes means to contrast the bad man not just with someone who takes all his cues from the law, but with someone who is guided by conscience outside the law as well as inside of it. In short, Holmes's "good man" is a man of conscience, and Holmes's "bad man" is not one.

The bad man does not figure in Holmes's supposed refutation of proposition (1) – his demonstration that moral rights need not be legal rights. Here he argues that "many laws have been enforced in the past, and it is likely that some are enforced now, which are condemned by the most enlightened opinion of the time, or which at all events pass the limit of interference as many consciences would draw it" (171). I call this a "supposed" refutation because it is not much of an argument. Almost nobody who seriously entertains the morality-in-law thesis denies that positive law can be immoral, nor that immoral laws are enforced. Rather, those who argue that moral rights are legal rights do not identify positive law with law as such. They argue, in the words of the classical natural law maxim, that unjust law is not law. Holmes, by contrast, believes the opposite: that unenforced law is not law – it is mere "empty words" (172). Holmes does not so much refute the natural lawyer's argument as assume it away.[29]

The bad man does put in an appearance in the discussion of (2), where Holmes notes that "our friend the bad man . . . does not care two straws for the axioms or deductions" of rules of law, "but . . . he does want to know what the . . . courts are likely to do in fact" (173). Here, the bad man comes closest to Attorney General Thornburgh's "client in need of legal advice." You do not have to be morally bad to lack interest in how a law that affects you fits in with the whole system of law; indeed, it is hard to imagine why a client would be interested in the whole deductive structure.[30]

But the most important use of the bad man is in Holmes's discussion of the nature of legal duty – his criticism of proposition (3). This is Holmes's famous argument that in much of private law – paradigmatically in contract law and tort law – the bad man regards damages as nothing more than a "tax" on conduct (breach, negligence). Of course, regarding damages as a tax removes any moral onus from the conduct: the income tax does not mean that earning an income is reprehensible, and thus the "tort tax" does not mean that tortious conduct is reprehensible. That is why the bad man's point of view removes a confusion between law and morality: if a fine is just a tax, then the supposed moral distinction between a penalty for wrongful conduct (the fine) and a levy on acceptable conduct (the tax) disappears, and with it the very point of calling one course of conduct wrong and the other acceptable.

The problem is that Holmes must show, not merely assert, that the bad man is right to regard a fine as just a tax. He must make the bad man's point of view plausible, and that is what the ensuing argument is about. Holmes's argument is an analysis of the logical form of law. In Holmes's words, "If you commit a tort, you are liable to pay a compensatory sum. If you commit a contract, you are liable to pay a compensatory sum unless the promised event comes to pass, and that is all the difference" (175). Holmes's point is that civil laws, or at any rate those protected by what are nowadays called liability rules, should not be read as categorical commands – "Fulfill contracts!" or "Take due care!" Rather, they are disjunctive in form: "Fulfill contracts, or pay compensation!" or "Take due care, or pay compensation for damage that results!"

Contrary to appearances, Holmes is not arguing here about whether we have a moral duty to obey the law, that is, whether a legal duty creates a corresponding moral duty. Any moral duty to obey a law in categorical form will be exactly the same if we recast the law in disjunctive form.

Holmes's own position in *The Path of the Law* acknowledges that laws can create genuine duties, whenever "equity will grant an injunction, and will enforce it by putting the defendant in prison or otherwise punishing him unless he complies with the order of the court" (175–76); presumably, the same would be true when conduct is enforced by criminal statutes, and indeed, Holmes states explicitly that his argument leaves "the criminal law on one side" (173). In contemporary parlance, Holmes is arguing that a law creates a genuine duty when it is enforced through a property rule rather than a liability rule.[31] Even in

Holmes's sense, a *very* bad man, who violates a contract *and* refuses to pay the fine *and* obstructs the effort to collect the fine, has violated a duty, because the court can throw him in jail to make him pay. But it is clear that the duties Holmes is discussing here, namely those that the law will enforce through punishment, are legal duties, not moral duties. For we have already seen him argue that laws are enforced that "pass the limits of interference as many consciences would draw it" (171).

Reading all of these passages together as a consistent whole, we see that Holmes's argument is not an attack on the moral status of legal duties. Rather, it is an attempt to eliminate a confusion within the concept of legal duty: a confusion between reading moral words appearing in legal texts in their moral sense, which suggests categorical obligations, and reading them in their legal sense, which (Holmes claims) implies only disjunctive obligations.

This reading meshes smoothly with Holmes's two final points in the discussion of proposition (3): that he is trying to warn us against "the trap which legal language lays for us" (179), and that it would avoid confusion to eliminate moral terms from the law entirely and replace them with artificial words carrying no extralegal connotations. His point is not to criticize the beliefs that law deals with moral issues and derives its content from moral principles. If that were his view, he would never assert that "[t]he law is the witness and external deposit of our moral life. Its history is the history of the moral development of the race" (170). Rather, his point is that the moral content of the law – the disjunctive duties it imposes – is simply different from what we would gather if we read moral terms morally. From the bad man's point of view, "the notion of duty shrinks and at the same time grows more precise," because we have "expel[led] everything except . . . the operations of the law" (174). By so doing, we lose nothing except "the fossil records of a good deal of history and the majesty got from ethical associations" (179) built into legal language.

Here, however, Holmes himself falls into confusion by overstating his point. On his own analysis, the moral and legal meanings of words are not simply unrelated, as they would be if it were really possible to replace morally loaded legal words with artificial terms. On the contrary, these meanings are systematically related. Suppose that in its moral sense negligence is wrong, so that the moral reading of tort law includes the categorical command "Don't be negligent!" On Holmes's analysis, the correct understanding of tort law would substitute "Either don't be negligent, or else pay for the damages that result." Here it is plain that the reanalysis leaves the meaning of the word "negligent" unchanged. The bad man trying to learn what kind of behavior will lead courts to make him pay compensation will have to know exactly what kind of behavior counts as negligent in the moral sense.

Holmes would respond that as they develop in the cases, moral words such as "malice," "intent," and "negligence" (his examples, 176) gradually change their meaning, and eventually become nothing more than homonyms of their ordinary-language counterparts. That is why it might "be a gain if every word of moral significance could be banished from the law altogether, and other words adopted which should convey legal ideas uncolored by anything outside the law" (179).

But Holmes exaggerates. As he himself argues, words initially enter legal language carrying moral baggage and nontechnical meanings. They may shed some of that baggage and acquire specialized senses as the case law develops them – but that proves very little, because words lose and gain connotations in any shift in context. There is actually no such thing as *the* ordinary meaning of a word: in different contexts, words lose some of their inference relations and gain others, without becoming mere homonyms.[32] Consider some everyday examples: *see*/light, *see*/point; *collect*/books, *collect*/friends, *collect*/debts, *collect*/barnacles; *make*/a sandwich, *make*/a bed, *make*/a mistake, *make*/time for, *make*/a plane, *make*/an appointment.[33] Meaning shifts permeate language. If we introduced a different word in each context, we certainly would not "gain very much in the clearness of our thought" (179), as Holmes suggests – just the opposite.

The bare fact that legal words diverge from their extralegal counterparts does not mean that they are different words with different meanings. Of course, some words, like "consideration," have acquired legal meanings having so little to do with their ordinary meanings that the two really are little more than homonyms. But such examples are few and far between, and the safest generalization is that if a word has moral connotations in ordinary usage, it probably has them in law as well. Holmes to the contrary, the word "negligence" remains a moral term even in tort law: to say that someone has fallen below the standard of care that a reasonable person would meet is a moral criticism, although it is not necessarily a moral criticism of the defendant's character.

Suppose we drop the homonym theory and ask why Holmes thinks that moral connotations in legal words are so misleading. In *The Path of the Law* he explains that "[m]orals deal with the actual internal state of the individual's mind, what he actually intends" (177). This explanation is perfectly in tune with his leading examples – the use of the term "malice" in the law of slander, and the will or meeting-of-minds theory of contractual obligation (176–78). His chief point in both of them is that in law the words lose their mentalistic connotations. But once we see this, we see that Holmes's attack on "confounding morality with law" (179) is much more modest in aim than it appears to be. Holmes does not demonstrate that law can be identified by its pedigree alone, without any reference to moral concepts – contemporary positivism's separation thesis. Instead, Holmes's explanations yield only his familiar theses that even ostensibly subjective concepts must be identified through objective tests, and that moral concepts in the law regulate conduct, not intentions.

Let me summarize the preceding discussion. I have been suggesting that Holmes's attack on the confusion of law with morality bears only a superficial resemblance to contemporary positivism's separation thesis. The resemblance is at its strongest where Holmes's argument is at its weakest – his question-begging attack on what I have called the morality-in-law thesis. Where his argument is at its strongest, it aims to defend conclusions that have nothing to do with modern positivism: first, that private-law rules should be analyzed disjunctively rather than categorically; second, that legal duties, properly so called, are only those enforced by property rules rather than liability rules; third, that the law relies on objective tests even when it invokes subjective concepts; fourth, that moral terms in the law are likely to mislead us unless we keep the first three points clearly in mind.

In addition, Holmes doubted that we have a moral obligation to obey the law, but that is only because he doubted that we have any moral obligations; he was certain that law cannot be deduced rationally from ethical principles; he doubted that ethical principles are rational; and he carelessly proposed a homonym theory of legal language that is not convincing. The first three of these ideas are central to Holmes's overall world-view, but none of the four is essential either to his attack in *The Path of the Law* on the confusion of law with morality or his discussion of the bad man.

On the reading offered here, it seems clear that the bad man is precisely Gordon's *homo law-and-economicus,* who, as Gordon says (Chapter 1), "treats all legal rules as prices on conduct, . . . , data for cost–benefit analysis. In Holmes, however, *homo law-and-economicus* is actually a pretty tame and law-abiding bad man, because even though he is willing to ask unsentimentally which disjunct in the "obey-or-pay" formula is cheaper, he is prepared to obey or pay.

For this reason, I have omitted one clause from Gordon's description, namely that the Gilded Age corporate client treats legal rules as "risks to be discounted by the probability of enforcement." There is no hint in *The Path of the Law* or elsewhere that Holmes understood that a genuinely bad man, "who cares only for the material consequences" (171), would think about enforcement probabilities as well as enforcement outcomes. If Holmes had appreciated this point, I suspect he would have seen straightaway that the bad man thesis is preposterous (for reasons I explain subsequently). Instead, he offers a bad man who asks his lawyer what a court would do if his conduct were litigated, but not how likely it is that his conduct will be litigated. The bad man chooses whichever disjunct in an obey-or-pay formula is cheaper but then complies with his legal duties, including court orders to pay, injunctions, and criminal statutes in categorical form.

Within the context of Holmes's argument, then, the bad man is a law-abiding rational calculator, and he functions as a rhetorical stick figure to bring to life the four major points in Holmes's analysis of legal duty.

The problem is that Holmes offers explicit definitions of the bad man that make him badder than the role he plays in Holmes's argument requires or – as I now suggest – even tolerates. These define him as someone who cares only about material consequences (and thus not about legal duties), and someone who, in contrast to the good man, is not motivated by conscience either inside or outside of the law. Regrettably, it is these definitions that remain most vivid in the hearer's and reader's memory – and it is these definitions that appear in Holmes's statement of the bad man thesis.

III. The Bad Man Thesis

This brings us back full circle to our earlier question: Why must we adopt the viewpoint of someone who cares only about material consequences and is unmoved by conscience, if we want to know the law? Let us consider the two most plausible answers.

1. THE BAD MAN THESIS AS AN EMPIRICAL HYPOTHESIS ABOUT CLIENTS. On one reading, as Gordon suggests, the bad man is a realistic picture of the usual corporate client of Holmes's day, who "treats all legal rules as prices on conduct, risks of sanctions to be discounted by the probability of enforcement, data for cost–benefit analysis." Gordon objects to this reading, and I agree with the objection, but for reasons slightly different from his. I doubt that many corporate clients – or noncorporate clients, for that matter – are really as reptilian as Holmes's bad man. Holmes cautions that it is not "advisable to shape general theory from the exception" ("Path" 176), and the bad man is the exception.

What is the harm in assuming that clients are Holmesian bad men? The problem is that if a lawyer assumes that every client is a bad man, the lawyer will shape the legal representation in a way that makes the assumption come true. Most of us, I expect, have known decent people going through a divorce who decided to retain a "bomber" to ensure that their interests were safeguarded – people whose decency quickly became irrelevant as the escalating battle of hired guns made life hell for their spouses and children, often for years on end.

2. THE BAD MAN THESIS AS A HEURISTIC DEVICE. What about the idea that the bad man is not supposed to be an operational assumption, but only a heuristic for analyzing the nature of legal duties? Gordon is right that Holmes's rhetoric, especially his explicit endorsement of the bad man's view of the law (173), appears to make the construct more than a mere heuristic. Nevertheless, there is something to the idea of viewing it as a heuristic, for the topic of Holmes's essay is the study of law, and Holmes's advice to take up the standpoint of the bad man seems clearly to be advice about how to study law, not how to practice it.

However, it is not very good advice about how to study law. Look closely at the bad man thesis: "If you want to know the law and nothing else, you must look at it as a bad man, who cares only for the material consequences which such knowledge enables him to predict" (171). There is something paradoxical on its face in Holmes's claim that to understand the law and nothing else you must look at it from the standpoint of someone who is interested only in extralegal consequences, that is, only in something else. How could it be that you cannot understand the law except from the standpoint of someone who does not give a damn about the law?

If Holmes's formula is right, then the lawyer whose client asks: "What are my legal obligations?" will advise the client about material consequences and nothing more. For example, a tax lawyer will answer the question not primarily by explaining the client's tax liability, but by explaining the audit lottery – the fact that the Internal Revenue Service selects only 2 percent of returns for random audits.

I am not arguing that the lawyer should withhold this information if the client asks for it, although I see no good reason for the lawyer to volunteer it. My objection is a conceptual one: it is that thinking of law from the bad man's point of view creates confusion, not clarity. It conflates advice about what the law requires with advice about how to violate the law without getting caught. More bluntly, it confuses advice about how to comply with the law with advice about how to evade the law. Holmes's protest (170) to the contrary, it is hard to imagine a more cynical theory of law. It calls to mind, of course, Ambrose Bierce's definition of a lawyer as one skilled in circumventing the law.

In short: there really is no good reason for adopting the bad man's standpoint, either in order to understand law or to practice it. If you adopt the bad man's standpoint to study law, you will learn little about law, although you may learn about consequences, including unintended ones. And if you adopt his standpoint to practice law, you will probably disserve your client. There is likewise no good reason for believing that the law has nothing to do with morality – and the more it has to do with morality, the less welcome your helpful advice will be, even to the bad man.

IV. The Good Lawyer

It seems that the basic elements of Holmes's jurisprudence in *The Path of the Law* – the bad man thesis and the critique of morality in law – incorporate serious confusions.[34] The implications of this for legal ethics are important. If there is no need to assume the bad man's point of view, and if legal duty has a moral dimension, then the lawyer's moral convictions about the rightness of law have a role to play in legal advice.

This is not quite a resurrection of the minister-of-justice argument, because basing advice on moral convictions is not the same as basing advice on the social purposes immanent in the law. But it is an explanation of why lawyers like Moorefield Storey and Louis Brandeis offer not only a more inspiring but also a more defensible ideal than Holmes's lawyer-thinker.

V. And Yet . . .

In the end, I am not confident that either Gordon or I have done Holmes justice by taking him at his word. Intuitively, it seems to me that Holmes is a more admirable, even lovable, lawyer than his own fierce rhetoric and tough talk would suggest. In the teeth of his own theoretical views, Holmes appears to have had an unselfconsciously decent notion of what lawyers should be. Indeed, he held a relatively decent notion of what clients are, for his bad man – who wants to know what the courts will do but not how to evade detection – is tamer than Holmes's definitions imply.

Consider a few passages in which Holmes conveys his sense of lawyers, the first from one of his eulogies:

> I am happy to think . . . that now it is the rule that a lawyer will try his case like a gentleman without giving up any portion of his energy and his force.[35]

Perhaps this is merely a formulaic puff for civility. But I think it more likely that Holmes really was happy that a lawyer would try his case like a gentleman. Let us proceed:

> I should say that one of the good things about the law is that it does not pursue money directly. When you sell goods the price which you get and your own interests are what you think about in the affair. When you try a case you think about the ways to win it and the interests of your client.[36]

And two passages from *The Path of the Law* itself:

> The practice of [law], in spite of popular jests, tends to make good citizens and good men. (170).

> Law is the business to which my life is devoted, and I should show less than devotion if I did not do what in me lies to improve it. (194)

Take the final passage first, with its easy to miss play on two meanings of the word "devotion," as preoccupation and reverence. Many lawyers "devote" their lives to the business of law without showing it the "devotion" of trying to improve it. In this passage Holmes describes law as a business, but he does not treat it as one.

Working backward to the second-last passage, notice that Holmes insists that the practice of law tends to make good men just one paragraph after he has introduced the bad man. The contrast must be intentional. The bad man always treats business as business, but Holmes once again seems to think that lawyers are different.

The preceding quotation states his reason why: lawyers, unlike businessmen, pursue money indirectly, putting the interests of their clients in the driver's seat. Gordon is clearly correct, then, when he suggests that Holmes's views would still have to travel a long way before they reached the ultimate reduction of lawyers' work our own day has achieved to evaluation by "a strictly commercial metric." Gordon's examples of what he means center on the relentless Babbittry of partners in large law firms who keep their eyes fixed on the AmLaw 100 while they run the meter on their clients, but the same could be said of plaintiffs' lawyers in settlements of class-action suits, who may bid down the value of their clients' rights in return for the franchise to sell them.[37] The ultimate reduction Gordon describes is nothing less than the transformation of the lawyer from Holmes's good man to Holmes's bad man. Indeed, one remarkable point about the opening of *The Path of the Law* is that although Holmes is willing to assume that the client is a bad man, it never seems to cross his mind that the lawyer might be one as well.

In these and other occasional passages in his writings, Holmes displays the ultimate sign of good character: it never even occurs to him to be dishonorable. In the end, Holmes's personality may be an argument against moral skepticism stronger than his philosophical arguments for it.

Notes

1 Robert W. Gordon, "Law as a Vocation: Holmes and the Lawyer's Path," Chapter 1, in this volume.
2 "I say . . . that a man may live greatly in the law as well as elsewhere; that there as well as elsewhere his thought may find its unity in an infinite perspective; that there as well as elsewhere he may wreak himself upon life, may drink the bitter cup of heroism, may wear his heart out after the unattainable." Oliver Wendell Holmes, Jr., "The Profession of Law," in *Collected Legal Papers* (New York: Harcourt, Brace, & Howe, 1920), 30.
3 Sheldon M. Novick, *Honorable Justice: The Life of Oliver Wendell Holmes* (Boston: Little, Brown, 1989), 223.
4 Oliver Wendell Holmes, Jr., "The Path of the Law," in *Collected Legal Papers,* ed. Mark DeWolfe Howe (Cambridge, Mass.: Harvard University Press, 1910), 167. (Cited hereafter parenthetically as "Path" by page number. *Collected Legal Papers* is cited hereafter as "CLP.") ("The Path" is reproduced with star paging in the Appendix of this volume.)

At the beginning of his argument for de-moralizing the law, Holmes writes: "I wish . . . to lay down some first principles for the study of this body of dogma . . . which we call law" (169). Later he refers to "the object of our study, the operations of the law" (174). He sums up his argument for basing legal decisions on social advantage by recommending that "the training of lawyers" focus on it (184), then turns immediately to "law as a subject for study" (185). Next he launches his historical attack on unthinking traditionalism, only to conclude that it shows "the part which the study of history necessarily plays in the intelligent study of the law as it is to-day" (194). His point about Roman law is that students should skip it. When he turns to jurisprudence, he describes it as "another study" (195), and in his coda, Holmes repeats: "I have been speaking about the study of the law" (200).
5 Sheldon Novick writes that Holmes's title "is probably a conscious reference to the Tao, a term that connotes both a path to understanding and a way of life: as in Bushido, the Way of the Warrior, a term Holmes almost certainly knew." Novick, *Honorable Justice,* 451n. I

am unsure on what basis Novick comes to this opinion, but the somewhat different double meaning I note in the text – "path" as evolutionary trajectory and "path" as way of life – seems closer to the surface of the English. Of course, the third meaning – path to understanding – may well be an overtone that Holmes also meant to sound.

6 See, e.g., William H. Simon, *The Practice of Justice: A Theory of Lawyers' Ethics* (Cambridge, Mass.: Harvard University Press, 1998); "Ethical Discretion in Lawyering," *Harvard Law Review* 101 (1988):1083; David Luban, "The Noblesse Oblige Tradition in the Practice of Law," *Vanderbilt Law Review* 41 (1988):717; Robert Gordon, *Lawyers as the American Aristocracy* (forthcoming); Robert Gordon, "Corporate Law as a Public Calling," *Maryland Law Review* 49 (1990):255. Simon argues that lawyers lie under an ethical obligation to achieve justice, which he identifies with the purposes underlying the law. In response to the obvious objection that some law has unjust purposes, he answers that if so, it is inconsistent with other, more fundamental legal values to which the lawyer must respond. William H. Simon, "Should Lawyers Obey the Law?", *William and Mary Law Review* 38 (1996):217; "Ethical Discretion in Lawyering," esp. 1115–16. Gordon paraphrases the functionalist view as "the belief that a legal system pursues, and its products reveal, immanent social purposes; that to all social conflicts there are efficient structural-functional solutions that harmonize with these purposes – the long-run needs of the society and its evolving public values." Gordon, *Lawyers as Aristocracy*, 15, 21–22. I have argued that versions of this view can be found in Tocqueville, Brandeis, Durkheim, and many contemporary public-interest lawyers.

7 See, e.g., 193. Holmes elaborates this argument more fully in "Law in Science – Science in Law," in CLP, 225–29.

8 Usually they are war metaphors: social purposes are "battle grounds" ("Path," 181), and "law embodies beliefs that have triumphed in the battle of ideas" ("Law and the Court" in CLP, 294). To Holmes, "while opposite convictions still keep a battle front against each other, the time for law has not come" (ibid., 295). In "Law in Science," he invokes the rise and fall of civilizations: "After victory the law of covenant and debt went on, and consolidated and developed their empire . . . until they in turn lost something of their power and prestige in consequence of the rise of a new rival, Assumpsit" (220–21). Occasionally the metaphor comes from physics: a judge's business is "to express . . . the resultant . . . of the pressure of the past and the conflicting wills of the present" ("Twenty Years in Retrospect," in *The Occasional Speeches of Justice Oliver Wendell Holmes*, ed. Mark DeWolfe Howe [Cambridge, Mass.: Harvard University Press, 1962], 156; cited hereafter as "OS"). At least once, the language is Darwinian as well as military: legal rules "show a lively example of the struggle for life among competing ideas, and of the ultimate victory and survival of the strongest" ("Law in Science," 220). The next sentence is ambiguously military.

9 Holmes, *Natural Law*, in CLP, 310.
10 Holmes, "Admiral Dewey," in OS, 109.
11 Ibid., 105.
12 Holmes, "The Soldier's Faith," in OS, 73.
13 Holmes, "George Otis Shattuck," in OS, 93.
14 Holmes, "Profession of Law," 28.
15 Holmes, "Remarks to the Essex Bar," in OS, 49; Holmes, "Sidney Bartlett," in OS, 53–54; Holmes, "Daniel S. Richardson," in OS, 57–58; Holmes, "Anonymity and Achievement," in OS, 59–61; Holmes, "Shattuck," 96.

16 Holmes, "Shattuck," 96.
17 Ibid.
18 See also Holmes, "Profession of Law," 29; Holmes, "Commencement Address, Brown University," in OS, 98.
19 Holmes, "Profession of Law," 28.
20 Holmes, "Bartlett," 54.
21 Holmes to James Bryce, 17 August 1879, quoted in G. Edward White, *Justice Oliver Wendell Holmes: Law and the Inner Self* (New York: Oxford University Press, 1993), 130.
22 Ibid.
23 Holmes to Frankfurter, 15 July 1913, in *Holmes and Frankfurter: Their Correspondence, 1912–1934,* ed. Robert M. Memel and Christine L. Compston (Hanover, N.H.: University Press of New England, 1996), 12. See also "Law in Science," 224; "Shattuck," 95; "The Use of Colleges," in OS, 62–63.
24 Holmes, "Law in Science," 224.
25 Gordon's fascinating comparison of Holmes with Max Weber leads me to observe that if Holmes was confused about what it is to be a thinker, Weber was more confused. Karl Jaspers offers the following recollection:
   [S]hortly after the publication of "Science as a Vocation" Max Weber, Thoma (a jurist) and I sat talking together one Sunday afternoon in the garden of the lovely house on the Ziegelhäuser-Landstrasse. Weber's talk, which had caused a great stir at the time, was of course the main topic of conversation. This talk was tough, implacable, and moving.
      I said something to this effect: You say nothing about the meaning of scholarship. If it is no more than what you say it is, then why do you bother with it? I spoke about Kant's "ideas" and said that every branch of science and scholarship acquires a meaning that goes beyond scholarship only by virtue of an idea. Max Weber knew next to nothing about Kantian ideas and did not respond. Finally, I said, turning to Thoma: "He doesn't know himself what meaning scholarship has and why he engages in it." Max Weber winced visibly: "Well, if you insist: to see what one can endure, but it is better not to talk of such things."
Karl Jaspers to Hannah Arendt, 16 November 1966, in *Hannah Arendt–Karl Jaspers Correspondence, 1926–1969,* ed. Lotte Kohler and Hans Saner, trans. Robert Kimber and Rita Kimber (New York: Harcourt Brace Jovanovitch, 1992), 660–61.
26 David Luban, "Justice Holmes and the Metaphysics of Judicial Restraint," *Duke Law Journal* 44 (1994):449.
27 "Despondency and Hope," in OS, 148.
28 H. L. A. Hart, "Positivism and the Separation of Law and Morals," *Harvard Law Review* 71 (1958):593.
29 But sometimes the natural lawyer bites back, as in Fuller's devastating criticism of positivism and realism, couched in language as strong as Holmes's, in Lon L. Fuller, *The Law in Quest of Itself* (Chicago: Foundation Press, 1940). Fuller shows that positivism and realism rely on unrealistic abstractions and occult entities – ironically, exactly the charge that their adherents usually level at natural law theories.
30 On the other hand, if law and ethics together form "a system of reason," then to say that the bad man does not care two straws about this system is to say that he is irrational, which, even Holmes would agree, is a criticism. Holmes does not take this possibility seriously enough to criticize; in his view, "morals are imperfect social generalizations expressed in terms of feeling," not truths of reason, and he was an instinctive ethical noncognitivist. See Holmes to Einstein, 21 May 1914, in Oliver Wendell Holmes, *The Holmes–Einstein Letters: The Correspondence of Mr. Justice Holmes and Lewis Einstein, 1903–1935,* ed. James Bishop Peabody (New York: St. Martin's, 1962), 93.

31 In this respect, Holmes's position in "The Path" has not changed from his early view that when a legislature has an "absolute wish" to prohibit conduct, the legal norm it creates is categorical, and the penalty attached cannot be regarded as a tax. See Oliver Wendell Holmes, "Book Notices," in *The Formative Essays of Justice Holmes: The Making of an American Legal Philosophy,* ed. Frederic Rogers Kellogg (Westport, Conn.: Greenwood, 1984), 91, 92–93.

32 Here I am following the contemporary view that identifies the meaning – the semantics – of an expression with the sum total of the inference relations it enters into. On this view, synonymy is a matter of degree: two expressions that share most but not all of their respective inference relations (or analogous inference relations) have similar meanings, and the fewer the shared inferences, the more dissimilar the meanings. If the two expressions are uses of the selfsame ideograph, then in the former case it makes sense to refer to them as alternative meanings of the same word, while in the latter case they are mere homonyms.

33 I take these examples from James F. Ross, *Portraying Analogy* (Cambridge: Cambridge University Press, 1981), 4–5.

34 So does the prediction theory – but showing why would take us too far afield. For a detailed argument, see the expanded version of this essay, Luban, "Bad Man and Good Lawyer," 1577–80.

35 Holmes, "William Crownenshield Endicott," in OS, 118.

36 Holmes, "The Bar as a Profession," in CLP, 153.

37 Susan P. Koniak, "Feasting While the Widow Weeps: *Georgine v. Amchem Products, Inc.,*" *Cornell Law Review* 80 (1995):1045; John C. Coffee, Jr., "Class Wars: The Dilemma of the Mass Tort Class Action Claim," *Columbia Law Review* 95 (1995):1343.

3

Why Practice Needs Ethical Theory
Particularism, Principle, and Bad Behavior

MARTHA C. NUSSBAUM*

> Innocence is indeed a glorious thing; but, unfortunately, it does not keep very well and is easily led astray. Consequently, even wisdom – which consists more in doing and not doing than in knowing – needs science, not in order to learn from it, but in order that wisdom's precepts may gain acceptance and permanence. . . . Thus is ordinary human reason forced to go outside its sphere and take a step into the field of practical philosophy, not by any need for speculation (which never befalls such reason so long as it is content to be mere sound reason) but on practical grounds themselves . . . Thus when ordinary practical reason cultivates itself, there imperceptibly arises in it a dialectic which compels it to seek help in philosophy.
>
> Immanuel Kant, *Groundwork for the Metaphysics of Morals*[1]

> Human beings, that exceedingly gentle type of being, are not ashamed to revel in the blood of others, to wage war, and to hand on the waging of war to their children, although even dumb and wild beasts keep peace among their own kind. Against this overmastering and widespread madness, philosophy has become more elaborate, and has taken on ambition and force in proportion to the growth in forces on the other side.
>
> Seneca, *Moral Epistle* 95

> For the apotheosis of Reason we have substituted that of Instinct; and we call everything instinct which we find in ourselves and for which we cannot trace any rational foundation.
>
> J. S. Mill, *The Subjection of Women*

---

* I am very grateful to Steve Burton for the occasion to develop these ideas, to Scott Brewer, Ken Kress, Dan Kahan, David Luban, and Catharine Wells for insightful comments at the Holmes conference ("The Path of the Law in the Twentieth Century," held at the University of Iowa College of Law on 24–25 January 1997) and to Eric Brown, Tracey Meares, Richard Posner, Eric Schliesser, and Cass Sunstein for valuable comments on an earlier draft. I am especially grateful to Bernard Williams for his lengthy comments, which I have tried to address in revising. I am sure, however, that I have not answered all of his questions.

I. Enemies of Ethical Theory

Ethical theory is under attack. That is nothing new: attacks on ethical theory began, in the Western tradition,[2] with the subject itself, which alarmed people who saw advantages in the unexamined life. No sooner did Socrates gain a following than he was indicted, convicted, and killed. Aristotle, fleeing a second time into exile, said that he did not want the Athenians "to sin twice against philosophy."[3] The emperor Nero knew Stoic moral theory too well to be content with its defense of liberty. After dispatching his mother, he turned, in 69 A.D., to his philosophical mentor Seneca, who was later to pattern his mandatory suicide closely on the death of Socrates. "Even in his last moments his eloquence did not fail him. He called scribes in and dictated a good deal, which, since it is published in his collected works, I shall not bother to adapt."[4] Marcus Aurelius philosophized with impunity until his death, but then he was the emperor. Other thinkers under the Empire were less fortunate. The fifth century saw the death of the eminent Neoplatonist philosopher Hypatia at the hands of a Christian mob in Alexandria, incited by a local bishop who said it was unchaste for women to argue in public. They dragged her from her litter and beat her to death with sticks; the bishop became Saint Cyril. Some time thereafter, again under Christian influence, the schools of philosophy at Athens were closed entirely.

The Middle Ages greeted philosophical theorizing with much skepticism; it was not until Thomas Aquinas that the subject established itself in Church-dominated universities. Renaissance humanists revived Greek ethical theorizing at a great personal and political risk. In the seventeenth century Grotius advanced his theory of the just war from exile after being smuggled out of Holland in a trunk by his wife and family.[5]

Nor did danger fail to greet his Enlightenment successors. The Scottish Enlightenment was relatively gentle in its restrictions: Hume's alleged atheism did not jeopardize his life or stop the publication of his works. But it did cause him to be denied the chair of philosophy in Edinburgh, a judgment approved by one contemporary opponent of ethical theory, on the grounds that ethical theory should derive its first principles from religious authority.[6] On the Continent, philosophers faced sharper opposition. In France, many works of ethical theory, viewed as anticlerical, had to be clandestinely circulated along with works of sexual pornography. A common genus, *philosophie,* covered both types of writing: Voltaire and Rousseau alongside the scandalous *Thérèse philosophe* and the *Histoire du Dom B. . . .*[7] In Germany the book trade was more decorous, but Kant, no friend of the pornographers, still had to fight for freedom of speech for philosophy. In 1795, writing on the conditions necessary for a lasting peace among nations, he cited as the "Secret Article of a Perpetual Peace" the freedom of speech of the moral philosophers, without whose aid, he argued, governments cannot succeed in making a productive plan for the containment of aggression. "Kings or sovereign peoples," he wrote, "should not . . . force the class of philosophers to disappear or to remain silent . . . This is essential to both in order that light may be thrown on their affairs."[8]

Nor, in our own century, has moral philosophy failed to threaten and be threatened. We have seen the political persecution of moral philosophers such as John Dewey and Bertrand Russell (imprisoned twice for his arguments against war and tossed out of a job at the City University of New York for allegedly "obscene" writings on marriage that were later praised in his Nobel Prize citation);[9] the stocking of Eastern European philosophy departments with drones and sycophants; the virtual impossibility of doing moral philosophy at all in Cuba, China, and many other parts of the world, even when other parts of the subject, such as logic and the philosophy of science, are permitted to proceed more or less as usual.[10]

It is nothing new, then, that ethical theory should be assailed from outside, by religion, politics, and custom, by power and anti-reason and sheer bad behavior. What is new, however, is that these days it is also under attack from within. During the past decade a number of prominent moral philosophers, including Bernard Williams, Annette Baier, Alasdair MacIntyre, and Cora Diamond, have assailed ethical theorizing, especially in its Enlightenment forms, as both useless and pernicious, as distorting practice and contributing nothing that could not be gained through more informal types of ethical reflection.

It might strike one that the external assault gives some evidence against the "uselessness" part of the internal charge. Any type of intellectual activity that is so vigilantly opposed by power is unlikely to be utterly without practical value. Nor do Williams and Baier, at any rate, want to yield the scene of social and personal decision making to the conservative and/or authoritarian forces that, in these various cases, opposed the philosophers.[11] One might suppose, then, that the persecution of philosophers would give these thinkers, too, at least some reasons to defend the influence of ethical theory as not altogether pernicious, and to hold not only that it has a practical impact but that this impact has done some good.

That they do not support the enterprise is, however, clear. Baier declares: "I want to attack the whole idea of a moral 'theory' which systematizes and extends a body of moral judgments" and inveighs against "that arrogance of solitary intellect which has condemned much moral theory to sustained self-delusions concerning its subject matter, its methods, and its authority."[12] For Williams, the major modern moral theories are "not well adjusted to the modern world" and are "governed by a dream of a community of reason that is too far removed . . . from social and historical reality and from any concrete sense of a particular ethical life – farther removed from those things, in some ways, than the religion it replaced."[13] Diamond's position is more elusive, since she doubts that we can succeed in finding any widely agreed account of what the enterprise of ethical theory is; but insofar as she does propose such an account, she concludes that "we should not take those rules seriously, or the conception of moral philosophy which they determine."[14] There are complexities in all of these thinkers' positions; it is not clear that any of them opposes all of the prominent ethical theories, or that the grounds of their opposition cannot be met by something that most of us would agree in calling a theory. I press these questions in what follows. Evidently, however, they all take themselves to be showing that, on at least some widely shared understandings of what ethical theory involves, ethical theory is both unimportant and, insofar as it does affect things, mostly damaging – a squeezing and deforming of particular experience that may actually prevent us from making the more valuable types of criticism of our daily lives.[15]

My purpose in this essay is to state these objections and to contest them. I begin by enumerating some of the central criteria of ethical theory, as it has been defined in debates both ancient and modern. I next introduce a distinction familiar in ancient Greek and Roman Stoicism but largely absent from the modern debate. The Stoics recognized not two categories – theories and concrete judgments – but three categories: theories, rules, and concrete judgments. I argue, with Seneca, that the distinction between theories and rules is an extremely important one, which enables us to avoid a number of confusions. I lay out some Stoic arguments for thinking that there is a natural alliance between theory and particular judgment, in that theory enables us to understand the limitations of general rules in ways we could not otherwise, therefore enabling us to correct the deficiencies inherent in any system of rules. Thus, criticism of systems of rules need not entail criticism of ethical theory and can, in fact, give us reasons for turning to an ethical theory.

With all this in place, I then identify the most prominent recent objections to ethical theory and argue that there is none that cannot be met by something still recognizably theory – although some of the more telling objections will lead us to reject theories that (unlike all ancient and most interesting modern theories) identify theory with a system of rules. Finally, I argue that we urgently need theory, for the reasons given by Kant and Seneca. In a world in which moral perception is corrupt and judgment likely to be thrown off track by temptations of all sorts, we need all of the explicitness and articulateness that we can muster if we are to elicit the best from ourselves, to identify defects in our social world, and to devise appropriate institutional and educational remedies.

This investigation should shed light on the contemporary legal scene, where anti-theoretical accounts of legal reasoning are increasingly in evidence, perhaps especially in my own university, so much so that Ronald Dworkin, the leading proponent of ethical theorizing in law, has recently spoken of a "new Chicago School" of legal anti-theory.[16] Some of the attacks on moral theory in law are based on specific arguments about the nature of legal reasoning and do not entail a rejection of ethical theory.[17] Others, however, do entail the more general attack and ground their arguments in anti-theoretical work in philosophy.[18] Here they also sometimes appeal to the influence of Oliver Wendell

Holmes, Jr., read in a particular way.[19] Holmes is often taken to be an ethical anti-theorist of a rather extreme kind, both about the law specifically and about ethical reasoning more generally. There are some statements in his writings that support this. The famous dictum, "The life of the law has not been logic: it has been experience,"[20] sounds, at least, like a rejection of abstract systems of thought, at least in the legal sphere. In a letter of 1899, Holmes made this rejection explicit, extending it to thought in general. He argues: "[A]ll the use of life is in specific solutions – which cannot be reached through generalities any more than a picture can be painted by knowing some rules of method. They are reached by insight, tact, and specific knowledge."[21] Elsewhere, however, he associates this very same idea of reasoning as picture painting with Aristotle, whom Holmes could not have considered to be an anti-theorist.[22] Indeed, he praises Aristotle's combination of general ideals with attunement to the complexity of particular cases, contrasting the *Nicomachean Ethics,* in this regard, with the "slapdash universals" of "ordinary Christian morality." These remarks suggest not a wholesale rejection of theory, but rather the acceptance of a particular type of theory. My purpose here, however, is not at all to mine Holmes's writings for the countless passages that bear on this question; it is to illuminate the general issue raised by Holmes's ambivalence toward theory, and to assess the contemporary philosophical debate that is invoked by the new Chicago-based legal movement.[23] Insofar as there are some good reasons for being skeptical about "slapdash universals," then, are these reasons to reject ethical theory or simply to prefer one type of theory to another? And are there other good reasons why we should not try to jettison theory in favor of "insight, tact, and specific knowledge"?

Two preliminary remarks. First, although I do have a preferred type of ethical theory, which combines elements of the Aristotelian and the Kantian approaches, I am not defending it here. My objections to utilitarianism do, however, become evident in many parts of the account. Nor do I defend my own preferred account of justification, which I share with Aristotle and John Rawls.[24] Inevitably, in the course of responding to attacks on theory, I give examples that I favor, but, where possible, I try to show how the attacks might be met by more than one sort of theory.

Second, there is an issue about the ethical and the political. In some recent qualifications to his anti-theory program, Williams has introduced a distinction between political and ethical theory, asserting that theory may serve useful purposes in the former domain but not in the latter. It is not easy to understand how this distinction is drawn, and I do not use that distinction here. It may be doubted, first, whether there are any elements of the ethical that are not political, but we do not have to establish that controversial proposition here, since we are not being urged to do ethics without political theory. We are being urged to do politics without ethical theory, so the real issue is whether there are useful political theories that do not have an ethical theory at their core – that would not be gutted of force by the removal of ethical theory. In *Ethics and the Limits of Philosophy,* Williams uses Rawls's theory of justice as a major example of a moral theory, defending it as such by saying, correctly, that although Rawls's theory is a political theory it has a moral foundation. One could hardly, it seems, have the political theory without this moral-theoretical foundation – any more than one could have Kant's arguments against aggressive war without the moral theory that makes them arguments rather than mere assertions, or Grotius's doctrine of the right of humanitarian intervention without the moral account of humanity as an end that gives it its substance, or Catharine MacKinnon's conclusions about sexual harassment without the moral account of objectification and the deformation of desire that makes them interesting.

One may, of course, insist, with Rawls, that citizens can agree on a partially comprehensive conception of value for political purposes and yet refrain from endorsing the entirety of the related moral theory as a fully comprehensive theory of value for all areas of life. Thus, as Rawls has recently insisted in *Political Liberalism,* one may endorse the Kantian ethical conception as a conception of justice for political purposes while remaining a Thomist or an economic utilitarian in respect of one's account of other goals and virtues. But that is a different point from Williams's, since the moral underpinnings of the political conception are still to be endorsed by all citizens as morally valid within the sphere to which they apply. This sphere includes the family, which is part of the basic structure of society. That full endorsement is crucial to the distinction between an overlapping consensus and a mere modus vivendi: citizens are to accept that the morality of justice is as Rawls describes it. So it seems inappropriate to deny that it is a moral conception or the theory a moral theory. Rawls has repeatedly emphasized that his political conception is in fact the articulation of a special type of moral theory. So I proceed on the assumption that a wholesale attack on moral theory disables political theory, at least political theory of the sort I have been discussing here. We should, however, leave open the possibility that in Williams's thought political theory of a different, non-Rawlsian kind (without foundations in an ethical theory) could still play a valuable role.

II. What Is an Ethical Theory?

Before we can begin, we need some account of the item in dispute.[25] This is tricky, since all sorts of different items have turned up in definitions of ethical theory, some so controversial that their acceptance would entail directly that ethical theory is in grave difficulty. (Thus, if it were granted that something is an ethical theory just in case it states that there are no moral dilemmas, or that there are no exceptions to generally binding rules, many people would immediately concur in the rejection of theory. But it seems implausible to make either of these stipulations, since something that most of us would agree to call theory can easily reject these contentions, as quite a few well-respected theories have.) Nor have the antagonists always been forthcoming with their criteria. Baier mentions "explicitness," "universality," "systematicity," and "hierarchical ordering" but offers no general definition of theory that shows which of these items she views as necessary and/or sufficient for it. Moreover, several of her concrete claims – for example, the claim that neither Aristotle nor Hume has an ethical theory – cast doubt on some of the criteria enumerated, insofar as they characterize the work of those thinkers as well; her historical remarks are more puzzling than helpful, in the absence of further evidence about the way in which she is interpreting the authors in question. Diamond, as I have said, rejects the whole enterprise of giving even a "rough story"[26] about what ethical theory is; it is therefore extremely difficult to tell what her anti-theoretical remarks are directed against.

Williams is much more direct, defining theory as follows: "An ethical theory is a theoretical account of what ethical thought and practice are, which account either implies a general test for the correctness of basic ethical beliefs and principles or else implies that there cannot be such a test."[27] But we need to ask what this statement means, for Williams grants that Rawls's theory is an ethical theory, and yet Rawls's theory, by his own description, holds that the process of justification is holistic, and that there is no single "test" for beliefs, the criterion of rightness being given by overall fit within the system as a whole. Moreover, Rawls holds that concrete beliefs sometimes test theoretical claims. So Williams's general definition must be intended to be elastic enough to include this more holistic sort of "testing."[28] Elsewhere, Williams mentions other criteria for theory: theory involves the attempt to "systematize" (ELP 116); it "looks characteristically for considerations that are very general and have as little distinctive content as possible"; it is a "structure of propositions" that "in part provides a framework for our beliefs, in part criticizes or revises them" (ELP 93). But it remains not fully clear which of these, if any, is intended as a necessary condition of theory.

I proceed in two ways: first, by mentioning examples of ethical theory that seem to me so clear that any account of theory that does not cover them is peculiar; second, by mentioning some of the features of theory that I take to be most pertinent to the contemporary debate – though here I do not include features that simply do not fit a significant number of the examples. The examples are Aristotle, the Greek and Roman Stoics, Aquinas, Hume, Kant, Adam Smith, Bentham, Mill, Sidgwick, and Rawls. (I select these in part for their obviousness, in part for the fact that they are the primary targets for the attackers. I myself would be happy to include Spinoza, Hobbes, Rousseau, and quite a few others; I later discuss Grotius, as one example of the Stoic tradition; but this list is sufficient for our purposes.)

An ethical theory, I suggest, might usefully be thought of as a set of reasons and interconnected arguments, explicitly and systematically articulated, with some degree of abstractness and generality that gives directions for ethical practice. I focus here on six criteria.[29] An ethical theory

1. *Gives recommendations about practical problems.* An ethical theory gives direction for practice: it shows us how to make progress on ethical problems. There is no reason to think that this progress need be easy or straightforward: one way of making progress is to identify complexities and difficulties. Nor is there any reason to suppose that this progress need involve direct application of theory to unreformed practice – as opposed, say, to instructions for the reform of institutions and of moral education.
2. *Shows how to test correctness of beliefs, rules, and principles.* I revise Williams's definition to make room for his own central case, Rawls's account of the search for reflective equilibrium, in which principles and judgments inform one another and none is held absolutely fixed. Some theories (e.g., those of Socrates[30] and, to some degree, Cicero) prefer to hold concrete judgments fixed and to use those as a test for principles; others prefer to use principles as a test for judgments; Rawls, like Aristotle and Sidgwick, allows illumination to travel in both directions. All of these seem acceptable ways for a theory to proceed; what is essential to its being a theory is that it give us some account of how to proceed in doing this; this account may allow a good deal of room for further interpretation and judgment, as it does in the case of Aristotle and Rawls.
3. *Systematizes and extends beliefs.* One of the major purposes of having an ethical theory is to bring the material of ethical experience into a perspicuous ordering, rendering the incoherent coherent (by suitable revision and discarding), and showing how one thing relates to another. This also makes it possible to extend the application of principles to previously unconsidered material, or to see how one concrete judgment can be extended to similar cases.
4. *Has some degree of abstractness and generality.* An ethical theory is only as abstract as its insights deem relevant: if we took as a necessary condition for an ethical theory that it regard all concrete situations and relationships as ethically irrelevant, we would omit virtually all of the theories on our list of examples. (For Kant, particular relationships are highly relevant to duties of beneficence; even utilitarians can admit such relationships as relevant to the strategies by which agents maximize universal happiness.) On the other hand, a theory cannot consist of simply a collection of reports on concrete particular judgments in concrete contexts. It is a theory only if it can give guidance for the future (see point 1); but this means that it must abstract, to at least some degree. There are obviously both good and bad ways to do this, and this concerns me in what follows.[31]
5. *Is universalizable.* An ethical theory should be applicable to all agents as such, rather than to agents simply in virtue of being members of a given com-

munity or religious group. This does not mean that an ethical theory cannot recommend latitude for people to pursue attachments to their communities or religious groups. It also does not mean (see point 4) that an ethical theory cannot allow its principles to be applicable only to people whose ethical situation is relevantly similar; any sensible theory has an account of relevant similarities and differences. These may or may not include family relationship, friendship, the character and propensities of the people in question, whether the agent is oneself or not, and so forth. Again, to say that a theory may not take these into account would be to make theory a virtually empty category. (In general, any categorization of theory according to which Kant does not have a theory should be condemned as empty rhetoric.) Universals may be, in this sense, highly concrete, and probably they must be to give appropriate guidance.[32]

6. *Is explicit.* A theory is, if it is anything, a set of explicit guidelines for practice: it is written down or otherwise promulgated and is available to be consulted by all. This does not mean that it may not take account of features of the inner world of people that cannot easily be made explicit, such as their loves and their religious attachments and convictions. Nor does it mean that it cannot say that in certain circumstances there is no explicit guidance it can give; most theories in fact contain an account of their own limitations. (Again, it is empty rhetoric to caricature all ethical theory as demanding explicit rules about everything, as if theories as such could not allow that human life has areas of mystery. But it is also a good idea to remember that to point to a mystery should not automatically be taken to immunize the area in question from the critical scrutiny of theory: thus Mill was correct that romantic views of love and sex can all too easily function to seal off that part of life from criticism, and that this move should be resisted for the sake of equality and justice.)

I treat these six criteria as both necessary and (jointly) sufficient for ethical theory. I do this for the sake of clarity in argument, not because I really believe the tradition has such a unified shape; in reality, certain characteristics have been regarded as more important in some eras than in others. But these six do seem to turn up in some form in all of the major examples, and they also appear to be among the characteristics most contested by the opponents of theory.

I have not included some characteristics mentioned in the debate because I do not think them essential to the major ethical theories: thus, the failure to recognize moral dilemmas is not included (though I comment on this later); nor is a lack of attention to concrete contexts, which may create exceptions to rules; nor is a lack of attention to moral psychology and the virtues of character; nor is an exceptionless hierarchical ordering of principles prior to context (an issue much disputed within the theoretical tradition). Few, I think, will dispute these omissions if they agree with my examples. More contestable, perhaps, is the omission of the idea that a theory is a system of general rules, since this is something that has sometimes been prominently mentioned, both by the defenders and the opponents of ethical theory.[33] But this seems to me a confusion, since one of the most important tasks of ethical theories has traditionally been to describe the point, function, and limitations of rules. This is well recognized by all of the writers on my list, but it is brought out with special clarity by the Greek and Roman Stoics, to whose observations on this question I therefore turn.[34]

III. Three Things, Not Two: Theories, Rules, Concrete Ethical Practice

No ethical theory is a system of rules. None of the examples on my list simply enumerates the rules governing conduct – for example, "Don't lie," "Don't kill," "Don't steal" – and then organizes these into a system. Indeed, it is obvious that we associate this way of proceeding with religion and custom far more than with ethical theory. We might, without much exaggeration, say that it was systems of rules that ethical theory came on the scene to displace. Why? What has ethical theory traditionally taken as its task that leads it to have reservations about the usefulness of rules and rule-governed conduct? I shall now draw on Seneca's *Moral Epistle* 95, as he attempts to answer this question.[35]

1. POINT AND PURPOSE. First of all, the maxims by which people usually guide their conduct are obtuse: without something more, they do not show their own point and purpose. "Don't lie" is all very well, if the person is docile, but if a person is inclined to want to lie for some particular purpose, she will need to understand something that the rule does not tell her: *why* she should not lie. Conventional systems of rules say: "Because this is the way we do things." Some religious systems of rules say: "Because God commanded you not to lie." Philosophical theories proceed in opposition to both of these answers. As Sidgwick puts it well, they recognize that a conventional moral code, even when it gives generally good guidance, is only "an accidental aggregate of precepts, which stands in need of some rational synthesis. In short, without being disposed to deny that conduct commonly judged to be right is so, we may yet require some deeper explanation *why* it is so."[36] Theories acknowledge the reasonableness of the agent's question, and they attempt to give her a good answer, giving *reasons for* the value of the rule in question. In so doing, they treat people as independent, thinking adults, rather than as children.

The form such answers take varies, of course, with the style of ethical theory being proposed. Some theories give the point of rules in terms of a single, highly general end that all good conduct is alleged to promote and give agents reasons for thinking this end the best one. (Utilitarianism is the most obvious example of such a theory.) Others give the point in terms of a plurality of (usually interconnected) ends, each of which is taken to have independent value;

they then set about showing agents that this list of ends is a reasonable one to adopt, and, if rules are the issue, that the rules in question promote those ends. (Aristotle's theory is an obvious example of such a theory.) Others give the point in terms of some more general imperatives and then try to show the point of those imperatives by convincing agents of their overwhelming importance. (Kant's is an obvious example of a theory of this type, although Kant is also concerned with the relation of duties to the happiness of agents and in that sense has a mixed theory.) What is important is that the reason of the agent is addressed with persuasive considerations that illuminate rules of conduct, giving an intelligent being something to go on in deciding whether she wants to adopt the rule in question.[37] Thus, in Kant, the rule "Don't lie" is made intelligent rather than obtuse by being linked to more general considerations about the ways in which one should treat a human being, as an end and not as a means;[38] thus, in Cicero and Seneca, the rule "Don't steal" is made intelligent by an elaborate set of considerations about the human community, designed to persuade an intelligent and independent person of the overwhelming importance of such laws. Opponents of theory need to consider, more than they typically do, what the alternative to this way of proceeding usually is.

2. MOTIVES AND CHARACTER. One of the most common complaints made by the ethical theory tradition against systems of rules is that they prescribe conduct without saying anything about the actor's state of mind and emotion. But – given, once again, that we are respecting people as adults, rather than treating them as children to be ordered about – we feel that people's conduct is right or wrong depending not just on the bodily movements they perform, but also on how their thoughts and emotions are working. If a person acts in a childlike way, fulfilling the rule because an authority figure says so, all major ethical theories agree that this is not a case of right conduct.[39] If the person fulfills the demands of the rule with great struggle and reluctance, many ethical theories also deny that this is a case of right conduct – those that hold that emotions and desires can and should be cultivated to love the good and right. Ethical theories undertake to specify the state of mind and emotion in which a suitably performed action counts as right and virtuous. Thus they need to answer questions about what the passions are, how and to what extent they can be cultivated, and to what extent we can expect them to agree with judgment. These issues are as much a preoccupation of Kant as they are of Aristotle, though Kant arrives at different (and, I believe, mistaken) conclusions regarding the malleability and intelligence of the passions. The tendency of the anti-theorists to caricature Kant as preoccupied with rules to the exclusion of moral psychology is a most unfortunate distortion. It is perfectly obvious that from page 1 of the *Groundwork* on he is preoccupied with motive and intention, and that the entirety of the *Doctrine of Virtue* is an attempt to describe virtuous states of mind.[40]

Seneca points out that this preoccupation with the soul gives ethical theory a big edge over systems of rules, or even over ordinary unsystematic practice, when it comes to vice. For theory's deep preoccupation with the passions inform us about the origins of the obstacles to right conduct, therefore about how we might address such obstacles through institutions and through moral education. For example, Stoic ethical theory has a developed account of anger and hatred that traces these socially divisive passions to an overvaluation of honor and status, as well as other "external goods." Thus they are deformations of thought, rather than natural expressions of a brutish part of the person. If we choose this analysis over the view (held by Kant and many Christian theorists) that bad passions are basically innate and brutish, we have a project on our hands. We know that if we want to minimize anger in our society we need to teach people a different set of ends and values; we can then ask whether doing this threatens other ends that we might legitimately pursue. Theory therefore takes us much farther than rules can.

3. EXCEPTIONS TO RULES. Systems of rules seem obtuse in another way: they do not mention special circumstances in which the rule may not give good guidance. This is connected with the fact that they do not describe their own point and purpose – so we cannot easily see from rules alone when that point is better served by a divergence from the rule. This is why the Stoics and Aristotle insist that there is a natural complementarity between theory and fine-tuned practice. If you have the illumination of theory, and you understand the point and function of the rules, then you will be able to see the new particular case more clearly, seeing, frequently, that this is a case where following the rule would not make sense. Cicero thinks it is obvious, for example, that if you promise to show up in court on a particular day to help a friend plead his case, and then when the day comes your child is very ill, you do not have to keep that promise, and your friend would have a false idea of morality if he complained.[41] Cicero thinks most people would act this way anyhow, but having a theoretical account of the importance of caring for one's family and its relationship to one's other duties will prevent someone from getting confused about the reach of the rule.

In other, more controversial cases, theory does more work. In killing Julius Caesar, Brutus and the other conspirators were killing a human being; they were also killing a friend. Cicero thinks, plausibly enough, that conventional systems of rules, and also conventional moral practice, would condemn their action. He believes also (I think plausibly) that his complex Stoic-based ethical theory[42] can show the point and purpose of the rules against killing and in favor of friendship, and that, when it has done so, we will see that the assassination was morally justified. This is so because the same theory shows the crucial importance of republican political institutions in giving people the liberty within which to cultivate their humanity and to pursue friendship. If, then, we agree with Cicero that Caesar's ascendancy represented a dire threat to republican institutions and that the assassination gave a reasonable hope for preserving them, we will agree that the assassination represents a rare exception to the usual rules.[43] The tyrannicides might have seen all of this without theory (though in fact they did not lack it: Brutus was a moral theorist); what is more important to Cicero is that theory could help the general populace to see the overwhelming importance of republican liberty, at a time when it was threatened with extinction and Antony's rhetoric was confusing the issue.

To take another historically salient example: Grotius, following Cicero, spends two books of *De Iure Belli atque Pacis* laying out the moral theory that governs proper conduct during war; its essentials are the keeping of agreements and a renunciation of aggressive warfare, which entails no tampering with the internal affairs of another state. Like Cicero, he traces the point of these rules to ideas about the intrinsic worth of human reason and human community. Then, in a chapter that has become the fountainhead of much of modern international law, he proposes an exception to the rule, citing Seneca. When a ruler is treating his people in a barbarous and inhumane manner, it is appropriate to intervene. The rightness of this conduct is seen from the theory, which gives as point and purpose of the rules the protection of human dignity and freedom. The community of human beings is usually best served by the renunciation of aggression against foreign powers; in the special case of oppression (deemed by Alberico Gentili, in a related text, to include the rape of women),[44] the case against intervention is removed, and a case for humanitarian intervention is created.[45]

In short, theory is not obtuse in the way that systems of laws can frequently be obtuse: by turning to theory, which gives us the point and purpose of rules, we learn when we may diverge from them. And we can go farther: divergence from a rule without point and purpose is itself obtuse. Theorists who license exceptions to generally good rules are legitimately anxious lest their permissions encourage bad behavior. They therefore plausibly insist that the exception should be taken only when an argument can be given that convincingly links the conduct in question to the overall purpose and point of human conduct. By imposing a stringent *and public* intellectual burden on the exception taker, these theorists discourage self-serving exception taking. Cicero is worried enough about assassination of leaders to insist repeatedly that this conduct is legitimate only when a convincing argument links it to the very possibility of liberty. (At the time he wrote *De Officiis,* he was moving from house to house in the Roman countryside to escape Antony's henchmen, who were bent on assassinating him as a key supporter of the republic. They succeeded six months later.) Grotius, too, is worried – as most international lawyers have been – that the recognition of a right of humanitarian intervention may be used as an excuse for projects of colonial conquest. And yet he – like Kant[46] and others who follow him – nonetheless upholds this right, commenting that "a right does not at once cease to exist in case it is to some extent abused by evil men."

4. ARGUMENTS. Theories, unlike systems of rules, address their recipients as reasoning beings. This means that, unlike systems of rules, they give arguments for what they conclude.[47] They begin by giving accounts or definitions of their key terms, and they proceed to lay out explicitly the course of their thought, showing how the general overview of human ends can be thought to dictate a particular course of conduct. This, theorists emphasize, is a way of respecting recipients. Nothing is hidden, everything is out in the open. If you do not like the definition, you are at liberty to object or to propose one of your own. If you do not like the way the conclusion is reached, find fault with the inferences or the premises, or bring in some other consideration that points in the opposite direction. All of these familiar philosophical maneuvers are made possible by the reasonableness and explicitness of theory, which addresses the recipient as an equal.

It cannot be emphasized strongly enough that this way of doing things is established in deliberate opposition to other ways of giving rules for conduct, those deriving from custom and religious authority. And this has been so since the beginning of the subject. Parmenides, writing early in the fifth century B.C., imagines the journey of a young person to the borders of the universe, where he is met by a goddess who promises a revelation of truth. Parmenides uses the language of mystery cult, and the poem generates the expectation that what will be revealed is a set of religious commandments. What happens? "Judge by reason the very contentious refutation," the goddess commands him. And, he is to keep his mind away from the "buzzing" of mortal opinion and custom while his does so. So too Socrates: he hears the oracle, but he will not allow it to govern his conduct until he has worked out the argument on his own. He sees himself and others as separate beings, centers of reflection and choice, possessed of the right to work out the purposes and patterns of their own existence. A life without that he sees as slavish and base. That is the message of philosophical theory in ethics, and it is for precisely this reason that it has been under attack ever since its beginning. Mental liberty is not popular with world leaders.

None of these points implies that ethical theories should dismiss rules as unnecessary. Typically, they do not. Most ethical theories draw heavily on the wisdom embodied in rules and conventions; from Socrates onward, they regard it as in general a point in favor of a theoretical account if it can preserve at least those general judgments that we regard as especially sound. Thus the rule against killing holds an important place in Stoic moral theory as one of the data of human moral experience on which theory goes to work, and which it would be surprising for a theory to reject wholesale. Indeed, a challenge to one well-entrenched rule is frequently given by showing that it conflicts with another that is regarded as more fundamental: thus, conventional rules mandating unequal education for girls and boys were opposed by the Stoics with arguments that held this rule to be incompatible with the rule that every human being deserves the maximal development of its powers toward virtue.

Rules are regarded as helpful in other ways as well.[48] They summarize the decisions of wise judges, whom we have some reason to trust as possibly shrewder and more experienced than ourselves. They keep us on track when we are likely to go astray through partiality to self or friends and the special pleading to which that can so easily give rise.[49] (This is an especially important function for rules in a system of law.)

Again, when we are faced with a complex particular situation, rules refresh our memory, shape and inform our vision, and focus our attention on aspects of the situation that we might otherwise have missed. On this basis Seneca argues that even the person who is familiar with the most general purposes and ends of human life, as given in a moral theory, still needs to hold onto rules of conduct: for our minds are often undertrained in discerning the salient features of a situation, and rules help us to see correctly.[50] (Again, this is a useful role for rules in a system of law, since situations can be described in indefinitely many ways, and rules give us a set of categories that are of at least prima facie relevance.)

Finally, rules save time. A Henry James novel may take six hundred pages to give an account of the relevant features of a practical situation; a legal system cannot afford such leisured description, and frequently our lives cannot either. We need to summarize, classify, subsume – even when we admit that this is not always the best way of doing justice to all features of the particular. This suggests that we will want to think hard about when this is correctly done and when it is most likely to prove inadequate – when, for example, a more complete narrative of a criminal defendant's life might usefully come into view, and when we might properly confine our vision to the time of the crime itself.

So we have three items: our concrete ethical practice, rules of conduct of various types, and ethical theories. (There are of course also other theories, such as religious theories and magical theories, which will be at work shaping practice, informing conventional rules, and competing with ethical theories. I return to these shortly.) The ethical theorist claims that an ethical theory gives valuable guidance for ethical practice and a set of guidelines for the proper use of rules, by sorting out the material of conduct in a more explicit and perspicuous way, giving the point and purpose of maxims of various types and providing an account of human psychology that can both direct programs of moral education and show when basically appropriate conduct is or is not fully virtuous.

IV. Objecting to Ethical Theory

One may, of course, object to philosophical theories in ethics on a number of grounds: because one holds a religious theory that objects to a large role for unaided human reason, because one is a believer in magic or astrology, or because one simply does not want too much scrutiny of conduct. These have been standard reasons throughout history for opposing ethical theorizing. As I have said, the reasons of the anti-theory philosophers are different. What are they, and how far can theory answer them? The current debate contains six primary charges.

1. **THEORIES NEGLECT AN AGENT'S OWN PARTICULAR PROJECTS AND HER SPECIAL RELATION TO THEM.** This is among Bernard Williams's principal complaints about ethical theories. Indeed, in an essay on Sidgwick, he has stated that theories demand neglect of our relationship to our projects, and that this fact "presents an insoluble problem to ethical theory."[51] By asking us to assess courses of action "from no point of view at all," these theories make an impossible and also inappropriate demand – for this simply is not how people live their lives and endow them with meaning.

To this we should reply, first, that although this may be an accurate characterization of Jeremy Bentham's and Henry Sidgwick's utilitarianism, it is far from being generally true of ethical theories. Even Kant's theory, while frequently asking us not to take account of our own particular situation and relationships, insists that we ought to do so when we are thinking of duties of beneficence. And there is always one special position, one's relationship to oneself, that occupies an absolutely fundamental structuring role in Kant's theory. The Stoics, Kant's mentors in many respects, also insisted that family ties, civic ties, and many other features of our situation should get special consideration, though not as much as many people give them. That Kantians typically deny the moral relevance of many other features of people's situations – for example, their race and gender – might be thought to be a point in the theory's favor; I am sure Williams thinks it is. As for Aristotle's ethical theory, it is entirely built up around the project of an agent who attempts to build a complete life for herself; this is a reason why Williams is more sympathetic to it than to other theories – though, despite his sympathy, he advances special reasons for dismissing it that seem to me inadequate.[52]

We might add that the demand that we see our situation from a point of view external to our own is a demand that arises within the ordinary point of view on ethical matters. Often we feel that we are too self-focused; even small children soon acquire the idea of a fair division of good things and criticize those who think only of their own goals and projects. The idea that a division should be impartial, made as if from the point of view of no particular individual, is more common on the playground (and at the family dinner table) than in politics. So it is not correct to say that in making the impartial perspective central the philosophers who do so are asking us to depart from ordinary life and practices. Whether they are right to make this one aspect of our practices central and to demote others is, as I have said, a disputed point within ethical theory itself. But Williams is surely shortchanging a part of ordinary life when he represents the nontheoretical agent as immured within a personal perspective on the world.

2. **THEORIES IGNORE MORAL PSYCHOLOGY AND THE IMPORTANCE OF EMOTIONS IN GOOD ACTION.** This objection is suggested in various ways by Diamond, Williams, and Baier[53] – but it seems, frankly, just mistaken. There is no major ethical theory that considers only an agent's reasoning processes important in arriving at correct choices. All have a deep interest in the passions, and

all have accounts of how institutions and moral education can shape the passions so that they are more likely to support good action. This is as true for Kant as for Aristotle, though his account of the passions is different. The Stoics are among the most profound psychologists in the entire history of philosophy, and the eradication of anger and hatred in favor of general human sympathy is a major part of what they propose. Adam Smith's ethical theory is entirely focused on the passions; Hume and Mill have a good deal to say about them too. Most of the theories, moreover, ascribe at least some positive value to the passions in the making of a good choice. Kant is no exception, as his ambivalent discussion of pity shows. The Stoics are indeed exceptions, urging a thorough extirpation of all anger, grief, pity, and the other items they call "passions," but they have arguments for this conclusion, and they do leave agents other affective motives, such as the love of humanity, and even a type of erotic love,[54] to steer them in choosing. If to some degree the Stoic life strikes us as bloodless, we need to grapple with their argument (which Spinoza develops further) that it is only in this way that society can be purified of hatred; we cannot simply dismiss them as people who do not see what passion can contribute to life.

3. THEORIES HOLD THAT THERE CAN BE NO MORAL DILEMMAS: THEY NEGLECT THE PLURALITY OF GOODS. There are actually two distinct points here, for a theory can accept the plurality of goods while giving us a decision rule that allows us to resolve every apparent moral dilemma. But at a deep level the two issues are linked, for the recognition that each of a plurality of diverse goods exerts its own sui generis pull on moral agency does seem incompatible with holding that this pull is altogether removed by a contingent conflict with another obligation. So a theory that recognizes distinct sources of value should recognize contingent moral dilemmas. Utilitarianism, especially in the version propounded by Sidgwick, does set out to remove moral dilemmas (clashes between right and right in which any course an agent might choose seems to involve some wrongdoing). The preferred strategy does indeed involve the homogenization of values. Kant seems determined to claim, as well, that there are no genuine moral dilemmas, though without proposing a single common coin of value. But this feature of his theory is difficult to integrate with the rest of it. Given his recognition that each human being is an end, of intrinsic worth, and given the obvious fact that society often makes it impossible for us to satisfy all of our responsibilities to all of the people with whom we have dealings, we might expect Kant to have recognized that contingent social facts can confront agents with moral dilemmas. This would provide an incentive to redesign the relevant social institutions (as Hegel saw).[55] So we may have a theory of basically Kantian type that does recognize moral dilemmas. Aristotle's theory does not give prominent recognition to moral dilemmas, but he probably does recognize them; his theory, recognizing plural sources of intrinsic value, is certainly compatible with that recognition, and there is some evidence that this is the right reading of his text.[56] Cicero tends to treat every prima facie conflict between obligations as resolvable by creating a suitable exception to one of the rules, but there is no necessity that he handle things in this way, and one might adopt a basically Ciceronian theory in ethics while recognizing that not all conflicts of value can be resolved in this way. Such a theory would make a lot more sense of the complex cases Cicero introduces.

In general, a moral theorist is not likely to defend a picture of the human good in which the distinct and plural goods recognized by the theory are intrinsically in conflict with one another; most moral theorists have been attached to consistency in that sense. But there is absolutely nothing to prevent the moral theorist from acknowledging that two goods that are in principle compatible – for example, one's attachment to one's children and one's attachment to one's work – may come into conflict in particular contingent circumstances. Indeed, that is exactly what a moral theorist who recognizes plural values (especially in an imperfect world) ought to say. The frequency and gravity of such conflicts is often the product of social arrangements: for example, societies that provide for parental leave have fewer and less grave conflicts between family and work than societies that do not. So recognition of the conflict often, and reasonably, provides the theorist with an occasion to propose institutional reform. But this surely does not mean that the theorist is attached to consistency in a perverse manner or refuses recognition of the texture of value in real human lives. In fact, people usually prefer not to face moral dilemmas, and if we can arrange things so that both of the good things they pursue are more securely within their grasp, that is a victory. Theory can contribute to that victory by articulating the features of the good in a perspicuous way and making the location of likely conflicts evident.

We must now speak about another type of value pluralism. Different cultures frequently endorse different lists of valuable things. Different groups within a given culture do so too. Ethical theory, as I have defined it, is in its nature antirelativistic: it says, that is, that at the most general level there is an account of ultimate ends that applies to all people as such and therefore implicitly denies that the norms of a given society or group are the court of last resort in ethical matters. This does not prevent theory from leaving spaces for local or personal specification of ends, and liberal theories of justice standardly do so, defending freedom of conscience and other types of liberty. Nor does it prevent theory from articulating its goals at a high level of generality, in order to allow for multiple specification even of the goals it does lay out. The theory I favor does exactly this.[57] With respect to the second type of conflict among ends, then, theory as I characterize it does constrain pluralism and repudiate relativism, but there is a lot of space inside it where legitimate types of pluralism can flourish.

4. THEORIES GIVE CRUDE GUIDANCE, FAIL TO DIRECT AGENTS IN HANDLING THE COMPLEX CONTEXTS OF LIFE. As we have seen, this criticism relies to some extent on confusing ethical theory with rules or systems of rules. Nor is there any major ethical theory that claims to have provided an algorithm that makes tough moral reflection about particular cases otiose. That, indeed, is why all of these theories have been preoccupied with moral psychology, positing that the best way to produce appropriate choice is to produce a certain type of agent. We may still feel that in certain areas some of the major theories are too crude to guide us well; that is why theories should consult good practice. Here Diamond's and Williams's interest in literature has real force, since literature can frequently, as Diamond suggests, cultivate our moral sensibilities and refine our ability to interpret complex situations. But literature can play this role as a partner of ethical theory;[58] one need not jettison theory in order to accept some of the most attractive suggestions of the anti-theorists.

5. THEORIES ASK AGENTS TO DELIBERATE ABOUT EVERYTHING, BUT GOOD ETHICAL PRACTICE IS FREQUENTLY INTUITIVE RATHER THAN REFLECTIVE. Again, this criticism, pressed vigorously by MacIntyre and implicit in the work of Williams and Baier, seems misguided. Ethical theories do demand critical reflection: on the whole, they demand that all agents reflect in some way at some time about the shape of their lives as a whole.[59] (That is not true of one version of utilitarianism, which requires reflection only for a utilitarian elite, but this inegalitarian and nontransparent character of deliberation seems to me, as it does to Williams, a grave defect in the view.)[60] But no ethical theory requires explicit reflection before each ethical choice. Theories vary in the amount of latitude they give well-trained agents to trust their own dispositions and sentiments; this variation depends on the theory's account of the passions. Thus Kant, who believes that bad inclinations can be suppressed but not very much modified, requires more testing and reflecting of agents than does Aristotle, who thinks it reasonable to expect well-brought-up people to come to love the good that they pursue. But even Kant urges agents sometimes to trust to their sentiments: for example, by strengthening our responses of pity through visits to hospitals and sick rooms, we acquire responses that guide us well when attention to duty might prove insufficient.[61] And Kant certainly thinks that people of good will need not work through Kant's moral theory every time they act; awareness of the idea of treating humanity as an end should infuse moral education very early, so that later in life the theory will serve to impart strength to a character that is already basically good. The passage I cite among my epigraphs states that good moral practice does not, as such, need theory at all; practice needs theory only because people are shaky about the good and need the systematicity and consistency of theory to steady them against the seductions of the bad.

6. THEORIES WILL NOT PERSUADE BAD PEOPLE AND THUS WILL PROVE IMPOTENT IN PRACTICE. It is unclear what this objection is supposed to show. The fact that a medicine will not cure everyone is usually not taken as a point against using it to cure those whom it will cure. Most ethical theories expect to improve practice not by winning universal adherence, but by improving the average of practice, so to speak, and, especially, by attracting the attention of people, such as legislators and judges, who are in a position to do something about the people who are not reached by reason. Kant did not expect to end war by convincing people to love one another; he expected to prevail on the governments of republican states to bind themselves to certain conventions of international law. Nor is there any doubt that his theories have greatly influenced the development of modern international law.[62] Similarly, feminist theorists do not expect to win universal support from men for their proposals regarding rape, sexual harassment, and domestic violence. But they do not need to: they need, instead, to work on two fronts, by raising the level of awareness in the population as a whole, and by focusing especially on the makers of laws. Again, there is every reason to think that they have succeeded in changing things on these two fronts, in areas such as sexual harassment, marital rape, and domestic violence. (I give examples in section 5.) More generally: in the history of Western politics, the philosophical theories of the Enlightenment have proven highly influential in shaping constitutions and laws, and at the same time in informing the moral education of people generally.[63] Of course, they have not persuaded everyone, but they have had a decisive impact even on the development of the religions within modern liberal democracies.[64]

But it is insufficient to rebut the objections to theory. For the attackers frequently make a further point: that theory is not necessary for the type of critical ethical reflection we need in our personal lives and in modern liberal society. Williams is very concerned to establish that when we do away with theory we are not left with mere convention or with unthinking experience. Although this may be the goal of some anti-theorists (there are elements of such a preference in MacIntyre, clearly), it is evidently not Williams's goal. He speaks of the "cruel superficiality" of everyday life, of the "distortions" involved in most ordinary experience and our need to "liberate" ourselves from these distortions. He plainly, then, endorses critical ethical thinking of some type. The question he poses to the defender of theory, then, is why the particular type of critical thinking involved in *theory* should be required in order to perform the critical task about whose value he and the theorist are in agreement. Why, then, do we want explicitness, universality, abstractness, systematicity, and a general account of how we may test our concrete judgments? In answering these questions I focus on two problematic areas of our lives that have, I believe, been profitably addressed by theory: aggression and world peace, and the nature of sex relations.

V. The Need for Ethical Theory

Anti-theorists claim that the exchange of ethical criticism in daily life is sufficient to uncover distortions in our practices. In so suggesting, they employ a tacit picture of everyday life that we should question. Williams conveys the strong impression of thinking that when we do away with theory we will be left with people like Bernard Williams: they will lack philosophical theory, but they will still be energetically critical and self-critical, not captive to any other theory, either, and alive to the possibility of distortion and hierarchy in the experiences that are the basis for their judgments. Life might then be like an Oxford common room in one of the more liberal colleges, or a Henry James novel with liberal politics thrown in.[65] Diamond, similarly, imagines that in the absence of formal arguments we will all be reading novels and expanding our moral sensibilities.

The first thing we should say, then, is that "ordinary life" is not (or not only) a place of cultivated sentiment, critical exchange, and refined imagining. That is a naive picture that even the anti-theorists do not seriously endorse. Certainly Williams, at least, does not endorse it. Thus, although he makes a valuable point when he stresses that good ethical practice has a lot to offer theory and can frequently be a better guide than the cruder sort of theory, it is somewhat odd that he is so confident that doing away with theory would leave good self-critical practice in the ascendancy in our daily lives. "Ordinary life" is in fact filled with theories about conduct, some sophisticated and some extremely crude. Some of these are religious theories, some theories based upon convention and habit, some involving magic, astrology, and new age views of the psyche. In the absence of philosophical theory, people live their lives, to a great extent, in accordance with unphilosophical theories, some of them ill considered and crude, many of them impeding sensitive perception by individuals.

Consider relations between men and women. People who do not think about the Kantian/Rawlsian theory that each human being should be treated as an end or the Millian theory criticizing women's subjection to men do not therefore simply go out and relate to one another in accordance with refined particular perceptions. Their mutual interactions are governed by a variety of theories, some metaphysical and religious, some customary. Stereotypes deriving from these theories prevent people from seeing what is before their eyes: thus, as Mill pointed out, we think we know all kinds of things about differences between the sexes, but when we put that knowledge to the test we discover that our knowledge rests on a totally inadequate foundation, one that we would never accept in many other domains. What a philosophical theory like Mill's does is to open our eyes to the defects of these other theories, bringing sharply into focus the empirical and logical inadequacy of a part of our daily life.

A vivid example of how it takes good theory to drive out bad is found in the history of the law of marital rape. For many centuries the conception of marriage dominant in the United States and most of the Western world made marital rape a conceptual impossibility. The theory, which entered the law from custom and religion, was that man and wife are a single person; in this compound person, the husband is the possessor of rights, and the wife is in his keeping. As Sir Matthew Hale expressed the dominant theoretical view, "The husband cannot be guilty of a rape committed by himself upon his lawful wife, for by their mutual consent and contract the wife hath given up herself in this kind unto her husband, which she cannot retract."[66] This theory was deeply internalized by many men in their daily conduct and was used to rationalize bad behavior.[67] The critical reflection of individuals and groups proved insufficient to dislodge this theory, deeply entrenched in our legal systems. It was only when feminist theory rebutted its presumptions with arguments and with an overall picture of women's dignity and autonomy that the legal system began to take notice. Between the 1950s and the present, the increasing influence of feminist theory (applying, we should note, insights gained from the tradition of Kantian moral philosophy) caused perceptions to shift and eventually routed the other theories of spousal duty and right. They could not have done this had unease not been present – had thoughts about women's dignity and rights not already been on the scene, conflicting with the theoretical judgment that women are merely chattel. But it took the reach and systematic power of a countertheory to put things in order in a new way. This theory ultimately had to become a legal theory – but it was of critical importance that it was a legal theory securely grounded in Kantian moral theory.[68]

Consider, again, our lives with respect to war and peace. When Cicero, Seneca, Grotius, and Kant theorize philosophically about limitations on aggression and the hope for lasting peace, they are not operating in a sphere governed, otherwise, by fine-tuned Jamesian perceptions. Their opponents are customary theories of manly honor, of the pride of nations, of the inferiority and rightlessness of aliens. To go against these theories they felt the need to produce something theory-like, something with an argument to answer each consideration on the other side, something that could connect people's deeply held intuitions about human dignity to determinate practical and political considerations about aggression, showing them that their own customary theories of manly honor are to some extent in conflict with their own views about human dignity. Perhaps this would not have been necessary had ordinary life not been distorted by such theories. Then intuitions embodying sound judgments could have come to the fore without opposition and connected themselves with action. But bad theories were blocking those connections. Theorizing about the just war would have had no impact if it had not tapped an already existing fund of thought about the worth of human beings and the badness of doing certain things to them. But to get those thoughts to have power required derailing the bad theories that overlaid and to some extent silenced those thoughts.

The first thing theory needs to do for practice is, then, to *defeat bad theories that silence important thoughts*. But it is not only bad theories that silence our thoughts. Often, as Kant saw, it is our self-interested desires and passions that pose a danger to practice, even in a culture that is relatively free of bad theory. His argument in the *Groundwork* in favor of ethical theory goes as follows. If we could live our lives on the basis of the sound thoughts that (let us suppose) a sound culture has taught us, we might not need philosophy. This much Kant grants, stating that "ordinary understanding in this practical case may have just as good a hope of hitting the mark as that which any philosopher may promise himself."[69] But that is unlikely to happen, Kant argues. That is so because we find within ourselves many counterweights to the moral demands that we recognize as legitimate. These counterweights come from our selfish inclinations and our aggressive feelings. (Kant thinks of these passions as innate and irremediable; his Stoic forebears think of them as culturally transmitted but ubiquitous. This difference means that for the Stoics, and for me, since I accept their view, the passions themselves are a kind of bad cultural theory, and this point is a further application of my previous point.)

When we feel these counterweights – when, for example, our deeply habitual conceptions of honor and personal prestige cause us to resent another person or group and to contemplate aggressive action against them – we may tell ourselves that we have good thoughts about the worth and dignity of human beings and that we recognize the badness of treating human beings as mere means to our ends. But what then happens, according to Kant, is that our passions begin to quibble with these good thoughts, telling us that it is ridiculous to think of dignity when someone has just insulted our own, or unnecessary to think of women as ends, given that they are parts of our very own household. These quibbles then start to eat away at the good thoughts: "Thereby are such laws corrupted in their very foundations and their whole dignity is destroyed – something which even ordinary practical reason cannot in the end call good."[70] (Such quibbling with the idea of equal worth misled Kant himself, clearly enough, as he vacillates oddly between ideas of equal human dignity that have proven highly fertile for feminist thought[71] and other ideas about women that treat them as chattel and deny their equal worth.)

Kant is right: in both areas of life from which I have drawn examples, quibbling does eat away at the good thoughts. In the area of sex and marriage, as Mill noted, men who lord it over their wives allow thoughts about the equal worth of persons and their liberty (which he plausibly thinks most of his fellow citizens have) to be silenced by aggressive desires that give rise to counter-thoughts and rationalizations: I have a right to this exercise of power, she is mine, and so forth. Such rationalizations even underwrite marital rape as right and proper, although, as Mill noted, such an act is flatly incompatible with other thoughts the man is likely to have. By the time such a rationalizer rapes his wife, he feels that it is right and proper for him to do so.[72] Again, men who harass women in the workplace are not in general evil through and through. Instead, they are likely to be self-indulgent rationalizers, people who have absorbed from society some rather good thoughts about women's equality and dignity, but when their desires and their interest in power gain the upper hand, those good thoughts are silenced.

Similarly in the area of war and peace: when we operate without an explicit theory as a test, desires for honor and distinction frequently quibble with the good thoughts, leading nations and individuals to think that it is perfectly all right to make war on this occasion and silencing the moral qualms that might otherwise have emerged. Kant here offers an especially instructive example. People generally agree, he says, that we have certain duties of humane and hospitable treatment to aliens. But if we now consider

> the *inhospitable* conduct of the civilised states of our continent, especially the commercial states, the injustice which they display in *visiting* foreign countries and peoples (which in their case is the same as *conquering* them) seems appallingly great. America, the negro countries, the Spice Islands, the Cape, etc. were looked upon at the time of their discovery as ownerless territories; for the native inhabitants were counted as nothing. In East India (Hindustan), foreign troops were brought in under the pretext of merely setting up trading posts. This led to oppression of the natives, incitement of the various Indian states to widespread wars, famine, insurrection, treachery and the whole litany of evils which can afflict the human race. China and Japan (Nippon), having had experience of such guests, have wisely placed restrictions on them . . . The worst (or from the point of view of moral judgments, the best) thing about all this is that the commercial states do not even benefit by their violence, for all their trading companies are on the point of collapse. The Sugar Islands, that stronghold of the cruellest and most calculated slavery, do not yield any real profit; they serve only the indirect (and not entirely laudable) purpose of training sailors for warships, thereby aiding the prosecution of wars in Europe. And all this is the work of powers who make endless ado about their piety, and who wish to be considered as chosen believers while "they live on the fruits of iniquity."[73]

We begin with decent moral practice. We then introduce the desires for gain, conquest, and power. These desires give rise to self-deception on a large scale: conquest is only "visiting," the native inhabitants are not really people. (Kant suggests that religious theories may aid and abet these self-deceptive stratagems: for the claim to piety was clearly underwritten by European religious leaders who saw Europe's mission as the Christianizing of the East.) The good thoughts about hospitality and universal humanity are silenced, and bad behavior ensues.

What happens next? If we remain at the level of untheoretical critical discourse and practice, as the anti-theorists recommend, we will always be left, Kant plausibly claims in the *Groundwork,* with some good thoughts, corrupted by selfishness, aggressiveness, and urges to dominate. Even if not utterly silenced, these thoughts will not steer practice in a consistent manner. Sometimes they may still prevail, but there will be no constancy to their victory.

For this reason, ordinary judgment reaches beyond itself to seek the help of philosophy, asking to have the good thoughts laid out perspicuously and systematically, so that it will be clear ahead of time exactly what they entail in the different areas of life. This way we steal a march on ourselves, building up bulwarks in thought against our all too pressing tendencies to slight the dignity of others. We get something to cling to, to look to when we are tempted, so that the self-deception of quibbling is less likely to prevail. From theories that connect and systematize the good thoughts, ordinary judgment, Kant concludes, derives "information and clear instruction regarding the source of its own principles . . . so that reason may escape from the perplexity of opposite claims and may avoid the risk of losing all genuine moral principles through the ambiguity into which it easily falls." This, he suggests, is one reason why a good ethical theory needs a theory of the passions: so that judgment can come to understand the origin of its own tendency to be led astray. His conclusion is, then, that ordinary reason seeks theory as an ally against its internal (as well as its external) enemies. *Theory, then, can help our good judgment by giving us additional opposition to the bad influence of corrupt desires, judgments, and passions.*

How does theory do this? First, it makes the good thoughts clearer and more explicit, so we cannot delude ourselves into thinking, say, that asking for sexual favors in the workplace is really compatible with equal treatment; that colonial conquest is really just "visiting." Kant thinks, plausibly, that self-deception is frequently involved in bad behavior, and that theory's clarity cuts like a knife through that sort of error. Second, theory gives us an account of error itself, showing us what our passions are and how they may incorporate bad cultural material or other types of bad tendencies. It shows us what we have to watch out for in ourselves. Finally, it pursues the good thoughts into areas we may not have thought about much; if we have thought about human dignity but not about foreigners and what they deserve, a good theory will force us to ask this question, connecting one thought with another. In this way too it puts us on our guard against our own selfish tendencies.

One device theory uses in pursuit of this project is that of *estrangement* or *defamiliarization*.[74] Our judgments frequently feel so natural to us that it is hard for us to doubt them. And of course these intuitions are one part of the data that good theory takes seriously. But by asking us to look at the logical form of our judgments, and by urging us to describe them in an unfamiliar theoretical language, theory offers us a perspective on them that can be valuable as we ask to what extent we have been engaging in self-interested rationalization. Just as Brecht famously urged the theatrical spectator to suspend identification with the theatrical characters and their lives in order to scrutinize the represented situation from a critical practical perspective, so good philosophy often gets us to do this with ourselves and our own lives. We look at the overall form of our judgments in new ways, and we use the unfamiliar language of "the kingdom of ends" or "the categorical imperative" to test reactions we usually do not even scrutinize. Often this can help us overcome our tendency to rationalize by getting us to see relationships that had eluded us in our daily thinking. Thus the very detachment and remoteness in theory that anti-theorists find problematic can serve a valuable practical function. Williams and Diamond are right to think that this sort of defamiliarization should not be pushed to extremes, and that more immersed and intuitive descriptions are also important. One good way of getting those more immersed descriptions while still maintaining a wise distance from our own immediate situation is, in fact, the turn to literature that Diamond recommends.[75] But we should see that even what strikes us as cold and forbidding in Socrates or Aristotle or Kant may be of significant practical value.

Does all of this mean that theory is necessarily hostile to the passions? Not in the least. Even Kant's theory is not generally hostile, as I have said: it asks us to cultivate our responses of pity or compassion. But it is inclined in that direction because of Kant's view that the passions represent an unthinking animal side of our personality and can never themselves be cultivated and made integral parts of a good character. If we were to select a theory such as Aristotle's or Adam Smith's, according to which appropriate passions can be cultivated as parts of good character, then we would find many occasions on which ordinary thought and judgment could trust the passions for guidance. (Indeed, once a theory is accepted, it can itself inform the structure of the passions, through self-criticism and especially through moral education.) But, as Aristotle and Smith show, the guidance of passion is never altogether trustworthy – no more than are the social norms that the passions embed or any other belief we might use in moral reasoning. Therefore we need critical scrutiny of our passions, especially where we feel that we are likely to be selfish or shaped by untrustworthy social forces. So even an Aristotelian can agree with Kant's perceptive point: we are driven to theory by our unwillingness to trust ourselves in many of the most vital matters. Even our compassion for human suffering, which may appear to be a reliable part of our emotional makeup, always rests on a foundation of social interpretation and therefore always needs reasoned scrutiny. The husbands described by Mill did not have compassion for the wives they were raping, nor did Kant's colonialists have compassion for those they enslaved. This was so because they had rationalized away the foundation of compassion, saying "I have a right to this," and "These heathen savages aren't really human." So even compassion is not a reliable bedrock, without the scrutiny of reason.

As Aristotle and John Rawls suggest, we should probably view the enterprise of justification holistically, testing theory by its fit with the most firmly entrenched of our ethical judgments and the related passions, but being prepared, as well, to alter concrete judgments and to criticize concrete passions in the light of a theory that integrates perceptions and judgments in a convincing manner.

At this point someone is bound to ask: "Why should we trust the moral philosophers? Are they particularly good, or particularly sensitive? Do we really want old Kant making decisions about sex relations, or even about foreign policy? Trusting theory when passions are likely to be corrupt seems odd: for aren't the theorists just as corrupt as other people, and isn't their striking failure (with the honorable exception of Mill) to say anything profound about the sexes a sign that they are not any better than the ordinary judgments of their era?"

Here we have to make a distinction. Of course no philosopher could create a distinguished moral theory without insight. To the extent that we allow ourselves to be guided by a great moral theory, we do thus far trust the reasoning of its creator. But of course people may say both profound and silly things together. Most great philosophers write badly about sex, and many have other significant gaps in human understanding. Many, prominently including Kant, have drawn from their own theory silly conclusions that the theory itself plainly does not imply. But the main thing is this: ethical theory does not ask us to trust a person at all. It asks us to listen to an argument and then to trust ourselves. It does not demand slavish adherence, it repels it. Insofar as we get insight from Kantian moral theory, well and good. But if we judge that Kant has bizarre things to say about sex, we do not have to believe them. Kant is our interlocutor, not our authority. We do have to consult the links between the theory and those judgments: if those judgments really are entailed by the theory, then we need to go back and question our acceptance of the theory. On the other hand, we should also ask what judgments the theory itself seems to generate – and in this case we are likely to find that they are quite different from the fallible concrete judgments of the very inexperienced philosopher. In other words, philosophers start a conversation in which the reason of each of us is the interlocutor. What we are trusting, insofar as we go for ethical theory, is this process and ultimately, therefore, our own reasoning powers. Theory is preferred to ordinary judgment not because it is more authoritative than ordinary judgment, but for the reasons that Kant gives: because, through it, we get the best out of ourselves.

Notice, then, that ethical theory does make a strong and controversial assumption: that people (at least a sufficient number of them) have a basic ability to recognize good reasons. Ethical theorists are followers of Socrates. In examining his fellow citizens, Socrates appears to assume that many of them, at any rate, could attain the right ethical answer by a process of self-examination. In so proceeding, he appears to assume (a) that the good ethical reasons are in them in some form, and (b) that when they are shown the inconsistency between two things they assert, their judgment will in general, at least over the long haul, make good choices about what to keep and what to reject.[76] Rawls follows Socrates here, assuming a certain degree of basic moral health, which need not be incompatible with recognizing that these capacities can be clouded by many interfering factors.[77] Kant, believer as he is in original sin and natural aggression, still feels able to follow this precedent, since he believes that the good will is also a reality, and that sound judgmental capacities can defeat bad modes of reasoning, at least often enough to make the enterprise of strengthening judgment by theory worthwhile. Thus, to follow the philosophers we need not reject the Christian idea of original sin; we need only counterbalance this notion with a certain degree of optimism about the moral capacity of ordinary people, seeing them not as a hopelessly venal bunch of predators or a hopelessly stupid herd or flock, but as the sort of beings of whom it might possibly be true that "the unexamined life is not worth living." And we need only think this about a sufficient number of people, in sufficiently favorable circumstances, in order to think that the project Kant proposes is likely to bear fruit.

This conception of theory does not, of course, imply that there is no such thing as a bad philosophical theory, or even one that is in principle hostile to humanity. But the bet is that in the holistic process of justification, good theories will drive out bad, show that the bad are only speciously attractive, or internally inconsistent, or simply not the best way of organizing our intuitions overall. This does require the somewhat optimistic view of humanity that I have just sketched – and it is here that we see the deepest difference between Williams and the theorists he opposes. People who follow Williams in his general pessimism about human life may have good reason to follow him, as well, in his skepticism about theorizing (although it would appear that this skepticism should extend equally to the good that may be done by critical reflection that does not take the form of theory). In the end it is impossible to prove that the optimistic view is more likely to be correct, and to that extent my position is based on what Kant would call a "practical postulate," which cannot be sufficiently justified by any real-world evidence.[78]

Kant imagines theory improving the practice of an ordinary individual. But he also envisages other roles for theory. It will *guide the moral education of children,* so that, one hopes, they will have fewer of the bad thoughts and more of the good thoughts as they embark on their own lives. We might emphasize this department of theory's operations more than Kant did. Because he thought that human nature was innately corrupt and that aggressive passions, for example, were not capable of being educated or changed, he did not hold out as much hope for moral education as we might if we conclude that many types of hatred and bad passion, at least, have a social origin in the images of self and other we use. We can aim to bring up children in whom the idea of the equal worth of persons is not derailed by racism and sexism; a good theory can be the benchmark by which we direct our efforts as parents and educators.[79] Good theory drives out bad social judgments at the level of early education, rendering our passions less hostile to the good of humanity.

Finally, *good theory shapes laws and institutions.* Kant does not think that world peace will come about because all people will ultimately concur in testing their maxims by the categorical imperative. It will come about, if it does, because enough people think this way to make good laws that will constrain the behavior of other people. And this is exactly how international law has evolved. The theories of Cicero and Grotius, developed by Kant, have had a formative influence on the conduct of governments and international agencies, so that by now, if we are not exactly progressing toward a state of "perpetual peace," we at least have in place many mechanisms to deal with egregious offenses against human dignity. In particular, the world community has become much more sensitive to the need to protest violations of basic human rights within nations, and that idea, first tentatively broached by Grotius citing Cicero, is now increasingly seen as a legitimate domain of international law. Bad behavior is still ubiquitous; good theory prompts us to create institutional mechanisms to get at it.

Once again, the anti-theory position looks naive. Innocence, as Kant says, is a glorious thing. But the world community is not innocent, nor is it especially reflective and self-critical. It takes an explicit theory to generate a crusade like the modern human rights movement. Had Kant sought to convey nuance, particularity, and mystery, rather than to give his writings the abstractly systematic character they actually have, he would not have had the formative influence he did on international law and on the conduct of the world community.[80] We needed to have an explicit, abstract, systematic proposal to debate in public, one that would codify and articulate many different judgments and intuitions, and one that would do so with a firm footing in a moral theory that would show the point and purpose of the political conclusions.[81]

Again, had Mill not been willing to make systematic and abstract and explicit claims about sex relations, his work would have had little impact on the shape of societies; because he constructed a theory, his moral perceptions have by now influenced the structure of sex relations in nations as distant as China. Had Catharine MacKinnon made a series of concrete critical judgments, rather than articulating a theory that offered a systematic, explicit, and abstract account of the structure of sex relations, the very concept of sexual harassment would not have been forged. Women would have gone on having experiences of it, but without an abstract and systematic conceptual structure we would not have been able fully to name what we were experiencing. The feminist theory organized perceptions and galvanized thought in a way that was continuous with prior experience, but that gave it new strength and efficacy. Some years ago, women's assertion that an asymmetry of power taints sexual behavior in the workplace would have seemed like self-interested whining and complaining. Now it is regarded as an essential part of the correct description of the "facts" of a case.[82] It is not that these experiences and the associated thoughts were not there before. But without an explicit theory we could not get far with them, in a world full of bad behavior.

We do not live in the innocent world of orderly ethical practice that Kant admiringly and Seneca nostalgically imagine. We live, as they well knew, in a world full of bad, crude theories, self-serving passions, and tainted judgments, where the good passions and judgments need all the help they can get to prevail, or even to survive. That is why we need theory. As Seneca says, when our enemies take up elaborate weapons, we need to make the weapons on the side of good more elaborate and systematic to keep up with them.

There are many obstacles in human life to this good role for theory, and to its practical success. Some of these obstacles are so deeply entrenched that we probably cannot get rid of them ever. As Seneca says of anger and hatred, "Slow is the resistance to evils that are continuous and prolific." But there is one obstacle that we can resist: it is the one Mill identified near the opening of *The Subjection of Women,* comparing his nineteenth-century culture to that of the eighteenth century: it is the tendency to mistrust argument and to prefer passion and intuition. It is always difficult, Mill says, to argue against deeply entrenched prejudice. But it is doubly so in an age that mistrusts Reason on principle, that substitutes instinct for Reason and calls by the name of instinct "everything which we find in ourselves for which we can trace no rational foundation."[83] Contemporary anti-theorists are not identical with the Romantic anti-theorists whom Mill attacks. Williams, at least, does not prefer "instinct" to reason, nor does he deny that we need some kind of rational scrutiny of what we find in ourselves. And yet there are tendencies in his thought that point in a Romantic direction, and his attack upon Enlightenment theories leaves Reason in a very reduced position. In a world in which irrational forces and their associated theories are increasingly getting the upper hand, it seems better to strengthen reason's bargaining position by allowing it to use all of the resources of which it is capable. Innocence is indeed a glorious thing – but the real world, being guilty, needs philosophy.

Notes

1 I am citing from the Ellington translation (Immanuel Kant, *Ethical Philosophy,* trans. James W. Ellington [Indianapolis: Hackett, 1983]), in which the title is translated as *Grounding.* But because both seem acceptable, I shall use the more conventional rendering *Groundwork* throughout. Translations of Latin are mine throughout.
2 I do not mean that these things did not happen in other traditions: Confucius, for example, was also an embattled figure. But I am focusing on the Western tradition here.
3 See I. Düring, "Vita Marciana," in *Aristotle in the Ancient Biographical Tradition* (Göteborg: Almqvist & Wiksell, 1957), 105. Like all the material in the ancient lives, this story is of dubious authenticity, but it shows what many people believed about the events.
4 See Tacitus, *Annales* 15.63. Seneca was implicated in the conspiracy of Piso, which, like other anti-imperial conspiracies, was inspired in part by Stoic ideals of *libertas.* Another prominent Stoic rebel was Thrasea Paetus, who committed suicide earlier in Nero's reign. For the relationship of Seneca's death to the *Phaedo,* see Miriam Griffin, *Seneca: A Philosopher in Politics* (Oxford: Clarendon Press, 1976); for the role of philosophy in anti-imperial politics, see Griffin, "Philosophy, Cato and Roman Suicide," *Greece and Rome* 33 (1986):64–77, 192–202.
5 Grotius was tried and imprisoned for Arminianism, a religious rather than a philosophical view, but his Christian and his Stoic/philosophical views are so mixed together that it seems impossible to isolate a purely religious aspect of his career.
6 Alasdair MacIntyre, in *Whose Justice? Which Rationality?* (Notre Dame, Ind.: University of Notre Dame Press, 1988).
7 See Robert Darnton, *The Forbidden Best-Sellers of Pre-Revolutionary France* (New York:

Norton, 1995); Darnton includes sales lists from the clandestine book-sellers; he also shows that the pornographic books contained many long stretches of anticlerical philosophizing, so in this way, too, the borders between genres were blurred. *Thérèse Philosophe* (from which Darnton translates long extracts) contains a remarkably progressive picture of women's sexual autonomy, defended by Enlightenment philosophical ideas: the central theme is that women are not mere reproducers, and that their sexual pleasure should be separated from reproduction, even when this is inconvenient for men. Whatever one may think of its odd mixture of pornography and argument, it is certainly a better Enlightenment account of women than anything in either Kant or Rousseau.

8 Kant, "Perpetual Peace," in *Kant: Political Writings,* 2nd ed., ed. H. Reiss (Cambridge: Cambridge University Press, 1991), 115.

9 Russell was in prison in 1918 and again 1961 (when he was eighty-six); *Marriage and Morals* was condemned as obscene by a New York court, causing Russell to lose his job at CUNY.

10 Bernard Williams (private communication) here makes two valuable points: first, that the attackers may not have been enemies of ethical theory as such, but only of a particular kind of (secular anticlerical) theory; they may well have been fond of some religious ethical theories. Second, he says that his own position does not entail the rejection of philosophical activity, and that an attack on philosophy as such is importantly distinct from his more limited assault on ethical theory, which retains a large role for the critical scrutiny of tradition.

The second point is true and important, and I try to deal with it in the last section of my essay. I believe that the attackers would have been far less worried about philosophers such as Kant and Rousseau if the latter had had no systematic views that contradicted received views, and so I continue to believe that the theoretical aspect of the theorizers' work was salient in motivating the attacks. (This was true even of Socrates, who was understood by his attackers, rightly or wrongly – I think rightly – to have a definite set of subversive views.)

About the first point, I have some doubt. We have to be careful here how we draw the line between a religious and an ethical theory; some ethical theories (such as that of Aquinas) have been housed within religious systems of thought. My own view is, however, that they cease to be ethical theories of a philosophical kind when they submit to temporal religious authority for their interpretation and further development. I doubt that the attackers were really friendly to any philosophical theory, even that of Aquinas, that they could not rigidify and codify in their own way.

11 Annette Baier, "Doing without Moral Theory?" in *Anti-Theory in Ethics and Moral Conservatism,* ed. S. Clarke and E. Simpson (Albany: SUNY, 1989), 33, claims that she does not share Alasdair MacIntyre's "very gloomy estimate of the prospects of a secular culture." Williams goes to considerable lengths to show that ethical reflections should criticize experience that is disordered: see his response to critics in *World, Mind, and Ethics,* ed. J. E. J. Altham and R. Harrison (Cambridge: Cambridge University Press, 1995), 218–19; see, however, his comment that I quote shortly, judging that in some respects moral philosophy is farther removed from social and ethical reality than religion is. Diamond's positions on political and religious authority have not yet been articulated, so far as I can see. MacIntyre's position is highly complex, since he recommends a large role for philosophical argument, but within bounds set by first principles handed down by religious authority. I do not discuss his views further in what follows.

12 Baier,"Doing without Moral Theory?", 46.
13 Bernard Williams, *Ethics and the Limits of Philosophy* (Cambridge, Mass.: Harvard University Press, 1985), 197 (cited hereafter as "ELP").
14 Cora Diamond, "Having a Rough Story about What Moral Philosophy Is," *New Literary History* 15 (1983):155–69, at 168. Diamond is here referring to an essay of mine on Henry James's *The Golden Bowl,* in which I try to show that this novel makes a valuable contribution to moral philosophy; in the process, I offer what I call "a rough story about what moral philosophy is." Diamond argues that on one common idea of what moral philosophy is (not the one I use in my article, as she recognizes), a project like mine (which she defends) would not be possible.
15 See Williams in Altham and Harrison, *World, Mind, and Ethics,* in Atham, pp. 218–19; theory "can be an effectively articulated expression of these distortions . . . blocking radical reconsideration of our morality."
16 For the Chicago anti-theorists, see especially Dan M. Kahan, "Theories, Anti-Theories, and Norms: Comment on Nussbaum," Chapter 4 of this volume; Richard Posner, *Overcoming Law* (Cambridge, Mass.: Harvard University Press, 1995), esp. "Legal Reasoning from the Top Down and from the Bottom Up," 171–97, "What Are Philosophers Good For?" 444–67, and "So What *Has* Pragmatism to Offer Law?" 387–405. For a critique, see Ronald Dworkin, "In Praise of Theory," *Arizona State Law Journal* 29 (1997):353–76, with replies by Posner, 337–88; more recently, see Posner, "The Problematics of Legal and Moral Theory," *Harvard Law Review* 111 (1998):1637. I reply to Posner in "Still Worthy of Praise: Comments on Richard Posner," *Harvard Law Review* 111 (1998):1776. Dworkin focuses on Posner but does not discuss Kahan, who would have been an especially suitable target for his critique; however, much of Kahan's work along these lines is not yet published, though there are clear signs of the position in "What Do Alternative Sanctions Mean?" *University of Chicago Law Review* 63 (1996):591–653 – a defense of punishments based on shame that does not cite Williams's work on this topic but does cite with approval earlier work of mine that was much influenced by Williams's thought. On the other hand, Dworkin discusses Cass R. Sunstein's position (see note 17 to this chapter) and emphasizes that Sunstein's views are not as far from his own as Sunstein sometimes suggests. Sunstein's reply accepts this characterization: see Sunstein, "From Theory to Practice," *Arizona State Law Journal* 29 (1997):389–404. Another prominent Chicago writer who might reasonably be cited is Lawrence Lessig (at The University of Chicago until 1997, now at Harvard). See Lessig and Kahan, eds., "Social Norms and Social Meaning," a special issue of the *Journal of Legal Studies* (1997). The term "new Chicago School" was coined by Lessig in connection with his and Kahan's shared views about the primary importance of social norms. Lessig – who has a degree in philosophy from Cambridge University – like Kahan, has been profoundly influenced by the philosophical movements attacking theory.
17 Cass R. Sunstein, *Legal Reasoning and Political Conflict* (New York: Oxford University Press, 1996).
18 See Kahan, Chapter 4 of this volume. Posner is less clearly indebted to these attacks, although in many respects his arguments are related to theirs. See especially "What Are Philosophers Good For?", which can be usefully compared with the views of both Williams and Baier.
19 The influence of Holmes on Posner is pervasive; for one clear example connected to Posner's philosophical anti-theory position, see "Top-Down and Bottom-Up," 195–97, where he uses Holmes as a foil for Dworkin.

20 Oliver Wendell Holmes, Jr., *The Common Law* (Boston: Little, Brown, 1881).
21 For discussion see Louis Menand, "Bet-tablitarianism," *New Republic,* 11 November 1996, 50–51.
22 Holmes to Lewis Einstein, 23 July 1906, quoted in *The Essential Holmes,* ed. Richard A. Posner (Chicago: University of Chicago Press, 1992), 58.
23 I have particular reasons for clarifying my position, since my own work has often been taken – mistakenly – as anti-theoretical. See, e.g., Stanley G. Clarke and Evan Simpson, *Anti-Theory in Ethics and Moral Conservatism* (Albany: SUNY, 1989), which includes an essay of mine under the "anti-theory" rubric.
24 See "Equilibrium," *Ancient Scepticism and the Sceptist Tradition,* Acta Philosophica Fennica 64 (1999):1–27.
25 I do not make a distinction between "moral theory" and "ethical theory." Some writers, such as Rawls, prefer the term "moral theory," while others use the term "ethical" for the same enterprise. Williams tends to reserve the term "moral" for what he attacks and continues to use "ethical reflection" for the nontheoretical use of reason he endorses: however, when he speaks of "theory," he tends to call the theory "ethical." Baier, by contrast, attacks "ethical theory." Since there seems to be no generally agreed-upon distinction between the two, it seems best to proceed by using a single term "ethical," and defining its use carefully.
26 As noted, "rough story" is my own term, in the article she has criticized.
27 ELP, 72.
28 Williams (private communication) has helpfully clarified this point: his phrase "implies a general test for the correctness of" was not meant to mean "implies that there is one single test which excludes holistic . . . argument."
29 Compare the very helpful list of twelve characteristics in R. Louden, "Virtue Ethics and Anti-Theory," *Philosophia* 20 (1990):93–113, and also in his book, *Morality and Moral Theory: A Reappraisal and Reaffirmation* (New York: Oxford University Press, 1992). My list is closely related to his, though shorter.
30 Of course, any claim about Socrates is bound to remain controversial. Some would deny that he had a theory at all. Moreover, my claim is complicated by the fact that on some occasions Socrates appears to hold fixed judgments, not only concrete judgments about action types and also some very general judgments, such as that a good person cannot be harmed. For my own current view of Socratic inquiry, together with a discussion of Vlastos's important account, see my review of Vlastos, "Socratic Studies," *Journal of Philosophy* 94 (1997):27–45.
31 See the illuminating discussion in Onora O'Neill, *Towards Justice and Virtue: A Constructive Account of Practical Reason* (Cambridge: Cambridge University Press, 1996), chapter 2.
32 On the concrete universal, see R. M. Hare, *Moral Thinking* (Oxford: Oxford University Press, 1981).
33 Thus Baier cites, critically, Alan Donagan's statement that the theory of morality is "a system of laws or precepts binding upon rational creatures as such, the content of which is ascertainable by human reason." See Baier, "Doing Without," 36, citing Donagan, *The Theory of Morality* (Chicago: University of Chicago Press, 1977), 7.
34 The main sources for the Stoic view of rules are Seneca, *Moral Epistles* 94 and 95, and Cicero, *De Officiis.*
35 See the related threefold distinction in Sidgwick, *The Methods of Ethics* (Chicago: Uni-

versity of Chicago Press, 1962), book 1, chapter 8, where he describes the transition from particular intuitions to rules of conduct, and from both of these to philosophical explanation. (Sidgwick, however, conceives of the more abstract as always being firmer than the concrete, not seeing the Stoic point that theoretical principles can help us identify exceptions to generally valid rules.)

36 Ibid., section 4.
37 See, for example, Seneca, *Moral Epistles* 95.12, where Seneca insists that theory is addressed to a rational being as such, and that rules by themselves are "rootless" if they do not attach to an overview of human life.
38 Most readers of Kant feel that Kant himself applied this rule in too rigid a way when he held that one should not lie to a would-be murderer who comes to the door asking for the whereabouts of his potential victim. But we should probably think that Kant has identified correctly one feature of this complex situation; where he goes wrong is in refusing to allow that other aspects, of greater moral urgency, conflict with it in this case. Either we should say that the case has the form of a moral dilemma, in which what one ought to do (all things considered) is to save the victim by lying, but where that lie itself is still a moral wrong; or we might say that the murderer, by his intent to kill, has forfeited his claim to be treated as the rule generally requires (a position that Kant does take concerning the issue of just war and duties not to kill). Certainly there is no reason to think that Kant's inadequate treatment of the case is a sign of deep difficulty for his moral theory.
39 See Seneca, *Moral Epistles* 95.40: purpose and manner are all-important, and these cannot be given in a system of rules.
40 For two convincing accounts, which show the close relationship between Kant's theory and Aristotle's, see Barbara Herman, *The Practice of Moral Judgment* (Cambridge, Mass.: Harvard University Press, 1993), and Nancy Sherman, *Making a Necessity of Virtue: Aristotle and Kant on Virtue* (Cambridge: Cambridge University Press, 1997). See also Onora O'Neill, *Constructions of Reason* (Cambridge: Cambridge University Press, 1989); Christine Korsgaard, *Creating the Kingdom of Ends* (Cambridge: Cambridge University Press, 1996), and S. Engstrom and J. Whiting, eds., *Aristotle, Kant, and the Stoics: Rethinking Happiness and Duty* (Cambridge: Cambridge University Press, 1996).
41 Cicero, *De Officiis* 1.32.
42 It is an interesting question whether Stoicism by itself could justify this conclusion, or whether Cicero is here, as often, relying on a hybrid version of Stoic and Academic ideas.
43 See Cicero, *De Officiis* 3.19; a similar example is at 3.40, where a different Brutus deposed his colleague Collatinus from office right after the expulsion of the kings, on the grounds that having a member of the royal family in high office was a threat to the founding of the Republic.
44 Alberico Gentili (1552–1608), *De Iure Belli Libri Tres:* "Further, to violate the honour of women will always be held to be unjust." Gentili holds aggression against rulers who permit this conduct to be legitimate according to "the common law of nations and of nature." (Gentili, an Italian Protestant, was professor of civil law at Oxford University.) This is a direct antecedent for the war crimes trials of Bosnian Serb leaders.
45 Hugo Grotius, *De Iure Belli atque Pacis,* II.xxv.
46 Kant, "Perpetual Peace," section 2, footnote (Reiss 98): A people who live "in a mere state of nature" do not deserve the same respectful treatment that "legal civil states" do. It emerges that Kant requires a republican constitution as the foundation of a "legal civil state": thus his exception seems far broader than that imagined by Grotius.

47 See Seneca, *Moral Epistles* 95.55, 61–62.
48 On this, see Seneca, *Moral Epistles* 94.
49 See, on this, my account of Bob and Fanny Assingham in Henry James's *Golden Bowl*, in "'Finely Aware and Richly Responsible': Literature and the Moral Imagination," in *Love's Knowledge* (New York: Oxford University Press, 1990).
50 See Seneca, *Moral Epistles* 94.32–33.
51 Bernard Williams, "The Point of View of the Universe: Sidgwick and the Ambitions of Ethics," in *Making Sense of Humanity and Other Philosophical Papers, 1982–1993* (Cambridge: Cambridge University Press, 1995), 153–71, at 170. The essay was first published in 1982 and thus predates the final version of *Ethics and the Limits*.
52 See our exchange in Altham and Harrison, *World, Mind, and Ethics*. Williams first made some of these criticisms in "Moral Standards and the Distinguishing Mark of Man," in *Morality* (Cambridge: Cambridge University Press, 1973); they are further developed in ELP.
53 Diamond, in "Anything but Argument?" *Philosophical Investigations* 5 (1982):23–41, focuses on Onora O'Neill's demand (in her review of a book on animal rights by Stephen Clark) that Clark "reach beyond assertion to argument." Diamond says some perceptive things about how works of literature can enlarge our moral sensibilities through imagination and emotion without presenting anything that an ethical theorist would call argument. True enough, but it is not clear that any moral theorist, including O'Neill, would deny this. (Presumably she is focusing on defects internal to Clark's own philosophical enterprise; Clark is not Dickens, and he is attempting philosophical arguments.)

Williams does not make the general claim that ethical theory neglects emotion, and indeed he has many valuable things to say about the role of the emotions in ancient Greek ethical theories and in Hume's ethical theory; he does, however, take the Kantian tradition to task for its neglect of emotion: see "Morality and the Emotions," in *Problems of the Self* (Cambridge: Cambridge University Press, 1973). Since for him, as for Baier, the primary targets are Kantianism and utilitarianism, he ends up saying little about how an ethical theory could respond to his criticisms, but his position here is subtle and does not seem to rule out the possibility of a (suitably constituted) ethical theory.

Baier prefers Hume's "psychological theory" to the rationalistic theories she finds elsewhere; she denies that Hume has any "normative theory," and by associating Aristotle closely with Hume and denying that Aristotle is an "ethical theorist," she appears to deny, most oddly, that he has a normative theory. She appears to think that we need to choose between normative theorizing, which must be "rationalistic," and moral psychology, which must be descriptive rather than normative. Aristotle, Kant, Adam Smith, Spinoza, Rousseau, and a host of other thinkers show that our options are more complex. Most normative proposals recognize that good descriptive psychology helps us to determine what our obstacles are and what we can demand. Baier takes the contemporary Kantian theories of Donagan and Gewirth as paradigmatic of "theory" in her sense; only thus is she able to claim that theory neglects emotion.
54 See Nussbaum, "*Erôs* and the Wise: The Stoic Response to a Cultural Dilemma," *Oxford Studies in Ancient Philosophy* 13 (1995):231–67.
55 See Ruth Barcan Marcus, "Moral Dilemmas and Consistency," *Journal of Philosophy* 77 (1980):121–36.
56 See Michael Stocker, *Plural and Conflicting Values* (Oxford: Clarendon Press, 1990).

57 See, e.g., "Aristotelian Social Democracy," in R. B. Douglass, G. Mara, and H. Richardson, *Liberalism and the Good* (New York: Routledge, 1990).
58 See Nussbaum, "Introduction," in *Love's Knowledge.*
59 On this aspect of ancient ethical theories, see Julia Annas, *The Morality of Happiness* (Oxford: Clarendon Press, 1994).
60 See Williams, "Sidgwick." Williams notes that neither act-utilitarianism nor R. M. Hare's version of utilitarianism raises this problem, though he objects to Hare's view on other grounds.
61 See Kant, *Doctrine of Virtue,* section 34.
62 See *Frieden durch Recht: Kants Friedensidee und das Problem einer neuen Weltordnung,* ed. Matthias Lutz-Bachmann and James Bohmann (Frankfurt: Suhrkamp, 1996); partial English version published as *Perpetual Peace: Essays on Kant's Cosmopolitan Ideal* (Cambridge, Mass.: MIT, 1997); with articles by Jürgen Habermas, Richard Falk (German edition only), Axel Honneth, Thomas McCarthy, and others.
63 See my criticisms of Williams's essay "Saint Just's Illusion" (*part of Making Sense of Humanity*), in *Ethics* (April 1997):526–29.
64 See John Rawls, *Political Liberalism* (New York: Columbia University Press, 1996), expanded paper edition.
65 There is room for much uncertainty here, since several figures prominently admired by Williams – the Greek tragic poets, Nietzsche, D. H. Lawrence – do not suggest the sensibility I describe at all. (Nor do they suggest liberal politics – although Williams plainly, and prominently, espouses liberal views.) The difficulty here comes from the fact that the sensibility expressed in Williams's text is to some extent at odds with the sensibilities of the figures he praises; my attempt to characterize the former has possibly shortchanged the role of the latter in his thinking.
66 Lord Chief Justice Sir Matthew Hale, *The History of the Pleas of the Crown* (London: Sollom Emlyn, 1778), vol. 1, 629. For the relevant texts, see Rebecca M. Ryan, "The Sex Right: A Legal History of the Marital Rape Exemption," *Law and Social Inquiry* 20 (1995):941–1001.
67 See Ryan's discussion of John Galsworthy's novel, *The Man of Property* (1908), in which Soames Forsyte calms his conscience by reflecting on his legal rights. The night of behavior that at first disturbed him becomes, as he reflects on theory, the "night on which Soames at last asserted his rights and acted like a man." Ryan, "Sex Right."
68 See now my "Rage and Reason," a review of Andrea Dworkin's *Life and Death: Unapologetic Essays in the Continuing War against Women, The New Republic,* August 1997, where I stress the Kantian ethical origins of Dworkin and MacKinnon's legal proposals. See also my "Objectification," *Philosophy and Public Affairs* 24 (1995):249–91. (Both essays have now appeared in my *Sex and Social Justice* [New York: Oxford University Press, 1999].) In the latter, I discuss the fact that Kant drew perverse and to some extent damaging conclusions from his own theory, and I argue that it was not the theory but Kant's own misapplication of it that was to blame.
69 Kant, *Groundwork,* trans. Ellington, Akad., p. 404.
70 Ibid.
71 See Susan Moller Okin, *Justice, Gender, and the Family* (New York: Basic Books, 1989), and Barbara Herman, "Can It Be Worth Thinking about Kant on Sex and Marriage?" in L. Antony and C. Witt, *A Mind of One's Own: Feminist Essays on Reason and Objectivity* (Boulder: Westview, 1993).

72 See E. Laumann et al., *The Social Organization of Sexuality: Sexual Practices in the United States* (Chicago: University of Chicago Press, 1994), on the discrepancy in numbers between women who report being forced sexually and men who report using force (many more women report being forced than men who report forcing) – the discrepancy being especially prominent within marriage. See further discussion of this discrepancy in chapter 5 of my *Sex and Social Justice*.

73 Kant, "Third Definitive Article of a Perpetual Peace: Cosmopolitan Right Shall Be Limited to Conditions of Universal Hospitality," in *Perpetual Peace,* trans. Reiss.

74 I owe this point to Scott Brewer, who develops it extremely well, in connection with the role of logic in moral and legal reasoning, in his excellent essay in this volume (Chapter 5). He appeals to Russian literary theory for clarification of the process; the Brecht analogy is my own, one that I develop, with comparison to Stoic moral theory, in "Poetry and Passions: Two Stoic Views," in *Passions & Perceptions,* ed. J. Brunschwig and M. Nussbaum (Cambridge: Cambridge University Press, 1993).

75 See my argument in "Introduction" in *Love's Knowledge* and also in chapter 3 in *Poetic Justice: The Literary Imagination and Public Life* (Boston: Beacon, 1995).

76 See Nussbaum, review essay on Vlastos.

77 See John Rawls, *A Theory of Justice* (Cambridge, Mass.: Belknap Press of Harvard University Press, 1971), 46: "Let us assume that each person beyond a certain age and possessed of the requisite intellectual capacity develops a sense of justice under normal social circumstances." On distorting factors, see 47.

78 See my "Rage and Reason" for further development of this idea in connection with the need for philosophy to turn, at times, to nonphilosophical modes of persuasion.

79 See my "Kant and Stoic Cosmopolitanism," *Journal of Political Philosophy* 5 (1997):1–25, published in German in ed. Lutz-Bachmann and Bohmann, *Frieden durch Recht* and in the English translation *Perpetual Peace.*

80 On this influence, see especially the articles by Richard Falk and Jürgen Habermas in Lutz-Bachmann and Bohmann, *Frieden durch Recht/Perpetual Peace.*

81 Williams could agree with the first part of this claim, but he would presumably disagree with this final stipulation: the systematic political theorizing he could favor, compatibly with his assault on ethical theory, would have to be a type less grounded in moral theory than modern international law is.

82 See *Carr v. Allison Gas Turbine Division, General Motors Corp.,* 32 F.3d 1007 (7th Cir. 1994), overruling the lower-court judge on the findings of fact because the "asymmetry of positions" between Carr and her male co-workers had not been considered.

83 John Stuart Mill, *The Subjection of Women,* ed. S. M. Vlein (Indianapolis: Hackett [1869], 1988), 4.

4

Theories, Anti-Theories, and Norms
Comment on Nussbaum

DAN M. KAHAN*

The jurisprudence of Oliver Wendell Holmes, Jr., embodies exactly the kind of anti-theoretical reasoning that Martha Nussbaum criticizes. Holmes, as Nussbaum recognizes, was notoriously hostile to generalization and abstraction. Consider his famous aphorisms: "[G]eneral propositions do not decide concrete cases";[1] "[T]he life of the law has not been logic: it has been experience";[2] The common law . . . decides the case first and determines the principle afterwards."[3] The same attitude informs the legal doctrines that Holmes championed. The "reasonable man" standard of negligence,[4] the "clear and present danger" test for speech restrictions,[5] and the "dangerous proximity" test for criminal attempts[6] – all reflect a calculated vagueness designed to preserve the freedom of the decision maker to adapt her judgment to an ever-shifting array of salient particulars.

So if Nussbaum is on target in her critique of anti-theory, we should be wary of Holmes's jurisprudence; indeed, we should be wary of the jurisprudence of a host of twentieth-century antiformalists, many of whom are indebted to Holmes. The most famous of these are the legal realists, who not only asserted the impossibility of formal deductive proofs in law, but who also defended what Karl N. Llewellyn called "situation sense" – a perceptive capacity born of a decision maker's immersion in the norms and practices of a particular field of law and social activity.[7] In describing the common law method, Holmes spoke of a similar perceptive capacity, which he characterized as "insight, tact, and specific knowledge," and which he contrasted to "rules of method."[8] The same confidence in intuition informs the work of many contemporary legal pragmatists and feminists.[9]

Nussbaum, in contrast, distrusts intuition because of its grounding in potentially corrupt social norms. Norms are what situate "situation sense": they stand behind decision makers' intuitive apprehension of what is appropriate and what

---

* I am grateful for the generous support of the Russell J. Parsons and Jerome S. Weiss Funds for Faculty Research at the University of Chicago Law School.

is not; they construct the goods that their emotions tell them are valuable. But that means, Nussbaum points out, that a decision maker's intuitions are no better than his or her community's norms. Before a decision maker can legitimately trust situation sense, she needs theory to tell her whether those norms are just or unjust.[10]

I want to suggest that this "bad norms" critique is completely inert. It does no damage to the anti-theory of Holmes, to the legal realists, or to anyone else. To be sure, bad norms are a big problem – an immensely big problem – for legal decision making. But they are no less a problem for theory-driven styles of legal reasoning than they are for anti-theoretical ones. Indeed, although it is hazardous, as Holmes reminds us, to generalize, there is a sense in which bad norms are an even bigger problem for theory than for anti-theory. Whereas particularistic decision making exposes contentious normative appraisals to plain view – where they can be challenged and attacked – theorized decision making tends to obscure such appraisals, thereby insulating them from competition with better ones and ultimately extending their life in the law.

To make this claim more concrete, I will recount a pair of stories. Both are about judges who followed the lead of their intuitions in sentencing.

The first story is about Judge Robert Cahill. Judge Cahill had to sentence a Maryland truck driver who shot his wife dead after he returned home unexpectedly and discovered her making love with another man. Judge Cahill expressed sympathy, stating the he could imagine nothing that would enrage "a happily married man" more than "to be betrayed in your personal life, when you're out working to support the spouse . . . I seriously wonder how many men married five, four years," the judge continued, "would have had the strength to walk away without inflicting some corporal punishment." So Cahill sentenced Peacock leniently: eighteen months of night-time custody with permission to continue driving his truck during the day.[11]

My second story is about a Texas judge named Jack Hampton, who had to sentence a man who killed a homosexual who allegedly propositioned him. "I put prostitutes and gays at about the same level," Hampton explained, "and I'd be hard put to give somebody life in prison for murdering a prostitute." Ergo, he imposed a far less severe sentence.[12]

Hampton's impeccable syllogism notwithstanding, I take these to be the kinds of anti-theoretical decisions that Nussbaum is anxious about. Both judges followed situation sense when it told them that mercy was in order. And it seems fairly obvious that this sense was constructed by social norms: norms relating to the subordination of wives to their husbands; norms relating to the dishonor of being a man who behaves too much like a woman; in a word, "bad" norms.

But would theorizing have caused Judge Cahill and Judge Hampton, or any other judge steeped in these bad norms, to decide these cases differently? The answer, I think, is no. For theory is fully up to the task of justifying the mercy of the Cahills and the Hamptons.

Common law jurists theorized mercy for vengeful cuckolds and dishonored homophobes by invoking principles of natural law. Natural law theory told them that adultery was "the gravest possible offence which a wife can commit against her husband"[13] and "the highest invasion of [his] property" by another man.[14] Common law authorities invoked similarly abstract principles to condemn homosexuality, which was in fact viewed as a "crime against nature."[15]

If that kind of theory sounds a bit quaint, let Cahill and Hampton try out the more secular theories that animate contemporary criminal-law jurisprudence. According to Jeremy Bentham's consequentialism, we punish if, and to the extent that, doing so increases social welfare.[16] Conesquentialists can argue (and have argued) that men who kill other men who proposition them, or who kill their unfaithful wives are less dangerous to society than those who kill in less extreme or unusual circumstances; mitigation is therefore appropriate for violent cuckolds and homophobes, because we get relatively less social benefit from incapacitating them.[17] Indeed, consequentialists could argue – and in fact have argued – that mercy toward provoked killers helps to deter the offensive behavior engaged in by their victims.[18]

Or, if these judges do not like consequentialism, they can consider H. L. A. Hart's voluntarism, which tells us that criminal offenders should be punished only if, and to the extent that, their conduct rests on choice.[19] This theory, too, can be (and has been) used to justify mercy for cuckolds and homophobes, on the ground that the intensity of their rage or disgust undermines their "volitional capacities."[20]

Nussbaum tells us that we must be sure to assess our intuitions according to "good" theories.[21] Any theory that justifies the mercy of Cahill and Hampton is definitely bad. But it is important to figure out why.

One thing we could be saying when we call a moral theory "bad" is that it is not a very good *theory*. Nussbaum gives us criteria for identifying what a theory is; presumably, these same criteria can be used to evaluate theories: ones that do not readily solve problems, that do not allow us to test and systematize our beliefs, or that are not sufficiently abstract and explicit are bad theories.

But I doubt that all of the theories that justify the mercy of Judge Cahill and Judge Hampton are bad in this way. It would be nice if only good norms, beliefs, practices, and so forth could be rationally theorized in the way that Nussbaum's criteria requires; but who believes that moral reality is this conveniently configured? Or, to put things another way, are theories like National Socialism, racism, communism bad because they are internally incoherent, or are they bad because they systematize bad norms and values?

Indeed, that is another thing we can mean when we say that a moral theory is bad: that the results the theory produces simply are not moral. That clearly *is* the problem for the theories that justify the mercy of Judges Cahill and Hampton.

But that sense of "badness" is not so good for Nussbaum. For if we are judging the goodness of a theory according to the results it produces, then we obviously have some pretheoretical way of perceiving which results are good, which bad. In that event, it is not theory that is normative for intuition, as Nussbaum maintains, but intuition that is normative for theory.[22] Or, to quote Holmes, we "decide ... the case first, and determine the principle afterward."[23]

If I were to stop here, the conclusion would be that the "bad norm" problem is a wash in the theory–anti-theory debate. Bad norms produce not just bad intuitions, but also bad theories.

In fact, though, I want to make a more ambitious claim. I am going to argue that anti-theoretical styles of legal reasoning are often, if not always, better than theoretical ones when we suspect that our decision makers are laboring under the influence of bad social norms. This is so because of the link that particularistic decision making forges between law and the forces that produce normative change.

Social norms are not static. Indeed, the transformation of norms is a pervasive phenomenon in contemporary political and social life. This is especially true, as Nussbaum notes, in the domains of gender and sexuality, where traditional hierarchical norms are now highly contested and in some cases completely discredited.

One of the most conspicuous mechanisms of such change is consciously orchestrated norm competition. The body of norms that construct a culture is almost always rich enough to underwrite an attack on one particular set of them in the name of the culture that they help construct. Think of Martin Luther King, Jr., and other civil rights reformers in the 1960s: they attacked American racism primarily by appealing to other distinctly American practices and values – pointing to a conflict that they made salient less through argument than through dramatic events that made it impossible for those who subscribed to the preferred norms to avert their eyes from the injustice of racism.[24]

To purge the law of bad norms, then, we should favor reasoning styles that facilitate this kind of norm competition in law or, more realistically, make the law responsive to such competition as it occurs elsewhere in society. Theory-pervaded styles of reasoning are unlikely to do that. That is because abstractions like social wealth and autonomy obscure the role that contentious norms play in legal decisions, allowing those norms to go on influencing law, unobserved and unremarked, long after they have become contested in society generally.

Matters are different, however, when decision makers speak in an anti-theoretical idiom. Then the norms that inform their judgments come boiling to the surface. The prospect of publicly owning up to reliance on anachronistic norms can itself shame decision makers into deciding on some other basis. Even more important, when we force decision makers to be open about their normative commitments, members of the public are fully appraised of what those commitments are. This outcome facilitates the kind of self-conscious norm competition that drives bad norms from the scene.[25]

To illustrate, let me go back to my two stories, both of which have relatively happy endings. Jack Hampton – the judge who announced that the life of a gay man just is not worth enough to justify life imprisonment – was formally censured for those remarks and then defeated at the polls.[26] In the wake of this and other incidents, moreover, the Texas legislature enacted a hate crimes statute that expressly enhances the penalty for crimes motivated by bias against any group.[27]

Judge Cahill's sentence and remarks about the dishonored Maryland truck driver likewise ignited a firestorm of controversy. Newspapers across the country ran critical editorials.[28] Protesters picketed the courthouse, calling for Cahill's removal. Members of the Maryland General Assembly introduced a resolution condemning him.[29] And the Maryland judiciary agreed to withhold new sentencing guidelines so that provisions relating to domestic violence could be reviewed and possibly strengthened.[30]

It seems much less likely that these decisions would have triggered this volume of public outrage had the judges used theory talk to rationalize them. For through the lens of theory, we see in those decisions not male sovereignty in the home, machismo honor, and related mysogynistic norms; we see instead sterile cost–benefit judgments, or pseudoscientific determinations about offenders' volitional capacities – propositions that most people are unlikely even to understand, much less get upset about. I am not just speculating here: theorized mercy for vengeful cuckolds and dishonored homophobes has been commonplace for decades, notwithstanding what we know about the contested status of the norms that these decisions embody.[31]

So what am I saying? I am not advancing the silly claim that anti-theory is good because it inevitably leads to outrageous decisions, which we can then use politics to correct; indeed, I would argue that at least where we think we have good social norms, intuition is more likely than theory to produce moral legal decisions. The argument I am making here, though, presupposes bad norms. And what I am saying is that, in that context, particularistic decision making is unlikely to make matters worse than theory would and could actually make them better, because of anti-theory's power to expose contentious norms to public scrutiny and attack.

But I do not want to insist on this point dogmatically. Maybe there are particular circumstances in which, strategically speaking, theory may seem to be a more potent weapon for attacking bad norms than does anti-theory. If we can sometimes trick bad decision makers into being just through theory rhetoric, I am all for that. My only target here is the broad-gauged claim that anti-theory is dangerous because of its peculiar vulnerability to bad social norms. That claim, to paraphrase Holmes, is exactly the kind of general proposition that does not decide concrete cases when we are trying to figure out how to make the law more just.

Notes

1 *Lochner v. New York,* 198 U.S. 45, 76 (1905) (Holmes, dissenting).
2 Oliver Wendell Holmes, *The Common Law* (Boston: Little, Brown, 1881), 1.

3 Oliver Wendell Holmes, "Codes and the Arrangement of the Law," *American Law Review* 5 (1870):1.
4 See generally Holmes, *Common Law*, 108–13, 120–24 (describing the use of an objective standard of liability by judges to conform results in particular cases to insights gained through "experience").
5 *Abrams v. United States*, 250 U.S. 616, 628 (1919) (Holmes dissenting) ("the present danger of immediate evil").
6 *Hyde v. United States*, 225 U.S. 347, 388 (1912) (Holmes dissenting); see also *Commonwealth v. Peaslee*, 177 Mass. 267, 272 (1901) ("the degree of proximity held sufficient [to distinguish preparation from attempt] may vary with circumstances").
7 See Karl N. Llewellyn, *The Common Law Tradition: Deciding Appeals* (Boston: Little, Brown, 1960), 59–61, 121–57, 206–8; see also Karl Llewellyn, *The Case Law System in America*, ed. Paul Gewertz, trans. Michael Ansoldi (Chicago: University of Chicago Press, 1989), 78–80.
8 Holmes correspondence, quoted by Louis Menand, "Bet-tablitarianism," *New Republic*, 11 November 1996, 50. Menand convincingly depicts Holmes as an anti-theorist.
9 For sources, and an insightful discussion, see Frederick Schauer, "Giving Reasons," *Stanford Law Review* 47 (1995):663, 650, and note 52.
10 See Martha Nussbaum, "Why Practice Needs Ethical Theory: Particularism, Principle, and Bad Behavior," Chapter 3 of this volume.
11 See Sheridan Lyons, "Court Panel to Probe Judge in Sentencing," *Baltimore Sun*, 20 October 1994, 1B; "She Strays, He Shoots, Judge Winks," *New York Times*, 22 October 1994, A22.
12 See Lisa Belkin, "Texas Judge Eases Sentence for Killer of 2 Homosexuals," *New York Times*, 17 December 1988, 8.
13 *Rex v. Greening*, 3 K.B. 846, 849 (1913).
14 *Regina v. Mawgridge*, 84 Eng. Rep. 1107, 1115 (1707). See generally Jeremy Horder, *Provocation and Responsibility* (New York: Oxford University Press, 1992); 71. Donna K. Coker, "Heat of Passion and Wife Killing: Men Who Batter/Men Who Kill," *Southern California Review of Law and Women's Studies* (1992):71.
15 William Blackstone, *Commentaries*, vol. 4, *215; see *Bowers v. Hardwick*, 478 U.S. 186, 196–97 (1986) (Burger, C. J., concurring) (canvassing relevant authorities). See generally Robert B. Mison, "Homophobia in Manslaughter: The Homosexual Advance as Insufficient Provocation," *California Law Review* 80 (1992):133.
16 See Jeremy Bentham, *An Introduction to the Principles of Morals and Legislation*, reprinted in *The Utilitarians* (Garden City, N.Y.: Doubleday, 1961), 162, 169–71.
17 See Herbert Wechsler and Jerome Michael, "A Rationale of the Law of Homicide: II," *Columbia Law Review* 37 (1937):1262, 1280–82; "Judge Draws Protest after Cutting Sentence of Gay Man's Killer," *New York Times*, 17 August 1994, A15 (reporting that the judge was "confident" that the man who shot another man between the eyes because the victim had made sexual advances to him would "not kill again").
18 See Alon Harel, "Efficiency and Fairness in Criminal Law: The Case for a Criminal Law Principle of Comparative Fault," *California Law Review* 82 (1994):1181, 1215–17.
19 See H. L. A. Hart, *Punishment and Responsibility* (New York: Oxford University Press, 1968), 46–49.
20 Joshua Dressler, "Rethinking Heat of Passion: A Defense in Search of a Rationale," *Journal of Criminal Law and Criminology* 85 (1982):421, 467; see Joshua Dressler, "When

'Heterosexual' Men Kill 'Homosexual' Men: Reflections on Provocation Law, Sexual Advances, and the 'Reasonable Man' Standard," *Journal of Criminal Law and Criminology* (1995):726 (defending the use of the provocation defense in "homosexual-advance" cases on this ground); *State v. Thornton,* 730 S.W.2d 309 (Tenn. 1987) (defending it in adultery cases).
21. Nussbaum, Chapter 3 of this volume.
22. This is one of the central insights of the ethical anti-theorists whom Nussbaum criticizes. See, e.g., Bernard Williams, *Ethics and the Limits of Philosophy* (Cambridge, Mass.: Harvard University Press, 1985), 112–17; Cheryl N. Noble, "Normative Ethical Theories," in *Anti-Theory in Ethics and Moral Conservatism,* ed. Stanley G. Clarke and Evan Simpson (Albany, N.Y.: State University of New York Press, 1989).
23. Holmes, "Codes and Arrangement."
24. Michael Walzer has written extensively on this anti-theoretical style of social criticism. See his *Interpretation and Social Criticism* (Cambridge, Mass.: Harvard University Press, 1987).
25. This is a theme that Nussbaum and I have jointly developed elsewhere. See Dan M. Kahan and Martha C. Nussbaum, "Two Conceptions of Emotion in Criminal Law," *Columbia Law Review* 96 (1996):269, 362–65.
26. See "Gay Rights Groups Hail Defeat of Judge in Texas," *New York Times,* 4 December 1992, B20; "Judge Is Censored over Remark on Homosexuals," *New York Times,* 29 November 1989, A28.
27. See Tex. Penal Code Ann. § 12.47 (West 1994); Tex. Code Crim. Proc. Ann., art. 42.014 (1997 Electronic Pocket Part Update, West Supp. 1996); see also Clay Robison, "Richards Signs Hate Crimes Bill into Law," *Houston Chronicle,* 20 June 1993, "State" section, 3 (noting that the purpose of the legislation was to enhance the penalty for "criminal offenses motivated by the victims' race, religion, ethnicity, sexual orientation or national origin").
28. See, e.g., "A Judge Who Dishonors the Bench," *Hartford Courant,* 21 October 1994, A16; "Justice Mocked in Maryland," *Boston Herald,* 24 October 1994, 26; "'Passion Killing' Sentence Absurd," *Sun-Sentinel* (Fort Lauderdale, Fla.), 22 October 1994, 18A; "She Strays, He Shoots"; Ann G. Sjoerdsma, "Eighteen Months for a Wife's Life," *Chicago Tribune,* 14 November 1994, 21; "Unequal Justice," *Saint Louis Dispatch,* 1 November 1994, 12B.
29. See John W. Frece, "Ouster of Judge Sought," *Baltimore Sun,* 8 December 1994, 1B; Sheridan Lyons and Robert G. Matthews, "Oust Judge Cahill, Protesters Urge," *Baltimore Sun,* 22 October 1994, 1B; editorial, *Baltimore Sun,* 13 December 1994, 18A.
30. See Janet Naylor, "Maryland Judges Delay Relaxation of Sentence Guidelines," *Washington Times,* 26 January 1995, A1.
31. See Coker, "Heat of Passion"; Mison, "Homophobia."

5

Traversing Holmes's Path toward a Jurisprudence of Logical Form

SCOTT BREWER

I. Holmesian Anti-Logic and the "Fallacy of Logical Form"

The life of the law is, and should be, logic suffused by experience and experience tempered by logic. That is the principal proposition I defend in this essay.

It is now a commonplace that Holmes's declaration "The life of the law has not been logic: it has been experience" is, as Thomas Grey has said, the "central slogan of legal modernism."[1] Holmes first offered it in 1880 in a review of C. C. Langdell's book on contracts,[2] and he repeated it prominently at the opening of *The Common Law,* published in the same year, where it serves as part of an extended admonition about the limitations of "logic" in the best explanation of common law doctrines:

> The object of this book is to present a general view of the Common Law. To accomplish that task, other tools are needed besides logic. It is something to show that the consistency of a system requires a particular result, but it is not all. The life of the law has not been logic: it has been experience. The felt necessities of the time, the prevalent moral and political theories, institutions of public policy, avowed or unconscious, even the prejudices which judges share with their fellow men, have had a good deal more to do than the syllogism in determining the rules by which men should be governed. The law embodies the story of a nation's development through many centuries, and it cannot be dealt with as if it contained only the axioms and corollaries of a book of mathematics.[3]

I refer to this basic thesis as Holmes's "anti-logic." The anti-logic thesis is not a passing fancy on Holmes's part. Rather, he maintained and repeated it (though not always in the same words) for at least twenty-five years, from the 1880 review of Langdell's book to his 1905 dissent in *Lochner v. New York,* in which he declared: "[G]eneral propositions do not decide concrete cases. The decision will depend on a judgment or intuition more subtle than any articulate major premise."[4] The anti-logic thesis is, of course, also a major emphasis in his essay of *The Path of the Law*.[5] I detail Holmes's anti-logic thesis in part I of this chapter and challenge it in several respects in part II.

A. Holmes's Anti-Logic in The Path of the Law

1. FOUR JURISPRUDENTIAL THESES. To understand the content of Holmes's anti-logic thesis in *The Path of the Law*, it is helpful to locate it among the other principal theses of the essay. Holmes was not a carefully systematic jurisprudential thinker, although he certainly had many flashes of brilliant jurisprudential insight, both with regard to relatively narrow doctrinal issues and with regard to the more abstract and traditional issues addressed by legal positivists and natural lawyers. Despite Holmes's lack of systemic attentiveness, the essay can profitably be read and examined for its insights into systemic jurisprudence. Holmes advances at least four principal theses, all of which concern one overarching topic: the best explanation of legal institutions, doctrines, and reasoning. The four theses – the prediction thesis, the separation thesis, the anti-logic thesis, and the rational reform thesis – may be characterized as follows:

1. *The prediction thesis:* Law (at least the law from the point of view of a lawyer) is a prediction of the decisions that courts will make, backed by the use of public force.
2. *The separation thesis:* Legal norms (e.g., rules, doctrines, principles) are not identical with moral norms, and their conflation has caused much confusion in the study of legal systems.
3. *The anti-logic thesis:* The law of a living legal system, such as that of the United States, cannot be adequately explained as an axiomatic deductive system, in large part because a significant role is inevitably played by the "inarticulate" in a judge's discernment and application of the law.

(Note that Holmes offers the (in)famous "bad man" as a heuristic device to illustrate and argue for theses 1, 2, and 3.)

4 *The rational reform thesis:* It is (a) possible and (b) normatively desirable to effect rational reform in the law – reform that is both properly attentive to and properly critical of history and tradition.

a. The Prediction Thesis. This thesis has received substantial jurisprudential attention. For present purposes, two observations about it will suffice. First, as scholars have long noted, Holmes's prediction thesis – the idea that law is a prediction of what *courts* will do – cannot serve as a complete account of "the law."[6] At best, the thesis accurately describes one very important, perhaps even dominant, aspect of what lawyers and clients care about, but it does not present a convincing account of what *constitutes* the law as a social and conceptual practice.[7] Indeed, if one applies the prediction thesis to a judge on the highest court in a jurisdiction, it seems to yield the absurd claim that such a judge, if he wishes to know what the law is, will be trying to predict his own behavior. In Holmes's defense, there is ample evidence in *The Path of the Law* that he intended to offer the prediction thesis not as a complete jurisprudential account of "the concept of law," but rather as a working explanation of the law from the limited *point of view* of the lawyer (which he reflects in the "bad man's point of view" ["Path" 174]).[8] Holmes clearly speaks from the point of view of a legal official who is *promulgating* rules, not *predicting* the behavior of public officials.

Second, even as an account of the dominant concern of clients and lawyers, the prediction thesis is far too narrow in its focus on the behavior of courts – a point also long remarked by scholars.[9] Even "the prediction of the incidence of [the use of] public force through the instrumentality of courts" requires accurate prediction of behavior by several other public "instrumentalities," such as the police, administrative-agency field officers and administrative-law judges, congressional committees, special prosecutors, and district and U.S. attorneys. There is little evidence that Holmes understood this.

b. The Separation Thesis and the "Bad Man." Holmes introduces the perspective of the "bad man" as a heuristic device to illustrate his "first principle for the study of law," namely, the separation thesis: "[N]othing but confusion of thought can result from assuming that the rights of man in a moral sense are equally rights in the sense of the Constitution and the law" ("Path" 171–72). Arguing for this principle occupies just over one quarter of the essay, in which Holmes first makes the point as a matter of abstract jurisprudence (169–78). In this part of the essay, Holmes discusses the bad man's view of the distinction presupposed in "the many discussions which have arisen in the courts on the very question whether a given statutory liability is a penalty or a tax" (173). In Holmes's view, courts tend to conflate legal norms and moral norms when they attempt to maintain and apply this distinction by assessing whether the conduct in question is "legally right or wrong." Were their views to be washed in the "acid bath" of the bad man's perspective, argues Holmes, legal reasoners would see no significance in the distinction. The real distinction could be found only in some additional difference in disadvantages (or other consequences) that judges attach to conduct in the name of a "penalty" compared to those they attach to conduct in the name of a "tax."

Holmes follows his more abstract jurisprudential argument about the separation thesis with three principal examples, two from contract law and one from tort law. Regarding contract law, Holmes argues that the "obligation" to keep a contractual promise is not moral; rather "[t]he duty to keep a contract at common law means a prediction that you must pay damages if you do not keep it – and nothing else" (175). Moreover, "[m]orals deal with the actual internal state of the individual's mind," whereas "all contracts are formal, and the making of a contract depends not on the agreement of two minds in one intention, but on the agreement of two sets of external signs" (178). Regarding torts, Holmes argues that such terms as 'malice' occasion a confusing conflation of legal and moral concepts. Properly understood, the legal concept of malice is not well understood "in the moral sense, as importing a malevolent motive," but "only signifies that the tendency of [a defendant's] conduct under the known circumstances was very plainly to cause the plaintiff temporal harm" (176–77). Holmes sums up his separation thesis with this striking comment: "For my own part, I often doubt whether it would not be a gain if every word of moral significance could be banished from the law altogether, and other words adopted which should convey legal ideas uncolored by anything outside the law" (179).

c. The "Anti-Logic" Thesis and the "Fallacy of Logical Form." After advancing and illustrating the separation thesis, Holmes turns to the second of his two "principles for the proper understanding of law," which he refers to as "the fallacy of logical form" (184). According to Holmes, the fallacy is "the notion that the only force at work in the development of the law is logic." This is a key argument, and I consider it in detail later.

d. The Rational Reform Thesis. To use William James's enduringly useful term, Holmes advanced many "tough-minded" skeptical sentiments in *The Path of the Law*: that "certainty generally is an illusion, and repose is not the destiny of man" (181); that "we do not realize how large a part of our law is open to reconsideration upon a slight change in the habit of the public mind" (181); that judicial decisions sometimes harbor "a concealed, half conscious battle on . . . question[s] of policy" (182); that "the very ground and foundation" of judges' judgments are frequently "inarticulate and often unconscious" (182). Yet there is a vitally powerful element in the essay that acknowledges – indeed celebrates and trumpets – the power of abstract rational ideas in general and declaims both the possibility and the normative attractiveness of imposing rational reform upon legal doctrines. Nearly half of the essay is devoted to this theme, which I summarize here briefly.

Holmes begins this part of the essay by asserting that the law of his day was "at the beginning of a philosophical reaction, and of a reconsideration of the worth of doctrines which for the most part are still taken for granted without any deliberate, conscious, systematic questioning of their grounds" (185). Holmes identifies the unquestioning imitation of the past and the undeliberated following of tradition as the chief "impediments to rational generalization" of the law (190). "Everywhere the basis of principle is tradition, to such an extent that we even are in danger of making the role of history more important than it is" (191). Time and again, he complains, "tradition . . . overrides rational policy" (192). Not that history has no proper place in "the rational study of law"; it does, both because "without it we cannot know the precise scope of rules which it is our business to know," and because an understanding of history "is the first step toward an enlightened skepticism, that is, towards a deliberate reconsideration of the worth of those rules" (186–87). Holmes warns, however, that despite the value of understanding the history of legal doctrines and institutions, there is also a grand danger in attending to history in the wrong way. "It is revolting," he says, in yet another of the essay's classic dicta, "to have no better reason for a rule of law than that so it was laid down in the time of Henry IV. It is still more revolting if the grounds upon which it was laid down have vanished long since, and the rule simply persists from blind imitation of the past" (187).

What is to be done to overcome the intellectually confining shackles of the traditionalist's overvaluation of history? Holmes's answer is succinct and programmatic:

> We must beware of the pitfall of antiquarianism, and must remember that for our purposes our only interest in the past is for the light it throws upon the present. I look forward to a time when the part played by history in the explanation of dogma shall be very small, and instead of ingenious research we shall spend our energy on a study of ends sought to be attained and the reasons for desiring them. (195)

Holmes places the "deliberated" study of the goals to be achieved by legal doctrines at the center of his exhortation to right-thinking legal moderns "to try to set some corner" of the legal world "in the order of reason" and collectively "to aspire to carry reason as far as it will go throughout the whole domain" (185). His axiological program, as one might call it (a program focused on the values at which legal doctrines are properly aimed), is designed to help lawyers, judges, and scholars make legal doctrines and institutions "more rational and more civilized"; this effect is achieved "when every rule . . . is referred articulately and definitely to an end which it subserves, and when the grounds for desiring that end are stated or are ready to be stated in words" (186).

Holmes offers some additional intellectual tools to fill out and complement the axiological program of rational reform. Economics is one. "Every lawyer ought to seek an understanding of economics," for such an understanding reveals that "for everything we have we give up something else, and we are taught to set the advantage we gain against the other advantage we lose, and to know what we are doing when we elect" (195). Jurisprudence is another tool. True to his earlier denunciation of "axiomatized" theories of law and his promotion of the prediction thesis, Holmes envisions "the study of what is called jurisprudence," the study of "law in its most generalized part" (195), not as "a striving for a useless quintessence of all systems," but rather as a means of providing an "accurate anatomy" (196–97) of one system – a device for "discern[ing] the true basis for [law's] prophecy" (196). Holmes summarizes these several elements of his "ideal" program for rational legal reform thus:

> In the first place, . . . follow the existing body of dogma into its highest generalizations by the help of jurisprudence; next, . . . discover from history how it has come to be what it is; and, finally, so far as you can, consider the ends which several rules seek to accomplish, the reasons why those ends are desired, what is given up to gain them, and whether they are worth the price. (198)

B. Five Senses of 'Logic' in The Path of the Law

There is much wisdom and insight in the four theses Holmes proffers, but along the path there are also some crucial missteps. Among them, in my view, is Holmes's analysis of the role of what he terms "logic"[10] in legal reasoning, doctrine, and institutions. That analysis comes in his treatment of the second of what he refers to as two "first principles for the study of this body of dogma or systematized prediction which we call the law" (169), principles that he also calls "two pitfalls" that "lie perilously close to the narrow path of legal doctrine" (178) and two "fallacies." The first of these first principles is the separation thesis. (The associated fallacy, apparently, is failure to recognize its truth.) The second of the first principles is the "fallacy of logical form" – "the notion that the only force at work in the development of the law is logic" (180).[11]

To assess the cogency of Holmes's arguments about this supposed fallacy, we must first discern what exactly Holmes meant in speaking of "logic" and "logical form." This is no small task, since Holmes used the term 'logic' in the essay in several different senses, without defining and explaining which sense he had in mind at different points.[12] This lack of systemic care is important. The anti-logic thesis has had such a misleading but powerful impact on the thinking of generations of law students, lawyers, judges, and scholars about the ways in which it is both possible and normatively desirable to recognize and promote the life of articulate reason in legal decision making.[13] Obviously Holmes did not explain his understanding of logic in legal decision making only in *The Path of the Law*; the discussion there reflects a view that Holmes repeatedly articulated, and it will be helpful occasionally to refer to passages in other works to discern how he defines various meanings of 'logic'.

In *The Path of the Law*, Holmes uses the term 'logic' in at least five different senses. What he says about "logic" is true of only some of the varied referents for that term. He thus slides quite close to a logical fallacy of his own (namely, equivocation). The five uses are these:

(i) 'Logic' as one of a set of roughly synonymous terms, including 'sensible', 'reasonable', 'warranted', 'advisable'. For example, "this really was giving up the requirement of a trespass, and it would have been more logical, as well as truer to the present object of the law, to abandon the requirement altogether" ("Path" 188); "there are some cases in which a logical justification can be found for speaking of civil liabilities as imposing duties in an intelligible sense" (175).

(ii) 'Logic' as syllogistic inference (or some other type of deductive inference). For example, "there is a concealed, half conscious battle on the question of legislative policy, and if any one thinks that it can be settled only deductively, or once and for all, I only can say that I think he is theoretically wrong" (182–83).[14]

(iii) 'Logic' as a formal *deductive system,* with axioms, rules of inference, and theorems, as in geometry. For example, "the danger of which I speak is . . . the notion that a given [legal] system, ours for instance, can be worked out like mathematics from some general axioms of conduct" (180).
(iv) 'Logic' as a rationally discernible pattern of cause and effect. For example, "The condition of our thinking about the universe is that it is capable of being thought about rationally, or, in other words, that every part of it is effect and cause in the same sense in which those parts are with which we are most familiar. So in the broadest sense it is true that the law is a logical development, like everything else" (180).
(v) 'Logic' as a set of *argument types,* individually invariant but distinct from one another. For example, "The training of lawyers is a training in logic. The processes of analogy, discrimination, and deduction are those in which they are most at home. The language of judicial decision is the language of logic. And the logical method and form flatter that longing for certainty and for repose which is in every human mind" (181).

C. *'Logic' in the "Fallacy of Logical Form"*

1. SENSES (I) AND (II) – UNPROBLEMATIC. Use (i) is a common, nontechnical use of 'logical' and plays no troublesome role in Holmes's anti-logic. Nor does use (ii) present any problem. In traditional logic deduction is, of course, an established type of logical inference (only one among several) and it would surely be a serious jurisprudential mistake to believe that "the only force at work in the development of law" is deductive logic. (*Pace* Holmes, it is difficult to find theorists who endorse this belief, and Langdell is pretty clearly *not* among them.) What Holmes labels the "fallacy of logical form" is what he takes to be a particular jurisprudential view *about* deduction – the view that an actual legal system can be formalized in a way that allows deductive inference of results in particular cases.[15] Thus, Holmes's real target is not deduction per se but some view – exactly what view we shall have to consider – about the role that deduction either does actually play in legal argument (a descriptive claim), or can possibly play in legal argument (a conceptual claim), or should play in legal argument (a conceptual and normative claim). The problems come with senses (iii) and (iv).

2. SENSES (III) AND (IV) – VERY PROBLEMATIC. It may seem that the target of Holmes's anti-logic is sense (iii), the view that actual legal systems are deductively axiomatizable. But here the assertions that comprise Holmes's anti-logic become problematically unclear. Holmes concedes that the proposition "[T]he only force at work in the development of the law is logic" is *true* "in the broadest sense" (broad along what metric, one wonders) for sense (iv) ("Path" 180). This proposition is true, Holmes seems to believe, by virtue of the rather

Kantian view that "the postulate on which we think about the universe is that there is a fixed quantitative relation between every phenomenon and its antecedents and consequents" (180).[16] As Holmes also seems to recognize, this concession is a significant threat to the coherence of his anti-logic and prediction theses. To see why, note that the prediction thesis relies, at least implicitly, on the idea that judicial behavior, like other motions and behaviors of the universe (whether products of the intentional mind or not) has a rationally discernible *causal* structure. The whole idea of "prophesying" the law seems to rely on the assumption that in discerning the causal structure of judicial behavior, the lawyer or judge must examine examples of judicial behavior encountered in experience and recorded in case reports, generalize *inductively,* and predict, or "prophesy," *on the basis of deduction* ('logic' in sense (ii)). Thus if 'logic' is used in sense (iv), Holmes's own prediction thesis is an instance of the fallacy of logical form, unless he can distinguish this use from a different use of 'logic' by other theorists, who, in Holmes's view, really do commit the supposed fallacy. Does he distinguish his thesis successfully?

I think not. He does *tell* us that the "danger of which I speak is not the admission that principles governing other phenomena also govern the law, but the notion that a given [legal] system, ours for instance, can be worked out like mathematics from some general axioms of conduct" ("Path" 180). That is, those who commit the fallacy of logical form, unlike Holmesian predictors, think that the law is, or could be, deductively axiomatized – sense (iii) of 'logic'. But this brings up a tricky issue for the anti-logic thesis. As many scholars have observed, Langdell was a chief target for Holmes's anti-logic.[17] It is also well remarked that Langdell, in the brief passages in which he discusses the matter (probably too brief to get a clear picture of his view), seemed to think of the system of legal concepts as one that is generated by means of *inductive* generalization from decided cases, rather than from some a priori axiomatic structure, and only later applied deductively.[18] Langdell, like Holmes, saw a crucial role for 'logic' in sense (iv) in the "legal scientist's" discernment of legal rules and principles. Langdell also saw a crucial role for the subsequent use of deductive inference ('logic' in sense (ii)), when the inductively discovered[19] rules and principles are later applied to individual cases; surely Holmes's prediction thesis sees an important role for deductive inference working on the rules and principles discovered from experience. In this way, Langdell's conception of the role of logic was much closer to Holmes's than Holmes acknowledged.

Despite these similarities, real differences of opinion about the role of logic in legal argument seemed to remain between Holmes and Langdell. Langdell was far more sanguine than Holmes about the possibility of organizing the inductively generated rules and principles into a coherent conceptual order that could later be applied to individual cases apodictically. In the helpful terms that Thomas Grey has brought to the analysis of "Langdell's orthodoxy," Langdell may have believed, along with other "legal scientists" of his day, that empirically (and inductively) generated legal rules and principles *could* in fact be organized into a system that is "complete" (i.e., such as to provide one right answer to every case), "conceptually ordered" (i.e., consisting of lower-level rules that can be *derived* from a smaller set of higher-order principles that are themselves coherent), and "formal" (i.e., such as to provide apodictic certainty for individual legal decisions).[20] Although Holmes himself aspired, in much of his work, to render areas of law into conceptually ordered systems, he was also quite skeptical of the ability of any "legal scientist," himself included, to organize legal rules and principles so as to allow for one right and certain resolution – such as deduction could in theory provide – of every case. For Holmes, blind, "inarticulate," and irrational forces are too powerfully present in legal decision making for Langdell's conceptualistic goals to be realizable:

[T]he logical method and form flatter that longing for certainty and for repose which is in every human mind. But certainty generally is an illusion, and repose is not the destiny of man. Behind the logical form lies a judgment as to the relative worth and importance of competing legislative grounds, often an inarticulate and unconscious judgment, it is true, and yet the very root and nerve of the whole proceeding. ("Path" 181)

This is a real disagreement, but if it is this view that Holmes was targeting as the fallacy of logical form, then the fit between the Langdellian ontology and epistemology of law (inductive discovery, conceptual ordering, deductive application) and the fallacy of logical form is tenuous at best. Again, in Holmes's terms, the fallacy is "the notion that the *only* force at work *in the development of law* is logic" (180, emphasis added). If 'logic' in this proposition is being used in either sense (ii) (deductive inference) or sense (iii) (a deductive system), then that proposition seems *not* to describe Langdell's view at all; as noted earlier, Langdell accorded a vital role to both *inductive* inference (close kin to 'logic' in sense (iv) – rationally discernible cause) *and* deductive inference ('logic' in sense (ii)), operating in a system conceptually ordered by the "legal scientist" ('logic' in sense (iii)). But Holmes concedes that in sense (iv), which Langdell thought a vital part of legal analysis, logic is a vital force in the development of law (indeed, he even suggests, "the only force," albeit only "in the broadest sense") (180). In sum, though there was genuine disagreement between Holmes and Langdell about the role of deductive logic in legal reasoning, the disagreement was not nearly as great as Holmes made out, in part because Holmes mischaracterized the complexity of Langdell's views about the role of different modes of logical inference in legal argument. (I discuss those different modes in some detail in the next section.)

3. SENSE (V) – MOST PROMISING. This brings me to a final point. Holmes seems unclear about what he himself understood to be within the scope of the kind of logic involved in the fallacy of logical form. The fallacy of logical form seems to be the view that law can be organized into an axiomatic system in such a way as to allow for apodictic resolution of individual cases. But at a crucial point in the anti-logic section of the essay, Holmes speaks as if it is neither solely deduction ('logic' in sense (ii)) nor solely a *deductive system* ('logic' in sense (iii)) that he has targeted, but rather something much more inclusive, namely, 'logic' in sense (v):

[J]udicial dissent is often blamed, as if it meant simply that one side or the other were not doing their sums right, and, if they would take more trouble, agreement inevitably would come.

This mode of thinking is entirely natural. *The training of lawyers is a training in logic. The processes of analogy, discrimination, and deduction are those in which they are most at home. The language of judicial decision is mainly the language of logic.* And the logical method and form flatter that longing for certainty and repose which is in every human mind. (181, emphasis added)

Now, it seems, the fallacious view about the possible role of logic in legal argument embraces not only "deduction" but also "the processes of analogy and discrimination" – that is, disanalogical argument! Such an inclusive critique of the role of logic in legal reasoning is surely a far cry from the narrower and much more plausible view that law cannot be organized into an axiomatic system that is deductively applicable in every case. One has to be not just skeptical, but skeptical to an implausible extreme, to deny that logic, in the broad sense of a patterned form of inference (including deduction and analogy), plays a vital role "in the development of law." And if the response on behalf of Holmes is that he is not critiquing the view that logic plays a vital role in the development of law, but is instead critiquing the literal belief that "the *only* force at work in the development of law is logic," well, we must ask who ever believed that logic, in any sense, was the *only* force at work in the development of law? If the proposition Holmes uses to describe the fallacy of logical form is taken literally, it seems no one, including the most formalist and deductivist of the legal scientists – German, British, or American – could have believed or endorsed *that*. The ball is in Holmes's court: if he really means it literally, he must show us that he is not attacking a straw theory.

Ironically, perhaps, it is this last of the five conceptions of logic that is the most promising for a cogent explanation of the role of different modes of logical inference in legal argument. As so often, even when Holmes is misguided and somewhat confused, his suggestions are fertile. In part II of this essay I take up that "suggestion" and explore the role, not just of logic in the narrow sense of deduction, but in the broad sense of patterned inference. Marking the different patterns of logical inference that *can* be used in legal argument, that *are* used in legal argument, and that *should* be used in legal argument comprises the work of an ongoing intellectual enterprise. I call that enterprise the "jurisprudence of logical form."

II. Anti-Anti-Logic: The Jurisprudence of Logical Form

A. Introduction: Central Tasks in the Jurisprudence of Logical Form

Holmes put the question of the relation between "logic" and "experience" on the jurisprudential map. This question, posed in *The Common Law* and in essays, including *The Path of the Law*, has had a powerful and lasting impact on succeeding generations of lawyers, judges, and scholars. His raising and framing of this issue, with typical stylistic grace, has been one of his most valuable contributions to jurisprudence, even though his views were either too unclearly expressed, too insensitive to significant distinctions, or too inadequately supported by accurate conceptual and descriptive analysis to be a useful guide to understanding the reasons and reasonings of law. In advancing the anti-logical thesis and descrying the fallacy of logical form as a fundamental jurisprudential error, Holmes posed an eristic challenge to the philosophical friend of legal rationality. That challenge can be met only by answering three questions that are central to understanding the role of logic in legal argument.

First, as a matter of accurate *description,* what roles does logic play in legal reasoning? This descriptive question motivates a second, *conceptual* question, namely, What is logical inference? – when does it occur? What is its structure? As I have argued earlier, Holmes's roughly sketched anti-logic was far too insensitive to this conceptual question, with the result that his own descriptive claim about logic and experience, while suggestive, is not convincing. Once we have a proper understanding of the conceptual terrain of logical inference and a clear description of how logical inference actually operates in legal reasoning,[21] we may then pursue the answer to a third question: In what way *ought* logic to operate in legal reasoning (and "ought" from what points of view – prudential, moral, aesthetic, other)? I take the ongoing project of answering these three questions to constitute the *jurisprudence of logical form.*

Analytically, the jurisprudence of logical form is firmly analytically connected to many other jurisprudential issues, including the nature and proper role of rule-of-law values, the explication of the concepts of law and legal institutions, the relations among legal, moral, and prudential reasoning, and the theory of formal and informal argumentation. Despite his insights and literary flair, Holmes had a baneful impact on this fundamental area of jurisprudence. Because of his insufficiently discriminative placement of "experience" in *opposition* to "logic," Holmes convinced many generations of lawyers, judges, and law professors (whether they trace the view back to Holmes or not) that the rigorous study of logical forms has virtually no proper place in a law curriculum. As a result, American legal culture – reflected in law schooling, lawyers' briefing, judges' opinion writing, law professors' jurisprudential musing – is rife with poorly articulated justificatory arguments and the belief that judges and lawyers either cannot or should not live up to a higher standard of rational articulateness. Indeed, from time to time law professors even glorify rational inarticulateness as a *virtue* of legal argument. One of the most important normative tasks for the jurisprudence of logical form is to combat this legal culture, both by showing the conceptual possibilities of logically articulate legal argument and by arguing its normative merits.

For the most part, I pursue answers to the two questions that I posed earlier in this section: (1) As a matter of accurate *description,* what roles does logic play in legal reasoning? (2) What *is* logical inference? When does it occur? What is its structure? I approach these two questions together because they can be conceptually linked in a simple but heuristically powerful way: in explicating the actual roles of different modes of logical inference in legal argument, one necessarily explicates its *possible* roles. (Everything actual is possible.) I conclude with only the briefest remarks on the third question: (3) In what way *ought* logic to operate in legal reasoning? I do not seek in this short essay to give comprehensive answers to any of these questions. I shall consider the essay useful if it frames the issues clearly and locates them in the larger framework of jurisprudential analysis and the Holmesian anti-logical corpus.

B. Descriptive and Conceptual Elements in the Jurisprudence of Logical Form

1. LOGICAL FORM (MODE OF LOGICAL INFERENCE). (1) An *argument* is an ordered pair, consisting of a set of premises, each of which is a proposition that bears a truth value, and (2) a conclusion, another proposition that bears a truth value. An argument's *logical form* (or *mode of logical inference*) is the relation between the truth of the argument's premises and the truth of its conclusion. There are four fundamental types of logical inference,[22] distinguished from one another by the relation that obtains between the premises of the argument and its conclusion when the argument yields the most warranted inference from premises to conclusion that it is logically capable of yielding. In a valid *deductive* argument, the truth of the premises guarantees the truth of the conclusion. In an *inductive* argument, the truth of the premises makes the truth of the conclusion (subjectively) probable but cannot guarantee it (the probability is always less than 1). In an *abductive* argument, the truth of the premises makes the conclusion a plausible candidate for further investigation and confirmation or disconfirmation. In an argument *by analogy,* the truth of the premises – itself already passed through a filter of confirmation or disconfirmation at an early stage of the multistep reasoning process – either guarantees the conclusion or makes it (subjectively) probable, depending on the method by which one of the premises is confirmed or disconfirmed.

2. ENTHYMEMATIC RECONSTRUCTION. Like most logically informal arguments, legal arguments, including arguments offered in judicial decisions, tend to be *enthymematic*. An *enthymeme* is any argument, valid or invalid, deductive or nondeductive, whose logical form (i.e., whose mode of logical inference) is not perspicuous from its original manner of presentation.[23] An enthymematic legal argument proffered by a judge becomes problematic – from interpretive, logical, and even perhaps some prudential or moral point of view – when, by virtue of the way in which it is presented, it is unclear which propositions are being offered to support which others, or which propositions are being inferred from which others, or what the claimed inferential relation is between what are identifiable as premises and conclusions.[24] The work of discerning the logical form of an enthymematic moving from its enthymematic form to a form in which its logical form is perspicuous – is *interpretive* work. Among the prima facie interpretive options for the interpreter of a legal enthymeme are the four basic logical forms: deduction, induction, abduction, and analogy. The task of an interpreter faced with an enthymematic argument is to select from among these prima facie interpretive options the one that offers the best explanatory interpretation, all things considered.

3. FOUR BASIC LOGICAL FORMS

a. Induction. In an *inductive* argument, the truth of the premises cannot guarantee the truth of the conclusion, but when the premises are well chosen their truth can warrant belief in the truth of the conclusion to some degree of probability. There are two varieties of inductive inference: inductive generalization and inductive analogy.[25] *Inductive generalization* involves generalizing from particular instances. The premises of this type of argument report features of the particulars, and its conclusion states a probabilistic generalization that is inferred from those particulars. Schematically, an inductive generalization looks like this:
Where

$\alpha_1 \ldots \alpha_n$' stands for a set of individual instances, and
  'ϕ' stands for one property that the individuals $\alpha_1 \ldots \alpha_n$ have been noted to possess, and
  'θ' stands for another property that the individuals $\alpha_1 \ldots \alpha_n$ have been noted to possess,

the pattern of inductive generalization is as follows:

(1) α_1 is both ϕ and θ (i.e., has both characteristics, ϕ and θ)
    [e.g., Yokel is a law professor, and Yokel is logorrheic.]
(2) α_2 is both ϕ and θ
    [Pokel is a law professor, and Pokel is logorrheic.]
(3) α_3 is both ϕ and θ
    [Jokel is a law professor, and Jokel is logorrheic.]

⋮

(n) α_n is both ϕ and θ
  [The nth individual observed is both a law professor and is logorrheic.]
($n + 1$) There were few or no observed instances of an α that was ϕ and also was not -θ.

∴ [Probably] all ϕ's are θ
  [Probably all law professors are logorrheic.]

The other type of inductive inference is *inductive analogy*. Instead of reaching a conclusion about a class of individuals, an inductive analogy offers a conclusion about one individual, based on a generalization about the classes to which that individual belongs; the generalization is that the individual (probably) has the characteristics that have been observed to be conjoined in the premises (e.g., from stated observations that one hundred law professors are logorrheic and that Jones is a law professor, one concludes that Jones is probably logorrheic as well).

Unlike valid deductive inferences, inductive inferences yield only a *degree of (subjective) probability* for the truth of the conclusion relative to the truth of the premises. How high a degree of probability a given inductive inference yields depends on several factors, including the number of instances in which individuals have been observed to exhibit the two (or more) characteristics that are the subject of the generalization, the explanatory relations that might obtain among the characteristics asserted in the inductive generalization, and various relevant similarities and differences among the individuals that are sampled in the premises. In law, a great many fact finders' decisions rely on inductive inferences, including the rather ubiquitous generalization-based judgments they are called upon to make regarding what is "reasonable" under the circumstances, what a trade usage or other community norm is, and what constitutes credible testimony by a witness. Judges also often rely on inductive inferences, and inductive judgments not infrequently become parts of authoritative common law doctrines, as in the presumption in contract law that services rendered between siblings are gratuitous.[26]

Despite its limited proper scope, the prediction thesis presents a nice opportunity to illustrate one role for inductive inference in legal argument. Consider the following bit of legal analysis, which, be it noted, reveals the triumph of Holmes-cum-legal realist quasi-skeptical thinking about the efficacy of legal rules:

[I]n the twentieth century, courts and commentators have advanced numerous doctrinal formulations in an attempt to provide judges with principled, clear, and administrable tests to determine when novel scientific evidence should be admitted or excluded. An examination of the history of this field, however, discloses that these doctrinal formulations possess very little *predictive* power regarding the decision to admit or exclude a particular piece of evidence. Much more powerful *predictors* of admission-exclusion decisions can be found by peeling away the layer of doctrine to reveal the underlying functional criteria that actually animate courts in these decisions, irrespective of what doctrinal standard a particular court purports to apply.[27]

The authors then offer what are apparently inductively generated rules specifying several factors to be used as "more powerful predictors of admission–exclusion decisions." I say "apparently" because this bit of legal analysis is enthymematic; it calls upon us as interpreters to discern the logical structure of the authors' argument from which these rule criteria have been generated.

Let us suppose that

'$\alpha_1 \ldots \alpha_n$' stands for a series of cases in which a court considered whether to admit or exclude proffered Novel Scientific Evidence (NSE) (in the "object language" presented here each individual series of cases is named '$a_1 \ldots a_n$');[28]

'ϕ' stands for a factor that has been observed to be present in the series $\alpha_1 \ldots \alpha_n$, that is a factor that the authors claim is a good predictor of courts' behavior (in the object language presented here, three factors are named F_1, F_2, and F_3); and

'θ' stands for an instance in which the court admitted the NSE or for an instance in which the court excluded the NSE (in the object language presented here these decisions are named P and P′, respectively).

Let us also assume, for the sake of argument, that the authors are presenting *warranted* inductive generalizations. Accordingly, we assume that (1) for each factor ϕ about which the authors offer an inductively generalized rule of the form 'All instances of ϕ are instances of θ', the authors had observed a series of cases $\alpha_1 \ldots \alpha_n$ in which ϕ was present and in which there were n decisions θ either to admit (P) or to exclude (P′) the evidence, and (2) that the generalization was supported by a sufficient sample, with sufficient control conditions, such as can be effected by the use of Mill's methods of agreement and difference. With these assumptions in place, we may reconstruct the pattern of inductive generalization as follows:

(1) In α_1 there was both ϕ and θ.
(2) In α_2 there was both ϕ and θ.
$\vdots$
(n) In α_n there was both ϕ and θ.
($n + 1$) There were few or no observed instances of an α that was ϕ and also was not-θ.

∴ Probably, all ϕ's are θ's.

Ideally, this argument pattern would underlie and justify the rules that the authors offer for each of the three factors they claim to be good predictors of courts' behavior in admitting or exclude NSE. Following the schema just presented, I proceed to represent one of the three rules for the factors that the authors present in their article. Note that the authors offer these rules as *sufficient conditions* for a court's decision to admit or to exclude NSE. Note also that each of the following rules is (presumably) the *conclusion* of an inductive generalization of the sort represented by the schema.

> *Enthymematic text:* "Some types of evidence convey essentially subjective determinations via a technique that enjoys the objective aura of 'science'. Such evidence is often subject to a high level of scrutiny, and is typically excluded."[29]
>
> *Reconstruction:* [*Probably,*] in a case in which a court considers a proffer of NSE (call this case a_i, i.e., some member of the observed series of cases $a_1 \ldots a_n$), *if* the NSE conveys an "essentially subjective determination via a technique that enjoys the objective aura of 'science'" (call this predictive factor F_1), *then* a court will exclude it (call this P); that is,
>
> [*Probably,*] *if* a_i is an instance of F_1, *then* a_i will also be an instance of P'.

b. Abduction. The conclusion of an abductive argument is an explanatory hypothesis (sometimes referred to as an *explanans*). The premises consist of (i) a proposition that describes some event or phenomenon that the abductive reasoner believes stands in need of explanation (the *explanandum*), and (ii) a proposition to the effect that, *if* the explanatory hypothesis that appears in the conclusion of the abductive inference were in fact *true* or otherwise warranted, then the explanandum would be sufficiently explained for the reasoner's purposes. The sufficient-explanation conditional asserts that, *if* the explanans were a valid theory in the jurisdiction, then it would explain the explanandum as a matter of course. I shall refer to this second premise as the sufficient explanation conditional." This premise appears in the form of a logical conditional (i.e., the form *If* Φ *then* Θ), in which the antecedent (Φ) is the explanatory hypothesis (the explanans) that the reasoner has "discovered" in the course of the abductive reasoning, and the consequent (Θ) is the explanandum that is asserted in the other premise of the abductive inference. Schematically, where

$\quad\quad\quad$ 'Θ' stands for an explanandum,
$\quad\quad\quad$ 'Φ' stands for an explanatory hypothesis (explanans), and
'If Φ then Θ' stands for a sufficient explanation conditional,

all abductive inferences have three basic steps, arrayed as follows:

1. Θ.
2. If Φ then Θ.
∴ 3. Φ.

A simple (but unpleasant) forensic example:

1. Θ.   Explanandum: The victim died as the result of a bullet-shaped puncture to the chest, but there was no exit wound, and the coroner recovered no bullet.
2. If Φ then Θ.   Sufficient explanation conditional: If it were the case that an ice bullet had been shot into the victim, it could cause his death and leave no trace other than water.
∴ 3. Φ.   Explanans: The victim was killed with an ice bullet.

Several observations are due here. First, as with all modes of logical inference, the defining feature of abductive inference is the relation between the truth (or other warrant) of the premises and the truth (or other warrant) of the conclusion. Typically, an abductive reasoner begins the abductive process by assuming or knowing that the proposition expressing the *explanandum* is true or otherwise warranted (a judgment made by observation, inference, memory). The ratiocinative centerpiece of abductive inference is the reasoner's "discovery" (creation, etc.) of a hypothesis that can explain the explanandum. It is critical to understand that the second premise of an abductive inference merely selects one from among several possible explanations. Though I say "merely," often great ingenuity, sometimes genius, is required even to see what kinds of explanatory hypotheses *might* provide an adequate plausible explanation of the explanandum. Charles Sanders Peirce, the first modern philosopher to highlight abduction and argue that it is a fundamental inference pattern along with deduction and induction, made the striking claim: "[A]ll the ideas of science come to it by the way of Abduction. Abduction consists in studying facts and devising a theory to explain them. Its only justification is that if we are ever to understand things at all, it must be in that way."[30]

Second, the pattern of abduction is *invalid* from a deductive point of view, because it commits the fallacy known as "affirming the consequent."[31] Nevertheless, abductive inferences have vital *epistemic* value in contexts in which reasoners must reason their way to an explanatory hypothesis. When properly attentive to the pattern of abduction, a reasoner asserts Φ in the conclusion of an abduction, only to settle on it *tentatively* as the proper explanatory hypothesis of Θ. This tentative "settling" on Φ is supported by neither deductive validity nor a probabilistically calculable inductive warrant. Just as a reasoner should understand that the conclusion of a valid deductive argument is held with certainty, and just as she should understand that the conclusion of an inductive argument is held with varying degrees of probability (the more cogent the argument, the higher the degree of probability), so she understands that the conclusion of an abductive inference (Φ) is asserted not as a truth, but as a tentatively held hypothesis that is *sufficiently likely to be the proper explanation of Θ* that it is worth the effort of confirming or disconfirming it. And the rational abducer recognizes that every abductive conclusion needs some kind of confirmation or disconfirmation. Thus, to return to my earlier example, from an epistemic point of view, in asserting the abductive conclusion "The victim was killed with an ice bullet," the abductive reasoner (a detective, let us suppose) is not warranted in believing that that conclusion is true whenever the premises are true (as he would be if the argument were a valid deduction), nor that any specifiable probability attaches to the conclusion; instead, the most he could be warranted in believing about this conclusion is that it is a sufficiently plausible working hypothesis to warrant the time that it will take to confirm or disconfirm it. He would not, in all likelihood, make that same judgment about the hypothesis "An invisible fairy came from nowhere and stole the deceased's spirit, killing him" – even though, if that proposition were true, it too might well explain the explanandum. Given the background theories of nature that I assume this abducer to have, he would not judge that hypothesis sufficiently plausible to be worth any (further) effort at confirmation or disconfirmation.

Third, all abductive inferences share the basic form noted earlier. (I shall refer to this as the *basic pattern.*) That basic pattern, while adequate for my purposes here, does not reveal the entire logical structure of the abductive inference, in that the typical conclusion of an abduction (the explanans) is itself an explanatory "proposition" that has considerable internal logical complexity. One kind of complexity that is common in the conclusion (Φ, the explanans) of an abductive inference is worth noting, since, it occurs in a quite typical pattern of abductive *legal* inference. Many abductive inferences have conclusions that are from a logical point of view *rules*. Abductive inferences in science are often of this type, where the "rule" abduced is a scientific law. As I shall explain shortly, one extremely common form of abductive inference in legal reasoning also adds this level of logical complexity to the basic pattern.

Fourth, there is of course a large literature discussing the concept of abduction, including debate about whether abduction is a distinct mode of inference and whether it has any role to play in rational inquiry, scientific or otherwise.[32] I believe that abduction is a distinct form of inference, and that it has a vital role to play in many reasoning processes, including legal reasoning. (In this context, I might be said to be abducing abduction as the best explanation for certain phenomena of legal reasoning. It stands in need of confirmation.)

Abduction is a ubiquitous pattern in legal reasoning. So far I have discussed its basic structure, its logical limits (as an invalid form of inference), and its concomitant pragmatic strengths (as a rationally disciplined method of discovery). I now explain that there are distinct settings of legal argument in which usefully distinguishable abductive inferences are made. The task of making legal arguments presents legal reasoners with different kinds of *explananda,* and, accordingly, they seek different kinds of explanatory hypotheses. According to the particular reasoning task the reasoner faces in a context of legal reasoning, the type of abductive inference will differ, although its basic structure is of course invariant in all settings. Three legal-reasoning settings, calling for three types of abductive explanans, are worth noting. I discuss two of them here and defer discussion of the third for my treatment of analogical argument.

(1) Fact Abduction. When the explanatory hypothesis "abduced" explains an empirical fact, the legal reasoner engages in *factual hypothesis abduction* or, as I refer to it, *fact abduction.* (I use this only as a convenient short form, since it is not the fact itself, but a hypothesis that explains the fact, that is abduced.) Fact abduction is the effort to discover an explanation, Φ, for some fact or event, Θ. Of course, as always with abductive inferences, once abduced, Θ must be confirmed or disconfirmed. Fact abduction is the familiar type of abduction used in philosophy of science, and it is what came to Peirce's mind when he himself abduced abduction.[33] I have already given a simple example ("the victim was killed with an ice bullet"). Fact finders in legal disputes are called upon to use abductive inferences to make judgments about the best factual explanation for events in the world that are the subject of legal dispute.[34] Sometimes these inferences are made on a nonexpert basis, where the fact finder relies on what she knows from personal experience and memory and on inference from that knowledge. Sometimes these inferences are made with the help of experts. In these cases the legal fact finder does something of a "meta-abduction" – inferring the best explanation of disputed facts by relying in significant part on abductions performed by scientific experts.

(2) Legal-Rule Abduction. In *legal-rule abduction,* the reasoner is once again faced with a set of empirically encountered facts that call for explanation. As in fact abduction, the explananda are facts that occurred in the world. But the type of explanation sought here is either not empirical explanation at all or, if it is, empirical explanation in a special "corner" of the empirical world, namely, the symbol-soaked doings of legally authorized officials and the populations subject to their laws.[35] Legal-rule abduction aims to explain its explananda by means of an intellectual apparatus consisting of the aims, methods, and judgments specific to *legal reasoning* as a distinct rational enterprise. In short, it aims to explain facts from a *legal point of view,* rather than, say, from a scientific, military, or business point of view.[36] It is a type of reasoning that every lawyer does, and must do, when a client walks through the door seeking legal redress for something that happened to him. The legal reasoner's task in legal-rule abduction is to "abduce" the legal rule (or the "theory of the case") that makes "legal sense," according to the rules of the jurisdiction, of the facts that have given rise to a potential legal dispute. Whereas in fact abduction the reasoner tentatively settles on an explanans as true (or otherwise warranted) from some empirical point of view, in legal-rule abduction the reasoner tentatively settles on a theory of the case that is true (or otherwise warranted) according to the laws of the jurisdiction in which the disputed event is to be litigated.

In most American jurisdictions, the same reasoning is also required of a judge before she can dismiss a complaint for "failure to state a claim on which relief can be granted." Rules of pleading (certainly federal rules, also most state rules) permit a complaining litigant to offer no more than a very vague summary of the "facts" that are the basis of his complaint. The rules do not require the characterization of those facts in legal terms – that is, a well-pleaded complaint need not present the litigant's own legal explanation of the facts. When it does not present such an explanation, the judge must try to abduce a legal rule that might give the complainant a sustainable cause of action if the facts alleged are later proven.

In legal-rule abduction, it is a legal rule that is "abduced" as the conclusion. Legal-rule abduction reflects the same basic pattern reflected in all abductive inferences:

1. Θ.
2. If Φ then Θ.
∴ 3. Φ.

where

'Θ' stands for the *explanandum* of a legal-rule abduction, namely, the set of facts the plaintiff thinks he can prove (or the judge thinks he might be able to prove), some of which have occasioned his petition for legal redress;

'If Φ then Θ' stands for the sufficient explanation conditional of a legal-rule abduction, namely, a proposition asserting that if the explanatory hypothesis Φ were true, Θ would be sufficiently explained for the legal reasoner's purposes;

'Φ' stands for the *explanans* of a legal-rule abduction, namely, a logically complex proposition that is a plausible theory of the case as well as a "valid" legal rule of the jurisdiction (e.g., violation of a statutory prohibition of sexual harassment, or violation of a constitutional right to equal protection); this explanans consists of a set of rules that links the "operative facts" that a plaintiff claims he can prove (namely, Θ) to a remedy he desires or might desire, as antecedent and consequent, respectively.

Some observations about legal-rule abduction: first, as with all abductive inferences, the rule abduced must be confirmed or disconfirmed. To "confirm" a legal rule (or legal theory) is to ascertain whether the legal rule (or theory) is a "valid" rule in the jurisdiction or is otherwise warranted.[37] Second, because Φ, the "theory of the case," is comprised of legal rules that are believed to be valid (or otherwise warranted) in the jurisdiction, Φ itself will contain a set of logically complex conditional propositions – as do the conclusions of abductive inferences to scientific laws. Third, closely related to the second point, in the context of legal-rule abduction, "sufficient explanation" means in part that the explanans Φ, a "theory of the case" consisting of legal rules expressed as a logically complex proposition, asserts a legal rule that has a special logical feature: Φ links the statement of facts the plaintiff claims to be able to prove to some legal remedy the plaintiff desires, as antecedent and consequent, respectively. This feature of Φ allows it to satisfy the special need of a legal reasoner who has sought to abduce the legal rule, namely, to find an explanation of the facts (Θ) from a legal point of view. This explanation must in turn produce a rule that the judge could apply deductively, at least in the final stages of reasoning (after any gaps have been filled, possibly by other modes of inference, such as analogy).

Fourth is a Holmesian point, closely related to the third point, about the strategic context in which a lawyer performs legal-rule abductions. Both fact abduction and legal-rule abduction can take place within a complex pattern of legal reasoning in a single case, and when a lawyer uses both types of inference they have a close holistic connection to one another. The connection arises from the strategic need of the lawyer to abduce (and then argue to the court) only those legal theories Φ (i) whose required factual predicate Θ he thinks he can prove, if and when necessary, and (ii) that imply consequents that are remedies the client desires. That is, for any theory Φ that the lawyer might abduce in legal-rule abduction, he will look ahead to what he thinks he could abduce *and* prove in *fact abduction,* as well as to the desirability for the client of the result of the abduced rule.

One typical example of legal-rule abduction occurs when a judge is faced with a motion to dismiss for failure to state a claim. Faced with such a motion, the judge must try to abduce at least one legal rule ("theory of the case") that will explain the complained-of facts from a legal point of view in such a way as to allow the plaintiff's case to survive the motion to dismiss. (This task is imposed on a judge in those jurisdictions that have replaced code pleading with notice pleading, as most have.) In *Searight v. New Jersey,* for example, a troubled man filed a *pro se* action complaining that the state of New Jersey had, more than a dozen years earlier, while he was in prison, injected him in the left eye with a radium electric beam, as the result of which someone began talking to him from inside his brain.[38] He brought an action in a federal district court, although it was doubtful whether that court had jurisdiction over his case. (There was no clear "federal-question" jurisdiction, and no diversity jurisdiction either.) Moreover, the state statute of limitations had run out on any tort claim he might have had, and the state moved to dismiss under Federal Rule of Civil Procedure 12(b)(6).[39] In effect, this rule required the judge to try to *abduce* the best legal rule that might be adduced to explain the facts of the case.

Before getting to the content of the abductions in *Searight,* let us remind ourselves of the basic structure of this case.

A Jurisprudence of Logical Form 115

Where

'P' stands for the *explanandum:* while the plaintiff was in custody, the defendant injected him with a radium electric beam,

'T→ P' stands for the *sufficient explanation conditional:* if T is indeed a valid (or otherwise warranted) theory within the jurisdiction (and one that links the facts that the plaintiff claims to be able to prove to some remedy that he desires),[40] then it would explain the plaintiff's case from a legal point of view in such a way as to allow the complaint to go forward,

'T' stands for the *explanans:* the state's behavior, described by P, was unlawful under some relevant overall legal theory that is valid (or otherwise warranted) in the jurisdiction,

the legal-rule abduction the judge performs has this familiar structure:

1. P.
2. If T then P.
∴ 3. T.

The judge's abductive task was to try to discover whether there really is any theory T that is both valid within the jurisdiction and implies a more specific rule P → Q such that P is a set of facts the plaintiff might be able to prove and Q is a remedy he might seek. In *Searight,* the judge abduced and then sought to confirm or disconfirm two possible theories of the case that might meet these requirements. One was the theory that the state violated the plaintiff's federal civil rights; the other was a sneering theory that there was an unlicensed radio communication to the plaintiff's brain (which the judge shamefully, albeit shamelessly, suggested the plaintiff could alleviate by trailing a string of paper clips from his pants' leg to the ground as a ground wire).[41] The judge *disconfirmed* both theories[42] and concluded that there was thus no legal rule that could be adduced to permit the complaint to go forward.

Fifth, there is no question that abduction, unlike other modes of logical inference, is a creative process. Peirce, who argued that abduction was a fundamental form of logical inference, also recognized that

[t]he abductive suggestion comes to us like a flash. It is an act of *insight,* although of extremely fallible insight. It is true that the different elements of the [explanatory] hypothesis were in our minds before; but it is the idea of putting together what we had never before dreamed of putting together which flashes the new suggestion before our contemplation.[43]

Although abduction thus relies significantly on flashes of insight, it is nevertheless a rationally disciplined process. The rational discipline comes largely from the explanatory context in which the abduction takes place. The explanation must both "fit the facts" and be confirmable or disconfirmable according to other theories that the reasoner brings to bear (scientific, legal, etc.). These rational constraints on abductive inference can be considerable.

An analogy: among (American) football kickers, whose task is to kick the ball through the goalposts, there is a great variety of kicking techniques. Creative variation is possible along many dimensions, including the manner of winding up the kicking leg and foot, placing the other foot, the approach to the ball, the contraction of stomach, back, neck, and arm muscles, even whether to wear a shoe on the kicking foot. But despite this room for variability and creativity, the task of getting the football through the goalposts operates as a substantial constraint on the methods that will be successful. So too with the rational constraints on the creative process of abduction.

Those rational constraints are to be understood as rational *logical* constraints on the various forms of legal-rule abduction. Recognition of those constraints is a crucial component of understanding one of the key roles of *logical inference* in legal argument. As we have seen, Holmes evinced a good deal of skepticism about the logical disciplinability of legal argument. In so doing he had a wavering, accordion-like conception of logic, now as limited to axiomatic deductive systems, now as embracing induction and even analogy. Nowhere, though, did he ever consider the vital *logically disciplining* role of abduction in legal argument – nor in scientific argument, for that matter, although the theory of abduction was available to Holmes, both in published essays and in lectures that he attended.[44]

c. Analogy and Disanalogy. The final basic logical form is analogical inference. As I have recently argued, argument by analogy is *not* best explained as a simple inference of a conclusion from a set of premises by means of one inference rule. Rather, it involves a series of three distinct reasoning steps that legal reasoners typically deploy when they are in doubt about the scope of a concept in a legal norm and use an analysis of examples to help resolve that doubt.

Step 1. In step 1, the analogical reasoner, surveying a set of examples to help in a context of doubt makes an *abductive* inference from those chosen examples to *a rule* that *could* resolve the doubt. Sometimes the examples are presented to the reasoner by others, as when a judge is presented with precedent cases that the litigants argue are "on point" for an instant case. Sometimes the examples themselves are chosen as part of the flash of abductive insight. This rule, to which I refer as the "analogy-warranting rule," is a proposition in the form of a logical conditional that offers either a necessary or a sufficient condition for a predicate or proposition in doubt.[45] The rule performs the crucial function of asserting what is relevantly similar about the "source" examples and the "target" case – the case that occasioned the analogical reasoner's doubt.

Regarding the kind of doubt that often triggers analogical analysis, it is hard to improve on Holmes's own description (emended by the addition of one word):

> I think it most important to remember whenever a doubtful case arises, with certain analogies on one side and other analogies on the other, that what really is before us is a conflict between two social desires, each of which seeks to extend its dominion over the case, and which cannot both have their way. The social question is which desire is stronger at the point of conflict. The judicial one may be narrower, because one or the other desire may have been expressed in previous decisions to such an extent that logic requires us to assume it to preponderate in the one before us. But if that be clearly so, the case is not a doubtful one. Where there is doubt the simple tool of [deductive] logic does not suffice, and even if it is disguised and unconscious, the judges are called on to exercise the sovereign prerogative of choice.[46]

Note that *analogy-warranting rule abduction* is the third type of abduction that pervades legal reasoning, along with fact abduction and *legal*-rule abduction. (When analogies are used to close gaps occasioned by the vagueness of legal rules or the silence of existing legal rules, analogy-warranting rule abduction is a special kind of legal-rule abduction.)

Step 2. The analogical reasoner confirms or disconfirms, by a process of reflective adjustment, the rule abduced in step 1. The confirmation disconfirmation process at work in step 2 has the same structure as the process identified in the work of Goodman and Rawls, known from the latter's work as "reflective equilibrium." In reasoning by analogy, however, that process is applied not to the justification of moral principles, but rather to the (analogy-warranting) rule that the reasoner has abduced in step 1 in the course of reasoning about what is relevantly similar among a set of example cases. At this crucial second step, the reasoner resorts to a *rationale* for adopting (or rejecting) the rule abductively hypothesized in step 1 (referred to in the theory as the *analogy-warranting rationale*). If in step 2 the rationales used by the analogical reasoner (whatever their content, whether drawn from a deductively justified system such as logic, or an inductively justified system such as empirical science, or from a moral or prudential system of practical reasoning) lead the analogical reasoner to *disconfirm* the rule abduced in step 1, she "goes back to the drawing board," abduces another rule that might serve the purpose of resolving the doubt by asserting what is relevantly similar about the source examples and the target case.

Step 3. The reasoner applies to the case that occasioned the doubt whatever (analogy-warranting) rule has been abduced in step 1 and sufficiently confirmed in step 2.

Reasoning by disanalogy has the same basic structure as reasoning by analogy. The main difference is that in reasoning by disanalogy the reasoner, still in a context of doubt about the scope of some term or phrase, uses examples that seem, at least prima facie, to be relevantly similar to the target case. The judge *abduces* a *disanalogy-warranting rule,* which specifies what is sufficiently and relevantly *dissimilar* in the source and target case such that she is not warranted in concluding that the target case should receive the same treatment that the source cases received. (This is *disanalogy-warranting rule abduction.*) As with all abductive conclusions, the reasoner must then confirm or disconfirm the rule. If confirmed, then, in step 3, the reasoner concludes that the source and target cases are not to be treated in the same way. Often, in cases in which the rule is *disconfirmed,* the reasoner goes back to the drawing board, seeking first to abduce and then to confirm or disconfirm a new analogy or disanalogy-warranting rule.

Holmes himself offers a fine example of reasoning by disanalogy in *McBoyle v. United States,* a case familiar to students of statutory interpretation.[47] In *McBoyle,* the U.S. Supreme Court considered the scope of the National Motor Vehicle Theft Act, a criminal statute. The issue in the case was whether the interstate transportation of a stolen airplane fell within the proscription of a statutory text that prohibited the interstate transport of "motor vehicles," defined to include "Sec. 2. . . . an automobile, automobile truck, automobile wagon, motor cycle, or any other self-propelled vehicle not designed for running on rails." The kind of doubt that occasioned the use of analogical/disanalogical reasoning in *McBoyle* was vagueness in the statutory phrase "any other self-propelled vehicle not designed for running on rails."

Holmes compared the airplane to the other individual items that the act included in the definition of "motor vehicle." His reasoning can be explained as an application of the *ejusdem generis* rule, which requires a reasoner to deploy analogical or disanalogical reasoning to decide what members of the "species" mentioned in a vague term are "of the same genus," that is, *relevantly similar to* the other specified items on a list. If the airplane is *relevantly similar to* "an automobile, automobile truck, automobile wagon, motor cycle," then the airplane falls within the scope of the statutory phrase "any other self-propelled vehicle not designed for running on rails." If not, then not. This judgment of relevant similarity or difference, in turn, calls upon Holmes to *abduce* a rule whose criteria (sufficient conditions, or necessary conditions) specify what is relevant. Holmes reasoned thus:

Section 2 defines the motor vehicles of which the transportation in interstate commerce is punished in § 3. The question is the meaning of the word 'vehicle' in the phrase "any other self-propelled vehicle not designed for running on rails." No doubt etymologically it is possible to use the word to signify a conveyance working on land, water or air, and sometimes legislation extends the use in that direction . . . But in everyday speech 'vehicle' calls up the picture of a thing moving on land. Thus in Rev. Stats. § 4, intended, the Government suggests, rather to enlarge than to restrict the definition, vehicle includes every contrivance capable of being used "as a means of transportation on land."

And this is repeated, expressly excluding aircraft, in the Tariff Act, June 17, 1930, c. 997, § 401 (b); 46 Stat. 590, 708. So here, the phrase under discussion calls up the popular picture. For after including automobile, truck, automobile wagon and motor cycle, the words "any other self-propelled vehicle not designed for running on rails" still indicate that a vehicle in the popular sense, that is a vehicle running on land, is the theme. It is a vehicle that runs, not something, not commonly called a vehicle, that flies. Airplanes were well known in 1919, when this statute was passed; but it is admitted that they were not mentioned in the reports or in the debates in Congress. It is impossible to read words that so carefully enumerate the different forms of motor vehicles and have no reference of any kind to aircraft, as including airplanes under a term that usage more and more precisely confines to a different class. The counsel for the petitioner have shown that the phraseology of the statute as to motor vehicles follows that of earlier statutes of Connecticut, Delaware, Ohio, Michigan and Missouri, not to mention the late Regulations of Traffic for the District of Columbia, Title 6, c. 9, § 242, none of which can be supposed to leave the earth.

Although it is not likely that a criminal will carefully consider the text of the law before he murders or steals, it is reasonable that a fair warning should be given to the world in language that the common world will understand, of what the law intends to do if a certain line is passed. To make the warning fair, so far as possible the line should be clear. When a rule of conduct is laid down in words that evoke in the common mind only the picture of vehicles moving on land, the statute should not be extended to aircraft, simply because it may seem to us that a similar policy applies, or upon the speculation that, if the legislature had thought of it, very likely broader words would have been used. *United States v. Thind,* 261 U.S. 204, 209.

Judgment reversed.[48]

Holmes's opinion goes through each of the three steps of disanalogical reasoning:

First, he compares the target case of the airplane with the source cases of the other types of vehicles mentioned on the statutory list – automobile, automobile truck, automobile wagon, motor cycle. At this stage, he acknowledges the prima facie force of the view that an airplane is indeed a vehicle, for purposes of this statute ("No doubt etymologically it is possible to use the word to signify a conveyance working on land, water or air, and sometimes legislation extends the use in that direction"). The rule he abduces – as it turns out, a *disanalogy*-warranting rule – makes it a necessary condition for being within the scope of "any other self-propelled vehicle not designed for running on rails" that the vehicle in question "run on land."

Second, having abduced this rule, Holmes moves to the stage of confirming or disconfirming it. He relies on one primary justificatory source – an "objective" reading of the statute, given normative force by the norm of lenity and the rule-of-law norm of fair notice. This objective reading, with its normative support, confirms the rule abduced in the first step. Holmes also observes that, insofar as he can discern them, the data that permit inferences about the intent of Congress are consistent with the objective reading. (Although Holmes may have regarded these "data" as an independent source of justification and confirmation of the rule he had abduced, it seems unlikely that he, the great early champion of objective readings across the board, in both contract and statutory interpretation,[49] would have accorded a "subjective" congressional intent much weight if it was, in his view, at odds with the objective reading.) Third, having confirmed the abduced disanalogy-warranting rule, Holmes applies it *deductively* to the case at hand. Since, for purposes of this case, per disanalogical inference, the only vehicles subject to the penalty are those designed for running on land, and since the airplane is not such a vehicle, the penalty does not apply to this defendant. (Holmes's overall opinion thus obeys what I have referred to as the "law of deductive form.")[50]

A model of analogy (and disanalogy) such as the foregoing helps give content to the wavering but warranted intuition Holmes had about the proper scope of logic, namely, that it embraces "[t]he processes of analogy, discrimination, and deduction." Moreover, it allows us to see that analogy, a vital organ of legal reasoning, is itself rationally disciplinable in its interaction with and reliance upon other methods of inference, including deduction, induction, and abduction.

d. Deduction. For our purposes, *validity* is the key defining feature of the relation between premises and conclusion in a deductively warranted argument. Informally speaking, in a *valid* deductive argument, the truth of the premises "guarantees" the truth of the conclusion. Slightly more formally, there are two ways to express the concept of formal deductive validity, one syntactic, the other semantic. According to the *syntactic* version, an argument consisting of a set of premises from which a conclusion is inferred is valid just in case the conclusion is *derivable,* by the rules of inference of that formal language, from the premises and the axioms of the formal language in which the proof is offered. According to the *semantic* version of the concept of validity, an argument consisting of a set of premises from which a conclusion is inferred is valid just in case the conclusion is true under all *interpretations* in which all of the premises are true.

Judges constantly rely on deductive inference in the course of making and evaluating legal arguments. They often rely on it even in the course of deploying other argument types, such as analogy and induction. They also rely on it when applying authoritative rules about which there is no active doubt about the meaning of a term or phrase that appears in the rule, nor doubt about which, if any, authoritative rule applies. The concept of "active doubt" is crucial for understanding the role of different modes of logical inference, and I pause to rehearse some perhaps familiar terminology. In speaking of "active doubt" I have in mind the critical distinction between the *vagueness* and the *open texture* of a term. A term is *vague* when, at a particular time, relative to a particular set of objects, a particular language user (or group of users) is undecided about whether the term applies to a given object among that set. A term is *open tex-*

tured when it yields the *possibility* of being vague at some time. Thus for a child learning the term 'dog,' once the child has been told something about its meaning and shown a few dogs, the term may not be vague for that child at time T_1 relative to the group of dogs the child has encountered and remembers. But if at time T_2 the child is shown a wolf or hyena, he may become uncertain about whether 'dog' properly applies to that animal as well. At T_1 the term dog was not vague for this child but was open textured. At T_2 it was vague (and open textured).[51]

Every legal rule is open textured, but not every legal rule is vague at the point of application in a particular case. When an open-textured legal rule is not vague at the point of application, it can be applied *deductively*. However, when it is vague (or is in some other way semantically underdeterminate,[52] such as by being logically, syntactically, or lexically ambiguous), the reasoner must first reason to a conclusion about how to resolve the underdeterminacy sufficiently for that case, and that supplemental reasoning often involves nondeductive modes of inference. Sometimes even the resolution of the meaning of a phrase that is vague at the point of application may be resolved by resorting to another *deductively* applicable rule, such as a rule of interpretation that is not vague at the point of application. Resolving a semantic underdeterminacy "sufficiently for a case" usually means articulating criteria (either necessary or sufficient conditions) for application of the doubtful phrase or concept in a legal rule, criteria that permit the rule, thus clarified, to be applied deductively in the final step of the judge's reasoning. As we have seen, Holmes himself offers a nice example of this "precisifying" reasoning in *McBoyle*. Failure to recognize this feature of legal rules has led some legal theorists (Edward Levi and Felix Cohen come to mind, but there are many others who have adopted this view)[53] to argue that legal rules are never deductively applicable. That is quite wrong. Typically, legal rules are deductively applicable, which is one reason why so many disputes that might be litigated, in our litigation-prone society, are not.

Though there is a good deal to say about the proper interpretive reconstruction of enthymematic judicial opinions into deductive form, a fairly simple example and some brief observations will have to serve. I offer an example of an enthymematic opinion, fairly typical in both its argumentative virtues and vices, that is fairly interpretable as the deductive application of a set of rules. In *Ray v. Eurice*,[54] the Maryland Court of Appeals considered a claim for breach of contract by a homeowner against a contractor. The contractor argued that, although he had signed every page of the final contract, he had not read it and should be excused from performance. The court's opinion calls for some interpretive work – it is truly enthymematic, in that the order of its reasoning is far from perspicuous. Nevertheless, it may be fairly reconstructed as the deductive application of a few authoritative rules that center on one rule, the duty-to-read rule, which provides a sufficient condition for the contractual liability of a person who has signed a contract. The court's basic reasoning was that because the defendant in the case did sign, and because none of the rule's own excusing conditions was satisfied, he was liable. The opinion also invokes and applies a few related rules that orbit around the duty-to-read rule, including rules regarding parol evidence, contract interpretation, and what constitutes a sufficient writing. One of the main bits of evidence supporting my interpretation of this argument as rule deduction is that the court did not seem to feel that any of the principal concepts was vague at the point of application here, though the rules are certainly open textured and could be vague in other contexts. Restating the main argument in the enthymeme in simplified form, it looks like this:

If (P) a party signs a contract when

(i) there is no fraud and no duress,
(ii) there is no mutual mistake,
(iii) the contract is integrated,
(iv) the language of the contract reflects a clearly expressed and unambiguous intent, according to a reasonable interpretation,
(v) the specifications of the whole contract are contained in several attached documents, but with clear cross-reference,

then (Q) that party is contractually bound, regardless of whether he

read or had it read to him,
placed a different subjective intent on the terms of the contract, or
can adduce parol evidence of his different subjective intent.

Slightly more abstractly, the reasoning is a *modus ponens:*

(1) If (P(i) & P(ii) & P(iii) & P(iv) & P(v)) then Q.
(2) P(i) & P(ii) & P(iii) & P(iv) & P(v).
∴ (3) Q.

Again, this is but one small example of the way in which deduction plays a role in judicial arguments. It is certainly not the only way in which deduction operates, and I must emphasize that I do not claim that all judicial enthymemes can best be reconstructed as the application of deductively applicable rules. *That* would indeed be a reproachable "mechanical jurisprudence." But mine is not reproachable. Therefore, mine is not that. Rather, in its descriptive aspect, the jurisprudence of logical form reveals, indeed emphasizes, that distinct types of logical argument, including but not limited to deduction, play vital roles in legal argument. In its conceptual aspect, it reveals the ways in which it is *possible* for modes of logical inference to serve the needs and solve the problems of legal argument.

I turn now from description and conceptual analysis to prescription, recommendation, and hortation. In its *normative* aspect, the jurisprudence of logical form calls upon judges and other adjudicating legal officials to be *rationally articulate* about the structures of (putative) justification in their decisions. This includes being rationally articulate about the role that the different modes of logical inference play in those putative justifications of the exercise of state power.

C. Normative Projects in the Jurisprudence of Logical Form

1. THE PRINCIPLE OF RATIONAL ARTICULATION. As a polity, we demand that the public exercise of adjudicatory power (and often, the private, too) be accompanied by a public putative justification. This demand is reflected, for example, in the practice of writing judicial decisions and in various norms of public law proscribing arbitrary decision-making behavior. The demand for rational articulation requires adjudicating legal officials to be clear about the structure of the putative justifications they offer. At the heart of that demand is a mandate that they be clear about the *modes of logical inference they are deploying in those putative justifications*. Members of the polity demand justification for the disposition of legal disputes but cannot know whether an argument and its conclusion *are* justified unless and until they can discern what that argument and conclusion are, and what logical relation is claimed (by the reasoner) to obtain between the argument's premises and conclusion.

In its normative aspect, the jurisprudence of logical form is most centrally concerned to insist on rational articulation and to provide an analysis of the values – prudential, political-moral, indeed, perhaps even aesthetic – that underwrite the mandate of rational articulation. As a mandate on an adjudicator's behavior, the norm of rational articulation has several dimensions, and the explication of *each* of these is part of the task of the jurisprudence of logical form. One dimension is that of political morality. The political-moral value of rational articulation is in the family of values explored, for example, in Kant's discussion of the (meta)right to a public declaration of rights,[55] in John Rawls's discussion of "public reason,"[56] in Ronald Dworkin's discussion of "articulated consistency,"[57] in Lon Fuller's explication of rule-of-law values,[58] and (perhaps more indirectly) in John Stuart Mill's promotion of critical public reflection in *On Liberty*.[59] In part, the mandate of rational articulation is a *prudential* value, one that Joseph Raz, for example, has explored, arguing that from a prudential point of view, it at least presumptively behooves a state that wishes to use legal rules as means of social control to adhere to the rule-of-law values that Fuller explicates, including those that are directly concerned with rational articulation.[60]

Despite his skepticism and his too pessimistic resignation to the realities of inarticulateness in judicial decision, Holmes himself may be counted among the friends of the normative jurisprudence of logical form and its core mandate of rational articulation. As I noted early in this essay, Holmes felt strongly the necessity of effecting rational reform in legal doctrine and legal decision making, and indeed his brief for rational reform occupies a much larger percentage of

The Path of the Law than do his skeptical musings. Immediately following his debunking discussion of the fallacy of logical form, Holmes argues for a "philosophical reaction" *against* potted-plantism in the development of the law,[61] and *for* "a reconsideration of the worth of doctrines which for the most part are still taken for granted without any deliberate, conscious, systematic questioning of their grounds" ("Path" 185). Holmes offers, for his immediate audience of law students and his mediate audience of posterity, something of a manifesto for the value of rational articulation:

> It does not follow, because we all are compelled to take on faith at second hand most of the rules on which we base our action and our thought, that each of us may not try to set some corner of his world *in the order of reason or that all of us collectively should not aspire to carry reason as far as it will go throughout the whole domain.* In regard to the law, it is true, no doubt, that an evolutionist will hesitate to affirm universal validity for his social ideals, or for the principles which he thinks should be embodied in legislation . . . Still it is true that *a body of law is more rational and more civilized when every rule it contains is referred articulately and definitely to an end which it subserves, and when the grounds for desiring that end are stated or ready to be stated in words.* (185–86, emphasis added)

Although I would characterize the content of what a judge ought to articulate rather differently,[62] Holmes is at least a fellow traveler in valuing rational articulation. I summarize my own view of the content of this norm in a *principle of rational articulation:* An officiating legal reasoner (judge or other public official) ought to clarify the logical form of each of the arguments that operate as elements in the overall justificatory legal argument he offers (or make sure that their form is readily "enthymematically recoverable" clear in context).

2. RATIONAL DEFAMILIARIZATION AND THE SOCRATIC MANDATE: THE UNEXAMINED DECISION IS NOT WORTH MAKING?

The discipline of rationally articulating the justification for a legal decision is a philosophical task, a Socratic task in which the judge is called upon to honor the maxim "Know thyself."" But as a maxim of public reason motivated by a concern for rule-of-law values, for promoting public understanding, and enabling and sharpening public political debate about the norms that guide legal decision making, the "self" involved is not that of the judge as a private person, but is rather the self of the judge as agent for the "public self" of government. As a norm, the value of rational articulation imposes a heavy but not irrebuttable presumption that it is *not* acceptable for a judge to rest on "inarticulate" beliefs and judgments when rendering a decision. *Sometimes* the urgency of circumstance – time constraints combined with a need for rapid resolution of a case – may allow a less than articulate decision to suffice. But it is worth observing that, over time, if we had a legal culture in which law students, later to become lawyers and judges, were systematically trained in the arts and philosophical sciences of justification (i.e., the arts and sciences of rational articulation), the amount of time it would take to produce rationally articulate judgments would substantially decrease. Right now, given the anti-logical culture in so much of the legal academy and bar, it is the far rarer lawyer or judge who comes equipped with these tools.

The normative presumption of rational articulation is related to, but importantly distinct from, the presumption that a judicial decision ought to be candid. For at least two reasons, these are not the same presumptive norms. A judge need not truly report the grounds of her decision in order to render a decision that is *justified according to law*. Many different motives – some noble, some base, some neutral – can motivate a judge to render a decision according to law. What counts is a rational articulation of *some* argument, not necessarily *the* argument that actually motivated the judge to render the decision. Moreover, rational articulation of even a disingenuous justification *sometimes* makes the disingenuousness easier to spot when held up to rational scrutiny. One of the great dangers of *inarticulate* decision making is precisely its ability to mask the abuse of power, a concern reflected in Hayekian rule-of-law norms concerned with the ability of rules to constrain government power.[63] Even though they are not the same norm, there is a sure consonance between the value of rational articulateness and the value of candor in judicial decision making. The presumption in favor of candor, like that in favor of rational articulateness, it is not irrebuttable. Candor is not required in all settings. The Nazi system, in which a judge might surreptitiously use the forms and procedures and institutions of law to undermine the power of that regime, is one that will strike many as a setting in which the presumption of rational articulation of the actual ground of decision is sufficiently rebutted. I shall not attempt here to provide the theory that undergirds these presumptions. I will observe that discerning the bounds of these presumptions is one of the most important normative projects in the jurisprudence of logical form.

One final observation about the content of the (prima facie) obligation on a judge to offer a rational articulation. I offer an analogy – perhaps a bit strained – to help explicate it. The literary theorists known as the Russian Formalists advanced a view of what art is and what, accordingly, art criticism should be. In their view (I adopt the words of their impresario, Victor Shklovsky), art operates by the process of "making strange," of "defamiliarizing" the everyday world by holding it up in art for a more lively examination, appreciation, investigation, and engagement than is possible with the workaday habitualized perceptions and conceptions on which we tend to rely in daily life. As Shklovsky put it,

The process of "algebrization," the over-automatization of an object, permits the greatest economy of perceptive effort. Either objects are assigned only one proper feature – a number, for example – or else they function as though by formula and do not even appear in cognition . . . And so life is reckoned as nothing. Habitualization devours works, clothes, furniture, one's wife, the fear of war. "If the whole complex lives of many people go on unconsciously, then such lives are as if they had never been." And art exists that one may recover the sensation of life; it exists to make one feel things, to make the stone *stony*. The purpose of art is to impart the sensation of things as they are perceived and not as they are known. The technique of art is to make objects "unfamiliar," to make forms difficult, to increase the difficulty and length of perception because the process of perception is an aesthetic end in itself and must be prolonged. Art is a way of experiencing the artfulness of an object; the object is not important.[64]

This concept of defamiliarization offers a heuristically useful description of the task of rational articulation. To lead the *examined life* is to make routinized everyday life somewhat strange, somewhat unfamiliar, if only because everyday life does not typically call upon us to reflect on the structures of language and reason and passion in which we live. This philosophical task is precisely to step back from that life, to make it strange, to make it examined, to articulate its structures. It is a deep philosophical enterprise. This task is a vital element of a judge's obligation of rational articulation. Far more than the average citizen, the judge must search his public soul, *defamiliarize,* the better to *examine* and *articulate,* his intuitions and instincts and gleanings and hunches and passions and prejudices. This baring of the public soul in the process of rational articulation is, in the judge's work, a jurisprudential task. Holmes was correct, in a way that he perhaps did not know, when he said in *The Path of the Law*: "Theory is the most important part of the dogma of the law, as the architect is the most important man who takes part in the building of the house." Through the never-ending task of discovering and articulating justification, the judge in the most mundane case can connect his decisions "with the universe and catch an echo of the infinite" and glimpse its not *fully fathomable* but nonetheless rationally investigable process. It is in *this* ratiocinative life of the law that the union of logic and experience occurs.

Notes

1 Thomas C. Grey, "Langdell's Orthodoxy," *University of Pittsburgh Law Review* 45 (1983):1, 1–3.
2 Oliver W. Holmes, Jr., review of C. C. Langdell, *Summary of the Law of Contracts* (1880), *American Law Review* 14 (1880):233–34.
3 Oliver W. Holmes, Jr., *The Common Law,* ed. Mark DeWolfe Howe (Boston: Little Brown, 1963), 5. Holmes iterates the assertion, with an application to contract law, about logic and experience: "The distinctions of the law are founded on experience, not on logic" (244). Again, in slightly different terms, he repeats it, observing optimistically that "the law is administered by able and experienced men . . . who know too much to sacrifice good sense to a syllogism" (32).
4 *Lochner v. New York,* 198 U.S. 45, 76 (1905). That this is the same theme as "law is not logic but experience" is revealed by comparing it to Holmes's second explicit reference to logic and experience in the chapter on void contracts in *The Common Law*. There he asserts that the "distinctions of law are founded on experience, not on logic" (244).

5 Oliver W. Holmes, Jr., "The Path of the Law" (1897), in *Collected Legal Papers* (New York: Harcourt, Brace & Howe, 1920), 167. Cited hereafter parenthetically in the text as "Path." "The Path" is reprinted in the Appendix to this volume with star paging.
6 See, e.g., William Twining, "The Bad Man Revisited," *Cornell Law Review* 58 (1973):275; Thomas Grey, "Holmes and Legal Pragmatism," *Stanford Law Review* 41 (1989):787.
7 Grey, "Holmes and Legal Pragmatism," 826–27.
8 See Grey, "Holmes and Legal Pragmatism," 826–27. Grey notes that the opening paragraph of Holmes's essay speaks only and explicitly from the perspective of a lawyer who "appear[s] before judges" or "advise[s] people in such a way as to keep them out of court" (174). Holmes repeats this theme of prediction and "prophecy" (moving easily between the more scientific term and the more biblical term for prognostication) several times within the essay's opening pages.
9 See Twining, "Bad Man Revisited," 281.
10 I follow the standard philosophical convention of using single quotation marks to mention a term and double quotation marks to quote a speaker's (or group of speakers') use of a term. (Thus, 'Logic' is a five-letter word; a good deal of talk about "logic" in American legal academia is misguided.)
11 The analysis of the "fallacy of logical form" takes up about five pages, about 14% of the total pages of the essay (180–84). This is *roughly* equal to the space Holmes devotes to the prediction thesis (168–73) and to the separation thesis (173–79). Of course discussions of these theses overlap substantially, so it is hard (and unnecessary) to fashion an accurate measurement of the space Holmes devotes to each. I offer the rough calculation only because it is worth nothing that Holmes devotes nearly 50% of the essay to arguing the possibility and desirability of rational reform and of sketching a program for it.
12 Holmes was, in many ways, a master of language, as witness the terse and powerful aperçus that have earned him that reputation. But on a broader scale his language is full of pitfalls. The meaning of the most central concepts in his writings, such as "philosophy," "principles," "logic," and "experience" would have to be clearly defined from within Holmes's own argument before an attempt to explicate his ideas in a more coherent and consistent way could possibly succeed.
Mathias Reimann, "The Common Law and German Legal Science," in *The Legacy of Oliver Wendell Holmes,* ed. Robert Gordon (Stanford: Stanford University Press, 1992), 146.
13 See the discussion in section II.C of the present chapter.
14 Although the interpretive evidence for it is indirect, Holmes does use the term 'logic' in "The Path" in sense (ii). At the start of page 180, Holmes introduces the concept of a "fallacy" in the "notion that the only force at work in the development of the law is logic." (Later, at page 184, he refers to this fallacy as "the fallacy of logical form.") Farther down the page, in what is clearly an explication of the "fallacious" view of "logic," he refers to the mistaken view that
> a given [legal] system . . . can be worked out *like mathematics* from some general axioms of conduct . . . So judicial dissent often is blamed, as if it meant simply that one side or the other were not doing their sums right, and, if they would take more trouble, agreement inevitably would come. (180, emphasis added)

The salient feature in Holmes's simile – legal reasoning is mistakenly thought to be "like mathematics" – is that mathematics (and "doing sums") are deductive processes. Thus, I take Holmes's reference to deduction at the end of page 180 to be an exegesis of his use of the term 'logic' at the start of that page, and in that way he uses the term in sense (i) (180).

15 See text accompanying note 21.
16 We know that Holmes admired Kant, at least to some degree, for at the end of "The Path" Kant figures prominently in Holmes's epideictic tribute to the power of intellect: "To an imagination of any scope the most far-reaching form of power is not money, it is the command of ideas . . . Read the works of the great German jurists, and see how much more the world is governed to-day by Kant than by Bonaparte" (201–2). Reimann argues that Kant, in the very influence he exercised over the "great German jurists," was at least the superficial target of Holmes's anti-logic thesis in *The Common Law*. His real target, suggests Reimann, was Langdell, but Holmes the mere Harvard Law School lecturer could not, for political reasons, directly attack the dean of the school where Holmes might want to have a permanent job. Reimann also points out that Langdell's view of the role of logic in law was quite different from that of many of the "great German jurists," and that the views of at least one of them, von Savigny, were consonant with Holmes's own views, though Holmes never conceded the point. See Reimann, "German Legal Science," 146.
17 See Grey, "Holmes and Legal Pragmatism," 818. In correspondence with Pollock, Holmes said of Langdell's book on contracts:
> A more misspent piece of marvelous ingenuity I never read, yet it is most suggestive and instructive. I have referred to Langdell several times in dealing with contracts because to my mind he represents the powers of darkness. He is all for logic and hates any reference to anything outside of it, and his explanations and reconciliations of the cases would have astonished the judges who decided them. But he is a noble old swell whose knowledge, ability and idealist devotion to his work I revere and love.

Holmes to Frederick Pollock, 10 April 1881, in *Holmes–Pollock Letters: The Correspondence of Mr. Justice Holmes and Sir Frederick Pollock, 1874–1932*, ed. Mark DeWolfe Howe (Cambridge, Mass.; Belknap Press, 1961), 16–17.
18 See M. H. Hoeflich, "Law and Geometry: Legal Science from Leibniz to Langdell," *American Journal of Legal History* 30 (1986):95. See also Reimann, "German Legal Science," 108–10; Grey, "Langdell's Orthodoxy," 29–30; Anthony J. Sebok, "Misunderstanding Positivism," *Michigan Law Review* 93 (1995):2054.
19 Actually, the inductions that both Holmes and Langdell contemplated relied on an initial "abductive" inference as well, as do all inductive inferences. See section II.B.3.b of this chapter.
20 Grey, "Langdell's Orthodoxy," 6–11.
21 We must be sensitive to the possibility that different legal systems, such as common-law–based and code-based systems, or even British and American common-law-plus-statute-plus-regulation–based systems, deploy the same basic modes of logical inference (deduction, induction, abduction, analogy) in different ways and to different extents. See P. S. Atiyah and Robert Summers, *Form and Substance in Anglo-American Law: A Comparative Study of Legal Reasoning, Legal Theory, and Legal Institutions* (Oxford: Clarendon Press, 1987).
22 Philosophers of logic dispute whether there really are four basic types of logical inference, and whether all of those on my list belong. Many would exclude abduction and analogy from the list, for example. For reasons beyond the scope of this essay, I follow Peirce in recognizing abduction as one of the fundamental types of inference. See, e.g., Charles S. Peirce, "Prolegomena to an Apology for Pragmatism," *Monist* 16 (1906):492; reprinted in *Collected Papers of Charles Sanders Peirce*, ed. C. Hartshorne and P. Weiss (Cambridge, Mass.: Belknap Press, 1960), section 541, note 1.
23 There are actually two types of enthymemicity that an informal legal argument can have,

which I have called "structural" and "practical." See Scott Brewer, "Exemplary Reasoning: Semantics, Pragmatics, and the Rational Force of Legal Argument by Analogy," *Harvard Law Review* 109 (1996):985.

24 One line of thought worth pursuing in the theory of the enthymeme is the way in which enthymematic arguments, including those that judicial decisions sometimes offer, violate pragmatic maxims of linguistic cooperation. The starting point for such an inquiry is Paul Grice's analysis of the general "Cooperative Principle," which, he argues, interpreters assume that speakers are consciously following ("Make your contribution such as is required, at the stage at which it occurs, by the accepted purpose or direction of the talk exchange in which you are engaged") and the more specific maxims concerning manner, the supermaxim "Be perspicuous," and such others as "Avoid obscurity of expression," "Avoid ambiguity," "Be brief (avoid unnecessary prolixity)," and "Be orderly." See Paul Grice, "Logic and Conversation," in *Studies in the Way of Words* (Cambridge, Mass.: Harvard University Press, 1989), 26–27.

25 This distinction is standard in accounts of inductive inference. See, e.g., Stephen F. Barker, *The Elements of Logic* (New York: McGraw-Hill, 1989), 186–95, and Irving M. Copi and Carl Cohen, *Introduction to Logic* (New York: Macmillan, 1990), 381–82.

26 See, e.g., *Brown v. Brown*, 524 A.2d 1184, 1188 (D.C. 1987) ("We believe that, *as a matter of common human experience,* such services are usually performed out of a sense of family responsibility, not pursuant to a contractual agreement with the legitimate expectation of payment"; emphasis added).

27 Ibid., 1490–91 (emphasis added).

28 There are two levels of abstraction here, one in a "metalanguage" (i.e., a language *about* a language), the other in a reconstructed and schematized version of the "object" language in which the *Harvard Law Review* authors offer their inductive arguments about the predictive factors. Even the "object" language is an abstraction, because I am offering a reconstruction of their enthymemes that seem, as a matter of interpretation, to underlie the analysis they offer. In the "metalanguage" occur the "metavariables" 'α', 'ϕ', and 'θ'. These metavariables represent (i) the distinct series of cases $\alpha_1 \ldots \alpha_n$ in which a predictive factor ϕ has been observed to occur, (ii) the different factors ϕ, and (iii) the decision θ to admit or exclude the NSE. In the object language, the distinct series of cases is represented by $a_1 \ldots a_n$, the different factors are represented by 'F_1', 'F_2', and 'F_3', the decision to admit NSE by 'P', the decision to exclude by 'P''.

29 "Development in the Law – Confronting the New Challenges of Scientific Evidence," *Harvard Law Review* 108 (1995):1498.

30 Charles S. Peirce, "Lectures on Pragmatism, Three Kinds of Goodness," in Hartshorne and Weiss, *Collected Papers,* sections 120, 145.

31 As does, for example, the following argument: "If Jones is a law professor, then Jones is logorrheic; Jones is logorrheic; therefore, Jones is a law professor."

32 One of the best recent thorough treatments of the subject is *Abductive Inference: Computation, Philosophy, Technology,* ed. John R. Josephson and Susan G. Josephson (Stanford: Stanford University Press, 1994).

33 For Peirce's view on the importance of abductive inference in science, see the text accompanying note 30.

34 Legal academics have in recent years begun to explore the role of abduction in legal reasoning, and most such treatments deal with it in the evidentiary, fact-finding context. See, e.g., David Schuman and Peter Tillers, "A Theory of Preliminary Fact Investigation," *Uni-*

versity of California at Davis Law Review 24 (1991):986–94; Marjorie Anne McDiarmid, "Lawyer Decision Making: The Problem of Prediction," *Wisconsin Law Review* No. 6 (1992):1899–1902.

35 On some positivist theories, indeed on some natural law accounts as well, legal explanations *are* a type of empirical explanation, or are at least in part a type of empirical explanation. Nothing in the text to this note, nor indeed in this essay, is intended to take a stand on that issue.

36 Half a century ago, in a rather Holmesian (Holmes the realist godfather, that is) and pragmatist analysis, legal realist Walter Wheeler Cook offered what remains one of the best explications of the difference between "facts" from a legal point of view and "facts" from other points of view. See Walter W. Cook, "'Facts' and 'Statements of Fact,'" *University of Chicago Law Review* 4 (1937):4. Whether the "legal point of view" is also a prudential, moral, or religious point of view is an enduring question debated by positivists and natural law theorists.

37 Positivist and natural law theories differ about what constitutes adequate confirmation.

38 *Searight v. New Jersey,* 412 F. Supp. 413 (D. N.J. 1976).

39 Ordinarily the judge would have allowed Searight time to file an amended complaint, because he had sued *pro se,* but Federal Rule of Civil Procedure 12(h)(3) allowed the judge to dismiss the claim if he found for other reasons that the court lacked jurisdiction.

40 This qualification goes to the internal structure of the explanans T.

41 *Searight v. New Jersey,* 415.

42 The judge first considered whether federal statutory civil rights law might afford the plaintiff a remedy. (He decided it would not, because a plaintiff must first bring an action in state court if the case does not "rise to constitutional levels," and the judge thought it did not) (ibid., 413). The judge next suggested that the facts, taken as true (as required at this early stage of the proceedings), showed, at most, "unlicensed radio communication" by someone, but that such transmissions were "within the sole jurisdiction of the Federal Communications Commission," and so the case did, after all, have to be dismissed (ibid.). The judge's best effort to abduce a legal rule that would "explain" this litigant's case from a legal point of view, in a way that would allow the case to proceed, failed to produce such an explanation.

43 Charles S. Peirce, "Lectures on Pragmatism, Pragmatism and Abduction," in Hartshorne and Weiss, *Collected Papers,* section 180.

44 As noted, it was Peirce who first identified and highlighted the importance of abduction as a mode of logical inference. Holmes knew Peirce from the Metaphysical Club meetings both had attended in Cambridge, Massachusetts, and was familiar with at least some of Peirce's work, though he does not seem to have admired it. The Metaphysical Club was a philosophical study group whose members included Holmes, Peirce, Chauncey Wright, and William James. See Max H. Fisch, "Introduction," in *Writings of Charles S. Peirce: A Chronological Edition* (Bloomington: Bloomington Indiana Press, 1986), xxi, xxx–xxxi. This group discussed the emerging principles of pragmatism during 1871–72 (ibid.). Grey, "Holmes and Legal Pragmatism" (788).

45 These two features define 'rule' in my account; the common (but in my view theoretically unhelpful) distinction between a 'rule' and a 'standard' does not play a role in my account of the analogy-warranting rule.

46 Oliver W. Holmes, Jr., "Law in Science and Science in Law," in *Collected Legal Papers* (New York: Harcourt, Brace & Howe, 1920), 210, 239.

47 *McBoyle v. United States,* 283 U.S. 25 (1931).
48 *McBoyle v. United States,* 26.
49 See Oliver W. Holmes, Jr., "The Theory of Legal Interpretation," in *Collected Legal Papers,* 203.
50 According to this "law" of judicial decision making, when, in a context of doubt about the scope of a legal concept (e.g., 'vehicle'), a judge is to conclude that a given party *has* satisfied the criterion for that concept, she will specify a *sufficient condition* for the application of that concept. Having done so, she may then deductively conclude that the party satisfied it. Similarly, when in a context of doubt a judge is to conclude that a given party has *not* satisfied the criterion for an applicable legal concept, she will specify a *necessary condition* for the nonapplication of that concept. Having done so, she may then deductively infer that the party did not satisfy it. See Brewer, "Exemplary Reasoning," 997.
51 See Israel Scheffler, *Beyond the Letter: A Philosophical Inquiry into Ambiguity, Vagueness and Metaphor in Language* (New York: Routledge & Kegan Paul, 1979), 50.
52 I use 'underdeterminate,' instead of the more commonly encountered 'indeterminate,' to indicate that although the meaning of the term or phrase is not *yet* determined at a point of application, it *can* be determined by some kind of supplemental reasoning process. (If by 'indeterminate' one means "not yet determined," then the two terms are synonyms.)
53 See, e.g., Edward Levi, *An Introduction to Legal Reasoning* (Chicago: University of Chicago Press, 1949), 1 ("It is important that the mechanism of legal reasoning should not be concealed by its pretense. The pretense is that the law is a system of known rules applied by a judge; the pretense has long been under attack"); and Felix Cohen, "The Ethical Basis of Legal Criticism," *Yale Law Journal* 41 (1931):201, 215 ("The confusion arises when we think of a judicial decision as implying a rule from which, given the facts of the case, the decision may be derived").
54 *Ray v. William G. Eurice and Bros.,* 93 A.2d 272 (Md. 1952).
55 See, e.g., Immanuel Kant, "On the Common Saying: 'This May Be True in Theory, but It Does Not Apply in Practice,'" in *Kant: Political Writings,* ed. Hans Reiss, trans. H. B. Nisbet (Cambridge: Cambridge University Press, 1991), 2d ed., 61, 84 n.
56 John Rawls, *A Theory of Justice* (Cambridge, Mass.: Belknap Press, 1971), section 23.
57 The constructive model, however, does not support the policy of submerging apparent inconsistency in the faith that reconciling principles must exist. On the contrary, it demands that decisions taken in the name of justice must never outstrip an official's ability to account for these decisions in a theory of justice, even when such a theory must compromise some of his intuitions. It demands that we act on principle rather than on faith. Its engine is a doctrine of responsibility that requires men to integrate their intuitions and subordinate some of these, when necessary, to that responsibility. It presupposes articulated consistency, decisions in accordance with a program that can be made public and followed until changed, is essential to any conception of justice.

Ronald Dworkin, *Taking Rights Seriously* (Cambridge, Mass.: Harvard University Press, 1978), 162.
58 Several of the rule-of-law values that Fuller explicates are directly concerned with rational articulation by public officials, including the values of *clarity* in legal rules; see Lon Fuller, *The Morality of Law* (New Haven: Yale University Press, 1964), 63. Heall discusses *generality* (46–49); *non-retroactivity* (51–62); *non-contradiction* (65–70); *congruence* (81–91); and *non-contradiction* (65–70). For further discussion, see Brewer, "Exemplary Reasoning," sections VI.A.1, 5.
59 Mill, *On Liberty,* chapter 2.

60 Joseph Raz, *The Authority of Law: Essays on Law and Morality* (Oxford: Oxford University Press, 1979), 223–26.

61 "The development of our law has gone on for nearly a thousand years, like the development of a plant, each generation taking the inevitable next step, mind, like matter, simply obeying a law of spontaneous growth" ("Path" 185).

62 I must concede, though, that Holmes himself appeared at times to exempt the judge from the group of those who "may . . . try to set some corner of his world in the order of reason or that all of us collectively should not aspire to carry reason as far as it will go throughout the whole domain." In an underjustified assertion in "Law as Science – Science as Law," he asserts:

> [I]nasmuch as the real justification of a rule of law, if there be one, is that it helps to bring about a social end which we desire, it is no less necessary that *those who make and develop the law should have those ends articulately in their minds. I do not think it desirable that the judges should undertake to renovate the law. That is not their province.* (238–39, emphasis added).

The highlighted portions of this passage seem to me to exhibit some tension, and the remainder of the reason he offers in the essay for exempting judges from the obligation to effect rational "renovation" of the law are to my mind quite unconvincing. In any event, if Holmes really believes judges are exempt in this way, the norm of rational articulation that I am advancing here is in that way fundamentally at odds with Holmes's conception of the judicial role.

63 See Friedrich A. Hayek, *The Road to Serfdom* (Chicago: University of Chicago Press, 1944), 72–73.

64 Victor Shklovsky, "Art as Technique," in *Russian Formalist Criticism: Four Essays,* trans. Lee T. Lemon and Marion J. Reis (Lincoln: University of Nebraska Press, 1965), 12.

6

Holmes on the Logic of the Law

THOMAS C. GREY*

Again and again throughout his long career, Oliver Wendell Holmes, Jr., seemed to be waging a jurisprudential campaign against something he called "logic." His first great one-liner (and it remains his most famous) was "The life of the law has not been logic; it has been experience."[1] In a much-quoted letter, he described Christopher Columbus Langdell, Dean of the Harvard Law School, as representative of "the powers of darkness" in legal thought, because he "is all for logic and hates any reference to anything outside it."[2] *The Path of the Law* includes six paragraphs denouncing the "fallacy of logical form" in legal thought.[3] In his dissent in *Lochner v. New York,* Holmes wrote that "[g]eneral propositions do not decide concrete cases," because judicial decision rests on a "judgment or intuition more subtle than any articulate major premise."[4] And in a later dissent also attacking Constitutional judicial activism, he deprecated "pressing the broad words of the Fourteenth Amendment to a drily logical extreme."[5]

These passages are well known and have been influential, but it is natural for readers with a background in analytical philosophy to find confusion in them. Scott Brewer's essay (Chapter 5 in this volume) does just that, arguing that Holmes was not clear on the target of his "anti-logic" campaign, for he seems to have meant various things by "logic": systematic coherence, deduction, induction, analogy, and even just plain common sense.[6]

Brewer is definitely onto something here, but after following out his suggestive leads, I still think that Holmes had a pretty consistent view of legal logic.[7] We can see this if we recognize that he gave the term a colloquial and not a technical meaning, and if we always take care to read him in context. A perhaps obvious second point, but one worth making in light of Brewer's coinage, is that Holmes was by no means generally "anti-logic" in legal theory. He thought that logic, in its various related senses, was a significant (but not the only) force in shaping the law,[8] and also that it supplied important (but again not the only) criteria for evaluating legal inquiry.[9]

---

* My thanks once again to Barbara Babcock for her many welcome editorial suggestions.

I. Fuzzy Logic

As it is for most of us in our everyday speech, "logic" for Holmes was a term that was somewhat vague and even a bit ambiguous, but certainly not meaningless. His prototype of legal logic was uncontroversial deductive reasoning based on systematic conceptual analysis. The idea that a legal system could be perfectly logical in this sense constituted the "fallacy of logical form" that he identified and criticized in *The Path of the Law*.

But he also used the term in at least three more limited senses.[10] First, a decision was based on logic if it involved the uncontroversial deduction of a result from a clear existing rule and a given set of past facts, whether or not the rule was derived as part of a conceptual system. Second, legal reasoning was logical if it was systematically based on general principles of the sort that were congruent with a perspicuous taxonomic classification of the law, even if the principles were used only as guidelines and not as deductive major premises. Third, he treated reasoning by analogy as logical because it was driven by the pursuit of internal consistency, even though it was neither deductively certain nor systematic. He contrasted decisions that were "logical" in any of these three senses to others that were "practical" and "legislative," in the sense that they were instrumental and contextual, aimed (without special concern for coherence) at achieving desired consequences in the light of situational details.[11]

This semantic efflorescence of overlapping and related senses of a single key word creates possibilities of confusion, of course. But if we pay attention to context – particularly to what Holmes contrasted to "logic" whenever he used the term – we find that he usually made pretty clear what he meant and stuck fairly close to usages familiar both in ordinary speech and among lawyers. We also find that Holmes disapproved of legal logic only in its most extreme and exclusive sense, what he called "the merely logical point of view" (*Common Law* 32), which is to say a jurisprudence committed above all else to the systematically deductive decision of every question of law. He thought that otherwise logic as he understood it played a valuable and important role in legal reasoning.

Parsing Holmes's various usages – the paradigm case and the three subsidiary senses of legal logic – is worth doing even now, because lawyers generally, including academic legal writers, still tend to talk about logic in the same loose way as he did. Logicians and analytical philosophers, by contrast, use a specialized and more rigorous terminology that develops a consistent but uncolloquially narrow sense of the term "logic." Unless the differences are made explicit, the divergent usages of the two groups are likely to breed misunderstanding. I leave unaddressed the question of whether lawyers and legal commentators would, ideally, be better off using the philosophers' technical vocabulary. In fact, they do not use it, and my guess is they are not about to.

II. Logic and Conceptual Analysis

In trying to clear up misunderstandings between lawyers and logicians, it is important to see that Holmes used the term "logic" to refer not only to formal canons of valid inference, but also to a priori arguments based on concepts or linguistic meanings. H. L. A. Hart made this point long ago, though he seemed to think that Holmes was simply mistaken in his deviation from the specialized idiom of analytical philosophy. Hart noted that Holmes (and the legal realist writers who followed him) tended to criticize formalist judges for making "an excessive use of logic" or going to a "drily logical extreme" in deciding cases. This could not be right, Hart argued, because "logic does not prescribe interpretation of terms" and "is silent on . . . the heart of judicial decision," which is "how to classify particulars."[12] Logic in the (philosophers') sense of purely formal rules of inference could not be a "force," something that (as Holmes and the realists portrayed it) struggled with policy or "good sense" and tended to be given too much weight by orthodox jurisprudence.

What Holmes and the realists were really complaining about, Hart said, was not logic but a particular style of interpretation. The formalist judge "either does not see or pretends not to see that the general terms of [a] rule are susceptible of different interpretations," so that the judge "has a choice left open." This opening (which Hart elsewhere analyzed in terms of the "open texture" of all natural language)[13] invited the judge to decide "in the light of social aims,"[14] and it was the formalist judge's failure to do this (or his doing it without acknowledging it) that the realist objected to. If we add to Hart's reference to interpretation a mention of the essentialist version of conceptual analysis that typically accompanies and supports it, we can see the main source of confusion. The disputes between realist and orthodox legal theorists are not about logic in its purely formal sense. No one who speaks of logic as a "force" that can be overemphasized in legal reasoning is objecting to judges making valid inferences or suggesting that they make too many of them.

As Hart suggested, Holmes was ascribing to the legal logician a particular and controvertible style of interpretation or conceptual analysis. The semantic and metaphysical assumptions behind this style are, in Holmes's view, roughly, that words have sense or meaning insofar as they connote independently existing concepts, which correspond to essences whose content is given by an Aristotelian definition *per genus et differentiam* or a statement of the necessary and sufficient conditions for application. Further, concepts follow bimodal logic and either apply or not – there are no differences in degree of applicability. If words appear to be vague, fuzzy in their applications at the edges, it must be either because we have not identified their proper meaning (their corresponding concept), or because of uncertainties in our factual knowledge.

By contrast with this classical approach, Holmes thought of words and their associated concepts pragmatically, as tools useful in identifying particulars for purposes of inquiry or communication. On this view, proper names denote individuals directly, and general terms are shorthand expressions that call up a group of more or less similar instances.[15] The similarity might or might not involve the sharing of necessary and sufficient conditions; what sorts of resemblance between particulars turn out to be useful in concept formation for purposes of thought and communication cannot be legislated in advance.[16] Human beings want to identify individual things for practical reasons, and outside the core of uncontroversial applications of a general term, whether it subsumes a particular often turns on questions of degree and depends on context and purpose.

III. Pragmatist and Classical Jurisprudence

Given his contextual and instrumental approach to concepts, it follows that if we are to understand Holmes's approach to legal reasoning – the use of concepts in law generally and in adjudication in particular – we need to know at least a little about what he thought law was for, and why we have courts. Here is a brief sketch of his general approach.

In political philosophy, Holmes was a preference utilitarian; he thought that people would naturally pursue their desires, and that the best system of government was one that gave them the most of what they wanted at the least cost. He was also a historicist, who believed that people were not solely driven by a universal desire for pleasure and aversion to pain, nor even by a small number of biologically given wants, but also by ideals and tastes that varied widely according to culture and history.

As one might expect from his historicism, Holmes was a skeptic about the possibility of accurate utilitarian evaluation. Human wants conflicted and were not easily commensurable, even in principle (because there was no single metric such as pleasure–pain), and certainly not in practice. For this reason, relatively crude practical measures were called for in the design of legal institutions. Fighting was the default mode of conflict resolution, and law was an alternative to violent disorder. Ideally, law would be shaped so as to maximize the satisfaction of intelligent desires, preferences purified by knowledge and self-criticism, but because people would fight for what they actually wanted, whether the wants were intelligent or not, and because in doing so they would inflict real evils on each other, as a practical second-best the law should correspond to actual desires, even unintelligent ones. And because even actual desires were not readily commensurable in cases of conflict, a practical third-best was that the law should at least be definite and knowable, so that people could shape their conduct to its demands, and that there should be ways of changing the rules in response to dominant preferences.

Courts exist mainly to decide disputes in an orderly and relatively nonviolent way, and in aid of predictability they should ideally do so by the application of known rules to the ascertainable facts of past events. Common law was the result of courts using the doctrine of precedent to create a body of rules out of individual decisions, and using fiction and equity to adapt those rules to gradual social change. When change accelerated under conditions of modernity, explicit forward-looking legislation became the main instrument of rule specification and legal reform. Elected legislatures responsive to public opinion made it more likely that law would correspond to the predominant wishes within the community. Courts were kept relatively independent so that they could carry out their specialized task of settling disputes with primary attention to stated law and established expectations; they were less well suited than legislatures to ascertain the balance of collective desire.

Coming down to the details of adjudication, Holmes thought that cases should be decided on the basis of the clear core meaning of existing rules, in aid of the primary policies of protecting expectations and satisfying collective desires. But all rules had a penumbra of doubtful application (vaguer standards having a proportionally larger penumbra), and the farther out from the core a case fell, the less power the rule had to generate expectations and the less evidence it provided about relevant collective preferences. For these reasons, at some point in the penumbra the court should give up interpreting and take over the role of sublegislator, formulating a ground of decision for the case that could take account of dominant wishes and the need for clear rules. In the name of predictability and clarity, Holmes thought courts should draw an artificially sharp line between the two modes of decision-rule-application and judicial legislation.[17] As context, we should note that Holmes did not have on his left flank any legal theorists (like the later "legal realists" or "critical legal scholars") arguing that adjudication was even more political or legislative than he said it was. His dispute was entirely with the shared presupposition of the Langdellian and older Blackstonian declaratory orthodoxy – that the judge's sole legitimate function was to declare existing law and apply it to facts, so that there must be determinate law for every case. The controversy was over whether the law left to judicial discretion a few cases (as Holmes, following John Austin, argued) or none (the orthodox view) – no one was arguing that judges had discretion in all or most cases.

Up through the middle of the nineteenth century, most commentators and common law judges (particularly American ones) had taken their declaratory theory with enough of a grain of salt to allow plenty of creative legal adaptation, under the guise of following existing law. But in Holmes's day there had emerged the more rigorous legal science that we associate with Langdell and his colleagues at the Harvard Law School. At the same time, during a period in which class conflict was mounting, conservative judges became (or pretended to become) increasingly confident that they were applying objective law and not just engaging in judicial politics when they used broad common law principles on the side of capital in its struggles with labor. It was against these two linked tendencies that Holmes directed the campaign that Brewer calls his "anti-logic."

On the classically orthodox view, law was conceived as a set of axioms from which legal principles were deduced as corollaries and rules as theorems, with the rules then applied to facts to produce determinate legal outcomes. Under such a conception, preexisting law deductively decided every case through the operation of an exact, consistent, and complete system, and thereby the Blackstonian ideal of an entirely declaratory judicial process was realized.[18] Such a Euclidean body of law could draw its axioms either from outside, by way of philosophy, in natural law style, or from within, as positivist legal scientists ascertained the simplest set of principles that could justify most of the decided cases. German neo-Kantian jurisprudence and American Langdellian legal science respectively represented these two tendencies for Holmes when he wrote *The Common Law*,[19] and later they both were found among the conservative activist judges with whom he contended throughout his judicial career.[20]

Explaining Holmes's theory of adjudication has required placing it in the context of his broader pragmatist (which is to say historicist and skeptically utilitarian) views of politics and society. One of the great strengths of the classical orthodox view of law is that it required no such external and debatable justification. It appeared to follow recursively from its own essentialist approach to conceptual analysis. No practical or philosophical answer had to be given, if someone asked why law should be a gapless logical system that left no room for judicial legislation or even judicial judgment. For the classically orthodox, it was simply a requirement of the inner logic of law that it had to take this form. As a result, any departure from a fully formal and conceptual jurisprudence was a violation of the very nature of law, and hence an abandonment of the ideal of the rule of law. While German legal theorists might give Kantian or Hegelian philosophical reasons why law had to be conceptual and formal, Langdellians gave no such reasons. In their philosophical silence they simply said: "If you want a government of laws and not of men – and whether you should want one is a political and philosophical question outside our jurisdiction – here is what it means to have one."[21]

With this understanding of the general approaches of Holmes and his opponents, we can now turn to the various senses of legal "logic" that he adopted in his writings. To schematize, we can say that Holmes identified legal reasoning as logical in the full sense when it was analytical or a priori, systematic, and consistency based – but also as logical, derivatively, when it was any of these three things.

IV. The Logic of Orthodoxy

Classical orthodoxy absolutely required that law should meet all three of these criteria: legal reasoning must proceed analytically, without consideration of consequences; each judgment must derive ultimately from a few basic abstract concepts, which must cover every case that could arise; and each correct legal judgment must be reconcilable with all others. Holmes attacked this orthodoxy on the two grounds that it could not be fully realized in practice, and that the attempt to realize it had bad consequences.

The first point was that the supposed deductions of controversial results from doctrinal generalities found in classical adjudication and commentary were never really ineluctable: "General principles do not decide concrete cases."[22] An example of Holmes's technique in showing this is his treatment of the issue of whether a contract by mail was formed when the acceptance was posted, as most courts had decided, or whether it had to be received and read. Langdell had notoriously argued that doctrinal logic dictated the "received-and-read" rule, and that as a result the alleged superior justice and convenience of the mailbox rule was entirely "irrelevant." Langdell's point was rooted in the systematics of contract doctrine, which in his view logically required that the acceptance must operate as a promise for it to serve as the consideration necessary for contract formation at common law, whereas the very nature of a promise required actual communication of its contents.[23]

In his response, Holmes not only asserted the relevance of justice and convenience, but also attacked the logic of Langdell's claim that consistency of doctrine demanded the received-and-read rule. He pointed out that at common law a covenant was treated as a binding promise when delivered and accepted, even if not read. The rationale was that once there had been mental assent to be bound on the part of a promisor, the contract was formed whenever a tangible sign of that assent was put into the control of the promise, whether or not its contents were actually communicated. By analogy, in the contract-by-letter situation, the offeree's posting of the letter of acceptance, by renouncing control over it, gave that control to the offeror and thereby completed the promise (*Common Law* 239–40).

This performance was quite typical. Again and again throughout his long career, Holmes took the trouble to show that he could "admit any general proposition you like and decide the case either way."[24] It was not that he thought general legal principles meaningless or unimportant; indeed, he was one of the great legal conceptualizers of his age. But he believed that although high-level generalizations could be very useful as presumptions and classificatory devices, they were invariably too vague to dictate particular legal conclusions.

If logical arguments from general principles did not settle hard cases, what did? Holmes was clear and consistent on this point. Left without a definite rule to control them, judges would "legislate," which is to say that they would decide by reference to their beliefs about "what is expedient for the community" (*Common Law* 32), following their "judgment as to the relative worth and importance of competing legislative grounds" ("Path" 397). And where the law failed to provide a determinate rule, judges should legislate, and should do so consciously and explicitly. Thus, because authority had not settled whether the mailbox or the received-and-read rule should govern contract by letter, Holmes thought that "[i]f convenience preponderates in favor of either view, that is a sufficient reason for its adoption" (*Common Law* 239).

One of the bad consequences Holmes saw flowing from orthodox jurisprudence was the temptation it created in jurists to misdescribe the living law as if it corresponded to the imagined dictates of principle. Thus a "characteristic yearning of the German mind" led Bruns, a civilian jurist, to derive property doctrines from "an internal juristic necessity" based on "the nature of possession itself." German statutes that recognized possessory rights in tenants were shunted aside as contrary to principle because Kantian philosophy made intent to own (which tenants lacked) essential to possession. In thus neglecting "the actual course of legislation" and the considerations of "convenience" that lay behind it, Holmes argued that orthodoxy violated "the first call of a theory of law," which was to "fit the facts" (*Common Law* 164–67).

A still worse consequence of orthodoxy was its power to delude judges into thinking that their rulings on politically charged subjects were derived by pure conceptual logic. This allowed them to leave "inarticulate, and often unconscious" the choice between competing policies that really dictated their decisions, all too many of which were based on "the prejudices which judges share with their fellow men" (*Common Law* 5), in this case fellow men who came from the same narrow segment of the community.

Thus it was that English judges allowed concerted boycotts by businesses but found labor boycotts unlawful, unaware that they were ruling on their biased weighting of class interests that were engaged in conflict on a social "field of battle." Believing that they were simply following the logic of the law where it led, they could not see that "judges with different economic sympathies might . . . decide such a case differently."[25]

Holmes concluded his assault on "the fallacy of logical form" in *The Path of the Law* with a surprisingly idealistic assertion of faith in the ability of judges, once freed of orthodox myths, to surmount class prejudices and decide impartially. "If the training of lawyers led them habitually to consider more definitely and explicitly the social advantage on which the rule which they lay down must be justified, they would hesitate where now they are confident, and see that really they were taking sides on burning and debatable issues" ("Path" 398).[26] He tried throughout his long judicial career to uphold this ideal of ideological impartiality in adjudication, and he never wavered in his view that its strongest enemies were the proponents of jurisprudential orthodoxy.

V. The Logic of Easy Cases

Though Holmes could never approve of the notion that a legal system "can be worked out like mathematics from some general axioms of conduct" ("Path"

396), he did think that judges should often decide cases by simple deduction, applying specific rules to definite findings of fact to produce uncontroversial results. Indeed, he believed that this was and should be the way judges decided most cases that came before them. Holmes thought that "judges do and must legislate, but they can do so only interstitially."[27] And, as suggested by the reasons he gave for bringing judges' legislative role out in the open, Holmes thought the interstices should be kept as narrow as possible. In the great mass of cases that did not involve gaps in the law, judges should look for a governing rule and syllogistically apply it. Thus he was always strongly deferential to existing precedents and to the plain meaning of statutes.

Holmes's modest approach to adjudication resulted from his skepticism about the prospects for utilitarian law reform. Because he had little faith that the consequences of competing legislative proposals could be accurately anticipated and then evaluated by reference to often mutable dominant preferences, he thought that "almost the only thing that can be assumed as certainly to be wished is that men should know the rules by which the game will be played."[28] As a result he was "very unwilling to increase the doubt as to what the court will do" by departing from precedent and contrasted his conservatism in this respect with the activist proclivities of those who "regarded our corpus juris as an image, however faint, of the eternal law."[29]

In his opinions, Holmes again and again insisted that the judge is bound to follow the "logic" of rules laid down in legislation or precedent, whether or not he thinks them wise, just, or convenient. Thus in *Olmstead v. United States,* one of the few cases in which he was willing to legislate judicially on an important question, he justified his action on the ground that the question had not been settled in previous decisions; if it had been, the Court would be "confine[d] to logical deduction from established rules."[30] In a Massachusetts case he insisted on following a common law rule established in precedent, even though "the grounds of policy on which it might be justified seem to us to be hard to find, and probably to have belonged to a different state of society."[31] In construing statutes, he wrote that the judicial task was "merely academic to begin with – to read English intelligently – and a consideration of consequences comes into play, if at all, only when the meaning of the words is open to reasonable doubt."[32] And he was not inclined to search hard to find doubts about plain meaning, or when dealing with case law to undermine with ingenious reasoning the evident thrust of precedents.

In fact, Holmes's few judicially creative forays were usually aimed not at any substantive legal reforms, but rather at subjecting areas of law that had previously been left to discretion to the discipline of determinate rules. On the common law side, his best-known reform effort was aimed at supplanting case-by-case jury application of the standard of reasonable care in negligence cases with judicially promulgated rules. Holmes did not think it appropriate that "our rights and duties throughout a great part of the law" should be left to "the necessarily more or less accidental feelings of a jury" (*Common Law* 101). Accordingly he undertook to lay down particular rules for the definition of due care in what he saw as recurring situations. Boston pedestrians were told that a heap of coal on the sidewalk gave them notice as a matter of law of the danger of an open coal hole,[33] and motorists at railroad crossings were told, also on pain of being found negligent as a matter of law, that they must get out of their cars to look up and down the track if they did not have a clear view from the driver's seat.[34]

In only one class of cases did Holmes exercise his ingenuity to widen the interstices left by existing precedent, but this effort too was ultimately in the service of judicial deference to rules laid down elsewhere. Where judge-made Constitutional doctrines limited legislative power, Holmes was quick to look past the (often reasonably clear) immediate precedents to the principles that were said to justify them, principles whose indefinite character he was always ready to emphasize. A vague Constitutional principle left a large penumbra of doubt in its application, and Holmes thought that where reasonable people could differ, the judgment of the legislature, which was possessed of popular sanction and equipped to draw arbitrary lines by virtue of the purely prospective operation of its decisions, deserved to prevail in all but the most extreme cases. The ultimate effect of his campaign against Constitutional judicial activism was to leave in place the enacted rules – the Constitutionally challenged legislation. Even if the substantive content of those rules was, as Holmes often believed, less than beneficial, still he thought it was better to have judges apply duly enacted law than to allow them discretionary authority, especially where they were inclined to exercise it under the illusion that they were following the logical dictates of neutral principles.[35]

On the other hand, in the few cases where Holmes thought the rules had run out, so that the decision could not be made by deduction, he believed in making entirely clear that the decision was legislative, and as such not a matter of logic but an exercise of the judge's "sovereign prerogative of choice." His language in the Olmstead case is characteristic: because the Court was not confined to "logical deduction from established rules," it followed that "we must consider the two objects of desire, both of which we cannot have, and make up our minds which to choose. . . . [F]or my part, I think it a less evil that some criminals should escape than that the Government should play an ignoble part."[36]

In other cases, when Holmes wanted to emphasize that he was exercising choice and not following the dictates of logic, he formulated the rule of decision in exaggeratedly imprecise terms. Thus in *Pennsylvania Coal Co. v. Mahon,* where Holmes was finally willing to invalidate a regulation of private property as a "taking," he laid down the notorious "general rule" that "while property may be regulated to a certain extent, if regulation goes too far it will be recognized as a taking." The question how far was too far was of course "a question of degree – and therefore cannot be disposed of by general propositions." The outcome was announced in distinctly "sovereign prerogative" terms: "[W]e regard this as going beyond any of the cases decided by this Court."[37]

Not only Constitutional and quasi-Constitutional questions such as those involved in *Olmstead* and *Mahon* called forth this kind of aggressively "anti-logical" language. In a simple Massachusetts nuisance case, the issue was whether leakage of acid fumes and sand from one business tenant's premises to those of another on the floor below was actionable. Instead of reciting the standard formula "sic utere tuo ut alienum non laedas" (Use your own property so as not to do harm to anyone else), Holmes made explicit that in cases of conflicting uses of property a "line of adjustment between conflicting rights must be drawn on practical grounds," and that where the line was drawn "may vary under different circumstances." For example, English courts took account of "the national importance of their great manufactures" and instructed juries that "in counties where great works are carried on, parties must not stand on extreme rights."

The general formula on the other side was that the plaintiff "took the risk" of this kind of damage because he had a choice whether or not to rent those particular premises. Holmes declined that gambit as well, pointing out its circularity: "[O]nce it is decided that a certain liability or risk shall be attached to a voluntary relation, the party entering into that relation takes that risk. But what risks shall be attached to any relation is a pure question of policy in the first instance." The real question was not a general one but was rather quite particular: whether there was a "right to invade lower premises with acid fumes and sand, in the mode described, in a manufacturing building, if the aggressor finds it necessary for his business." And the conclusion was again peremptory: "We are not prepared to admit the existence of such a right."[38]

Holmes believed that legislation, including the interstitial kind enacted by judges, was generally based on guesswork, not science or logic. He could imagine a world in which policy decisions were made on the basis of precisely predicted consequences, the value of which was accurately measured, so that legislative decision followed mechanically from the application of the utilitarian calculus. But he was clear that the real world was not like that, and might never be. Conscious effort to guess at consequences and estimate values could sometimes produce better decisions than blind adherence to habit, but in general social decision makers could not accurately foresee the consequences of new policies, and even if they could, there was no precise metric for weighing losses against gains.[39]

As he wrote of the judge-made tort doctrines that preferred the interests of capital to those of labor in boycott cases, "judges do not like to discuss questions of policy," because "the moment you leave the path of merely logical deduction you lose the illusion of certainty which makes legal reasoning seem like mathematics." A question of policy "cannot be answered by generalities," but "the worth of the result, or the gain from allowing it to be done, has to be compared with the loss which it inflicts." Beliefs about the value of those gains and losses were "taught by experience of the interests of life" on society's "fields of battle."[40]

Holmes had in fact shaped his own view of forward-looking practical judgment as a young officer on the battlefields of the Civil War, where human intellectual and moral capacities were dwarfed by the chaos and terror that afflicted every choice, but where duty demanded that choices must be made nonetheless and responsibility taken for them. Though he had moments of optimism about the possibilities for the progress of the law through rational reform,[41] he also had an existentialist side that saw this duty of decision as a commitment "blindly accepted," like a soldier's absurdly noble duty to go forward "in a cause which he little understands, in a plan of campaign of which he has no notion, under tactics of which he does not see the use."[42]

In law, as in the war for which law was the civilized alternative, it was often a comfort and a practical blessing to be subject to a rule (or a superior's order) whose interpretation required only understanding the words of the language. But where no such rule applied, the judge should understand that, like a soldier operating beyond the scope of his orders, he faced an existential situation and had to "make up [his] mind upon a living question at [his] peril, for purposes of action."[43] This was Holmes's dominant view, simple if crude, an essentially military conception of the judicial task.

As a somewhat hyperbolic corrective to the Blackstonian myth so dominant in his time, it was bracing and effective. If he had held such a view without qualification, though, it would be properly subject to the critique implicit in the old saw that military justice is to justice as military music is to music. As we shall see, Holmes did soften and qualify his martial view by giving to the informal logic of principle and analogy a role in the adjudicative process that mediated between the otherwise starkly opposed alternatives of mechanical deduction and sovereign legislative choice.

VI. Legal Systematics, Principles, and Standards

Holmes's main point against classical orthodoxy was that general principles cannot decide concrete cases. Why, then, have them at all? Later on, legal realists would argue that the generalities only provided emotive ammunition to advocates and logical cover for judges,[44] and that they should be swept away and the law should be rearranged according to "narrow categories" and real-world situations.[45]

Though many realists took Holmes as their progenitor, he would not have agreed with this aspect of their program. He devoted his early legal career to a reclassification of the common law into substantive categories designed to replace both the rough-and-ready practical pigeonholes of the vanishing writ system and the loose taxonomy of law into personal and property rights used by Blackstone and Kent. Holmes's first significant piece of legal scholarship,

"Codes and the Arrangement of the Law," argued for the necessity of a system of "philosophical" (i.e., abstract) legal categories and principles that could be used in the exposition of any legal system.[46] Later, his historical studies convinced him that each body of law had evolved in so path dependent a way that the pursuit of a "useless quintessence of all systems" should be replaced by "an accurate anatomy of one" ("Path" 403).

Holmes's aim in *The Common Law* was just such an anatomy, a structured and logical exposition that could rival the great synthetic works performed by civilian scholars on the body of Roman law. "The business of the jurist," Holmes wrote, was "to make known the content of the law; that is to work upon it from within, or logically, arranging and distributing it, in order, from its summum genus to its infima species, so far as practicable" (*Common Law* 173, see also 64–65). He classified the common law into the primary categories of crime, tort, property, contracts, and succession,[47] and within each category suggested simplifying concepts and principles meant to help organize established doctrines and bring out the history and policies behind them. Perhaps his most impressive achievement along these lines was his organization of the nascent common law of torts around the negligence action (treating negligence objectively as conduct rather than as a state of mind), with the array of traditional causes of action distributed into two peripheral categories, intent on one side, and strict liability on the other (*Common Law* 63–129). His ultimate ambition was to reduce the whole of tort law to a "philosophically continuous series," with the categories of fraud, malice, intent, and negligence all analyzed along the single dimension of the degree of objective risk of harm created by an action, given the circumstances known to the actor (*Common Law* 104).[48]

In his project of arranging and reformulating the substance of the common law, Holmes insisted that the categories used should be abstract and general, and specialized to the law rather than drawn from practical life. He inveighed against the proliferation of digests and textbooks on "practical" subjects such as "railroads or telegraphs," or "historical subdivisions" such as "shipping or equity." In his mind, private law was properly divided into the abstract categories of contract and tort ("Path" 403).

How did Holmes reconcile his devotion to abstract systematization of the law with his insistence that general principles do not decide concrete cases? The answer was that the categories, concepts, and principles of high-level doctrine were not meant to decide cases, in the sense of supplying major premises from which answers to concrete legal questions could be deduced given findings of objective fact. The purpose of the taxonomy was to arrange doctrine in such a way as "to make the law easier to be remembered and to be understood" ("Path" 391).[49]

Thus it turned out that contracts to sell land, labor, and goods were all governed by substantive legal rules that shared a good deal of content, so it made sense to classify them together and formulate their shared elements as general principles of contract law. Creating a new legal category in this way would draw attention to the idiosyncratic features of previously separate doctrines and would create pressure to smooth out anomalies up to the point at which genuine policy grounds justified separate treatment, taking account of the rule-of-law virtue of transparency through simplicity.[50]

Here we see logic, in the sense of taxonomy or rational classification, operating as a "force" on the law – through what Holmes, borrowing from Spencer's account of "integration," regarded as a progressive "evolutionary process." "[T]he generalizing principle will prevail," he predicted of his own favorite project of reducing tort law to a few principles, "as generalization so often prevails, even in advance of evidence, because of the ease of mind and comfort which it brings."[51] And for this reason "[t]he law constantly is tending towards consistency of theory."[52] Logic in the sense of rational taxonomy pressed the body of doctrine in the direction of a kind of consistency that had more to do with simplicity and uniformity than with deduction or the absence of contradiction.

Holmes's reference to pedagogic motives, "ease of mind and comfort," as the rewards that drive the progress of "the generalizing tendency" reminds us of his well-known psychological diagnosis of the appeal of classical orthodoxy in *The Path of the Law*. Holmes said there that lawyers were tempted by the Langdellian siren song because "the logical method and form flatter that longing for certainty and repose that is in every human mind." Against this powerful temptation he rhetorically counterposed the rigorous appeal of the strenuous life, urging that "certainty generally is illusion, and repose is not the destiny of man" (396–97).

Juxtaposing the passages on "the generalizing tendency" and "the logical fallacy," we can see that Holmes thought the fallacy involved simply an excessive indulgence in the (otherwise laudable) tendency. To generalize and simplify a legal system so as to make its requirements easier to learn, understand, and apply, advanced the rule of law. And it was also good to smooth out discrepancies exposed by the amalgamation of previously separate bodies of doctrine. But insofar as the generalizing impulse only served the psychological and aesthetic needs of lawyers and jurists, it should yield to substantive convenience.[53] And in any event, absolute certainty and repose are false goals, and reasonable predictability is more likely to come from the enactment of specific and often relatively arbitrary rules than from the systematizing work of abstract conceptual jurisprudence.

So far I have treated the general categories and concepts of the law as if they served only a classificatory purpose for Holmes. But general legal concepts are typically put to work in legal principles, which take the form of directives and are cited by judges in justification of decisions. Holmes did not believe that principles generally dictate results in cases, but he did give them normative force, as presumptions or guidelines that could properly incline a judge toward one side of a case.

Thus in the *Lochner* dissent, when Holmes said that "general principles do not decide concrete cases," he had himself just stated the general principle that a "[c]onstitution is not intended to embody a particular economic theory, whether of paternalism and the organic relation of the citizen to the state, or of laissez faire." Though the principle did not decide the case, if given proper weight it could "carry us far toward the end." And indeed it established a presumption that Holmes relied on in arguing for the constitutionality of the maximum-hour law for bakery workers.[54]

So it was with the doctrinal principles of private law for which Holmes contended throughout *The Common Law*. He argued vigorously that, for example, the standard of liability in the typical case of accidental injury should be objective negligence rather than either strict liability, on the one side, or actual subjective fault on the other (66–89, 73).[55] But these three competing standards were just that, standards; they were not precise rules, and so on Holmes's theory could not dictate results. Holmes would no doubt say of these standards what he had said about general principles, that he could decide any particular case either way under any of the three of them. And yet he certainly believed that they had guiding force, so that it mattered to the overall run of outcomes which standard was chosen.

Holmes's legal universe thus contained both general principles and openended standards, which supplied reasons for the decision of cases that fell within their scope. This point blurs the stark battlefield dichotomy he sometimes posed between the mass of decisions that followed deductively from the rules laid down and the few decisions in which judges exercised their sovereign prerogative of choice. The doctrinal principles and standards that he worked so hard to formulate through the early years of his legal career did not leave him uninfluenced during his half century on the bench.[56] Though he did not always acknowledge it, judges had available to them a middle ground between strict rule bondage and absolute freedom, an area in which the choice of rule might be influenced but not dictated by a principle, or a decision guided but not determined by a general standard.

VII. Analogy and Local Consistency

In Holmes's legal theory, principles and standards emerged in the doctrinal enterprise of formulating general legal categories and concepts, an enterprise meant to make the law easier to remember and understand. He saw the work of systematization as being done mostly by legal theorists and doctrinal commentators. Judges, on the front line resolving practical disputes, could not often afford to devote time and energy to readjusting the larger doctrinal structure.[57]

Still, judges could be influenced in reaching particular decisions by arguments derived from that structure, as Holmes was influenced to dissent in *Lochner* by the principle he cited there, and ultimately by the Constitutional theory that lay behind it. Similarly, an American common law judge with formalist leanings might be convinced by Langdell's theoretical case for the logical necessity of the received-and-read rule, or a German judge might construe a statute to reject a possessory action by a tenant on the basis of Bruns's argument that to allow it would violate Kantian first principles. In these examples, both the pragmatist Holmes and the American or German formalist would find "logic," in the sense of the overall consistency of the law working as a force on particular decisions, though only the formalists would believe that their decisions followed deductively from the law conceived as a system.[58]

In other cases, and much more commonly, Holmes recognized that judges are influenced not by arguments derived from an overall legal system or theory of law, but by coherence-based arguments of a less global kind, arguments based on analogy. These are claims that consistency with decisions and doctrines in the taxonomic vicinity of the case at hand press toward one outcome rather than another.[59] For Holmes, a lawyer's "training in logic" included practice in "analogy and discrimination" as well as "deduction" (which implicitly included conceptual analysis) ("Path" 397). Yet analogy lacked the certainty of deductive or analytical reasoning; in cases that had "certain analogies on one side and other analogies on the other," the honest judge had to recognize that "the simple tool of logic"[60] was not sufficient to dictate decision.[61]

While analogies did not typically give certainty, they did offer a mode of reasoning that was distinct from forward-looking policy balancing, and that was "logical," in the sense that it rested on a search for internal consistency. Indeed, an argument from analogy had force similar to that of an argument from principle of the sort considered in Section VI of this chapter; it supplied a presumption, a directive guiding decision where other things were equal.

Holmes illustrated the use of analogy in *Fairbanks v. Snow*, a Massachusetts case that posed the question of whether duress of a promisor by a third party was a good defense to a contract claim by a promisee who had no notice of the duress.[62] The law was clear that where the promisee's claim was fraud by a third party rather than duress by a third party, notice to the otherwise innocent promisee was required to establish the defense. Holmes argued that the analogy was controlling; both defenses were based on the subjection of the defendant to "an improper motive for action" – false belief in one case, and fear in the other. A defense based on the promisor's motives should not defeat the claim of a promisee who "neither knows them nor is responsible for their existence."[63] The similarity Holmes saw between the two doctrines led him to give a restrictive interpretation to precedents that could have been read to allow duress as a defense even in the absence of notice. He wrote to Frederick Pollock that to decide *Fairbanks* as he did, he had had to "get away" from the precedents, so as to "establish what principle and analogy required."[64] He did not treat his decision as resting on ineluctable reasoning, nor did he try to show that the principle governing third-party fraud and duress flowed from some larger doctrinal framework.

Holmes went out of his way to stress the logical as against the legislative character of argument by analogy in *Kepner v. United States,* one of his first Constitutional dissents after he joined the U.S. Supreme Court. The Court held that to allow a retrial after a successful government appeal from a verdict of acquittal on the ground of misdirection would be to put the defendant in jeopardy twice. Holmes alluded to a policy ground that could support his dissent: "At the present time in this country there is more danger that criminals will escape justice than that they will be subjected to tyranny." But then he elaborately disavowed reliance on it: "[S]uch considerations are not supposed to be entertained by judges, except as inclining them to one of two interpretations, or as a tacit last resort in case of doubt."[65]

He argued instead that allowing the government appeal followed by analogy (and so followed "logically and rationally") from the established doctrine that the double jeopardy doctrine did not bar retrial of a defendant whose conviction had been reversed on his own claim of error. Against the analogy – the standard distinction that where the defendant raised the claim of error, he waived his claim of former jeopardy – Holmes argued that this rested on pure fiction: "Usually no such waiver is expressed or thought of." Further, if the Constitutional right against double jeopardy were really at stake, it would be wrong to force a defendant to waive that right as a condition of appealing his conviction on the basis of a legal error in his trial.[66] Holmes's analogical argument was based on logic in the sense of consistency with doctrines prevailing in closely related cases, but he made no pretense that he was deducing his result from an established rule, or that in reaching the opposite conclusion the majority justices were "not doing their sums right" ("Path" 396). And again, he made no claim that consistency with some overall doctrinal framework favored his side of the dispute.

In *Gompers v. United States,* the main issue was whether a residual federal three-year statute of limitations applied in cases of criminal contempt. Holmes thought it did apply in terms but admitted that the interpretation was debatable and added an analogical argument. Even if the statute did not directly apply, still "[t]he power to punish for contempt must have some limit in time, and in defining that limit we should have regard to what has been the policy of the law from the foundation of the Government." Therefore, "by analogy if not by enactment the limit is three years." Though analytical and deductive logic did not dictate three years as the limit, the informal logic of analogy favored it over the alternatives. In some cases where the penumbras of competing concepts overlapped, Holmes sometimes thought logic left the issue in equipoise, so that a judge could only legislate. But in other cases of conflict between vague principles or standards, a prior decision along the same continuum could provide a basis for argument *a fortiori,* a form of analogical reasoning, and so avoid the need for arbitrary judicial line drawing. "The line which is drawn must be justified by the fact that it is a little nearer than the nearest opposing case to one pole of an admitted antithesis."[67] Logic does not dictate when day ends and night begins, but if a particular hour has been set as within nighttime, a later hour cannot (other things being equal) consistently be considered daytime.

Like principles and standards, analogies did not fit into the simplified military version Holmes sometimes gave of his judicial universe, in which all decisions were either a matter of rigidly following orders, on the one hand, or free legislative choices on the other. And yet he often argued analogically in judicial opinions – in contexts where it was clear he regarded this form of argument as less certain than deduction, but as involving consistency with past decisions more than forward-looking policy prescription. Again, we see that Holmes recognized a middle ground between rule-governed decision and legislation, a ground occupied by the informal logical tools of analogies, principles, and standards. And as already mentioned, in theoretical writings as well we find him acknowledging that the lawyer's training in "logic" encompassed not only "deduction" but "analogy and discrimination" ("Path" 397).

Decisions driven in the three ways we have reviewed – by rules, by principles, and by analogies – were all in different but related senses based on legal logic as Holmes saw it. The senses differed: rules were logical because they dictated results by deduction; even inexact but principled reasoning was based on the logical enterprise of systematic taxonomy; analogies were logical though neither determinative nor systematic. The unifying thread was the appeal to internal coherence or consistency among decisions (and their grounds), as distinguished from the legislative criterion, which was external, the correspondence of the decision and its consequences with the dominant desires of the community. A deduction serves consistency because its negation implies a contradiction. Conceptual legal systematics promotes the simplicity and transparency of the whole of the law and thereby helps to enable the detection and correction of inconsistency over the whole field. An argument by analogy says that when case A is more like case B than case C, it should be decided by the rationale of case B, in order to comply with the requirement of consistency that like cases should be decided alike.

VIII. Formalizing the Informal?

Both in his essay in the present volume (Chapter 5) and elsewhere, Scott Brewer has pursued a project of making explicit what he calls the "logical form" of the nondeductive modes of argument found in judicial opinions and other legal contexts.[68] Among these are arguments based on induction and Peircian "abduction," and arguments by analogy, which Brewer further analyzes as a complex sequence of abduction, reflective adjustment, and deduction.

The question is whether the game is worth the candle. In defense of his project, Brewer argues that Holmes could have avoided the confusion created by the disparate senses he gives to the term "logic" if he had been equipped with a taxonomy and expository apparatus that made explicit the different logical forms used in informal legal argument. I am a bit doubtful, as I do not see that Holmes's variations in usage, analyzed here, are likely to confuse readers who approach them alert to context.

In a letter to Felix Frankfurter, Holmes commented on Hohfeld's schema of legal relations in a way that raises the doubts one naturally has about the utility of regularly taking the trouble to formalize the not-exactly-rocket-science kinds of arguments that lawyers and judges commonly make.

I must admit . . . that I saw but limited advantage in the elaboration of cycles and epicycles. Like the rules of logic or good manners or painting, they may help to make an insight articulate once in a while, but the idea of bothering oneself with all that hocuspocus for daily purpose seems to me superfluous. You don't learn to reason, or behave, or paint, in that way. A man of accurate thoughts will have avoided the pitfalls without the guides.[69]

But against this, many have thought that Hohfeld's disaggregation of the intuitive but vague legal notions of "right" and "duty" really did usefully change the angle of vision from which lawyers saw important substantive legal issues.[70] With his appeal to the virtues of "defamiliarization"[71] Brewer suggests that similar gains may await us if we follow his lead and try to formalize modes of argument that we have previously left informal. The proof will come when the logical apparatus gives us fresh insights into real legal problems.

Notes

1 Oliver Wendell Holmes, review (1879) of Christopher Columbus Langdell, *A Summary of the Law of Contracts* (Boston: Little, Brown, 1880) (hereafter "Langdell review"), in *The Collected Works of Oliver Wendell Holmes,* ed. Sheldon Novick (Chicago: University of Chicago Press, 1995), vol. 3, 102 (hereafter "CW"); Oliver Wendell Holmes, *The Common Law* (1881), ed. Mark Howe (Cambridge, Mass.: Harvard University Press, 1963), 5 (hereafter "*Common Law*"). I cite writings in Novick's *Collected Works* by title, original date, and page, except for *The Common Law,* which I cite to the more accessible Howe edition.
2 Holmes to Frederick Pollock, 10 April 1881, *Holmes–Pollock Letters,* ed. Mark Howe (Cambridge, Mass.: Harvard University Press, 1941), 1, 17.
3 O. W. Holmes, "The Path of the Law" (1897), in CW, vol. 3, 391, 396–98 (cited hereafter parenthetically in the text as "Path" with page number). ("The Path" is reprinted in the Appendix to this volume with star paging.) On how this passage fits into the overall structure of the essay, see Thomas C. Grey, "Plotting 'The Path of the Law,'" *Brooklyn Law Review* 63 (1997):19, 22–25.
4 *Lochner v. New York,* 198 U.S. 45, 76 (1905) (dissenting opinion).
5 *Noble State Bank v. Haskell,* 210 U.S. 104, 110 (1911).

6 Scott Brewer, "Traversing Holmes's Path toward a Jurisprudence of Logical Form," Chapter 5 of this volume.
7 The present essay resurveys in somewhat more detail, and with changes that take account of Brewer's fruitful suggestions, the terrain that I earlier mapped in Thomas C. Grey, "Holmes and Legal Pragmatism," *Stanford Law Review* 41 (1989):787, 816–26.
8 "[T]he whole outline of the law is the resultant of a conflict at every point between logic and good sense – the one striving to work fiction out to consistent results; the other restraining and at last overcoming that effort when the results become too manifestly unjust." Oliver Wendell Holmes, "Agency" (1891), in CW, vol. 3, 340, 341.
9 "It is something to show that the consistency of a system requires a particular result, but it is not all." *Common Law*, 5.
10 And there may have been other senses not particularly relevant to legal theory. As Brewer notes, Holmes sometimes uses "logical" as a simple synonym for "rational" or "sensible" and also describes the assumption of universal causality as presupposing (Kant-style?) the operation of "logic."
11 In Ronald Dworkin's terminology, legal reasoning that was "logical" in any of Holmes's three senses would be consistent with "integrity," whereas reasoning that was "legislative" or "practical" in Holmes's sense would be "pragmatic" (and hence, according to Dworkin, not properly judicial). Ronald Dworkin, *Law's Empire* (Cambridge, Mass.: Harvard University Press, 1986), 176–275. Dworkin's distinction between "local integrity" and more general integrity (250–54) roughly corresponds to the distinction between Holmes's second and third (systematic and analogical) special senses of "logical" legal reasoning. Holmes's overall theory of adjudication was "pragmatic" in Dworkin's sense, in that Holmes treated coherence (Dworkin's "integrity") not as a side constraint but as a goal to be pursued for its instrumental (heuristic) value. See note 49 and the accompanying text.
12 H. L. A. Hart, "Positivism and the Separation of Law and Morals," *Harvard Law Review* 71 (1958):593, 610.
13 H. L. A. Hart, *The Concept of Law* (Oxford: Clarendon Press, 1961), 124–25.
14 Hart, "Positivism," 611.
15 "[T]o make a general principle worth anything, you must give it a body; you must show in what way and how far it would be applied actually in an actual system; you must show how it has gradually emerged as the felt reconciliation of concrete instances no one of which established it in terms." Oliver Wendell Holmes, "The Use of Law Schools" (1886), in CW, vol. 3, 474, 477.
16 The modern development of the idea of "nonclassical" concepts stems from Wittgenstein's celebrated account of the concept "game" as involving not necessary and sufficient conditions shared by all of its applications, but rather "family resemblances" among them. From this Wittgenstein drew the lesson that the structure of a concept could not be assumed to be classical; the investigator had to "look and see." Ludwig Wittgenstein, *Philosophical Investigations* (Oxford: Blackwell, 1963), vol. 1, 66–67. Wittgenstein's view of concepts, like Holmes's, was pragmatic: "Language is an instrument. Its concepts are instruments. Concepts lead us to make investigations; are the expression of our interest, and direct our interest" (569–70). For empirical work on the shape of concepts following Wittgenstein's lead, see *Categories and Concepts,* ed. Edward Smith and Douglas Medin (Cambridge, Mass.: Harvard University Press, 1981); George Lakoff, *Women, Fire, and*

Dangerous Things: What Categories Reveal about the Mind (Chicago: University of Chicago Press, 1987).
17 For more on this point, see Thomas C. Grey, "Molecular Motions: The Holmesian Judge in Theory and Practice," *William and Mary Law Review* 37 (1995):19, 43–44.
18 For a full account, see Thomas C. Grey, "Langdell's Orthodoxy," *University of Pittsburgh Law Review* 45 (1983):1.
19 See Holmes, *Common Law,* 32; Grey, "Holmes and Legal Pragmatism," 818–19.
20 A good example of a conservative activist judge animated by natural law theory was Holmes's predecessor as chief justice of the Supreme Judicial Court of Massachusetts, Walbridge Abner Field. See Oliver Wendell Holmes, "Walbridge Abner Field" (1899), in CW vol. 3, 494, 496 ("[H]e seemed to me to conceive of the law as ideally, at least, embodying absolute right. It was part of the same habit of mind that he should be free to the point of innovation in applying convenient analogies to new cases"). Holmes's great contemporary, Thomas Cooley, both as Constitutional commentator and judge, was a conservative activist who adopted a positivistic legal-science approach to the ascertainment of overriding legal principles.
21 Cf. Ernest Weinrib, *The Idea of Private Law* (Cambridge, Mass.: Harvard University Press, 1995), 5 ("Private law, I will claim, is to be grasped only from within and not as the juridical manifestation of a set of extrinsic purposes. If we must express this intelligibility in terms of purpose, the only thing to be said is that the purpose of private law is to be private law").
22 *Lochner,* 198 U.S., at 76.
23 Christopher Columbus Langdell, *A Summary of the Law of Contracts,* 2d ed. (Boston: Little, Brown, 1880), 15, 20–21.
24 Holmes to Harold Joseph Laski, 2 February 1920, in *Holmes–Laski Letters,* vol. 1, 243.
25 Oliver Wendell Holmes, "Privilege, Malice, and Intent" (1894), in CW, vol. 3, 370, 375–76 ("When socialism first began to be talked about, the comfortable classes of *the community were a good deal frightened. I suspect that this fear has influenced judicial action both here and in England, yet it is certain it is not a conscious factor in the decisions to which I refer.") See also "Path," 398.
26 See also *Vegelahn v. Guntner,* 167 Mass. 92, 107, 44 N.E. 1077 (1896) (dissenting from labor injunction on the ground that the law's policy favoring "the free struggle for life . . . is not limited to struggles between persons of the same class competing for the same end"); Oliver Wendell Holmes, "Law and the Court" (1913), in CW, vol. 3, 505, 507:
    It is a misfortune if a judge reads his unconscious or conscious sympathy with one side or the other prematurely into the law, and forgets that what seems to him to be first principles are believed by half his fellow men to be wrong. When twenty years ago a vague terror went over the earth and the word socialism began to be heard, I thought and still think that fear was translated into doctrines that had no place in the Constitution or common law. Judges are apt to be naif, simple-minded men, and they need something of Mephistopheles.
27 244 U.S. 205, 221 (1917). I say more about Holmes's pervasive judicial deference to precedent and legislation in "Molecular Motions," 26–33.
28 Oliver Wendell Holmes, "Holdsworth's English Law," in CW, vol. 3, 434, 436.
29 Oliver Wendell Holmes, "Address: Banquet of the Middlesex Bar Association" (1902), in CW, vol. 3, 535, 536. Holmes probably had in mind Chief Justice Field (see note 20).
30 *Olmstead v. United States,* 277 U.S. 438, 469–470 (1928) (dissenting opinion).
31 *Dempsey v. Chambers,* 154 Mass. 330, 331–332, 28 N.E. 279, 280 (1891).

32 *Northern Securities Co. v. United States,* 193 U.S. 197, 400 (1903) (dissenting opinion).
33 *Lorenzo v. Wirth,* 170 Mass. 596, 49 N.E. 1010 (1898).
34 *Baltimore and Ohio R.R. Co. v. Goodman,* 275 U.S. 66 (1927).
35 Holmes reiterated this pattern of decision in dozens of opinions over his long career, from *Hubbard v. City of Taunton,* 140 Mass. 467, 5 N.E. 157 (1886) (municipal ordinance consistent with state statute: "We know of no simple and merely logical test by which the limit can be fixed. It must be determined by practical considerations. The question is one of degree"), to *Baldwin v. Missouri,* 286 U.S. 586, 595 (1930) (dissenting opinion) ("[W]e . . . should be slow to construe the [due process] clause in the Fourteenth Amendment as committing the Court, with no guide but the Court's own discretion, to the validity of whatever laws the states may pass").
36 *Olmstead,* 277 U.S. 438, at 470.
37 *Pennsylvania Coal Co. v. Mahon,* 260 U.S. 393, 416 (1922). Holmes once wrote in a letter, "[T]he present swing toward government activity is exaggerated – . . . it expects too much, and will lead to things being worse done. But the only limits I would fix are practical, not logical." Holmes to Laski, 12 September 1916, in *Holmes–Laski Letters,* vol. 1, 243.
38 *Boston Ferrule Co. v. Hills,* 159 Mass. 147, 150–51, 34 N.E. 85 (1893).
39 "Propositions as to public policy rarely are unanimously accepted, and still more rarely, if ever, are capable of unanswerable proof." *Vegelahn v. Guntner,* 167 Mass. 92, 105, 44 N.E. 1077 (1896). "[I]t is for science to determine, so far as it can, the relative worth of our different social ends. . . . Very likely it may be that with all the help statistics and every modern appliance can bring us there never will be a commonwealth in which science is everywhere supreme. But it is an ideal, and without ideals what is life worth?" Oliver Wendell Holmes, "Law in Science and Science in Law" (1899), in CW, vol. 3, 406, 420.
40 Holmes, "Privilege," 370, 375; 373; 373; 375–76.
41 Most of the things we do, we do for no better reason than that our fathers have done them, or that our neighbors do them, and the same is true of a larger part than we suspect of what we think. The reason is a good one, because our short life gives us no better, but it is not the best. It does not follow, because we all are compelled to take on faith at second hand most of the rules on which we base our action and our thought, that each of us may not try to set some corner of his world in the order of reason, or that all of us collectively should not aspire to carry reason as far as it will go throughout the whole domain. ("Path" 398–99)
42 Oliver Wendell Holmes, "The Soldier's Faith" (1895), in CW, vol. 3, 486, 487.
43 "Law in Science," 412.
44 See Max Radin, "The Theory of Judicial Decision: Or, How Judges Think," *American Bar Association Journal* 11 (1925):357.
45 For the "narrow-category" aspect of the realist program, see Karl Llewellyn, "Some Realism about Realism," *Harvard Law Review* 44 (1931):1222.
46 Oliver Wendell Holmes, "Codes, and the Arrangement of the Law" (1870), in CW, vol. 1, 212.
47 Holmes may have adopted the categories used in Sir Henry Maine, *Ancient Law* (London: John Murray, 1869), whose concluding chapters take up "successions," "property," "contracts," and "delict and crime" in that order. See also the extensive tables and accompanying notes on the arrangement of the law in John Austin, *Lectures on Jurisprudence,* ed. Sarah Austin (London: John Murray, 1861), vol. 2, 916–88, which certainly also influenced him.
48 Cf. "Privilege," 370, 371–72 ("The law of torts as now administered has worked itself into

a general theory"); "Path," 400–401 ("Take the law of tort.... Is there any theory for such liability, or are the cases in which it exists simply to be enumerated...? I think there is a general theory to be discovered, though resting in tendency rather than established and accepted"); "Law in Science," 411–12 (describing integration of tort law from discrete and unrelated causes of action to "a true living branch of the Common Law," though it would be "bold" to say "that the integration was complete, that it did not rest partly in tendency"). Tort law as conventionally presented today is actually less integrated than Holmes conceived it, as we have never followed his suggestion that we unite negligence with all of the traditional tort actions, many of which require intent, to form the "philosophically continuous series" that he advocated.

49 See also Langdell review:
[I]t is to be remembered that the book is published for use at a law school, and that for that purpose dogmatic teaching is a necessity, if anything is to be taught within the limited time of a student's course. A professor must start with a system as an arbitrary fact, and the most which can be hoped for is to make the student see how it hangs together, and thus to send him into practice with something more than a rag-bag of details. (104)

And see "Law in Science":
I sometimes tell students that the law schools pursue an inspirational combined with a logical method, that is, the postulates are taken for granted upon authority without inquiry into their worth, and then logic is used as the only tool to develop the results. It is a necessary method for the purpose of teaching dogma. (414)

50 See Holmes's discussion of the relatively recent creation of the general category "contract" to cover what had previously been disparate doctrines, in "Law in Science" (409).
51 Ibid., 411–12.
52 *Hanson v. Globe Newspaper Co.,* 159 Mass. 293, 302, 34 N.E. 462 (1893).
53 Holmes stressed the aesthetic, and hence in practical terms relatively trivial, virtues of the ideal of system in the law by calling it "elegantia juris," or legal elegance (Langdell review, 103).
54 *Lochner,* 198 U.S., at 75. See the more extended discussion in Grey, "Holmes and Legal Pragmatism," 820–21.
55 I distinguish (conventionally) between a legal principle and a standard as follows. Both are legal directives stated at a level of generality or vagueness that requires a further act of judgment or specification before they can determine the outcome of a case when applied to a given set of facts; this distinguishes both from a rule. A *standard,* such as "reasonable care" for negligence cases, is the primary criterion for decision of a case, and the further specification or exercise of judgment required for its application is left tacit. A *principle,* by contrast, is a higher-level criterion used in the justification of more particularized (but still general) legal directives. Hence the principle invoked in *Lochner,* to the effect that choices in political economy are not generally made in our system at the Constitutional level, was cited in justification of the more particular doctrine permitting maximum-hour laws in bakeries that Holmes thought should have decided the case.
56 In a valuable study, Patrick Kelley details Holmes's persistent but only sporadically successful judicial efforts to inject the doctrinal theories he had worked out in *The Common Law* into the case of law of his state. See Patrick Kelley, "Holmes on the Supreme Judicial Court: The Theorist as Judge," in *The History of the Law in Massachusetts: The Supreme Judicial Court, 1692–1992,* ed. Russell Osgood (Boston: Supreme Court Historical Society, 1992), 275–352.
57 "I ask myself, what is there to show for this half lifetime that has passed?... I... find

about a thousand cases, many of them upon trifling or transitory matters . . . when one would have liked to . . . generalize it all and write it in continuous, logical, philosophical exposition, setting forth the whole corpus with its roots in history and its justifications of expedience real or supposed!" Oliver Wendell Holmes, "Speech to the Bar Association of Boston" (1900), in CW, vol. 3, 498.

58 Holmes was particularly prone to give high-level theoretical justifications for concrete decisions in cases where he could oppose his own positivist jurisprudential views to the natural law overtones he often detected in orthodox doctrinal arguments and formulations. See *Kawananakoa v. Polyblank,* 205 U.S. 347, 353 (1907); *American Banana Co. v. United Fruit Co.,* 213 U.S. 347, 357–358 (1909); *Kuhn v. Fairmont Coal Co.,* 215 U.S. 349, 372 (1910); *Southern Pacific v. Jensen,* 244 U.S. 205, 221–222 (1916) (dissenting opinion); *The Western Maid,* 257 U.S. 419, 432 (1921); *Black and White Taxicab Co. v. Brown and Yellow Taxicab Co.,* 276 U.S. 518, 533–535 (1928) (dissenting opinion).

59 Cass Sunstein suggests some interesting reasons why it might sometimes be desirable for judges to decide on grounds that are "incompletely theorized" and yet not straightforwardly legislative – and how argument by analogy fits this description. See Cass Sunstein, *Legal Reasoning and Political Conflict* (New York: Oxford University Press, 1995), esp. 91–100.

60 "Law in Science," 418–19.

61 Compare the discussions of analogy by Austin, Holmes's primary teacher in legal theory, in Austin, *Lectures on Jurisprudence,* vol. 2, 638–41, 1001–20. Austin wrote that where no rule of the system controlled a case, "the judge virtually makes one," deriving it from "custom" or "a maxim of international law," or "his own views of what the law ought to be" (639), but

> perhaps, mostly commonly . . . he derives the new rule by a consequence built on analogy, from a rule or rules already part of the system. And it is to the creation of law thus derived from pre-existing law, that the competition of opposite analogies to which judicial legislation is liable, is peculiarly, if not exclusively, incident. (639)

62 *Fairbanks v. Snow,* 145 Mass. 153, 13 N.E. 596 (1887).

63 Ibid., at 154.

64 Holmes to Frederick Pollock, 4 March 1888, in *Holmes–Pollock Letters,* vol. 1, 32.

65 *Kepner v. United States,* 195 U.S. 100, 134 (1904) (dissenting opinion). The case actually involved the application of a federal statute passed for the governance of the Philippines, but because it incorporated the double jeopardy prohibition, the Court's construction would be binding for domestic constitutional cases.

66 Ibid., 135.

67 *Haddock v. Haddock,* 201 U.S. 562, 628 (1905). See also *Pennsylvania Coal,* 260 U.S. 393, 416:

> As we already have said, this is a question of degree – and therefore cannot be disposed of by general propositions. But we regard this as going beyond any of the cases decided by this Court. The late [rent control] decisions upon laws dealing with the congestion of Washington and New York, caused by the war, dealt with laws intended to meet a temporary emergency and providing for compensation determined to be reasonable by an impartial board. They went to the verge of the law but fell far short of the present case.

68 In addition to Chapter 5, see Scott Brewer, "Exemplary Reasoning: Semantics, Pragmatics, and the Rational Force of Legal Argument by Analogy," *Harvard Law Review* 109 (1996):925.

69 Holmes to Felix Frankfurter, 20 February 1922, in *Holmes and Frankfurter: Their Cor-*

respondence, 1912–1934, ed. Robert Mennel and Christine Compston (Hanover, N.H.: University Press of New England, 1996), 136.
70 See Walter Wheeler Cook, "Privileges of Labor Unions in the Struggle for Life," *Yale Law Journal* 27 (1918):779; Walter Wheeler Cook, "The Associated Press Case," *Yale Law Journal* 28 (1919):347; and Morton Horwitz, *The Transformation of American Law, 1870–1960* (Cambridge, Mass.: Harvard University Press, 1992), 151, 156.
71 Chapter 5, section II.C.2.

7

Holmes versus Hart
The Bad Man in Legal Theory

STEPHEN R. PERRY

I. Theory versus Anti-Theory

In *The Path of the Law* Oliver Wendell Holmes advances a number of propositions about the law that have a distinctly theoretical flavor to them. The following six seem to be the principal ones:

1. Law is properly characterized in terms of prediction; more particularly, it is to be characterized by reference to predictions about the use of court-sanctioned force. "The object of our study, then, is prediction, the prediction of the incidence of the public force through the instrumentality of the courts" (457).[1] "The prophecies of what the courts will do in fact, and nothing more pretentious, are what I mean by the law" (461).
2. Law is properly characterized from the point of view of what Holmes calls the "bad man." "If you want to know the law and nothing else, you must look at it as a bad man, who cares only for the material consequences which such knowledge enables him to predict, and not as a good one, who finds his reasons for conduct, whether inside the law or outside of it, in the vaguer sanctions of conscience" (459).
3. The predictions mentioned in proposition 1, or at least the means for making these predictions, are found in case reports, statutes, and legal treatises. "In these sybylline leaves are gathered the scattered prophecies of the past upon the cases in which the axe will fall. These are what properly have been called the oracles of the law" (457). "The number of our predictions when generalized and reduced to a system is not unmanageably large. They present themselves as a finite body of dogma which may be mastered within a reasonable period of time" (458).
4. Rights and duties, as well as the law itself, are to be understood as predictions of the incidence of the use of public force. "[A] legal duty so called is nothing but a prediction that if a man does or omits certain things he will be made to suffer in this way or that by judgment of the court; – and so of a legal right" (458).

5. Law is, in some sense, distinct from morality. "The first thing for a businesslike understanding of the matter is to understand its limits, and therefore I think it desirable at once to point out and dispel a confusion between morality and law" (459). "[N]othing but confusion of thought can result from assuming that the rights of man in a moral sense are equally rights in the sense of the Constitution and the law" (460).
6. It is a fallacy to think that the only force at work in legal reasoning is logic. Although courts employ the language of logic, they are in fact making legislative decisions based on considerations of policy. "Behind the logical form lies a judgment as to the relative worth and importance of competing legislative grounds, often an inarticulate and unconscious judgment, it is true, and yet the very nerve and root of the whole proceeding" (466).

These propositions all have, as I say, a certain theoretical flavor to them. But Holmes tosses off the observations encapsulating these propositions in a fairly casual manner, making little or no attempt to relate them to one another in a systematic way. He does not, in other words, appear in *The Path of the Law* to be developing a comprehensive *theory* of law. There are, moreover, passages in the essay that cast at least some of these propositions in a light that is more antitheoretical than theoretical. At times "our friend" the bad man is described with such enthusiasm that it is difficult not to conclude that Holmes introduced this figure solely for his shock value. In other passages, Holmes appears with a wave of his hand to be repudiating the theoretical presumptions of analytical jurisprudence in their entirety: "You may assume, with Hobbes and Bentham and Austin, that all law emanates from the sovereign, even when the first human beings to enunciate it are the judges, or you may think that law is the voice of the Zeitgeist, or what you like. It is all one to my present purpose" (465). It is this debunking, apparently anti-theoretical tone that has, quite understandably, led to *The Path of the Law* being widely read as an early but forceful articulation of some of the more skeptical themes emphasized by the legal realists.

While there is no question but that *The Path of the Law* is in part a debunking exercise, it is far from clear that it constitutes an outright rejection of analytical jurisprudence. After all, at a number of points in the essay Holmes praises both theory and jurisprudence: we have too little theory in the law rather than too much, he writes; and, the way to get to the bottom of the subject is to follow the existing body of dogma into its highest generalizations by means of jurisprudence (476). The trouble with Austin was not that he was a theorist, but, we are informed, that he did not know enough English law (475). Despite that deficiency, Holmes acknowledges that it is a practical advantage to master Austin, not to mention his predecessors Hobbes and Bentham, and his "worthy successors," Holland and Pollock (475). Still, doubts remain about Holmes's jurisprudential bona fides. Some commentators have thought that by "theory" he had in mind the methodological precepts of the empirical sciences of his day,[2] or those of the philosophical pragmatism of James and Peirce,[3] and that this was his reason for placing so much emphasis on prediction in the law. As for jurisprudence, it is characterized by Holmes, in a curiously Dworkinian turn of phrase,[4] as "simply law in its most general part": "Every effort to reduce a case to a rule," Holmes continues, "is an effort of jurisprudence" (474). But this sounds more like doing law than theorizing about it, a charge that, in our own time, has sometimes been leveled against Ronald Dworkin as well.

So where does that leave us on the question of whether Holmes was putting forward a theory of law in a jurisprudential sense, as opposed to a would-be scientific theory of some kind or a pure exercise in realpolitik and demystification? Is there, implicit in the various theoretical-sounding but discrete observations about the law that Holmes offers in his essay, a theory of law that can be said to join issue with the preceding theories of Hobbes, Bentham, and Austin, or with the contemporary theories of H. L. A. Hart, Joseph Raz, and Dworkin? The text of *The Path of the Law* does not provide a definitive answer as to Holmes's own intentions on this score, but there is a sense in which his intentions are simply beside the point. The crucial question is, surely, whether or not we can construct an intelligible and coherent jurisprudential theory from his various aphorisms and pronouncements about the nature of law, while remaining true to what Holmes had in mind in advancing them. I argue that we can. More specifically, I argue that there emerges from the six propositions just enumerated a theory of law that can appropriately be described as Hobbesian in character. I do not mean to suggest, of course, that Holmes's theory of law is the same as, or just an abbreviated version of, Hobbes's theory; in detail, it is quite different. It is of course possible that Holmes's views about law were in part directly inspired by Hobbes, with whose writings he seemed to have had at least a passing familiarity, but my concern in this essay is not with Holmes's intellectual influences. My central claim is, rather, that Holmes and Hobbes share an essentially similar view of the nature of human beings – in the modern jargon, they share an essentially similar conception of the person – which constitutes a core feature of their respective theoretical accounts of law. In Holmes's work, this conception of the person enters in the form of the bad man.

In order to answer the question of whether we can construct an intelligible and coherent jurisprudential theory from Holmes's various pronouncements about law we need to have some idea of what constitutes an intelligible and coherent jurisprudential theory. We require, in other words, some appropriate account of methodology in jurisprudence. Because jurisprudence lies within a rather unstable area of intersection between philosophy and social theory, methodological questions tend to be as controverted as substantive questions, and often the two become inextricably entangled. Bearing these points in mind, I propose to proceed in this essay in the following way. From a jurisprudential point of view, one of Holmes's strongest critics is H. L. A. Hart, who uses

Holmes as a stalking-horse at a number of key junctures in his book *The Concept of Law* (1961). After drawing out the implicit methodological assumptions on which Hart's own theory of law can be seen to rest, I argue that if we bring this methodology to bear on Holmes's six propositions, we can see the following: first, the Hartian criticism of the Holmesian position often fails to find its mark; second, the Holmesian propositions hang together, in accordance with Hart's own methodological assumptions, as a distinct and more or less unified theory of law. As I suggested earlier, this theory can appropriately be characterized as Hobbesian. I discuss each of Holmes's six propositions in turn, making clear how each fits into the larger picture and taking account, where appropriate, of Hart's specific criticism.

The key methodological notions that are at work in Hart's theory of law, and that I argue can be used to construct a Holmesian theory, are the following: a conception of the person, an attribution to law of a point or function, and an understanding of the impact that law has upon the practical reasoning of those who are subject to it. These notions are, within the internal structure of each theory, systematically related. It is in connection with the impact of law upon practical reasoning that Hart's famous notion of the "internal point of view" enters into jurisprudential methodology.[5] I argue, among other things, that Hart's own characterization of this point of view is too narrow, and that the concept of the bad man represents another version of the internal viewpoint that cannot be ruled out, contrary to what Hart implicitly suggests, on methodological grounds alone. None of this is meant to demonstrate that Holmes was right about the nature of law and Hart wrong; in fact, I think they were both wrong. The idea, rather, is to show that each can be understood to be advancing the same type of theory, that those theories join issue rather than speak past one another, and that the case for the Holmesian view is rather stronger than is often allowed by contemporary legal theorists.

II. Prediction and the Bad Man

The first of the six propositions from *The Path of the Law* that were enumerated in section I is that law is a matter of predicting the incidence of the use of public force through the instrumentality of the courts. The second is that law is to be characterized from the point of view of the bad man, whose only reasons for action are self-interested reasons and whose only concern with law is to predict when the public force might descend upon him. These two propositions may seem to be two different ways of saying the same thing, but that is not necessarily true. Consider Holmes's initial formulation of the first proposition: "The object of our study is prediction, the prediction of the incidence of the public force through the instrumentality of the courts" (457). This statement is quite consistent with, and when considered in isolation suggests, a theory in which law is studied, as it were, from the outside. The theorist, an actual or notional outsider to the social practices under scrutiny, is the one who wishes to do the predicting; his interest, presumably, is similar to that of a scientist who wishes to be able to predict other sorts of empirical phenomena in the world. It is possible to formulate such a theory without reference to any such figure as the bad man, and indeed, from the point of view of a scientific, normatively neutral description of the world, the morally freighted concept of a "bad" man seems quite out of place.

Not only does a purely predictive, externally oriented theory not require reference to the bad man, but it might even be possible to make predictions about the future behavior of courts or citizens without overtly introducing the notions of agency or acting for a reason. Perhaps all that is required to formulate such a theory is the concepts of stimulus and response, and indeed Holmes has in the past been accused of paving the road to behaviorism.[6] Theories of this kind, which are most readily viewed as adopting a methodology rooted in the scientific positivism of the late nineteenth century, are criticized by Hart in *The Concept of Law*. Hart says that an observer who took up this "extreme external" point of view could learn to correlate deviation from certain of a group's social practices with hostile reaction, and on that basis would come to be able to predict, with some measure of success, the behavior of the subjects he is studying.

However, in a passage worth quoting at length, Hart argues that the observer who "keeps austerely" to the extreme external point of view will be leaving out something important from his theory, namely, the manner in which the members of the group view their own behavior. As a result,

[the observer's] description of [the group's] life cannot be in terms of rules at all, and so not in the terms of the rule-dependent notions of obligation or duty. Instead, it will be in terms of observable regularities of conduct, predictions, probabilities, and signs. For such an observer, deviations by a member of the group from normal conduct will be a sign that hostile reaction is likely to follow, and nothing more. His view will be like the view of one who, having observed the working of a traffic signal in a busy street for some time, limits himself to saying that when the light turns red there is a high probability that the traffic will stop. He treats the light merely as a natural *sign that* people will behave in certain ways, as clouds are a *sign that* rain will come. In so doing he will miss out on a whole dimension of the social life of those whom he is watching, since for them the red light is not merely a sign that others will stop: they look upon it as a *signal for* them to stop, and so a *reason* for stopping in conformity to rules which make stopping when the light is red a standard of behaviour and an obligation. To mention this is to bring into account the way that the group regards its own behaviour. It is to refer to the internal aspect of rules seen from their internal point of view. (87–88, emphasis in original)

As noted earlier, Holmes's initial characterization of law in terms of prediction seems to suggest just such an extreme external theory of the kind that Hart criticizes. Hart's objection to such a theory is that it leaves out of account "the internal point of view," which is the point of view held by those who accept social rules. A social rule exists, according to Hart, when a certain pattern of behavior is general, deviations from the pattern give rise to criticism, deviations from the pattern are regarded as justification for such criticism, and, finally, there is associated with the pattern an "internal aspect" (54–55). The internal aspect involves a "reflective critical attitude" toward the relevant pattern of behavior, which means that the pattern is regarded by members of the group in question as a standard to which they have reason to conform. This standard is viewed as legitimizing criticism of deviations from the pattern and as justifying the use of a wide range of normative language: you must (or must not) do such and such; doing such and such is wrong. In the case of a rule for which "the general demand for conformity is insistent and the social pressure brought to bear upon those who deviate is great," the rule is regarded as giving rise to an *obligation* (84). The internal point of view is the point of view of those in the group, consisting of at least a majority, who accept that the rule is binding upon all members of the group in the manner suggested by the rule's internal aspect.

Hart's analysis of the concept of law employs the notion of a social rule, as characterized in the preceding paragraph. The core element of law is, Hart argues, the "rule of recognition," which is a fundamental social rule that is accepted as binding by a group of officials whom, for present purposes, we can equate with judges. The rule of recognition sets out criteria of validity for other rules in the legal system and imposes an obligation on judges to enforce the valid rules. Judges hold the internal point of view toward the rule of recognition and hence regard the rule as "a public, common standard of correct judicial decision" (112). Other members of the society may or may not share the internal point of view, although it is a general requirement for the existence of a legal system that there be at least a minimal level of general compliance with the system's rules. Some citizens comply because they themselves hold the internal point of view toward the rule of recognition (and, by extension, toward the rules it identifies as valid), but others only pay attention to the rules and comply with them to the extent that they have to "because they judge that unpleasant consequences are likely to follow violation" (88). These persons are, of course, Holmes's bad men. Hart maintains that such persons have adopted the "external point of view" toward the rules of their society and continues: "At any given moment the life of any society which lives by rules, legal or not, is likely to consist in a tension between those who, on the one hand, accept and voluntarily co-operate in maintaining the rules, and so see their own and other persons' behaviour in terms of the rules, and those who, on the other hand, reject the rules and attend to them only from the external point of view as a possible sign of punishment" (88).

I suggested earlier that the theoretical perspective of an external observer who is interested, as a scientific matter, in predicting behavior within a given society does not necessarily implicate any such figure as the bad man. Yet Hart seems to suggest, as we have just seen, that the bad man adopts the "external point of view" that Hart had earlier associated with the outside observer. It is true that, as a practical matter, the bad man might go about avoiding having the public force used against him by making predictions similar to those made by the external theorist, and on the basis of considerations similar to those that the external theorist would take into account. Of course the theorist would presumably be interested in general predictions, whereas the bad man would be interested in predictions concerning his own well-being. But this is not a particularly significant distinction in itself, especially since the bad man might find it most useful to advert to theoretical generalizations about the behavior of courts in order to determine when court-sanctioned force was most likely to descend on him in particular.

However, despite this possible pragmatic connection between the activities of the external observer and those of the bad man, their respective points of view are quite different. The external observer is engaged in an exercise of *theoretical* reason. His concern, in other words, is with the truth or falsity of the behavioral generalizations that he attempts to formulate, and with the truth or falsity of the predictions that he makes on the basis of those generalizations. The bad man, on the other hand, is engaged in a process of *practical* reason. He is trying to decide what he *ought* to do, in a prudential sense, in order to avoid being visited with a fine, imprisonment, or some other form of legally sanctioned unpleasantness. To see the distinction from another perspective, recall that one possible type of extreme external theory abstracts from all reasons for action and simply pays attention to the relationship between stimulus and response, or even to the pure correlation of event types in the world, with no concern at all for whether those event types involve an exercise of agency. ("[The observer] treats the light merely as a natural *sign that* people will behave in certain ways, as clouds are a *sign that* rain will come.") The bad man, on the other hand, is very much concerned with reasons for action, namely, reasons of prudential self-interest, and with the question of how he ought to exercise his own agency on the basis of those reasons. He differs from the theorist in that he has no inherent interest in prediction as such; he does not, in other words, care about knowledge for the sake of knowledge. He is concerned with prediction purely for instrumental reasons, as a means to help him avoid unpleasantness of a certain sort.

Hart, however, argues that an adequate theory of jurisprudence must take account of the internal point of view. Extreme external theories are unsatisfactory precisely because they fail to do this. The internal point of view involves the acceptance of social rules by at least some persons within a society; on Hart's account of law, judges must, at a minimum, accept the particular social rule that Hart calls the "rule of recognition." Thus any adequate theory of jurisprudence must make essential use of the concept of a social rule. A Holmesian theory, based on the perspective of the bad man, is unsatisfactory because it fails to do this. Moreover, it cannot help but fail in this respect, because it places the extreme external point of view at the core of its account of law. As Hart at one point puts the objection, predictive theories define the internal point of view out of existence (88). But this argument is a bad one, for the following two related reasons: first, it depends on an equivocation in the characterization of the external point of view; second, it presupposes too narrow an understanding of the internal point of view. The equivocation I have already remarked upon: Hart conflates the viewpoint of the external observer, who is engaged in an exercise of theoretical reason, with the viewpoint of the bad man, who is engaged in an exercise of practical reason. In light of this equivocation, Hart's conclusion that a jurisprudential theory cannot be based on the perspective of the bad man simply does not follow from his premises. The Holmesian account does not rest on the extreme external point of view that Hart regards as an unacceptable foundation for any satisfactory theory of law.

The second problem with Hart's argument, which is that he characterizes the internal point of view too narrowly, takes the line of thought underlying the first criticism farther by making clear that the Holmesian and Hartian theories are in fact of the same general character. The salient claim here is that the viewpoint of the bad man should be generically associated, not with the point of view of an external observer, but rather with the very same internal viewpoint that Hart says lies at the core of jurisprudence. In order to avoid any ambiguity in terminology, let me relabel Hart's understanding of the internal point of view – that is, the understanding he describes as based on the acceptance of social rules – and call it the "socialized" point of view. This label is appropriate because the viewpoint in question is that of a person who has accepted the conventional thinking on some matter, as embodied in the relevant social rule. The perspective of the bad man we can call the "prudential" point of view.

With this terminology at our disposal, we are now able to argue that both the socialized and the prudential points of view should properly be characterized as internal in nature. To see this, consider the role that the socialized point of view plays in Hart's own theory of law. As he himself remarks in the passage quoted at length earlier, what the observer who takes the extreme external perspective misses is that those whom he is watching look upon the red light as "a *reason for stopping* in conformity to rules which make stopping when the light is red a standard of behaviour and an obligation." In other words, to take up the socialized point of view involves coming to see the social practice that constitutes the relevant "rule" as giving one a *reason for action* of a certain kind. Let me call such (perceived) reasons for action "social" reasons. Whether social reasons for action really exist (as opposed to being perceived to exist), and, if so, what kind of reasons they are, are important questions, but ones that for the moment we can set aside. The point to be emphasized for present purposes is that the bad man also regards the social practices Hart calls "rules" as reason giving. It is true that the bad man is concerned with a different kind of reasons for action, namely, prudential reasons, but the nature and motivating force of such reasons is in fact more readily apparent than in the case of social reasons. Furthermore, prudential reasons are analytically, not just contingently, associated with the practices Hart "calls social rules," since, as his own characterization makes plain, an essential element of such practices is that deviations will be met with criticism, social pressure to conform, and possibly some type of punishment. It is precisely these forms of unpleasantness that the bad man wishes to avoid.

Hart is quite right that the bad man does not look upon the social practices in question as rules, since his sole concern is with avoiding the unpleasantness to which deviation from such a practice gives rise. But it is solely because Hart assumes that the socialized viewpoint is the only possible internal point of view that he is able to treat this fact about the bad man as a criticism of the Holmesian theory. In fact, as we have seen, the bad man's perspective is best regarded as a distinct form of internal point of view. The bad man, after all, is not an outsider, let alone an external observer; he is a member of the relevant society, even though he has not internalized its practices in the way that Hart claims is true of other members. But the bad man still treats those practices as reason giving, and according to Hart's own account it is reason givingness, or at least perceived reason givingness, that is the essential characteristic of the internal point of view. So far as jurisprudence is concerned, the important question does not involve a choice between an internal and an external point of view, but rather a choice between two points of view that are both internal. The question is, in effect, which type of reason, social or prudential, best typifies law as law? To put it another way, which characterization of the relevant social practices, the one that sees them as rules or the one that sees them as exercises in coercion, best captures the true nature of law?

It is time to return to Holmes. I have argued that, contrary to what Hart suggests, the perspective of the bad man is an internal rather than an external point of view and hence, by Hart's own lights, the basis for a possible theory of law that would be competitive with Hart's own. Did Holmes in fact view the bad man along similar lines? As noted earlier, it has been suggested by some commentators that Holmes emphasized prediction in his characterization of law because he wished to make the study of law as scientific as possible.[7] We have already seen that his initial characterization of law as prediction is entirely consistent with what Hart calls an "extreme external theory," which would definitely have a descriptive and a scientific orientation. It is thus at least conceivable that Holmes introduced the bad man as a "heuristic" in order to make clear, in a typically colorful way, that the object of studying this particular phenomenon, as in the scientific study of all empirical phenomena, is to discover testable regularities that permit the prediction of future events. After all, even without actually being committed to the viewpoint of the bad man, an external observer could look at law from the bad man's perspective in order to formulate prediction-facilitating generalizations that might be of scientific interest.

There are, however, a number of strong reasons to doubt this scientific interpretation of the prediction theory. First, the introduction of an overtly normative notion such as the bad man makes little sense from a scientific perspective. Second, why should we be particularly interested, scientifically speaking, in the prediction of the use of court-sanctioned force as opposed to other recurring phenomena in the legal world? Why not attempt to predict the behavior of legislators, for example, or the behavior of the population at large, as citizens react to the activities of legislators, courts, and other legal actors? From a jurisprudential perspective, however, an emphasis on force makes some sense, since the potential use of force gives rise to a specific type of reasons for action, namely, prudential reasons, and reasons for action are, at least according to Hart, the pith and substance of the jurisprudential enterprise. (Of course, Hart left prudential reasons for action out of his own picture of this enterprise, but without clear warrant for doing so.)

Third, Holmes himself explicitly draws attention to prudential reasons for action and contrasts them with another type of reason that bears at least a family resemblance to social reasons: "If you want to know the law and nothing else, you must look at it as a bad man, who cares only for the material consequences which such knowledge enables him to predict, not as a good one, who finds his reasons for conduct, whether inside the law or outside of it, in the vaguer sanctions of conscience" ("Path" 459). From a scientific point of view, though, there is no obvious or necessary rationale for bringing in the concept of a reason for action at all here, let alone for contrasting one type of reason with another. So far as predicting the use of court-sanctioned force is concerned, perhaps the best scientific theory would not even mention the concepts of agency or reasons for action. Again, however, so far as jurisprudence is concerned, reasons for action seem to be central.

As the discussion in the preceding two paragraphs makes clear, the understanding of law that Holmes propounds in *The Path of the Law* emphasizes the effect that law has on persons' practical reasoning. A fourth, textually based reason for doubting the scientific interpretation of the prediction theory arises from the contrast between this approach and the strictly scientific study of law that Holmes describes elsewhere. In "Law in Science and Science in Law" Holmes writes that it is possible to study law "simply as a great anthropological document," with no practical end in view, and that it is this form of study that "becomes science in the strictest sense."[8] As Thomas Grey has suggested, Holmes seems here to be describing the study of law from a truly external perspective that is to be distinguished from the "practical" and "internal" point of view that he adopts in *The Path of the Law*.[9]

The final and principal reason for rejecting the scientific interpretation of the prediction theory is that Holmes believed that in an important sense people really are "bad men." More accurately, he believed that people generally act in a completely self-interested manner, and that in the last resort they can be expected to use force to try to get their way. Thus the figure of the bad man was not for Holmes just a colorful heuristic for establishing a point about the scientific study of law or, as has also been suggested, for making clear how an effective lawyer advises his client.[10] Holmes was convinced that the notion of the bad man captured something fundamental about human nature, and such a thesis could not help but affect the views he held concerning the theoretical character of law. Thus, whether or not Holmes consciously intended to sketch the outlines of a systematic theory of jurisprudence, we have some reason to think that he regarded the bad man as important from a jurisprudential perspective. Bearing that in mind, we may continue with our task of constructing a general theory of law from the six propositions that Holmes propounded in *The Path of the Law*.

III. The Bad Man and the Function of Law

I argued in the preceding section that the Holmesian and the Hartian views about the nature of law are on the same footing: each is based on a different view of which (perceived) reasons for action best capture the true nature of law. But how are we to choose between these competing theories? Hart's main argument against so-called predictive theories is that they define the internal point of view out of existence. As we have seen, this argument is misconceived. Hart does have another argument, however, which does not depend on the conflation of the point of view of the bad man with that of the external observer. After referring to Holmes's claim that the law should be characterized from the bad man's point of view, Hart continues:

> Why should not law be equally if not more concerned with the "puzzled man" or "ignorant man" who is willing to do what is required, if only he can be told what it is? Or with "the man who wishes to arrange his affairs" if only he can be told how to do it? It is of course very important, if we are to understand the law, to see how the courts administer it when they come to apply its sanctions. But this should not lead us to think that all there is to understand is what happens in courts. The principal functions of the law as a means of social control are not to be seen in private litigation or prosecutions, which represent vital but still ancillary provisions for the failures of the system. It is to be seen in the diverse ways in which the law is used to control, to guide, and to plan life out of court. (39)

The following two points should be noted about this response to Holmes. First, Hart offers an alternative conception of the person in place of the bad man, namely, the "ignorant man," who is willing to do what is required, if only he can be told what it is. Second, Hart explicitly invokes the idea of the "function" of law. These two points are related, and both bear on Hart's implicit assumptions about methodology in jurisprudence. Hart states at the beginning of *The Concept of Law* that the book can be regarded as an essay in descriptive sociology (v), which suggests that he conceived of his theory of law as a purely descriptive, nonnormative enterprise. As I have argued at length elsewhere,[11] however, in relying on the notion of function, Hart is introducing evaluative, and indeed moral, considerations into his theoretical account of law. Moreover, this was not a move that Hart could have avoided; he requires the notion of function in order properly to define his own theory, not simply in order to respond to Holmes. Hart asserts that the chief function of law is to guide and plan life out of court. As this suggests, and as Hart makes explicit in an earlier passage, he has in mind here the guidance of ordinary citizens.[12] But such guidance is possible only if (a sufficiently large number of) ordinary citizens are the type of person who will respond to such guidance, and not just to threats of force: hence, the ignorant man, who is willing to do what is required, if only he can be told what it is. This view of law, and the related conception of the person, have the further consequence that sanctions are not an essential element of law at all, but are rather a secondary method for achieving social control when the primary method fails. (Unlike the bad man, the ignorant man is, by hypothesis, willing to do what is required.) This is a consequence that Hart accepts.[13]

Hart's understanding of the function of law clearly supposes that (a sufficiently large number of) ordinary citizens adopt the socialized, as opposed to the prudential, point of view. The ignorant man who is willing to do what is required has clearly internalized the "official" view associated with the legal system in question; in this he is very different from the Holmesian bad man, who responds to the law only in order to avoid the unpleasantness of sanctions. There is, it seems to me, at least a minor embarrassment for Hart here, since he maintains that the only persons who *must* be regarded as having adopted the socialized point of view are judges.[14] So far as ordinary citizens are concerned, Hart says, as we have seen, that the life of any society that lives by rules is likely to involve a tension between those who adopt the socialized and those who adopt the prudential perspectives (in Hart's terminology, between those who adopt the internal and those who adopt the external point of view). But if both points of view exist among ordinary citizens, on what basis does Hart pick out one as determinative of the nature of law? He must be saying either that bad men are few and far between, which is a fairly implausible empirical claim and in any event not one for which he argues, or else that the conception of the person that he advocates is in part a regulative ideal with a normative content. If the latter possibility is the one Hart would opt for, then his claim to be engaging in "descriptive sociology" is rendered somewhat suspect.

But that claim is rendered suspect anyway, regardless of how Hart would choose to respond to the dilemma just described, because in order to delineate a precise concept of law, he requires value judgments concerning how well (or badly) the function he assigns to law is served by different social practices. Hart plainly has in mind the function of providing guidance for the conduct of ordinary citizens when he excludes from the province of law pure systems of customary or "primary" rules, as opposed to systems based on a rule of recognition: systems of the former type do not guide conduct well, he says in effect, because they are too uncertain, too static, and too inefficient in the provision of social incentives for conformity (89–96). Hart thus cannot plausibly maintain that in theorizing about law he is merely describing social reality: the concepts he employs cut up that reality in the manner they do – excluding one type of social practice, including another – because the excluded social practices have been judged to be, in the light of Hart's understanding of the function of law, defective.[15]

Nor does the failure of pure description end there, for even if, implausibly, the conception of the person on which Hart relies is taken to be based on purely empirical considerations, we still must ask what reason we have for accepting that law has the particular function Hart attributes to it. After all, the conception of the person he sketches makes it possible for a social institution to serve the function of guiding behavior by means of an internalized form of socialization, but it does not obviously restrict the functions that lawlike institutions could serve to just this one and no others. The most plausible answer to the question of why we should accept Hart's characterization of the function of law is that serving that function has potential moral value: a social institution whose purpose is to guide conduct is capable of realizing great social good, if the valid rules of the system have an appropriate moral content. Hart himself appears to think that law obviously does serve the function of guiding conduct and no other, but the controversies of contemporary jurisprudence make clear that this view of the matter is untenable.[16] Since Hart offers no other argument as to why we should accept his account of the function of law, and since there does not appear to be any other plausible argument on the horizon,[17] we do best by Hart's own substantive theory if we regard it as resting on the methodological precept that the function of law is to be determined in accordance with judgments of moral value that originate with the theorist him- or herself.

That the value judgments in question are to be made from an external perspective (rather than, say, from the perspective of members of the relevant group) is consistent with Hart's claim that he has based his theory on a certain type of statement, which, though distinct from the extreme external statements discussed earlier, is still properly characterized as "external."[18] This second type of external statement, to which I have elsewhere given the label "engaged," takes account of the group members' own internal point of view but is not itself offered from that point of view. Thus, although Hart rejects the extreme external perspective, and with it what he terms "the methodology of the empirical sciences"[19] – perhaps surprisingly, he goes so far as to accept the term "hermeneutic" as applicable to his own approach – it is evident that his theory of law is the theory of an external observer. That being so, if the theory involves value judgments of a certain kind, we would naturally expect those judgments to be made from the observer's perspective. It is worth noting at this point that the existence of such value judgments does not entail that the concept of law, once it has been formulated, cannot be employed to describe the world in a morally neutral way. But since theorizing about law is, for Hart, essentially just a process of concept formation, legal theory itself, as he engages in it, cannot be morally neutral.

Hart is, of course, a legal positivist; he believes that any overlap in content between morality and law is a contingent rather than a necessary state of affairs. It may seem that a normative methodology for legal theory would be at odds with Hart's professed positivism, but that is not so. It is true that positivists often maintain that legal theory must be a purely descriptive, nonnormative enterprise; as we have seen, Hart himself claims to hold that view. But there is a distinction to be drawn between substantive and methodological legal positivism. The former is concerned to deny a necessary connection between moral value and law, while the latter is concerned to deny a necessary connection between moral value and theories of law.[20] These are logically independent positions. I have suggested that, contrary to his own understanding of the matter, Hart is not a methodological positivist; *The Concept of Law* is not the pure exercise in descriptive sociology that he says it is. But the fact that Hart has implicitly adopted a normative methodology does not mean that he cannot employ that methodology to defend a version of substantive positivism. The implicit argument would be, roughly, that law can serve the function of guiding conduct only if there is some overarching social practice that determines which norms are to provide the requisite guidance. But the content of that social practice – the rule of recognition – is by hypothesis determined socially, and hence only contingently overlaps with morality. Some positivists go farther. Joseph Raz maintains – on the basis of an argument that I have elsewhere suggested is moral in character[21] – that law can usefully guide conduct only if the criteria that the rule of recognition employs to determine the validity of individual legal norms are themselves purely social, not moral, in nature (the "sources thesis").[22] But these differences among the various versions of legal positivism need not concern us here. The essential point for present purposes is that it is possible to defend a substantive positivist theory on the basis of a nonpositivist methodology.[23] This observation is as applicable to Holmes's version of positivism as it is to Hart's.

Now that we have clarified the methodological foundations of Hart's own theory of law, we are in a position to ask how Holmes might have responded to Hart's critique. Holmes, or at least a defender of a theory built up from Holmes's views, would no doubt begin by arguing that Hart is making use of an inappropriate conception of the person. Here, it seems to me, Holmes has available two possible lines of argument. The first holds that although human beings are capable of responding to reasons for action other than those that are purely prudential or self-interested, it is only by appealing to reasons of the latter kind that law can truly be effective. The argument would presumably be twofold: first, a large proportion of people just are bad people – that is, they respond only, or mainly, to considerations of prudential self-interest – and second, even good persons, who act or are capable of acting for moral or social reasons, also respond to reasons of self-interest. In other words, prudential reasons are reasons for everybody, but moral or social reasons are reasons for some people only; the bad man is the lowest common denominator. If you wish to maintain social control, you therefore do better to appeal to prudential reasons for action, which are universally effective. Now this line of argument, which acknowledges the possibility of different kinds of reasons for action, is to some extent suggested by the text of *The Path of the Law*. Recall that Holmes contrasts the bad man, who cares only for the material consequences that he can predict might befall him, with the good one, "who finds his reasons for conduct . . . in the vaguer sanctions of conscience." And Holmes seems relatedly to be appealing to the universal efficacy of prudential reasons over moral or social reasons when he says that "[y]ou can see very plainly that a bad man has as much reason as a good one for wishing to avoid an encounter with the public force" ("Path" 459).

However, a second line of argument is available to Holmes, and it is suggested by other works that he wrote both before and after "The Path of the Law." Consider the following passage from *The Common Law,* published in 1881:

The ever-growing value set upon peace and the social relations tends to give the law of social being the appearance of the law of all being. But it seems to be clear that the *ultima ratio,* not only *regum,* of private persons is force, and that at the bottom of all private relations, however tempered by sympathy and all the social feelings, is a justifiable self-preference. If a man is on a plank in the deep sea which will only float one, and a stranger lays hold of it, he will thrust him off if he can. When the state finds itself in a similar position, it does the same thing.[24]

These sentiments are echoed in a letter written to Frederick Pollock in 1920:

I think that the sacredness of human life is a purely municipal ideal of no validity outside the jurisdiction. I believe that force, mitigated so far as may be by good manners, is the *ultima ratio,* and between two groups that want to make inconsistent kinds of world I see no remedy except force.[25]

Consider, finally, the following passage from Holmes's essay "Natural Law," published in 1918:

Deep-seated preferences can not be argued about – you can not argue a man into liking a glass of beer – and therefore, when differences are sufficiently far-reaching, we try to kill the other man rather than let him have his way. But that is perfectly consistent with admitting that, so far as appears, his grounds are just as good as ours.[26]

These passages suggest very strongly that all human beings are, ultimately, bad men. More specifically, they suggest that human beings act only on the basis of reasons of prudential self-interest. This is the Humean position that desires are the sole motivators of human action, combined with the Hobbesian thesis that all desires are in some sense, or at some level, self-regarding.[27] There is also evidence in these passages that Holmes believed that when desires conflict in a fundamental way, cooperation among persons is impossible and force will ultimately settle the issue. This thesis can also be called Hobbesian, since it bears at least a family resemblance to Hobbes's own view that in the absence of an absolute sovereign, cooperation of any kind is impossible among persons, so that the state of nature is a state of perpetual war. Holmes was not a philosopher, and neither in these passages nor elsewhere in his writings does he approach the philosophical sophistication or power of Hobbes's work. But he clearly shared with Hobbes a rather bleak understanding of human nature, a fact that is perhaps not surprising, given that each man lived through a particularly ferocious civil war. In any event, the conception of the person that emerges from the passages just quoted is sufficiently close to Hobbes's own to justify our characterizing it as Hobbesian. The same label can likewise appropriately be attached, as we shall see, to Holmes's theory of law.

Which of these two lines of argument should we attribute to Holmes: the one that sees the bad man as merely the least common denominator among human beings, or the one that sees him as the human archetype? The answer to this question depends in part on what we take Holmes's conception of morality and moral reasons to be, and I shall have something to say about that issue in section V. But the passages just quoted, from work spanning the greater part of his career, suggest what seems to me to be the right view: morality, for Holmes, is either a socialized version of the dominant group's self-interest or, at best, a thin social veneer that amounts to little more than good manners, and that is incapable of preventing the forces of self-interest from operating when fundamental matters are at stake. If that is right, then the best overall interpretation of the bad man is the Hobbesian view that he is the human archetype.

For present purposes, however, the answer to the question just posed does not really matter, since either way Holmes is clearly supposing that law can be effective only by appealing to reasons of prudential self-interest. He thus seems to be setting up the bad man as a kind of regulative ideal, in much the same way that Hart does the ignorant man. But this makes sense, from the perspective of the methodology we found reason to attribute to Hart, only if we can discover a Holmesian view of the function of law that serves as an analogue to Hart's notion of guiding conduct. Although Holmes does not expressly discuss the function of law, there is a view of the matter that one is led naturally, and indeed almost inevitably, to attribute to him. Recall that Hart argues that the principal function of law, "*as a means of social control*" (emphasis added), consists in the ways it is used to control, guide, and plan life out of court. This suggests that the ultimate function of law is social control, a proposition with which one can readily imagine Holmes concurring. But he would then add that such control can be achieved only through the threat of force; social or moral reasons, supposing they exist and are capable of motivating people, are not capable of doing so to the degree required to preserve social order. I am suggesting, then, that the appropriate Holmesian view is that the function of law is to maintain social control by means of the threat of force.[28] I take the concept of "social control" to include both the bare preservation of social order – the prevention of anarchy and widespread violence – and the channeling of behavior in ways that are potentially welfare enhancing.

I said while discussing Hart that introducing the notion of function into legal theory brings with it a normative methodology. The theorist who relies on such a methodology, whether explicitly or implicitly, cannot claim to be offering a neutral description of reality and nothing more. The suggestion that Holmes is implicitly relying on such a methodology may seem to be at odds with the undeniable strands in his thought that are concerned to make the study of law as scientific as possible. I do not deny that there may be some tension here, but remember that there is a similar tension in Hart's own work; *The Concept of Law* is not the straightforward exercise in descriptive sociology that he himself said it was. In order to make sense of Holmes's theoretical account of law it might likewise be necessary to attribute a methodology to him that he would perhaps have repudiated if it had been put to him directly. It should, in any event, be borne in mind that I am not so much attempting to elucidate Holmes's theory of law as trying to construct from his various observations about law a theory that can appropriately be called Holmesian. That having been said, however, I am not so sure that Holmes would reject the idea of a normative methodology for jurisprudence, and I am certain that he would find it less repugnant than would Hart. As I shall discuss in the following section, Holmes sets for law a certain ideal and makes suggestions for the reform of legal language that do not square very readily with an enterprise of pure description but that make a great deal of sense if we take his implicit starting point to be the idea that law has the function of maintaining social order by means of threatened force.

Holmes does not, as I say, explicitly rely on the idea that law has a function. But there is a passage in his late essay "Natural Law" which, while even bleaker in tone than anything else I have quoted so far, can readily bear that construction. Holmes first states that "as an arbitrary fact" people wish to live, and that they can do so only on certain conditions. After noting that the necessity to eat and drink is absolute, he continues:

It is a necessity of less degree but practically general that they should live in society. If we live in society, so far as we can see, there are further conditions. Reason working on experience does tell us, no doubt, that if our wish to live continues, we can do it only on those terms . . . If I do live with others they tell me that I must do and abstain from doing various things or they will put the screws to me. I believe that they will, and being of the same mind as to their conduct I not only accept the rules but come in time to accept them with sympathy and emotional affirmation and begin to talk about rights and duties.[29]

Although Holmes does not put the point in quite this way, this passage can easily be read as saying that people can live in society only if there is some person or group who can control the predilection to resort to violence that, he has already told us in the same essay, is inherent in everyone. But that person or group can exercise control only by credibly threatening to use force on – put the screws to – anyone who does not comply with their "rules." The law is comprised of just those threats, and its function is to maintain the social control that will permit persons to live together and, hence, to survive. As Holmes said in an 1899 speech, "[T]he law does not mean sympathetic advice which you may neglect if you choose, but the stern monition that the club and the bayonet are at hand ready to drive you to prison or to the rope if you go beyond the established lines."[30]

The passage just quoted from "Natural Law" is of further interest because it is here that Holmes seems to come closest to Hobbes's own political philosophy and theory of law. Hobbes's view, stripped to its essentials, is that individuals desire self-preservation above all; that the state of nature is a state of perpetual war; that peace and the conditions for cooperation among persons can be secured only by an absolute sovereign; that it is therefore in each individual's interest to institute such a sovereign; and that the benefits of absolute sovereignty can be achieved only if the sovereign's commands are treated as the sole source of law (one form of legal positivism). When the passage from "Natural Law" is read together with those outlining Holmes's conception of human nature, some of which were quoted earlier, it is not in the least difficult to imagine him assenting to most of these propositions, although he would probably deny that the benefits to be derived from the existence of law and the state require absolute sovereignty. Of course the subtlety and power of Hobbes's theory reside in the detailed discussions of human nature, rationality, and strategic behavior that he offers in support of these propositions,[31] and Holmes's work contains nothing similar; he offers the rhetoric of Hobbes's philosophy, but without its sophistication. Even so, if we are to understand Holmes as advancing a theory of law at all, that theory is clearly Hobbesian in character.

However, a note of caution is in order. The passage quoted from "Natural Law" comes closest to Hobbes's own position, insofar as it suggests that it is in each individual's own interest to enter into association with others in a state governed by a person or group that is in a position to keep order by means of credible threats of force. The passage also suggests that each individual would be aware of the fact that it is to his or her advantage to live in such an association and would act accordingly. The general impression left by Holmes's discussion in *The Path of the Law*, however, is that the bad man is, in Jon Elster's phrase, "parametrically" rather than "strategically" rational.[32] He sees the law as a force that constrains *him,* and hence as something that is not in his interest, rather than as a force that constrains *him and everyone else,* and hence as an institution that might well be in his interest.[33] Although Holmes does not explicitly say as much, one gets the impression that the bad man in the state of nature would not see that there could be anything to be gained by entering into political association with others. This bears on the methodological issue of how to determine the point of view from which a function should be attributed to law. If the bad man is only parametrically rational, then the relevant point of view would have to be external rather than internal: it would be the viewpoint of an observer rather than a participant. Holmes's theory would then resemble Hart's in that regard: as I suggested earlier, we do best by Hart's own substantive theory if we suppose that the attribution of a function to law is made in accordance with value judgments originating with the theorist himself. A truly Hobbesian theory of law, however, would inquire into the function of law from the perspective of the bad man, along the lines suggested by the passage quoted from "Natural Law." I return briefly to these methodological issues in section VI.

It is worth drawing attention, finally, to some rather un-Hobbesian passages elsewhere in Holmes's work where he suggests that the state is, in Hart's phrase, just a gunman writ large. In other words, the state is just that person or group that happens to be more powerful than anyone else around, and it will behave just as individuals behave when their interests are threatened. Consider, for example, the passage quoted earlier from *The Common Law,* in which Holmes writes that the state will always act like the individual who shoves another off a plank at sea.[34] Or consider the following passage, also from "Natural Law":

> The most fundamental of the supposed preexisting rights – the right to life – is sacrificed without a scruple not only in war, but whenever the interest of society, that is, of the predominant power in the community, is thought to demand it. Whether that interest is the interest of mankind in the long run no one can tell, and as, in any event, to those who do not think with Kant and Hegel it is only an interest, the sanctity disappears.[35]

For Hobbes, the sovereign is not inherently more powerful than anyone else, and indeed it is a premise of Hobbes's political theory that there are no significant mental or physical differences among persons. Rather, the Hobbesian sovereign is instituted and maintained in power because it is in everyone's strategic interest that this be done. The passage just quoted from "Natural Law" is certainly consistent with the thesis that it is in an individual's *ex ante* interest to live in a political association rather than outside one, even if *ex post* the state does sacrifice the lives of some of its citizens to secure its own interests (i.e., the interests of the most powerful person or faction in the society). But there is a certain fatalistic, un-Hobbesian flavor to this passage, and indeed to the "Natural Law" essay generally, which suggests that an individual really has no choice about whether to live in such an association; he will be forced into it by someone with power, whether he likes it or not. In that case, the distinction between parametric and strategic rationality would have no practical significance. However, as I shall suggest in section VI, it may still have significance for legal theory.

IV. Prediction, Dogma, and Duties

The third of Holmes's six propositions about law is that the predictions that constitute the law are to be found in case reports, statutes, and legal treatises. The fourth is that rights and duties, as well as the law itself, are to be understood as predictions of the incidence of the use of public force. In this section, I discuss these two propositions and show how they fit into the larger Holmesian theory of law that I have been developing in this essay.

Holmes makes quite clear in *The Path of the Law* that the law does not consist of just any prediction of the exercise of the public force, made on whatever basis. Law is, rather, associated with predictions that are made by reference to what we might call the traditional sources of law, namely, statutes and judicial precedents. (Holmes also mentions legal treatises, but treatises just summarize legislation and cases; they are not an independent source of law.) Holmes repeatedly refers in *The Path of the Law* to the rules and propositions that are derivable from these sources as a "body of dogma," and most of the time he writes as though these propositions simply *are* the predictions that he says constitute the law – that is, they are themselves the law. Thus he writes, for example, "of this body of dogma or systematized prediction which we call the law" (458).

Holmes's position that the predictions he says constitute the law are to be discovered in judicial decisions and statutes may, on first impression, strike one as rather at odds with the general tenor of *The Path of the Law*. The idea that the law consists of propositions and rules found in case law and legislation is hardly startling or unconventional, and if that is all that Holmes ultimately has to say on the subject, why does he make such a fuss about it? Why does he announce, with such evident iconoclastic relish, that "[t]he prophecies of what the courts will do in fact, and nothing more pretentious, are what I mean by the law" (461)? Why the emphasis on prediction in the first place, if the predictions he has in mind turn out to be the same old thing that most people have always meant by the law? Holmes's apparent iconoclasm, together with the central role he assigns to prediction, have led many commentators to see him as a forerunner of extreme legal realism, whose proponents in the 1920s and 1930s thought that prediction could in principle be as readily based on what the judge had had for breakfast as on the contents of law reports. This interpretation of *The Path of the Law* is related to the view that Holmes wished to base the study of law on the methodology of the empirical sciences, since the most promising scientific basis for predicting how judges will decide cases might well be sociological in nature, or even physiological. Even the bad man would be interested in such techniques for prediction, if it would help him to avoid an encounter with the use of the public force. Why, then, does Holmes apparently limit the bad man to studying the lawbooks?

Holmes does not directly address this question in *The Path of the Law*, but he had had something to say about it in a "Book Notice" he published in 1872.

Holmes begins the essay by stating that in the English law journal Holmes was supposedly reviewing, Pollock discusses Austin's definition of law, but that is the last we hear of either the journal or Pollock. Holmes devotes the entire essay to presenting his own critique of Austin, based on a series of lectures on jurisprudence that Holmes had given at Harvard. (Apparently he felt more constrained to get his own views into print than to tell his readers about Pollock's.) Holmes observes that Austin had said that custom became law only by the consent of the sovereign, so that before adoption custom "was only a motive for decision, as a doctrine of political economy, or the political aspirations of the judge, or his gout, or the blandishments of the emperor's wife might have been."[36] After arguing that cases and statutes are as much "motives for decision" as custom, and that it is not the will of the sovereign that makes "lawyers' law" but rather what the judges *say* is the sovereign's will, Holmes continues:

> The only question for the lawyer is, how will the judges act? Any motive for their action, be it constitution, statute, custom, or precedent, which can be relied upon as likely in the generality of cases to prevail, is worthy of consideration as one of the sources of law, in a treatise on jurisprudence. Singular motives, like the blandishments of the emperor's wife, are not a ground of prediction, and are therefore not considered.[37]

We have in this "Book Notice," then, an early statement of Holmes's thesis that law is a matter of predicting what judges will do. But more about this statement is of interest than its date, since Holmes makes clear that the predictions in question must be *general* in nature; "singular motives" are not to be considered. In *The Path of the Law* itself Holmes similarly emphasizes not just prediction but "*systematized* prediction," prediction "generalized and reduced to a system," where that system is clearly supposed to be based on "the finite body of dogma" that is associated with case law and legislation (458).[38] Considered from the point of view of the bad man, however, this emphasis on dogma is rather odd. The bad man would be extremely interested in hearing about the blandishments of the emperor's wife, if this would tell him how the judge was going to decide in *his* case. He has no interest in general predictions as such, but only in predictions of how the public force will affect his own well-being.

We can begin to resolve this puzzle if we accept as a premise that Holmes regards law as serving the function of maintaining social control through the threat of force. Law is thus not to be characterized solely from the point of view of the bad man. The bad man is significant because he represents a certain conception of the person and thereby makes clear the kind of reason for action to which the law must appeal if it is to be effective. But the implicit point of law is, as it were, to keep the bad man in line – "to drive [him] to prison or the rope if [he goes] beyond the established lines" – and this means that law must always strive to make as clear as possible to the bad man, first, what the limits on conduct are, and second, what will happen to him if his conduct exceeds those limits. That end is best achieved, in turn, by setting out a systematized set of general "predictions" that are as clear and precise as possible. This is what the lawbooks are supposed to do.

It is true that, at certain points in *The Path of the Law* Holmes seems to be suggesting that the predictions that he says constitute the law are made from the point of view of the bad man and those who are giving him legal advice. But that could not really be Holmes's position. He presumably begins with the picture of a lawyer advising his client because he was speaking to a group of law students about their future profession. But Holmes clearly transcends this rather parochial perspective in order to address broader theoretical concerns. If that were not the case – if he were continuing to look at law solely from the point of view of the bad man and his lawyer – then Holmes could hardly speak of law as systematized prediction set out in lawbooks. For one thing, it is not the bad man who can plausibly be thought to be speaking through these books; it is the courts and the legislature, or, if you prefer, the law itself. For another thing, the contents of the lawbooks are, as we have already noted, only one source of concern to the bad man. If he thought it would help him to predict the outcome of his case, he would be intensely interested in knowing what the judge had had for breakfast or discovering what blandishments the emperor's wife had whispered in the judge's ear. Even more importantly, the bad man would be very keen to know the antecedent probability that he would be brought to court in the first place – the probability, that is, that his transgression would be detected and, if it were, that he would be prosecuted or sued. The bad man would also want to know what the probability was that any judgment rendered against him would be enforced. The substantive content of the law books is, at best, only the starting point for the bad man as he goes about maximizing his expected utility.

It is quite striking that Holmes never mentions any of these other considerations that the bad man would as a matter of course take into account, and in particular never mentions the probabilities of his being sued or having a judgment enforced against him. It seems unlikely that this was because Holmes simply failed to realize, in however rough a way, that the concept of probability plays a role in calculating self-interest. In fact, the reason why Holmes never discusses a realistic calculus of self-interest is quite straightforward. The predictions that constitute the law are made, not from the bad man's point of view but from that of the courts or the legislature, or perhaps both. Holmes is rather vague about this, and for present purposes it is enough to speak of the point of view of the law itself. If the law hopes to keep the bad man in line, it probably does not want to give him accurate information about the probability of enforcement. It will express its predictions in absolute terms: if you do such and such, you *will* be put in prison for ten years. Furthermore, since it is the courts themselves or some related agent of the state that have the task of putting the bad man in prison, this is really an expression of intention: it is, in other words, a *threat,* and the most effective threats are, generally speaking, those expressed as forcefully as possible.

I am suggesting, then, that for Holmes the law is more accurately characterized as a generalized system of threats than as a generalized system of predictions, although he himself seems to have regarded these as interchangeable notions. In at least one of his formulations of the prediction idea he makes this explicit:

> Law is a statement of circumstances in which the public force will be brought to bear upon men through the courts. But the word commonly is confined to such prophecies or threats when addressed to persons living within the power of the courts. A threat that depends upon the choice of the party to bring himself within that power would hardly be called law in the ordinary sense.[39]

A prediction is not, of course, the same thing as a threat, but they are related notions. What Holmes appears to be getting at is something like this. The concept of law begins with the idea of a public and general threat, and if the threat is credible we can think of it as being associated with an unqualified prediction that the threatened consequence will come about if the persons threatened do not stay within the designated bounds of conduct. Such threats will induce bad men to engage in systematic prediction of their own concerning when the public force will affect them (although they will still try, of course, to discover what are the true probabilities of enforcement). Since the threat of force is, for Holmes, the only possible glue that is capable of holding together a society of self-interested beings with a natural tendency to violence, it is only by such means that social order can be maintained. In this way, law can be seen to have a point or function along essentially Hobbesian lines.

Holmes is often described as a forerunner of extreme legal realism, but although he may have had some influence on the development of that movement, he was not an extreme realist himself. The last thing the realists cared about was prediction that is systematically rooted in the lawbooks. They were concerned with prediction from the point of view of someone affected by the law, such as the bad man. Prediction thus regarded can focus on any discoverable regularity, such as the correlation (if it exists) between what the judge had for breakfast and how he will decide the case. But Holmes himself is not interested in prediction of that kind. His concern, rather, is with threats, which are a form of communication made with an *intention* to publicize a certain, canonical, form of regularity: do such and such, and we will force you to pay money, go to prison, or whatever. These threats are just the same old propositions and rules that everybody else, or at least all other positivists, regard as law. Holmes's iconoclasm consists not in his having focused on prediction, which is not conceptually limited to the "dogma" of the law, but rather in interpreting this dogma as a body of threats which appeal to prudential rather than to social or moral reasons.

For Holmes, I suggest, law is best regarded as a generalized system of threats, and that conceptualization of social practice makes most sense if it is regarded as flowing from a certain view of the function of law. As I said earlier, Holmes does not explicitly state that law serves a function; I am using that notion to construct a theory of law that is, if not Holmes's actual view, the strongest theoretical interpretation of what he actually wrote. That having been said, the following two points about the notion of function bear mention. First, to make use of it, a Holmesian does not have to say that the persons who make and enforce law do so with the intention of maintaining social order for the greater social good. It is in keeping with Holmes's conception of human nature that those who make and enforce law do so because it is in their own interest to do so. I am supposing, in line with the methodological precepts on which we saw Hart to be implicitly relying, that a Holmesian would attribute a function or point to law from the outside, as it were. The institution of law can be seen to have some point or function – to have moral value, one is tempted to say, although that is not a very Holmesian notion – even as the relevant actors assiduously pursue their own self-interest. An analogy with the invisible hand, as envisaged in the classical conception of the free market, is almost unavoidable here. The second point is that attributing a function or point to law does not undermine the positivist character of Holmes's view of law. Just as we saw in connection with Hart's theory, it simply means that a nonpositivist methodology is being employed to defend a version of substantive legal positivism.

The idea that law has a point or function does entail, however, that there is a regulative ideal of a certain kind built into the very idea of law.[40] Holmes states explicitly in *The Path of the Law* that he wishes to point out an ideal that law has not yet attained, but that is relevant to the study of law for those who wish to use it to make their own prophecies (458). Later in the essay, he articulates this ideal as follows: "[A] body of law is more rational and more civilized when every rule it contains is referred articulately and definitely to an end which it subserves, and when the grounds for that end are stated or are ready to be stated in words" (469). This ideal is not concerned with any particular ends, moral or otherwise, that Holmes thinks law should pursue, since he did not believe that human societies have necessary or inherently desirable ends; there are only competing desires or interests that must fight it out on the social battlefield.[41] Rather the ideal is to make the end–means relationship as clear as possible. It is an ideal of instrumental rationality. Given Holmes's initial statement that the ideal he has in mind bears on the study of law from the perspective of those who wish to prophesy in their turn, it seems that at bottom the concern is with making prediction as straightforward and simple as possible: the more clearly the end one desires to achieve by a threat is articulated, the clearer the threat itself. This is, if you like, Holmes's version of the rule of law: make your threats as rationally motivated, and therefore as precise, as you can, so that people will be able to predict as readily as possible when the public force will be visited upon them.[42]

This brings us to the fourth of Holmes's six propositions about law, which is, it will be recalled, that rights and duties, as well as the law itself, are to be understood as predictions of the incidence of the use of public force. This thesis is often thought to be a reductive analysis of the concept of duty (together with the associated concept of a right) along Austinian lines.[43] Certainly Hart, for one, thinks Holmes's view is essentially the same as Austin's (243). In *The Concept of Law* Hart offers a number of devastating criticisms of Austin's analysis, all of which are to the effect that it is completely unsuccessful in capturing what we mean in speaking of a "duty" (79–88). If Austin's view were correct, for example, it would be a contradiction in terms, as it obviously is not, to say that someone has an obligation but that, owing to his having bribed the relevant official, there is not the slightest chance that he will suffer any penalty. Holmes, however, is not plausibly interpreted as offering an Austinian reductive analysis of the concept of duty. He does make use of conceptual analysis, but in a way that to some extent obscures the real thrust of what he is saying about rights and duties. Let me explain.

Holmes writes in *The Path of the Law* that the common law, understood as excluding criminal law and equitable remedies, does not impose duties "in an intelligible sense" (462). Although I will not undertake the task here, a close comparison of the relevant passages of *The Path of the Law* (461–63) with the 1872 "Book Notice" makes it quite plain that Holmes is relying on an analysis of the concept of legal duty that he first put forward in the latter work. In the course of rejecting Austin's reductive analysis in terms of sanctions, Holmes offers there the following alternative account:

> The notion of duty involves something more than a tax on a certain course of conduct. A protective tariff on iron does not create a duty not to bring it into the country. The word imports the existence of an absolute wish on the part of the power imposing it to bring about a certain course of conduct, and to prevent the contrary. A legal duty cannot be said to exist if the law intends to allow the person supposed to be subject to it an option at a certain price. The test of a legal duty is the absolute nature of the command . . . The imposition of a penalty is therefore only evidence tending to show that an absolute command was intended (a rule of construction).[44]

Holmes goes on to say that even if a penalty is imposed, there is no such absolute command unless a breach of it is deprived of the protection of the law. This would be shown by the existence of "collateral consequences," such as the invalidity of contracts to do the forbidden act or the denial of a remedy when the illegal act is part of the plaintiff's case.

In the 1872 "Book Notice" Holmes employs this analysis of legal duty to reach the following conclusion:

> Liability to pay the fair price or value of an enjoyment, or to be compelled to restore or give up property belonging to another, is not a penalty; and this is the extent of the ordinary liability to a civil action at common law. In a case of this sort, where there are no collateral consequences attached (which is perhaps the fact with regard to some contracts, to pay money, for instance), it is hard to say that there is a duty in strictness.[45]

Notice that Holmes is making precisely the same point when he says in *The Path of the Law* that it is not "intelligible" to speak of legal rights and duties at common law. And he argues for that conclusion in very much the same way, by pointing to the relatively few collateral consequences that attach to breach of a supposed "duty" (461).[46] But both equity, which acts *in personam,* and the criminal law, which purports to prohibit certain acts outright, can plausibly be regarded as giving rise to the "absolute commands" that in the 1872 "Book Notice" Holmes says are the mark of a duty.

Holmes's thesis that much of the common law can be understood as imposing liability conditional upon a person's acting in a certain way, without reference to whether the action breached a categorical duty or even fell below some standard of conduct, is historically significant and justly renowned.[47] It allowed for an understanding of the common law that differed significantly from Austin's blameworthiness-oriented interpretation and lent a new respectability to strict liability. In the 1872 "Book Notice" Holmes discusses the possible desirability of strict liability for "injuries from extra-hazardous sources," and he pursues similar themes along surprisingly modern lines in *The Common Law* and in *The Path of the Law* itself (467).[48] When all is said and done, however, this is still a thesis about the common law, and not about law as such. Moreover Holmes does not need the bad man to formulate or defend this thesis. In the 1872 "Book Notice" he gets the same view across using just his analysis of a legal duty, and he could have done without even that. The key idea he wished to convey was, after all, simply this: the law can legitimately impose liability on conduct even where it does not purport to treat that conduct as in any sense morally wrong or blameworthy.

So far as this thesis about the common law is concerned, bringing in the bad man in fact proves too much. The bad man would of course be concerned with any collateral consequence that the law attached to his actions, but he would just fold these into his calculation of expected utility, together with his consideration of the main consequence (e.g., penalty or damages award). The main characteristic of the bad man, as Holmes himself portrays him in *The Path of the Law*, is that he cares only about the material consequences of his actions. It simply does not matter to him whether the law also purports to issue an absolute command. So far as the impact on his practical reasoning is concerned, Holmes's own rhetorical question says everything that needs to be said: "But from [the bad man's] point of view, what is the difference between being fined and being taxed a certain sum for doing a certain thing?" (461). This question points, not to a limited thesis about the common law, but to a general thesis about law: the essence of law is the threats that it makes, and the quintessential legal reasons for action are those to which a bad man would respond. There is simply no room here for distinguishing between those threats that are supposedly accompanied by an absolute command and those that are not.

Holmes's retention in *The Path of the Law* of his 1872 analysis of legal duty shows quite clearly that he cannot be lumped in with Austin as a proponent of the conceptual reduction of duties to sanctions; the 1872 analysis was, after all, offered precisely as a critique of Austin.[49] At the same time it is somewhat puzzling, for the reasons canvassed in the preceding paragraph, that he would wish to retain that analysis at all. In fact I think that Holmes was groping toward a different view of legal rights and duties, which he did not quite formulate in *The Path of the Law* but stated clearly on several subsequent occasions. This view, to the effect that the concepts of legal right and legal duty are empty, or redundant, emerges, for example, in a letter Holmes wrote to Pollock in 1928. After first writing that his account of a right begins with his definition of law as the circumstances in which the public force will be brought to bear upon men through the courts – "the prophecy in general terms" – Holmes continues:

> Of course the prophecy becomes more specific to define a right. So we prophesy that the earth and the sun will act towards each other in a certain way. Then as we pretend to account for that mode of action by the hypothetical cause, the force of gravitation, which is merely the hypostasis of the prophesied fact and an empty phrase. So we get up the empty substratum, a *right,* to account for the fact that the courts will act in a certain way. We have got used to our phraseology and might find it hard for a time to do without it; but in that as in other cases I think our morally tinted words have caused a great deal of confused thinking.[50]

Leaving aside the bad physics, the point here is clearly that the concepts of legal right and duty are at best redundant and at worst a source of confusion. As Holmes put the point in a letter written to John Chipman Gray in 1914, "I became convinced that the machinery of rights and duties was a fifth wheel."[51] The confusion to which talk of rights and duties in law gives rise has its source, Holmes says, in the fact that "[w]e fill the word[s] with all the content which we draw from morals" (461). But this is a separate and distinct problem from any confusion that might arise in sorting out when there exists a true *legal* duty in an intelligible sense, since Holmes nowhere makes the implausible suggestion that moral duties should be understood along the lines of his 1872 analysis, that is, in terms of commands of some sort. In subsequently putting forward the redundancy idea Holmes was explicitly drawing the conclusion toward which the main arguments of *The Path of the Law* implicitly point: the concepts of right and duty have to be confined to the moral sphere, because they have no application whatever to law. In law, the only reasons for action that have any theoretical significance are prudential reasons. It is therefore misleading even to talk of law as giving rise to rights and duties, since this way of speaking suggests an appeal to social or moral reasons for action.

Hart's critique of Austin has no bite against the position just outlined, which, instead of offering a conceptual analysis of legal rights and duties, rejects those concepts outright. If I am correct, Holmes's starting point is a deeper thesis about the function of law. He is saying, in effect, that when law is viewed in terms of its function it must be pictured as a set of threats, and that to try to redescribe those threats using concepts that have been inappropriately borrowed from morality only confuses the picture. Of course, the attempt to force the law into the straitjacket of rights and duties is a deeply embedded aspect of our legal practices, as Holmes recognizes. That he nonetheless recommends abandoning that attempt is strong evidence for the thesis that at bottom his account of law is not purely descriptive but is in some measure normative in character, ultimately informed by a certain conception of law's point or function.

V. Law, Morality, and Adjudication

The fifth of the six propositions about law that I attributed to Holmes in section I is that law is in some sense distinct from morality. The sixth is that behind the logical form in which courts cast their judgments, they are in fact making legislative decisions on grounds of policy. In this section, I show how these final two propositions fit into the general Holmesian theory of law that I have been developing.

In order to understand what Holmes means when he says that law is distinct from morality, it would of course help to have some idea of what he thinks morality is. Unfortunately, this is a topic on which Holmes is anything but clear. The normative arguments in *The Common Law* are mainly (although not entirely) utilitarian in nature, and Holmes subsequently acknowledged that he was relying in that work on "the criterion of social welfare as against the individualistic bill of rights."[52] But at many other points in his work Holmes suggests that morality is a matter of social convention, or fashion, or majority agreement.[53] On such a view, moral reasons for action might well be thought to coincide with, or at least to constitute a subset of, the reasons for action I earlier called "social reasons." It seems quite possible, however, that Holmes did not distinguish between utilitarianism and some form of conventionalism; that he regarded the "social desire" that is "stronger at the point of conflict"[54] as simply the prevailing morality in the society in question. There are also passages in his work, particularly in *The Path of the Law*, where he could easily be interpreted as saying that there are moral reasons for action that are not reducible to social reasons. He certainly does not regard such independent moral reasons as universal but seems to hint that they could have their source in the conscience or idealism of the individual.[55] This perhaps suggests an even more thoroughgoing form of relativism than conventionalism. Finally, there are passages, such as the one quoted from "Natural Law" earlier, in which Holmes suggests that there are no moral reasons for action of any kind; that morality is just a form of self-deception in which the weak identify emotionally with the interests of the strong because that offers them their only (slim) chance of survival.[56]

Holmes's views on the nature of morality are, in short, a mess. There is almost nothing of philosophical interest here, and trying to tease out a coherent theory from his various pronouncements on the topic is almost certainly a game not worth the candle. For what it is worth, Holmes seems to me to be saying something like this: People generally act on the basis of their own self-interest and always do so when fundamental matters are at stake. As a result, there is a constant battle among "social" desires or interests. The stronger such interest generally prevails, and social welfare is maximized as a result, although (one way or another) individuals are sacrificed along the way. But although people generally act in their own self-interest, they are, in limited circumstances, also capable of acting for non-self-interested reasons that we can call "moral." The nature and source of these reasons are not at all definite, except that they do not form a universally valid system; their content varies from time to time and place to place. For present purposes, all that we need to know is that there are such reasons. Let me therefore refer to the propositions setting out the actions these reasons require, at a given time and place, as "morality."

It is obvious enough that one thing Holmes means when he says that law and morality are distinct from one another is just the standard thesis of legal positivism that the content of legal "dogma" does not *necessarily* coincide with morality. Although the law "is the witness and external deposit of our moral life" (459), this is a contingent fact only. Holmes would probably also endorse a version of Raz's sources thesis, which says that individual laws must be identified solely by reference to social facts and not by means of moral propositions or arguments. I have argued that Holmes is best interpreted as holding that laws are threats – communications issuing from those who wield power – and not predictions made by those who might be affected by the law. If that is right, it seems to entail a version of the sources thesis. A threat is just a certain kind of social fact, and the threats that constitute the law are, according to Holmes, recorded in the statute books and case reports. That is another kind of social fact. Hart rejects the sources thesis, because he thinks the rule of recognition can incorporate morality by reference. But it is difficult to see how a theory that conceptualizes law as a system of threats could give rise to an analogous notion.

There is, however, more to Holmes's claim that law and morality are distinct than these standard theses of legal positivism. It is sometimes suggested that Holmes meant that law and morality *should* be kept apart, and I think there are three senses in which this suggestion is correct. The first takes us back to the sources thesis: Holmes probably did believe that we should keep *the means for identifying law* distinct in our minds from morality, because conceptually the two just are different; the particular type of threat that constitutes law can be identified as such only as a matter of social fact, even where the action the threatener hopes to induce is required by morality. The second sense in which Holmes thought that law and morality should be kept distinct concerns the content of law, rather than just its sources. It is, however, a limited point, and not of general jurisprudential significance. It concerns Holmes's thesis in *The Common Law* that "the tendency of the law everywhere is to transcend moral and reach external standards,"[57] where by "moral standard" Holmes means a standard of evaluation that takes account of a person's state of mind, and by "external standard" a standard that assesses conduct without regard to state of mind (e.g., the "reasonable-person" standard in negligence law). The particular example Holmes gives in *The Path of the Law* is malice, which in law, he says, no longer imports a malevolent motive but "only signifies that the tendency of [a person's] conduct under known circumstances was very plainly to cause the plaintiff temporal harm" (463). This limited point is, however, concerned with morality not in the broader sense that Holmes clearly acknowledges to exist, but only in the limited sense in which morals "deal with the actual internal state of the individual's mind, what he actually intends" (463).

The third sense in which Holmes thinks morality and law should be kept distinct also concerns the language of law, but at issue this time are the more fundamental terms "duty" and "right." There is a general problem in jurisprudence, often called the problem of the "normativity" of law, that asks, *inter alia,* whether these and similarly fundamental normative terms have the same meaning in legal discourse as they have in moral discourse. A defender of natural law is almost inevitably committed to saying that they do mean the same thing in both contexts, but positivists have more leeway. Hart holds that the meaning of fundamental normative terms is different in the two types of discourse, since the meaning of "duty" or "obligation" in law is dependent on the notion of a social rule.[58] Raz, by contrast, thinks that such terms carry the same meaning in moral and legal contexts, but that it is possible to use normative language in a "detached" sense that does not commit the speaker to believing in the correctness of the normative propositions he asserts.[59] On this issue Hart and Holmes are, for once, on the same side, although their solutions to the problem differ. Holmes's approach was outlined in my section IV. His basic claim is that the terms "right" and "duty" not only do not bear in law the same meaning as in moral contexts, but are, generally speaking, "empty" terms; there are no such things as legal rights and duties.

This brings us to the sixth and final proposition that Holmes advanced in *The Path of the Law*, which is that judicial judgments, though clothed in a logical form, involve legislative decisions based on considerations of policy. This proposition is on its face somewhat different from the others, since it concerns adjudication rather than the nature of law as such. In its terms it does no more than reject the Langdellian version of formalism, according to which judicial decisions never involve extralegal, policy-based considerations. But the rejection of pure formalism naturally leads us to ask whether judicial decisions ever do *not,* for Holmes, turn on considerations of policy. That is a question that does have implications for the theoretical characterization of law, since if all or most judicial decisions (potentially) turn on the judge's views of policy, then the law is indeterminate or, at the least, is not of a nature to bind courts. This is one aspect of a more general question that asks how, on a Holmesian view of law, we should understand the theoretical relationship between law and adjudication.

Hart famously criticized Holmes's view that law is a prediction of what judges will do, on the grounds that a judge does not look upon a legal rule as a statement that he and others are likely to punish offenders, but rather as his *reason* and *justification* for punishment (10–11, 102). The picture of adjudication that Hart draws here fits well with his own conception of the nature and function of law. Law consists of rules, identified as valid by an overarching rule of recognition, that are intended to guide the conduct of ordinary citizens. The rule of recognition imposes a duty on judges to assess the conduct of citizens in accordance with those same rules. Judges consequently treat the rules as a reason for decision and a justification for reaching a certain result. Hart of course acknowledges, like Holmes, that judges at least sometimes decide on the basis of policy considerations, but only when they are not bound by existing law; that is when they have the "discretion" to legislate.

Hart's criticism of Holmes is, in effect, that if law is a prediction of what judges are going to decide, they will have to predict what they themselves are going to do. This is problematic because (a) it will probably lead to logical conundrums of one sort or another, and (b) it seems far removed from our pretheoretical sense of what it is that judges in fact are doing. One way that Holmes, or a Holmesian, could avoid this difficulty would be to say that it begs the question against Holmes. More specifically, Hart is assuming that judges are bound, or at least regard themselves as bound, by existing law, so that if one defines law as a prediction of what judges will do, it follows that a judge is bound to try to predict what it is that he is going to do. But Holmes can break out of this circle simply by saying that judges are not bound by existing law, so that this theory about the nature of law would have no bearing on his theory of adjudication (i.e., his theory of how judges should decide cases). On this view the judge is a pragmatist, in Dworkin's sense of that term in *Law's Empire*.[60] He is, in essence, a morally free agent; he can take account of what courts have done in the past, but for strategic or policy reasons only and not because he is bound in principle to do so. This response to Hart leads in the direction of a certain strand of legal realism, according to which *all* judicial decisions – not just some – are made on grounds of policy.

This is not, however, the route that I think Holmes would take, nor is it the appropriate direction for the Holmesian theory of law. Recall that Holmes is not best understood as saying that the predictions that constitute law are made at large, or from the perspective of the bad man. The state, through the legislature, the courts, and perhaps other agents, is the one doing the predicting, and its predictions have been enshrined in the lawbooks. Holmes is, in effect, simply offering a new interpretation of what he and everyone else agrees is the law, namely, statutes and judicial decisions. Moreover, the predictions do not so much concern what the judge is going to do as what will happen to the ordinary citizen if he or she exceeds the designated limits on conduct. When we add the element of intention, we arrive at the idea of a threat. If we think of law as a threat, the potential logical difficulties disappear, and we see also that there is a sense in which the law "binds" judges, or at least gives them reasons for action. If the state is threatening its citizens and the judge is an agent of the state, the judge has reason to give effect to those threats that the state has made in the past.

This is of course only an initial sketch of a theoretical view of adjudication. Many details would need to be filled in and many objections addressed. These matters cannot, for the most part, be considered here. There are however, two issues to which I would at least like to draw attention. The first concerns the theoretical status of the courts: Do they simply play a role in enforcing threats that for the most part are made by some other entity, which for the moment we can refer to as "the state," or are they the ultimate threateners? This is something that Holmes is rather vague about. At times, especially in his earlier work, he suggests, in anticipation of John Chipman Gray, that all law is really made by judges. Thus in the 1872 "Book Notice" he writes that "in a civilized state it is not the will of the sovereign that makes lawyers' law, but what a body of subjects, namely, the judges, by whom it is enforced, *say* is his will."[61] If one takes seriously the idea that law is a system of threats, however, it is rather implausible to envisage judges as the ultimate threateners. After he had been on the bench for a while, Holmes, in any event, began to take a much more conservative view of adjudication. Judges only legislate "interstitially,"[62] and it is not generally desirable that they should "undertake to renovate the law."[63] Beyond that, the courts are no more than "an instrumentality established by the United States to carry out its will"; they are "simply directors of a force that comes from the source that gives them their authority."[64] This suggests that Holmes came to hold that the real source of law – the true threatener – is the state. Given the basic premise that law consists of threats, this is clearly the more plausible view. But it is evident that a great deal more has to be said about the relationship between this abstract entity and the various persons in a society who actually have power of one kind or another.

The other issue to which I would like to draw attention concerns the motivation of judges in those cases in which they are free to make policy decisions. At one point in *The Path of the Law* Holmes suggests that judges "have failed adequately to recognize their duty of weighing considerations of social advantage" (467). This suggests that judges have a duty, and therefore presumably a capacity, to decide cases on the basis of a selfless utilitarian determination of what is in the general social interest. But can this suggestion be reconciled with Holmes's apparent view that most people, most of the time, are motivated purely by self-interest? If judges could consistently act on the basis of moral or social reasons, then presumably many others could as well, and the conception of the person on which Holmes's theoretical edifice rests – the bad man – would have to be drastically modified or rejected. Another possibility, however, is that judges do in fact decide on the basis of self-interested reasons. They are not, of course, generally coerced into deciding this way or that by threats of force, but perhaps there are more general pressures at work that ensure that it is in the judge's own interest to decide in favor of the "social desire" that is "stronger at the point of conflict."[65] In other words, the judge is merely a foot soldier and not a general in the "concealed, half-conscious battle on the question of legislative policy" (467).[66] At most the judge can give effect to Holmes's ideal for law of articulating as clearly as possible the end which each rule subserves (467). But so far as the choice of one end over another is concerned, that is generally beyond his control.

VI. Conclusion

I have argued that Holmes's various discrete observations about law in *The Path of the Law*, when viewed in light of the methodological assumptions of one of his strongest critics, H. L. A. Hart, can be seen to hang together as a comprehensive and more or less consistent theory of jurisprudence. I have not argued that that theory is correct, nor do I think that it is. But I believe that it is a much more powerful theory than Holmes is often given credit for. For example, it is commonly thought that Hart's critique of Austin's theory of law was as devastating for Holmes's theoretical views as it was for Austin's, but this is not so; Holmes survives the Hartian onslaught much better than Austin. Hart's most potent criticisms of Austin are generally concerned with the inadequacy of the latter's conceptual analyses, such as his analysis of a law as a command backed by threats of evil,[67] or his analysis of an obligation in terms of a sanction. Since Austin is most plausibly interpreted as offering these definitions as analyses of our ordinary concepts of law, obligation, etc., Hart's criticisms have a great deal of force. If Holmes were arguing that what we ordinarily *mean* by law is a threat, then he would be subject to similar criticisms. But I do not think that that is what he should be understood to say. The Holmesian claim, when placed in its most favorable light,[68] is that the only effective reasons for action to which law gives rise are reasons of prudential self-interest, so that regardless of how law is at present conceptualized, it is in terms of such reasons that it *should* be conceptualized. Holmes is entitled to this "should" because, again when his theory is placed in the most favorable light, it can be seen to rest on a normative methodology similar in essential respects to the one that Hart himself implicitly employs.

According to that methodology, the theorist ascribes a point or function to law, but from the outside; any views on this question that the "participants" in law might hold are not regarded as theoretically significant. Hart of course rejects extreme externalism but accepts that theories of law are external in the sense that I earlier called "engaged": they take account of the effect of law on participants' practical reasoning, but without taking up the participants' point of view. I have argued that Holmes can plausibly be interpreted along similar lines. Since Hart's own methodology advocates an external perspective, he is hardly in a position to complain that the Holmesian conceptualization of law departs from the conceptualization of participants. This is not to say, of course, that the blunt characterization of law as a system of threats will not run into conceptual problems even from an external perspective,[69] but any such obstacles are clearly much less formidable than those facing Austin's theory. Besides, a certain degree of ingenuity can undoubtedly overcome many of these difficulties,[70] and Hart's theory faces a few analogous obstacles of its own.

In fact the dispute between Holmes and Hart becomes something of a stalemate, unless we modify the methodological approach to jurisprudence upon which the substantive theory of each is best understood to rely. Both Hart and Holmes appear to regard any reflection about the point or function of law by those who participate in legal practices as irrelevant to jurisprudence. We can, however, make a start toward overcoming the stalemate if we suppose, as seems plausible, that law is the sort of social institution whose nature is in part determined by *internal* debates about what its point or function should be taken to be. This requires, in turn, that the theorist him- or herself adopt a certain kind of internal viewpoint rather than simply, as in Hart's theory, take account of such a viewpoint. The adoption of the appropriate internal viewpoint makes participants' conceptualization of law and legal practice, or, more accurately, their competing conceptualizations, a crucial factor in theorizing about law. In this way we are led to endorse a methodology for jurisprudence that is similar to Ronald Dworkin's interpretivist approach.[71] This does not, of course, settle the key questions of jurisprudence. But it does permit us to ask those questions in a more satisfactory manner and to formulate more sophisticated Holmesian and Hartian answers to them.

The more sophisticated Holmesian theory was of course advanced by Hobbes three centuries ago. Hobbes in effect treats the bad man as strategically and not just parametrically rational[72] and argues that from such a person's internal perspective it is rationally desirable that there should be a sovereign who wields absolute power. The more sophisticated Hartian theory has been developed in recent years by Raz, who argues that under certain circumstances it can be seen to be rational, from the internal perspective of an ordinary citizen, to be guided by the directives of a legal authority. Those circumstances are, essentially, that the ordinary citizen is likely to comply better with the reasons for action that apply to him if he follows the authority's directives than if he acts on his own judgment.[73] Raz argues, in effect, that it can be explained to the ignorant man who is willing to do what he is told that it can at least sometimes be rational for him to do what he is told, and that this explanation properly figures in our understanding of the concept of law.

The Hobbesian and Razzian theories are two versions of legal positivism, and of course other substantive theories of law can be formulated from the appropriate internal perspective. This is not the place to enter into those substantive debates or to address the further methodological issues that arise when legal theory adopts an internal point of view. I have been concerned in this essay simply to show that the methodological assumptions on which Hart implicitly relies in *The Concept of Law* can be employed both to develop a distinctively Holmesian theory of law and to neutralize at least some of Hart's criticisms of Holmes's theoretical views. The manner in which those methodological assumptions must be modified in order to permit adequate versions of each theory to be formulated and assessed is not a task for the present occasion.[74]

Notes

1 Oliver Wendell Holmes, Jr., "The Path of the Law," *Harvard Law Review* 10 (1897):1457. Cited hereafter parenthetically in the text as "Path." "The Path" is reprinted in the Appendix to this volume with star paging.
2 David Rosenberg, *The Hidden Holmes: His Theory of Torts in History* (Cambridge, Mass.: Harvard University Press, 1995), 46–50.
3 Frederic Rogers Kellog, *The Formative Essays of Justice Holmes: The Making of an American Legal Philosophy* (Westport, Conn.: Greenwood, 1984), 69.
4 Ronald Dworkin, *Law's Empire* (Cambridge, Mass.: Belknap Press, 1986), 90. "[N]o firm line divides jurisprudence from adjudication or any other aspect of legal practice . . . Jurisprudence is the general part of adjudication, silent prologue to any decision at law."
5 See H. L. A. Hart, *The Concept of Law* (Oxford: Clarendon Press, 1961), 87–88. Unless otherwise noted, all citations of Hart (by page number only) are to this source.
6 See Henry M. Hart, Jr., "Holmes' Positivism – An Addendum," *Harvard Law Review* 64 (1951):929, 933.
7 Cf. Rosenberg, *Hidden Holmes,* 48–49:
> [Holmes's] new jurisprudence's antidote to cognitive and linguistic distortions in formulating general legal theories was to "substitut[e] a scientific foundation for empty words." The prescription was to focus on the rudimentary sensate conditions, the facts which are likely to trigger judicial action and the resulting coercive effects, whether imposed directly by the court judgment or indirectly by social stigma . . . Accordingly, any statement worthy of study must be capable of yielding empirical predictions of what the courts will do in fact (or explanations of what the courts have done). Those predictions must then be compared to the law in operation – the actual requirements, effects, and consequences of decisions and rules . . . To facilitate testing legal concepts and theories in the "dry light" of experience, Holmes advocated the "bad man" heuristic – examining the requirements and effects of the law as one who cares only about avoiding its sanctions.

8 Oliver Wendell Holmes, Jr., "Law in Science and Science in Law," in *Collected Legal Papers* (New York: Harcourt, Brace & Howe, 1920), 121. *Papers* is cited hereafter as "CLP."
9 Cf. Thomas C. Grey, "Holmes and Legal Pragmatism," *Stanford Law Review* 41 (1989):787. On my reading of Holmes, Holmes the theorist takes account of the bad man's internal, prudential point of view, just as Hart takes account of the ignorant man's internal, socialized point of view, but, again like Hart, Holmes is not committed to taking up the internal point of view himself, *qua* theorist. See the discussion in section III of the present chapter. Grey's own interpretation of the prediction theory is that Holmes has in mind a "heuristic purpose" defined by "a limited but particularly important legal perspective, that of a private lawyer counselling a client" (828, 826). I agree with Grey that this perspective

informs Holmes's discussion in *The Path of the Law*, but, for the reasons I present in section III, I believe it merges into a more general and comprehensive theory of law.
10 Grey, "Legal Pragmatism."
11 Stephen Perry, "Interpretation and Methodology in Legal Theory," in *Law and Interpretation,* ed. Andrei Marmor (New York: Oxford University Press, 1995), 97; Stephen Perry, "The Varieties of Legal Positivism," *Canadian Journal of Law and Jurisprudence* 9 (1996):361.
12 "The idea that the substantive rules of the criminal law have as their function (and, in a broad sense, their meaning) the guidance not merely of officials operating a system of penalties, but of ordinary citizens in the activities of non-official life, cannot be eliminated without jettisoning cardinal distinctions and obscuring the specific character of law as a means of social control" (38–39; cf. 134).
13 "In the case of the rules of the criminal law, it is logically possible and might be desirable that there should be such rules even though no punishment or other evil were threatened . . . We can, in a sense, subtract the sanction and still leave an intelligible standard of behaviour which it was designed to maintain" (34).
14 Is it really possible, on Hart's theoretical account of law, that "[i]n an extreme case the internal point of view with its characteristic use of legal language . . . might be confined to the official world"? (114)
15 "The remedy for each of these three main defects [uncertainty, rigidity, and inefficiency] in this simplest form of social structure consists in supplementing the *primary* rules with *secondary* rules which are rules of a different kind" (91). Hart's definitions of primary and secondary rules, which are complicated and somewhat confused, need not be considered here. All that matters for present purposes is that the rule of recognition is a secondary rule.
16 See Hart's discussion in the postscript to *The Concept of Law* (248–49). In Perry, "Interpretation," 129–31, 135, I argue that Hart is wrong to assume that there is no controversy about the idea that the function of law is the guidance of conduct.
17 W. J. Waluchow argues that ascriptions of function to law can be understood in "descriptive-explanatory" terms. W. J. Waluchow, *Inclusive Legal Positivism* (New York: Oxford University Press, 1994), 119. I argue in Perry, "Legal Positivism," 369–74, that that is not so.
18 "Statements made from the external point of view may themselves be of different kinds. The observer may, without accepting the rules himself, assert that the group accepts the rules, and thus may from the outside refer to the way in which *they* are concerned with them from the internal point of view" (86–87, emphasis added). Cf. Hart, "Comment," in *Issues in Contemporary Legal Philosophy: The Influence of H. L. A. Hart,* ed. Ruth Gavison (New York: Oxford University Press, 1987), 35, 39.
19 H. L. A. Hart, Introduction, in *Essays in Jurisprudence and Philosophy* (New York: Oxford University Press, 1983), 13.
20 Cf. Perry, "Legal Positivism," 361–62, 369–74.
21 Perry, "Interpretation," 131–32.
22 Joseph Raz, *Ethics in the Public Domain* (New York: Oxford University Press, 1994), 194–204.
23 Austin is clearly a methodological as well as a substantive positivist. Austin's and Bentham's legal theories are often thought to be similar in most respects, but Postema argues persuasively that Bentham explicitly adopted a normative methodology in order to defend

his version of substantive positivism. See Gerald Postema, *Bentham and the Common Law Tradition* (New York: Oxford University Press, 1986), 328–36. The same is also clearly true of Hobbes.
24 Oliver Wendell Holmes, Jr., *The Common Law* (Boston: Little, Brown, 1881), 44.
25 Quoted in *The Essential Holmes,* ed. Richard A. Posner (Chicago: University of Chicago Press, 1990), 102–3.
26 Holmes, "Natural Law," in CLP, 312.
27 Jean Hampton denies that Hobbes held this thesis in *Leviathan.* Jean Hampton, *Hobbes and the Social Contract Tradition* (Cambridge: Cambridge University Press, 1986), 20–21. However, it is a view sufficiently identified with Hobbes to justify calling it "Hobbesian."
28 In fact I implicitly introduced this idea earlier, when I attributed to Holmes the thesis that it is only by appealing to reasons of self-interest that law can truly be effective.
29 Holmes, "Natural Law," 313.
30 Holmes, "Admiral Dewey," in Holmes, *Occasional Speeches of Justice Oliver Wendell Holmes,* ed. Mark DeWolfe Howe (Cambridge, Mass.: Belknap Press of Harvard University Press, 1962), 109.
31 The best philosophical exposition of those discussions of which I am aware is in Hampton, *Hobbes and the Social Contract.*
32 Jon Elster, *Ulysses and the Sirens,* rev. ed. (Cambridge: Cambridge University Press, 1984), 18:
> The parametrically rational actor treats his environment as a constant, whereas the strategically rational actor takes account of the fact that the environment is made up of other actors, and that he is part of their environment, and that they know this, etc. In a community of parametrically rational actors each will believe that he is the only one whose behaviour is variable, and that all the others are parameters for his decision problem.
33 I thus agree with Brian Leiter, "Holmes, Economics, and Classical Realism," Chapter 13 in this volume, in the text associated with note 98, that the bad man is not only selfish but stupid. Leiter argues that Holmes, in accepting this view of human nature, falls within the philosophical tradition that Leiter calls "classical realism."
34 See quotation in the text at note 24 to this chapter.
35 Holmes, "Natural Law," 314.
36 "Book Notice," *American Law Review* 6 (1872):593 reprinted in Felix Frankfurter, "The Early Writings of O. W. Holmes, Jr.," *Harvard Law Review* 44 (1931):717, 788–91 at 789. All references are to this reprint.
37 Ibid., 790.
38 Emphasis added.
39 *American Banana Co. v. United Fruit Co.,* 213 U.S. 347, 356–57 (1909). This case is interesting for reasons beyond the explicit equation of predictions and threats. Holmes makes practical use of the idea that the efficacy of a threat does not ordinarily depend upon the choice of the party threatened in order to propound a principle of statutory construction that says that all legislation is prima facie territorial. This principle is no doubt defensible on grounds of both principle and policy, but it must be said that this particular line of reasoning has a curiously formalistic air to it.
40 Hart inevitably builds an analogous ideal into his concept of law: in order to guide conduct well, legal rules should be clear, public, general, prospective. These are, not coincidentally, the virtues traditionally associated with nonsubstantive versions of the ideal of

the rule of law. Cf. Joseph Raz, *The Authority of Law* (New York: Oxford University Press, 1979), chapter 11.

41 "[Policy] matters really are battle grounds where the means do not exist for determinations that shall be good for all time, and where the decision can do no more than embody the preference of a given body in a given time and place. We do not realize how large a part of our law is open to reconsideration upon a slight change in the habit of the public mind" ("Path" 466). Many similar passages are to be found throughout Holmes's work, in which the metaphor of battle, if it is a metaphor, is pervasive.

42 Holmes has in mind precisely the same ideal when he writes that "the whole meaning of every new effort of legal thought is to make these prophecies more precise, and to generalize them into a thoroughly connected system" ("Path" 457–58).

43 John Austin, *The Province of Jurisprudence Determined,* ed. Wilfred E. Rumble (Cambridge: Cambridge University Press, 1995), 24–25:
> It also appears from what has been premised, that *command, duty,* and *sanction* are inseparably connected terms; that each embraces the same ideas as the others, though each denotes those ideas in a peculiar order or series. "A wish conceived by one, and expressed or intimated to another, with an evil to be inflicted and incurred in case the wish be disregarded," are signified directly and indirectly by each of the three expressions. Each is the name of the same complex notion. . . . When I am talking *directly* of the chance of incurring the evil, or (changing the expression) of the liability or obnoxiousness of the evil, I employ the term *duty,* or the term *obligation:* The liability or obnoxiousness to the evil being put foremost, and the rest of the complex notion being signified implicitly.

44 "Book Notice," 790.

45 Ibid., 791.

46 In *The Path of the Law*, Holmes uses the term "further disadvantages" instead of "collateral consequences."

47 "The duty to keep a contract at common law means a prediction that you must pay damages if you do not keep it, – and nothing else. If you commit a tort, you are liable to pay a compensatory sum. If you commit a contract, you are liable to pay a compensatory sum unless the promised event comes to pass, and that is all the difference" ("Path" 462).

48 In a recent book, David Rosenberg has rightly emphasized Holmes's defense of what amounts to "enterprise liability," an aspect of Holmes's work that has been neglected in recent years. See Rosenberg, *Hidden Holmes.*

49 Postema argues convincingly that Bentham also was not offering an Austinian reductive analysis of the concepts of right and duty but rather was advancing a *substitute* for the ordinary conception, based on the notions of command plus sanction. See Postema, *Bentham,* 323–24.

50 Holmes to Pollock, quoted in Posner, *Essential Holmes,* 179. Cf. "Natural Law," 313.

51 Quoted in Rosenberg, *Hidden Holmes,* 189.

52 Holmes, *Common Law,* 307.

53 Ibid., 213, 310–11.

54 Ibid., 239.

55 "[W]hen we speak of the rights of man in a moral sense, we mean to mark the limits of interference with individual freedom which we think are prescribed by conscience, or by our ideal, however reached" ("Path," 460).

56 See text accompanying note 29 to this chapter. It is worth contrasting this suggestion of Holmes's with Hart's view. Hart clearly regards moral reasons for action – reasons rooted in what he calls "critical morality" – as distinct from, although likely to overlap in con-

tent with, social reasons – reasons that flow from, or at least are perceived to flow from, social rules. Hart thinks that people can adopt the socialized point of view, and therefore subject themselves to (perceived) social reasons, for a variety of other types of reasons, including in particular moral reasons and reasons of self-interest. H. L. A. Hart, *Essays on Bentham* (New York: Oxford University Press, 1982), 256–57. Holmes, in the passage referred to, might be taken as saying that the socialized point of view can be adopted *only* for reasons of self-interest.

57 Holmes, *Common Law,* 135. This thesis is clearly related to Holmes's view, discussed in my section IV and developed by him in connection with the common law in particular, that law can legitimately impose liability on conduct even where it does not purport to treat that conduct as morally wrong or blameworthy.
58 Hart, *Bentham,* 159–61. See also Raz's commentary on Hart in Joseph Raz, "Hart on Moral Rights and Legal Duties," *Oxford Journal of Legal Studies* (1984):123, 129–31.
59 Raz, *Authority of Law,* 137–45, 153–57.
60 Dworkin, *Law's Empire,* 147–75.
61 "Book Notice," 789 (emphasis in original).
62 *Southern Pacific Co. v. Jensen,* 244 U.S. 205, 221 (1917) (Holmes dissenting).
63 Holmes, CLP, 239.
64 Holmes to Harold Laski, January 29, 1926, quoted in *Essential Holmes,* 235.
65 Holmes, CLP, 239.
66 This is essentially the view of Brian Leiter, in Chapter 13 of the present volume, when he argues that Holmes is a quietist, i.e., someone who thinks that it is better to keep quiet about normative matters than to theorize in ways that make no difference to practice.
67 Hart employs the term "orders backed by threats" to avoid the sense of legitimacy that accompanies the word "command." Austin himself says that law is a species of command and then defines "command" as a "signification of desire" directed from A to B, where B is "liable to evil" from A if B does not comply with the desire (*Province of Jurisprudence,* 21–22).
68 That is, the light that lends the greatest plausibility to Holmes's views.
69 For example, one of Hart's criticisms of Austin is that his definition of law does not satisfactorily show how law, understood as orders backed by threats, can bind the sovereign (41–43). A similar point obviously applies to law understood as threats *tout court*. In his judgment in *The Western Maid,* 257 U.S. 419, 431 (1922), Holmes says the following: "[W]e must realize that the authority that makes the law is itself superior to it, and that if it consents to apply to itself the rules that it applies to others the consent is free and may be withheld." It is difficult to see, however, how one can consent to threaten oneself, from which it seems to follow that a lawmaker simply cannot bind himself by law. This looks unsatisfactory, even from the engaged external perspective. It seems that Holmes will have to say something to the effect that the *paradigmatic* instances of law are threats and then perhaps help himself to the concept of rules to explain other cases. This is not necessarily an implausible strategy.
70 See, e.g., Robert Ladenson, "In Defense of a Hobbesian Conception of Law," *Philosophy and Public Affairs* 9 (1980):134.
71 Dworkin, *Law's Empire,* 45–113.
72 Elster, *Ulysses.*
73 Raz, *Ethics in the Public Domain,* 195–204.
74 I have begun to address some of these issues in Perry, "Interpretation."

8

The Bad Man and the Internal Point of View

SCOTT J. SHAPIRO*

Before H. L. A. Hart, every major figure in the legal-positivist tradition subscribed to a sanction-centered theory of law. Famously, John Austin conceived of legal rules as threats backed by sanctions, and he viewed statements of legal obligations as predictions that the threatened sanctions would be carried out. Although Hans Kelsen sought to explain legal rules and obligations in terms of norms, these norms were understood to be directives to courts requiring that sanctions be applied. Adopting a hybrid position, Alf Ross understood legal rules as norms addressed to courts directing the use of sanctions, and he understood statements of legal validity as predictions that these norms would be followed.

In *The Concept of Law,* Hart showed that sanction-centered accounts of every stripe ignore an essential feature of law. This feature he termed "the internal point of view." Seen from the internal point of view, the law is not simply sanction-threatening, -directing, or -predicting, but rather obligation-imposing.

Though the internal point of view is perhaps Hart's greatest contribution to jurisprudential theory, this concept is also often and easily misunderstood. It is commonly thought that the internal point of view is synonymous with the "insider's" point of view. According to Stephen Perry, "[T]he general idea of the internal point of view is that an adequate jurisprudential account must at some point take into consideration how the practice looks to at least some of the practice's participants, from the inside."[1] Legal theories must resonate, as it were, with the shared experiences of legal natives. To many commentators, Hart's introduction of the internal point of view in *The Concept of Law* initiated the "hermeneutic turn" in modern jurisprudence.

---

* I would like to thank Arthur Jacobson for the many enjoyable and illuminating conversations we have had about H. L. A. Hart's *The Concept of Law.* Thanks are also due to Peter Hilal for his usual help. A mere acknowledgment, however, would not express my gratitude to Jules Coleman for all of the assistance he has given me with this essay. I refrain from detailing the extent of it, not only because it is embarrassing, but also because I fear the reader would think that I was simply exaggerating.

On this reading, legal theories that take into account the internal point of view are to be contrasted with ones that ignore the beliefs and attitudes of those who live under the law. The clearest examples of "external" legal theories are those motivated by the concerns of philosophical behaviorism or naturalism. Many sociological theories of law are external accounts, in this sense, insofar as they limit the observer's role to recording the frequency of compliance with the law in a given population and correlating its absence with the appearance of sanctions.[2]

On the other hand, the internal point of view may refer to a specific kind of normative attitude held by an insider. In that case "internal" is not synonymous with "inside" but with "internalized." Someone takes the internal point of view toward the law when he treats it as obligation-imposing. According to this interpretation, legal theories that take into account the internal point of view are to be contrasted with theories that fail to capture the experience of those who recognize the law's claim to authority. All sanction-centered theories are external accounts in this sense.

Quite obviously, one's interpretation of the internal point of view determines how one views Hart's critique of his predecessors. If the internal point of view is the insider's point of view, sanction-based accounts are inadequate, because they fail to reflect a cardinal feature of the insider's legal understanding: in every culture with a legal system, virtually everyone regards the law as a normative institution. The law not only claims to make a practical difference in their lives, but ordinarily it does. It affects people's practical reasoning by providing them with reasons for acting in ways the system deems desirable and for not acting in ways the system deems undesirable. An adequate legal theory must recognize that the law claims to be, and is generally treated as, a creator of obligations, not simply a harbinger of harm.

In his essay "Hart versus Holmes: The Bad Man in Legal Theory" (Chapter 7 of this volume) Stephen R. Perry seems to understand Hart's critique in just this way.[3] As a result, Perry claims that Hart's argument is ineffective against Holmes's "bad man" theory, because Holmes also took into account the insider's point of view. After all, the bad man, by definition, is someone who sees the law as a normative institution – he is an insider whose curiosity about the law is piqued solely by his aversion to sanctions. Although this practical interest may not be commendable, it is nevertheless genuine. Hart's misleading characterizations notwithstanding, Holmes's theory is every bit as hermeneutic as Hart's.

However, Perry continues, if Hart were to concede that Holmes also took into account the insider's point of view, Hart's criticism of Holmes for ignoring those who accept the law on its own terms would beg the question. For if Holmes was being myopic by overlooking the "good" or "puzzled" man (Hart's terms), then Hart was also being myopic by neglecting the bad man. Hart did not realize that there is not just one way to see the law from the internal point of view; there are at least two!

According to Perry, the real issue between Hart and Holmes was not about how to do jurisprudence. Both were convinced that the legal theorist must adopt the hermeneutic stance and therefore understand the law as a normative institution. Perry believes, however, that they developed divergent legal theories because they had different moral conceptions. Although Hart claimed to be engaged in a descriptive analysis, his account belies a normative vision of the person and the proper function of the law. Hart emphasized the point of view of those committed to the legal system not because he thought that most people *do* treat the law as imposing obligations, but because he thought that they *ought* to. The point of legal institutions, therefore, is to guide conduct through rules, insofar as this is a worthy goal for the law to pursue.

Hart's dispute with Holmes, according to Perry, is in essence a moral disagreement over how people ought to act and how social institutions ought to be structured. Holmes privileged the role that sanctions play in the law because he believed that most people are "bad" in the sense of being self-interested, and that they have no reason to be otherwise. Because an appeal to rules and obligations would be ineffective with such people, the proper function of law is to control self-interested behavior through threats and sanctions.

Perry has offered an ingenious interpretation of *The Concept of Law,* but his view stems from a misunderstanding of (1) the role of the bad man in Hart's argument, and (2) the nature of the "internal point of view." Contrary to Perry's assumption, the main object of Hart's criticisms in the sections that Perry discusses was not Holmes. Rather, Hart was concerned with contemporary legal theorists such as Alf Ross and Hans Kelsen, who offered sanction-based accounts as part of an effort to rework jurisprudence as a scientifically respectable discipline. These theorists did not premise their jurisprudential accounts on Holmesian grounds; rather, their *legal* positivism was based on their *logical* positivism.

Hart's objections were leveled primarily at these supposedly "scientific" theories of law. The reduction of legal obligations to predictions of sanctions, Hart argued, fails to account for the normative role that such predictions play in society in the guidance and evaluation of conduct. The reformulation of laws addressed to ordinary citizens as norms directed at legal officials masks the fact that the laws do in fact shape the conduct of ordinary citizens as well as that of legal officials.

Hart introduced the bad man at this point in his discussion solely in order to consider one defense of these positivists as he proceeded to attack them. Sanction-based accounts, Hart suggested, may indeed capture an aspect of the law's normativity. Since the bad man is concerned only with the penalties for disobedience, sanction-based theories illustrate in a striking fashion how the law guides this sort of person.

Hart still considered Holmes's methodology to be hermeneutic in nature. In fact, Hart was able to enlist the bad man in defense of sanction-centered theories of law precisely because he thought that the bad man regards the law as a normative institution. Hart invoked the internal point of view, however, in order to point to the limitations of Holmes's hermeneutic perspective. Sanction-centered theories, he argued, may characterize some members of the community, but they inevitably neglect people who heed the law because they are committed to it. Some take the internal point of view and see the law as imposing obligations, not just threatening sanctions.

Hart, therefore, did not understand the internal point of view simply as the perspective of a legal insider; rather, he meant it to refer to the perspective of an insider who accepts the law's legitimacy. The problem with all sanction-based accounts, on this reading, is that they disregard those who treat the law as imposing obligations. Bad man theories, as well as naturalistic ones, ignore the internal point of view and, as a result, fail to account for the range of normative attitudes that people may, and actually do have toward the law.

This interpretation of Hart's argument has many virtues. Because this reading does not regard the bad man view of the law as Hart's main target, it is not necessary to conclude, with Perry, that Hart mischaracterized Holmes's argument or begged the question. Because Hart's sights were fixed on the logical positivists, the critical comments in these sections do not apply to Holmes, who did not share their methodological commitments. Moreover, since Hart defines the internal point of view as the perspective of those committed to the law, he was right to conclude that all sanction-centered theories, including bad man ones, are external accounts. Finally, there is no need to see Hart's rejection of sanction-centered theories as resting on a moral conception of the person. Hart's complaint is premised on his methodological commitment to theoretical generality: theories of legal institutions should account for *all* of the ways in which the law guides conduct, not simply focus on one technique at the expense of all others.

I. The Internal Point of View

The first mention of "the internal point of view" in Hart's *Concept of Law* occurs in chapter 5, during his discussion of the predictive theory of legal obligation. To see claims of obligations as statements about the likelihood of sanctions, Hart argued, is to disregard the way that members of the group normally see the effect that law has on their behavior. Members do not see legal rules simply as *signs* that some evil will befall them if they disobey, but also as *signals* to obey. From the internal point of view, the law is seen to impose obligations rather than simply to threaten sanctions. The predictive theory is inadequate because it defines this point of view "out of existence."[4]

Hart's criticisms, Perry claims, rest on a caricature of Holmes's theory. Hart would have been justified in condemning the bad man theory if it had failed to consider the insider's point of view. Since every jurisprudential theory must account for the way that the law appears to those who are subject to it, a purely behavioristic theory of law would be inadequate. Clearly, legal rules are reasons for, not just causes of, action.

However, Perry continues, Hart's accusation is meritless, because Holmes's theory is hermeneutic. Contrary to Hart's misleading characterization, the bad man is a genuine practical reasoner, just like Hart's "puzzled" man. They both respond to reasons, albeit reasons of different sorts. The bad man should not, therefore, be seen as if he were merely an "external observer" of "signs" rather than "signals." Hart, Perry says,

> conflates the viewpoint of the external observer, who is engaged in an exercise of theoretical reason, with the viewpoint of the bad man, who is engaged in an exercise of practical reasoning. In light of this equivocation, Hart's conclusion that a jurisprudential theory cannot be based on the perspective of the bad man simply does not follow from his premises. The Holmesian account does not rest on the extreme external point of view that Hart regards as an unacceptable foundation for any satisfactory theory of law.

Because the bad man, *pace* Hart, is a genuine practical reasoner, Perry argues that there are really two ways of describing the law from the internal point of view. Insofar as this perspective is supposed to track the way that people who are subject to the law understand it, a person might either take the "socialized" or the "prudential" point of view. Hart's puzzled man takes the socialized point of view, according to Perry: he "accept[s] the conventional thinking on some matter, as embodied in the relevant social rule" and "internalize[s] the 'official' view associated with the legal system in question." By contrast, Holmes's bad man adopts the prudential point of view: his sole motivation for following the law is to avoid legal sanctions. Hart's conception of the legal actor's self-understanding is therefore too narrow; it overlooks the possibility that others may take the prudential point of view toward the law.

Although Perry is surely right that people may maintain different normative attitudes toward the law, his characterization of Hart's puzzled man as taking the socialized, as opposed to prudential, point of view is unfortunate, for Hart explicitly allowed for the possibility that the "good man" may be committed to the law for self-interested reasons:

> [T]he dichotomy of "law based merely on power" and "law which is accepted as morally binding" is not exhaustive. Not only may vast numbers be coerced by laws which they do not regard as morally binding, but it is not even true that those who do accept the system voluntarily, must conceive of themselves as morally bound to do so, though the system will be most stable when they do so. In fact, their allegiance to the system may be based on many different considerations: *calculations of long-term self-interest;* disinterested interest in others; an unreflecting inherited or traditional attitude; or the mere wish to do as others do. (198, emphasis added)

To be subject to a duty-imposing rule simply indicates, for Hart, that there are strong social reasons for preventing people from engaging in the activity prohibited by the rule (85). This does not imply that those who recognize their legal obligations are motivated to act for these strong social reasons. They need not "accept the conventional thinking on the matter" or "internalize the 'official' view associated with the legal system in question." People can have any number of reasons for being committed to the law. They may be guided by the law because they think that it is in their long-term self-interest to be so committed. Judges may apply the law simply in order to pick up their paychecks. Nonetheless, for a person to be committed to the law requires that she treat its rules as rules, that she is committed to following them regardless of her assessments of the merits at any given time.

For Hart, therefore, to accept the law's authority is simply to treat the law as a set of mandatory rules; it does not imply anything about one's personal reasons for being committed to the rules. Nor was Hart particularly interested in the sociological question of whether the majority of people are good or bad. The principal jurisprudential issue is not *why* people are guided by the law, but *how* they are guided by the law. Hart could not have privileged the socialized over the prudential point of view, because that would have amounted to taking sides in an issue that is not the jurisprude's principal concern.

If we reformulate Perry's objections to take these points into account, we can characterize his view as follows: Hart's presentation of Holmes's theory as behavioristic is inaccurate. The bad man is not a crude social scientist but a *bona fide* practical reasoner. To see the law as the bad man sees it, therefore, is to take a hermeneutic stance toward the law. Once this is recognized, Hart's privileging of the committed point of view can no longer be sustained. Holmes's theory describes a normative response to the law every bit as genuine, albeit not as pretty, as the one depicted by Hart.

Perry's objections can be answered, however, once it is realized that the predictive theory of obligation can be motivated in several ways, not all of them Holmesian. Hart characterized the predictive theory as the product of a narrowly empiricist world-view because his targets were logical positivists who sought to pattern the legal sciences after the social sciences and the social sciences after the physical sciences.[5] One of them, the Scandinavian realist Alf Ross, for example, was deeply concerned about the cognitive status of legal statements – he regarded talk about the existence of rules and obligations as "mystical" and "metaphysical" – and proposed a reductive account of the law in order to naturalize the law's ontology. "The interpretation of the doctrinal study of law presented in this book rests upon the postulate that the principle of verification must apply also to this field of cognition – that the doctrinal study of law must be recognized as an empirical social science."[6] Statements of legal validity were taken to be empirical predictions about the behavior or feelings of legal officials rather than "metaphysical constructions built upon a false interpretation of the 'binding force' experienced in the moral consciousness."[7] The bad man played no part in his motivations for proposing the predictive theory.

Because Hart's target was Ross, not Holmes, Hart was justified in depicting the predictive analysis in crudely empiricist terms. Later Hart, in discussing the predictive theory of legal validity, wrote:

[T]he motive for advancing this predictive theory is the conviction that only thus can metaphysical interpretations be avoided: that either a statement that a rule is valid must ascribe some mysterious property which cannot be detected by empirical means or it must be a prediction of future behavior of officials.[8]

The empiricist accounts are inadequate because they see rules exclusively as the grounds for predicting, rather than guiding or evaluating, action. Therefore these theories are unable to account for the existence of rule-governed behavior. When a social rule exists, it is not simply the case that social behavior will track the rule's prescription. The rule is normally taken to be a reason for conformity and a reason to criticize deviations from the rule. Predictive theories of obligation, Hart showed, reduce all rule-governed behavior to mere group habits.[9]

Hart conceded that the predictive theory may "very nearly reproduce" (87) the bad man's experience of the law. Since the bad man is interested only in the private costs of his activities, he is likely to make extensive use of causal predictions of official behavior. Nevertheless, Hart argued, this defense of the predictive theory is inadequate, because it renders the concept of obligation superfluous. If the bad man uses these causal generalizations in his practical reasoning, he does not need deontic concepts. He can describe his situation as the state of being "obliged," rather than "obligated," to conform to the law. The normative language of duty and obligation, however, is appropriate whenever people recognize the existence of rules as common standards of behavior and use these rules in the guidance and evaluation of conduct. The predictive theory of obligation cannot explain the special role that deontic claims play in the social life of a community.

As I have noted earlier, Hart introduced the bad man as a way of defending the predictive theory against his own initial criticisms. Hart was trying to save the theory by replacing its empiricist justification with a hermeneutic one. Predictive analyses of legal statements, he offered, might help to illuminate the way that some agents view the law. The bad man would regard predictions about official conduct not merely as inductive conclusions of theoretical inferences, but also as major premises in practical inferences.

To be sure, Hart rejected this somewhat half-hearted defense, but not because he concluded that the bad man perspective is behavioristic in nature. Rather, the problem with this reinterpreted version of the predictive theory is that it is too blinkered an account of how the law guides conduct. It implies that everyone is interested in the rules because of their attendant costs. It denies that at least some people regard the rules as legitimate standards of public behavior.

When Hart complained, therefore, that the predictive theory of legal obligation defines the internal point of view "out of existence," he was not referring to the insider's point of view. As we have seen, the predictive theory can be accepted by those with very different methodological commitments; it can be endorsed either by hermeneutic theories such as Holmes's or naturalistic theories such as Ross's. Rather, Hart was referring to the internal point of view as a particular type of normative attitude. The internal point of view was specifically defined as the perspective of those who comply with the rules because they regard the rules as legitimate standards of conduct, that is, those who respect the "internal aspect" of legal rules. "For it is possible to be concerned with the rules, either merely as an observer who does not accept them, or as a member of the group which accepts and uses them as guides to conduct. We may call these respectively the 'external' and the 'internal points of view'" (86). The predictive theory of legal obligation is deficient because it cannot account for the fact that some follow the rules because they are committed to them. It cannot account for this fact because it characterizes the concept of obligation in terms of sanctions rather than rules.

II. Guidance of Conduct

The bad man makes his first appearance in *The Concept of Law* during Hart's discussion of power-conferring rules (38–41). In these sections, Hart attempted to show that the reduction of power-conferring rules to duty-imposing rules distorts the various social functions that the law aims to achieve. Hart began by arguing that certain extremely reductive accounts, such as Hans Kelsen's, were nonstarters, because they employed seriously inadequate analyses of duty-imposing rules. Kelsen had argued that all legal norms should be recast as imperatives directing legal officials to impose sanctions on citizens under certain conditions. Kelsen thought it best, for example, to construe the rule against murder as if it were a direction to legal officials to punish anyone who commits an act of murder, even though the law is typically formulated as a rule addressed to the population at large.

Kelsen opted for a sanction-centered theory because he rejected the possibility of giving a natural law account of legal systems. Given his logical-positivistic belief that justice is "an irrational ideal,"[10] he sought to ground the concept of law in the amoral category of sanctions. Kelsen rejected Austin's analysis of duty-imposing rules, however, because he did not think that it was true that in every legal system every breach of law is subject to a sanction.[11] In international law and in some primitive legal systems, for example, the rules directing officials to sanction behavior are not themselves backed by sanctions. Kelsen therefore opted for an account which requires that every law be one that stipulates, rather than is subject to, a sanction.

Hart objected to Kelsen's account of duty-imposing rules because he thought it gave a misleading picture of the legal system's priorities. Kelsen's reformulations made it seem as if the law's chief concern was with the guidance of official conduct. Rather, Hart argued, the provision of rules requiring legal officials to sanction certain conduct is merely "ancillary" to the "primary" function of the law, which is to guide the conduct of ordinary citizens. The law provides its citizens with rules that they are supposed to discover and follow. The rules directed at legal officials are merely remedial measures provided by the law when the primary aim of guidance has failed.

Hart suggested at this point that the distortion created by the Kelsenian reformulation might be justified by the Holmesian concern that the law be viewed from the bad man's perspective. A reconstruction of the law that highlights the existence of sanctioning mechanisms portrays the law as the bad man sees it. Hart, however, rejected this suggestion. Why, he rhetorically asked, should the law not also care about the "'puzzled man' or 'ignorant man' who is willing to do what is required, if only he can be told what it is?" (39). The Kelsenian reformulation masks, rather than clarifies, the primary technique that the law uses for guiding conduct. Its guidance is seen by the fact that it can obviate the need for punishment out of court rather than by the fact that it authorizes punishment in court. "The principal functions of the law as a means of social control are not to be seen in private litigation or prosecutions, which represent vital but still ancillary provisions for the failures of the system." They are "to be seen in the diverse ways in which the law is used to control, to guide, and to plan life out of court" (39).

Perry makes two criticisms of Hart's argument here. First, by claiming that the principal function of the law is the guidance of ordinary citizens, Hart seems to be making a strong and unwarranted assumption about human nature. If the law's chief concern is with the guidance of ordinary citizens, not officials, then it must follow that a significant number of people will heed the law's claim to authority. Hart seems to assume, in other words, that a large number of people are good, at least from the law's point of view. "Hart asserts that the chief function of law is to guide and plan life out of court . . . But such guidance is only possible if (a sufficiently large number of) ordinary citizens are the type of person who will respond to such guidance, and not just to threats of force." Not only is such a claim controversial, Perry argues; it is also likely to be false, at least in the strong form in which Hart presented it. It is highly implausible that so many people in *every* legal system would respond to the law's claim of authority. The bad man cannot be defeated simply by assuming his prominence out of existence.

Second, Perry argues, not only did Hart make an implausible empirical assumption about human nature; he drew a fallacious inference from it. Hart's warrant for privileging the good man cannot be the mere fact that Holmes privileged the bad man – for if Holmes was being myopic, then so was Hart. According to Perry, Hart did not give a reason for thinking that it would be better to build a legal theory around one kind of person at the expense of the other. On the contrary, Perry claims, it is Holmes who justified his methodological choice, not Hart. First, Holmes pointed out that even good people are concerned about sanctions. Although legal rules per se are not universally capable of motivating, sanctions, at least, are. Second, Holmes felt that most, if not all, people are self-interested and, therefore, can be deterred only by the threat of sanctions. Rules are not central to jurisprudence because, given the way human beings are, rules cannot motivate.

In order to answer Perry's powerful criticisms, it is necessary to examine more closely what Hart meant by claiming that the primary function of the law is the "guidance" of conduct. As he explained, the distinctive method that law employs to control society is the provision of rules:

What is distinctive about this technique, as compared with individuated face-to-face orders which an official, like a policeman on traffic duty, might give to a motorist, is that the members of society are left to discover the rules and conform their behavior to them; in this sense, they "apply" the rules themselves to themselves, though they are provided with a motive for conformity in the sanction added to the rule. (38)

According to Hart, rules enable legal officials to guide behavior indirectly: citizens are expected to learn what the rules are and apply them to their own conduct. This indirect guidance is contrasted with the direct control of conduct via face-to-face orders. Using rules, the law is able to guide conduct from a distance, dispensing with the need for a throng of legal officials directing behavior at every turn.

As Hart characterized it, the guidance of conduct provided by rules has two components. The first is "epistemic": a rule guides conduct when the agent learns of his obligations from the rule, rather than directly from an official. The second component is "behavioral": the rule guides conduct when it is conformed to:

[T]he characteristic technique of the criminal law is to designate by rules certain types of behavior as standards for the guidance either of members of society as a whole or of special classes within it: they are expected without the aid or intervention of officials [1] to understand the rules and to see that the rules apply to them and [2] to conform to them. (38)

Notice that, for Hart, guidance does not contain a direct "motivational" component:[12] it does not require that people are motivated to follow the law simply because the law requires them to do so. It is possible, therefore, for the rules to guide conduct even though the motive for conformity is the threat of sanctions. Hart's claim that the primary function of the law is the guidance of ordinary citizens does not presuppose, in other words, that ordinary citizens take the internal point of view toward the law. The law is not particularly interested in the reasons people have for conforming: they may be motivated by their concern for their fellow men or simply by their wish to avoid being punished. The law simply cares that its citizens learn what it is that is expected of them and act accordingly.

Given this epistemic notion of guidance, it is clear why Hart thought that Kelsen's theory was defective. Kelsen made it seem that the law is solely interested in the guidance of official conduct. As Hart pointed out, the law is concerned with such matters only when there has been a "breakdown or failure of the primary purpose of the system" (38). Rather, the law's primary interest is the guidance of its citizens: it cares only that they act as they are supposed to. In fact, it would prefer that its authority were never challenged and sanctioning mechanisms never triggered. Rules directing officials to sanction are "ancillary" not in the sense of being "less important" than the rules directing citizens, but in the sense of being "subservient" to such rules. The existence of sanctioning institutions may indeed be "indispensable" (38), but their importance can be understood only relative to how well they enable the primary guidance function to be satisfied.

Perry's charge that Hart presupposed a "thick" conception of human nature is therefore ungrounded. The primary aim of the law is satisfied for Hart irrespective of the reasons why people guide their conduct according to the law. The only assumption made is that people are capable of learning what the law expects of them and can conform to its requirements. Perry seems to attribute to Hart a much stronger notion of guidance, that is, where conformity is motivated by the rules themselves rather than by sanctions. If Hart had thought that the primary function of the law was to ensure that people adopted the internal point of view, then Perry would be correct to maintain that this presupposes that people are generally able and willing to respond to the law's demand for conformity. As we have seen, however, there is no reason to take Hart's claim in this way.

We should, for similar reasons, reject Perry's second criticism of Hart. Hart did not repudiate the bad man *in favor of* the puzzled man. He simply thought that the bad man perspective should not be allowed to distort the fact that the law is interested in the guidance of all of its citizens, not just the bad ones. As Hart readily acknowledged, some might learn which activities to avoid by inferring this information from the rules directed at legal officials. Given that the sole motivation of these citizens is to avoid sanctions, their conduct can be guided solely by such rules. However, citizens may be willing to cooperate with the authorities and act in exactly the way that the law requires of them. The way that they learn what the law expects would be completely lost by a Kelsenian recasting of the law. Kelsen's theory of norm individuation is pernicious because it ignores the existence of citizens who are willing to live up to their obligations, if only they could be told what they are.

We can see that the bad man plays the same role here that he did in Hart's discussion of the predictive theory of obligation. The bad man is not the protagonist of the story; he is simply a famous villain brought in for brief cameo appearances. The bad man's walk-ons are confined to suggesting a possible hermeneutic justification for Kelsen's theory of duty-imposing rules. Hart's dismissal of the bad man, therefore, is not a direct assault on the Holmesian picture of law. It is merely a parry of the attempt to revive Kelsen's theory by having the main character's lines read by an actor known for his hermeneutic roles.

III. The Incoherence of Sanction-Centered Theories

Even though bad man theories are not the focus of Hart's critique in *The Concept of Law,* it is obvious that Hart opposed these views, for the reasons we have reviewed. The bad man perspective is myopic in two respects. First, it assumes that people are motivated to follow the law simply in order to avoid sanctions, rather than out of respect for the rules. The bad man view therefore defines the internal point of view out of existence. Second, the bad man view focuses exclusively on one technique that the law uses to motivate conduct to the exclusion of all others. The law not only threatens and punishes those who do not want to comply with the rules, but provides guidance for those who want to live up to their obligations.

We might say, therefore, that Hart's rejection of sanction-centered theories stemmed from his desire to develop a *general,* not a *moral,* theory of law. Hart insisted that a jurisprudential theory take into account and study all of the methods that the law provides for the guidance of conduct. It must include within its ambit the fact that the law may guide conduct either through its rules or through the sanctions attached to its rules.

To be sure, Hart did privilege the internal point of view in his explication of the concept of law. Although he thought that everyone in a given group might take the internal point of view, he claimed that it is impossible for everyone to take the external point of view. At the very least, legal officials would have to be committed to the law in order for us to say that a group had a legal system.

In *The Concept of Law,* Hart offered many arguments in favor of this asymmetry between the internal and external points of view. Hart showed, for example, that the very concept of sovereignty depends on the concept of rule-guided behavior. Rex I is not the sovereign simply because he is habitually obeyed and habitually obeys no one else. The sovereign is the one upon whom the rules confer sovereignty, and his edicts can survive only if these power-conferring rules do. Therefore, even when Rex I dies and Rex II's ability to enforce his own will has yet to be established, Rex II may still have the legal power to make laws (50–60). Likewise, the edicts of Rex I may still be legally valid during Rex II's reign, even though Rex I no longer has the power to sanction behavior he deemed undesirable (60–64). As Hart brilliantly proved, the continuity and persistence of legal systems requires that at least some people in the community accord the sovereign the authority to make law. Some must, in other words, take the internal point of view.

Perry is certainly right when he claims that the arguments Hart offers in support of this position presuppose the truth of certain normative principles. Insofar as all hermeneutic theories seek to understand human thought and behavior as intelligible, conceptual arguments made from this perspective tacitly assume that those being observed actually adhere to certain basic norms of rationality. Pursuant to the principle of charity, coherence is imputed to concepts being studied, so that the beliefs of the interpretees are not seen as obviously contradictory and their actions not clearly self-defeating.[13]

Because it would be incoherent to conceive of a legal system in which no one took the internal point of view, Hart concluded that our concept of law presupposes that at least some do take the internal point of view toward the law. The notion of coherence used here is clearly normative in some sense, but its normativity is epistemic, not moral. Hermeneutic theories need not assume at the outset that the attitudes held, the actions taken, and the institutions established are morally acceptable or desirable; they simply assume that, in some respect, they make sense.

Although these types of arguments do presuppose a certain normative framework, it would be misleading to label them "normative arguments." The legal theorist does not offer conceptual analyses in order to show people how they ought to think about the law or to portray their thought processes in the "best light." Rather, the theorist's aim is to represent the way that people actually think about the law. The theorist could not portray their thoughts as thoughts, however, unless he assumed that the people being studied follow certain norms of rationality, at least to some degree. For when beliefs and actions cease to be describable as the products of rational agency, they become mere neural events and muscular contractions. Necessarily, therefore, these interpretations must be charitable, or they fail to be interpretations.

Charity does not require that our concepts be put in their best light; the theorist must simply be confident that, at the very least, they can be put in some light, even if this illumination fails to flatter. A radically unjust concept of law, therefore, may still be a concept of law; however, a radically incoherent concept of law cannot be.

Notes

1 See Stephen R. Perry, "Interpretation and Methodology in Legal Theory," in *Law and Interpretation,* ed. Andrei Marmor (Oxford: Clarendon Press, 1996), 99. See also Gerald Postema, "Jurisprudence as Practical Philosophy," *Legal Theory* 4 (1998) ("The law, like other similar social practices, is constituted not only by intricate patterns of behavioral interactions, but also by the beliefs, activities, judgments and understandings of participants. The practice has an 'inside,' the 'internal point of view' of participants"); Brian Leiter, "Rethinking Legal Realism: Toward a Naturalized Jurisprudence," *Texas Law Review* 76 (1997):315 ("According to [Hart's model], we do not look for lawful regularities in the external behavior of social actors; rather, to understand social actors we must adopt their 'internal' point of view and understand, for example, what their reasons mean to them") (315, note 126).
2 See, e.g., Donald Black, *The Behavior of Law* (London: Academic Press, 1976), 6–8.
3 Stephen R. Perry, "Hart versus Holmes: The Bad Man in Legal Theory," Chapter 7 of this volume. Perry does say that Hart understood the internal point of view to be the internalized point of view. However, Perry does not claim that Hart took this to be an analytical

truth. According to Perry's interpretation, the internalized point of view is the *reference,* not the *meaning,* of the internal point of view. That he understands Hart in this way is made clear by Perry's claim that the bad man also takes the internal point of view. If the "internal" point of view were synonymous with the "internalized" point of view, it would be contradictory to argue that the bad man's attitude is also internal in nature. Indeed, Perry's major complaint is that Hart should have realized that the internal point of view has more than one reference because there is more than one type of legal insider.

4 H. L. A. Hart, *The Concept of Law* (Oxford: Clarendon Press, 1961), 88. (Cited hereafter parenthetically in the text by page number.)

5 In 1958, two years before *The Concept of Law* was published, Hart criticized the predictive theory for emphasizing the external aspect of rules in a review of Alf Ross's book *On Law and Justice* (Berkeley and Los Angeles: University of California Press, 1958). The piece, which he entitled "Scandinavian Realism," is reprinted in H. L. A. Hart, *Essays in Jurisprudence and Philosophy* (Oxford: Clarendon Press, 1983). In introducing this review into the collection and setting out its critique of the Scandinavian realists, Hart says: "In *The Concept of Law* these ideas are elaborated further, though not wholly to my own satisfaction or that of those of my critics who, complaining of various detailed aspects of my exposition, have generally welcomed my introduction of these ideas into jurisprudence as constituting an appropriate hermeneutic approach" (14).

6 Ross, *On Law and Justice,* 40.

7 Ibid., 68.

8 Hart, in *Essays in Jurisprudence and Philosophy,* 101. See also Ross, *On Law and Justice,* 11.

9 Although technically Ross proposed a predictive theory of legal validity, not a theory of "obligation," Hart thought that his claim was "not very different from [those of] the cruder American Realists which treat statements of legal rights and duties as predictions of official action." Hart, 165.

10 Hans Kelsen, *General Theory of Law and State,* trans. Anders Wedberg (New York: Russell & Russell, 1945), 13.

11 Ibid., 60.

12 Guidance does have an indirect motivational component, insofar as any epistemic change might potentially affect the actions someone is motivated to perform.

13 On the role of charity in the interpretation of human behavior, see Donald Davidson, "Radical Interpretation," in *Inquiries into Truth and Interpretation,* ed. Donald Davidson (Oxford: Clarendon Press, 125, 136–37).

9

Oliver Wendell Holmes, Jr., and William James

The Bad Man and the Moral Life

CATHARINE PEIRCE WELLS*

Why has there been so much controversy about Holmes – why so much disagreement over the nature of his views? On one level, he was exceptionally articulate. The sharpness of his wit left little doubt about where he stood on particular issues. But on another level, he was often obscure. Despite the seeming lucidity of his prose, scholars have been unable to agree even on a general description of his theoretical views: they have variously described him as a realist, a positivist, an instrumentalist, a utilitarian, a pragmatist, a liberal, a conservative, a fascist, a critical theorist, a cynic, an idealist, and even a nihilist. Among this wealth of labels, two have seemed especially appropriate. The first – "legal realist"[1] – seems plausible because of Holmes's well-known disagreement with the logical methods of Christopher Columbus Langdell. In reviewing Langdell's book *Cases on the Law of Contracts,* Holmes made his disagreement clear: "The life of the law," he wrote, "has not been logic: it has been but experience."[2] In addition, the notion of Holmes as a realist gained credibility from the fact that the realists themselves frequently regarded him as a leader of their movement. Nevertheless, a thoroughgoing realism seems inconsistent with many of his articulated views. If he was a realist, then how would we explain his insistence that legal doctrine be properly categorized, his close attention to legal precedent, and his continuing interest in the process of legal reasoning?

The second alternative – Holmes as a legal positivist – fares no better. Again, the label seems plausible. Much of his essay *The Path of the Law*[3] is concerned with arguing for a sharp distinction between law and morals. For example, he writes:

I think it desirable at once to point out and dispel a confusion between morality and law ... You can see very plainly that a bad man has as much reason as a good one for wish-

---

* I am especially grateful to Ruth Anna Putnam, who not only introduced me to James but also imparted to me so much of his spirit. I am also grateful to the Boston College Summer Research Fund for a grant supporting this research.

ing to avoid an encounter with the public force, and therefore you can see the practical importance of the distinction between morality and law. (169–70; 992)

But as positivistic as such passages may seem, other passages point in different directions. For example, following this passage, Holmes seems to contradict himself by declaring: "The law is the witness and external deposit of our moral lives" (170; 992). Equally hard to digest under the positivist label is the essay's big finish:

> Read the works of the great German jurists, and see how much more the world is governed today by Kant than by Bonaparte. We cannot all be Descartes or Kant, but we all want happiness. And happiness, I am sure from having known many successful men, cannot be won simply by being counsel for great corporations and having an income of fifty thousand dollars . . . The remoter and more general aspects of the law are those which give it universal interest. It is through them that you not only become a great master in your calling, but connect your subject with the universe and catch an echo of the infinite, a glimpse of its unfathomable process, a hint of the universal law. (202; 1009)

In this essay, I offer a reading of *The Path of the Law* that makes sense of these seeming inconsistencies. Despite its ambiguities, Holmes's essay has had a powerful influence on American law. Its supposed "legal positivism" stands as a needed counterweight to the tradition of American naturalism.[4] But the essay, in addition to its "positivism," carries an inspiring – if somewhat obscure – message, and my task here is to articulate that message in a way that is consistent with what is understood as Holmes's "positivism." To do this, I use the normative views of William James – particularly the views set out in his essay "The Moral Philosopher and the Moral Life"[5] – as a kind of study guide for reading *The Path of the Law*.

I adopt this approach for two reasons. The first is that Holmes and James were close friends during their young adulthood. This was a time when both men were struggling with the large questions of life: How should they make their way in the world? What should be their goal? What would be the ultimate meaning of their lives? And, for Holmes: What was the point of studying law? Where was the road to fame and fortune? Holmes and James spent a great many evenings together – drinking whisky, smoking cigars, and discussing philosophy well into the early morning.[6] Certainly such discussions – held between intimate friends during a formative period in their lives – often lead to a lifelong resonance between the views of the participants. The second reason is that this way of reading Holmes seems to work: it reconciles some of the more obvious contradictions; it provides concrete meanings for some of the more obscure passages; and it even makes sense of the inspirational passage at the end of the essay.

I proceed as follows: in section I, I discuss pragmatic ethical theory as formulated by William James. In section II, I dissect *The Path of the Law*, identifying Holmes's four major claims about the nature of law and analyzing them within the normative framework described in section I. Finally, in section III, I address three further questions about *The Path of the Law*: (1) Who is the bad man? (2) How should we understand the big finish at the end of the essay? and (3) What about Holmes? How does this understanding of his most famous essay help us to assess his influence in American law?

I. Reading James: Understanding the Nature of Pragmatic Ethical Inquiry

There is a certain amount of skepticism about the idea of a pragmatic ethic. People often think that being pragmatic is only a few steps short of being unethical. For example, in common speech, when we say that a person is pragmatic, we mean that the person is so intent upon obtaining the desired result that she does not think enough about the morality of her action. This understanding of pragmatism seems to be supported by Charles Sanders Peirce's pragmatic maxim

> Consider what effects, that which might conceivably have practical bearings, we conceive the object of our conception to have. Then our conception of these effects is the whole of our conception of the object.[7]

But this "anything goes" view of pragmatism is based on a misunderstanding. Although the maxim identifies the meaning of a concept with its practical effects, it does not direct us to disregard the ethical. Rather it suggests that we should – whether we are concentrating on our own desires or on our moral responsibilities to others – favor practical considerations over abstract principles. Thus a pragmatic actor thinks about a proposed action in terms of its practical effects, not in terms of the correctness of the principle that it supposedly instantiates.[8] But this way of analyzing action does not leave ethical questions out of the picture. The idea that human conduct should be assessed in the context of a concrete situation does not mean that it cannot be assessed at all. In fact, part of the context of any human action is the ideal[9] or purpose for which it is done. And this notion of purposeful action, in turn, raises a number of normative questions: Does the act promote the actor's purpose? Is this purpose an appropriate one for this particular actor? Is it worth pursuing in this particular situation? Thus, whether one is a pragmatist or not – whether one favors results over principles or not – ethics remains a central touchstone for assessing human conduct.[10]

In section A, I explore the poorly understood realm of pragmatic ethics. To avoid the common confusions about what pragmatism is and what it is not, I sketch a simple account of pragmatic method and its use in ethical inquiries. Specifically, I suggest that this method results in an ethic that is situational and relativistic but not necessarily awash in subjectivity.[11] Pragmatists – at least classical pragmatists such as Peirce and James – were believers in a "truth beyond," and the "truth beyond" with respect to ethics had to do with intersubjective agreements and the development of community values. Thus, at the end of section C, I talk about the role of the philosopher in defining and defending community values.

A. Pragmatic Empiricism and Ethical Judgment

Pragmatism can be understood as an extreme form of empiricism. The traditional debate between rationalism and empiricism is a dispute over the role of experience in producing knowledge. On the one hand, the rationalist says that we can learn from experience, *but only if* we have a prior understanding about the nature of human reason and the proper role of experience in a reasoned investigation of the world.[12] On the other hand, the empiricist says that all knowledge comes from experience and that everything we know – if we truly know it – can be traced to some form of empirical observation.[13] With respect to this division, the pragmatist is an empiricist. He differs, however, from the traditional empiricist in the way in which he analyzes the concept of experience.

Traditional – nonpragmatic – empiricists normally begin their analysis with a description of what it means for knowledge to be empirical. Whether the description is in terms of sense data or observation statements, the effect is to start the analysis with a stipulation about the nature and limits of experience. The effect of this stipulation is similar to the a priori analysis of the rationalist. It requires that we commit ourselves, in advance, to a certain understanding about what counts as experience. Thus, for example, many empiricists start by limiting experience to information obtained by one of the five senses; in effect, they say that if your information does not come from sight, sound, taste, smell, or touch, then it does not qualify as legitimate information. The pragmatist, on the other hand, suggests that we examine this stipulation more closely. The organization of experience into five senses, he would argue, is itself an empirical hypothesis that is subject to review whenever it fails to provide an effective way of interpreting experience. Thus, pragmatism makes no exception to its empiricism; there are no foundational frameworks that are beyond the test of ongoing experience.

This "no exceptions" form of empiricism makes a big difference when it comes to doing ethics. For one thing, it means that our understanding of ethics must be derived from experience.[14] For another, it leaves us free, at least initially, to take a broad view of what counts as experience. Pragmatism begins with two simple ideas: first, that we seek knowledge by intelligently observing the world around us, and second, that we remain willing to revise our beliefs in the face of new experience. This means that our investigations must proceed in a self-correcting way. Thus, we must

1. observe the empirical facts,
2. analyze the data into general categories,
3. form a tentative hypothesis that will explain the observed data,
4. use the hypothesis to form expectations about the future, and
5. revise our opinions in the face of defeated expectations.[15]

The rationale for this process is that it gives us an ongoing way of learning from experience, but since it holds all beliefs subject to continuing reexamination, it does not irrevocably commit us to any false interpretations of the empirical data.

There are clear similarities between this description of pragmatic theorizing and standard accounts of the scientific method. Like the scientific method, pragmatic theorizing is centered on the formulation of an experimental hypothesis and the attempt to confirm or disprove the hypothesis through the collection of experimental data. But the pragmatic approach is different, in two ways: first, in its application to all kinds of investigations – whether scientific or normative; whether formal or informal – and, second, in its emphasis on the fact that hypotheses produce predictions only in the context of many background assumptions. Thus, unexpected outcomes give rise not only to a reevaluation of the designated hypothesis but also to a review – more cursory or less cursory, depending on the circumstances – of all of the "facts" that supported the original expectation.[16] Just as a scientist tracks many factors in the laboratory, so too the moral philosopher must consider the many factors that contextualize human conduct. In both areas, every detail has potential significance. Thus, an ethicist proceeds by examining an action in many different ways: What is our feeling about the action? How are others responding? What does the act tell us about the actor? What are the consequences of this action? How does it affect other people? Who gains? Who loses? Who is happy? Who is not? Answering these questions is the beginning of knowledge about the moral dimension.

There are major differences between James's approach and other empiricist ethics. The traditional empiricist analyzes ethics in one of two ways: either she explains ethical constructs in terms of their role in producing bodily pleasure and pain, or she endorses those acts that seem to maximize certain kinds of preferred outcomes. At first glance, it appears that James falls into the latter category. For example, in "The Moral Philosopher and the Moral Life" he writes:

Since everything which is demanded is by that fact a good, must not the guiding principle for ethical philosophy . . . be simply to satisfy at all times *as many demands as we can?* That act must be the best act, accordingly, which makes for the *best whole,* in the sense of awakening the least sum of dissatisfactions. In the casuistic scale, therefore, those ideals must be written highest which *prevail at the least cost.* (80)

But to peg James as a consequentialist is a fundamental misunderstanding of his views.[17] Consequentialism bases its ethical judgments on comparative assessments of the value of certain outcomes. This comparative assessment, in turn, is based on a hierarchy of goods – a hierarchy that is obtained by weighing individual goods on a single scale of essential goodness. For James, however, the reduction of the multitude of human goods to a unitary framework is simply not possible:

> There is really no more ground for supposing that all our demands can be accounted for by one universal underlying kind of motive than there is ground for supposing that all physical phenomena are cases of a single law. The elementary forces in ethics are probably as plural as those of physics are. The various ideals have no common character apart from the fact that they are ideals. No single abstract principle can be so used as to yield to the philosopher anything like a scientifically accurate and genuinely useful casuistic scale. (77)

And, if we cannot count all good things on a single casuistic scale, then determining right conduct cannot be a question of maximization. The irreducible fact is that each person has her own ideals and her own feelings about what constitutes an ethical life. And, since these feelings are part of the empirical world,[18] they are entitled to respect; they cannot be trumped by the philosopher's own feelings about what is worth doing and what is not.

B. Viewpoint and Perspective

Although the basis for James's ethics is respect for the perspective of others, this does not commit him to the passivity of relativism. To understand why this is true, we should begin with his distinction between moral questions as they arise in one's own private sphere and moral issues as they are (or should be) be viewed by the community.[19] In an essay entitled "On a Certain Blindness in Human Beings"[20] James dramatizes the difficulty of entering into another's perspective by describing the enormous gap that separates his own world from that of his dog:

> We are practical beings, each of us with limited functions and duties to perform. Each is bound to feel intensely the significance of his own duties . . . But this feeling is in each of us a vital secret, for sympathy with which we vainly look to others. The others are too much absorbed in their own vital secrets to take an interest in our own . . . Take our dogs and ourselves, connected as we are by a tie more intimate than most . . . and yet . . . how insensible, each of us, is to all that makes life significant for the other – we to the rapture of bones under hedges . . . , they to the delights of literature and art. As you sit reading the most moving romance you ever fell upon, what sort of a judge is your fox terrier of your behavior? With all his good will toward you, the nature of your conduct is absolutely excluded from his comprehension. To sit there like a senseless statue, when you might be taking him to walk and throwing sticks for him to catch! What queer disease is this that comes over you every day, of holding things and staring at them like that for hours together, paralyzed of motion and vacant of all conscious life.[21]

The obvious thing about this kind of moral isolation is that it creates a certain pointlessness in judging other people's conduct. Were my dog to say to me:

"You're not interested enough in sticks, Catharine," I would be amazed. And were I to say to my dog: "But Layla, you don't read enough fine literature," that would seem silly too. But, when it comes to other people, these kinds of judgments abound. Think how frequently we make judgments such as "Susan does too many dangerous things" or "Paul is wasting his time at the bowling alley." One reason why these judgments seem less pointless when directed at people is because people, unlike dogs, are sometimes persuaded by argument. Nevertheless, if arguments prove unpersuasive, the worth of these activities is ultimately a question for Susan or Paul.

The reason why James emphasizes the inherent solitude of moral life is not that he is a relativist; rather, it is that it will help us to arrive at a better understanding of the "perspectival" nature of moral experience. With respect to the physical world, we are able to make sense of the idea that we all live in the same world, even though the appearance of that world differs significantly from person to person. We do this by relying upon the concepts of perspective and viewpoint to explain the many different ways in which the same object appears to different people. The concepts of perspective and viewpoint are part of an abstract model that helps us to translate our private perceptions of a physical world into public reality. But we do not just live in the physical world. In fact, we experience reality as a complex composition of the physical, the emotional, the ethical, the cognitive, the attitudinal, and so forth.[22] In each of these realms, experience is shaped by a variety of perspectival factors. With respect to physical observations, perspective may only be a matter of the relation between the physical location of the observer and the physical location of the object. But in more complex cases, perspective is subject to many influences. For example, whether one sees a book on the table depends upon one's physical location, one's familiarity with books, and sometimes the clarity of one's vision. And further, some cognitions depend on mood – "That was a lovely party; everyone had such a fine time!" – while others depend upon the nature of one's prior beliefs – "That bird quacked like a duck"; one's attitudes – "That can wait until tomorrow"; or one's agenda – "It's important that Charles does not think of himself as stupid." Whenever we think about how to act or how to respond to the conduct of others, we inhabit a moral viewpoint that is shaped by some of these factors.

It is important not to confuse perspectivism – the claim that all observations are relative to the viewpoint of the observer – with moral relativism. The privacy of one's individual moral world – like the privacy of individual sensation – is the beginning, not the end, of moral inquiry. The end of moral inquiry is a form of truth – not the truth about a world of noumenal objects but the truth about an intersubjective world of human agreement. When we seek the truth, we seek to understand our experience in the same terms in which others use to interpret their own experience. This means that we can no longer be satisfied with the limits of our individual perspective. I like books, and my dog likes sticks, but these are worlds of solitude. Even when I reflect upon what it takes to lead a truly good life, I am still within the confines of my own individual world. The question is about me and what it would take to make my life good for me. Moral truth has to do with the moral life of the community. The question it poses is this: "How do we live our shared lives in ways that meet our individual needs and our collective ideals?"

C. Pragmatism and the Truth Beyond

James begins his discussion of ethics in "The Moral Philosopher and the Moral Life" by distinguishing among three types of ethical inquiries: the psychological, the metaphysical, and the casuistic. The psychological inquiry seeks to uncover the origin of our moral ideals and judgments; the metaphysical inquiry asks about the meaning of ethical terms; and the casuistic inquiry poses the question "What is the measure of the various goods and ills which men recognize?" with the hope that an answer will assist moral philosophy in settling "the true order of human obligations" (66).

In "The Moral Philosopher and the Moral Life," James turns first to the psychological question. Like Jeremy Bentham and John Stuart Mill, he believes that many human ideals derive significance from their role in producing pleasure and avoiding pain. But James disagrees with these philosophers when they attribute all of our ethical feelings to practical considerations. Thus he writes:

> Association with many remote pleasures will unquestionably make a thing significant of goodness in our minds; . . . But it is surely impossible to explain all our sentiments and preferences in this simple way. (66–67)

It is often the case, he argues, that we have a sense of "fitness" about things that has little to do with pleasure or utility.

> The moment you get beyond the coarser and more commonplace moral maxims . . . you fall into schemes and positions which to the eye of common-sense are fantastic and overstrained. The sense for abstract justice which some persons have is as eccentric a variation from the natural-history point of view, as is the passion for music or for the higher philosophical consistencies which consumes the soul of others. The feeling of the inward dignity of certain spiritual attitudes as peace, serenity, simplicity, veracity; and of the essential vulgarity of others, as querulousness, anxiety, egoistic fussiness, etc. – are quite inexplicable except by an innate preference of the more ideal attitude for its own pure sake. (67)[23]

And this conclusion is an important part of James's moral philosophy. It is the nonreducibility of some of life's ideals that make them doubly worthy of respect. They deserve respect not just because respect honors individual autonomy but also because they represent the originality and depth of the human spirit.

The starting point for James's attempt at answering the metaphysical question is the observation that there could be no meaning to moral terms in a world devoid of sentient beings.[24] It follows, for James, that the good cannot be an abstract quality that exists without reference to conscious life. Instead, he argues that moral obligations are best understood in relation to the underlying claim:

> The moment we take a steady look at the question, *we see not only that without a claim actually made by some concrete person there can be no obligation, but that there is some obligation wherever there is a claim.* Claim and obligation are, in fact, coextensive terms; they cover each other exactly. (72)

This conclusion follows from James's pragmatism. If we apply Peirce's pragmatic maxim to determine the meaning of these terms, then James's conclusion seems to follow: the practical meaning of a claim is the sense of obligation it engenders, and the practical meaning of a moral obligation is the motive it gives to actions that will satisfy the underlying claim. This way of looking at claims and obligations leads James to formulate the casuistic question in a particular way.

Thus far, James has defined the boundaries of ethical inquiry – first, by focusing on ideals of conduct and, second, by linking ideals to the specific claims they generate. Therefore, when he comes to the casuistic question "What do we do about moral conflict?" he is committed to understanding the question in terms of the need to adjudicate among the competing claims that arise in the context of many individual perspectives. And, as James describes them, these conflicts are both plentiful and hard to reconcile:

> The wars of the flesh and the spirit in each man, the concupiscences of different individuals pursuing the same unshareable material or social prizes, the ideas which contrast so according to races, circumstances, temperaments, philosophical beliefs, etc. – all form a maze of apparently inextricable confusion with no obvious Ariadne's thread to lead one out. (75)

One way of resolving all of this conflict is to create a hierarchy of goods that would determine the relative merit of individual claims. But, given the presumptively equal claim for respect that attaches to each ideal, such a hierarchy could be obtained only by arbitrarily preferring one set of ideals over another. Thus, James's moral philosophers seem to be stuck with a familiar dilemma: on the one hand, they must provide answers, and, on the other, they are not allowed to privilege their individual ideals by consulting their own opinions as to what is right and what is wrong.

The way out of this dilemma is to be sure that we have posed the appropriate question. We must keep in mind that the mere fact that individual interests are noncomparable does not mean that there is no sense in talking about a community's interests. The question for ethics is not "What works for me?" but "What works for us as a community?" This is not necessarily a matter of looking for a uniquely correct set of ideals. It is the matter of looking for those ideals that accommodate one another, that allow us to live in harmony and to pursue our ideals in peace. James poses the question in these words:

The philosopher, then, *qua* philosopher, is no better able to determine the best universe in the concrete emergency than other men. He sees, indeed, somewhat better than most men what the question always is – not a question of this good or that good simply taken, but of the two total universes with which these goods respectively belong. (83)

So issues about judging what is good for us as a society are issues about inclusiveness, accommodation, efficient organization, and smooth coordination – all for the purpose of facilitating the simultaneous efforts of each member of the community in pursuing their chosen ideals.

II. Reading Holmes: *The Path of the Law* as a Pragmatic Analysis of Legal Decision Making

In *The Path of the Law*, Holmes proposes a strict separation between law and morals. "Nothing but confusion of thought," he warns, "can result from assuming that the rights of man in a moral sense are equally rights in the sense of the Constitution and the law" (171–72; 993). Despite this warning, we find that, even for Holmes, there are strong similarities between the two disciplines.[25] Both disciplines are engaged in normative inquiries; they each address questions such as "What should we do?" and "How should we decide?" Further, just as James believed that ethics must be founded upon empirical observation, so also Holmes believed in an empirical method for law.

We have noted that James divided ethical inquiry into three separate inquiries: (1) psychological inquiry – determining as a psychological matter the kinds of ideals that motivate human behavior; (2) metaphysical inquiry – determining as a definitional matter how moral terminology should be used; and (3) casuistic inquiry – determining as a strategic matter how a community should arrange its affairs. Looking at Holmes, we can see a similar structure in his approach to legal theory. We note, for example, that much of his book *The Common Law* (1881)[26] is taken up with what James called the "psychological question." In addition, we can also see that Holmes's emphasis on the separation between law and morals is part of an answer to the "metaphysical" question "How should we use the terms 'law' and 'morality'?" And further, we can see that "casuistic" questions are at the center of the legal enterprise, since judges routinely decide cases by determining, under the particular facts and circumstances of each case, what is the best outcome from the community perspective.

A close reading of *The Path of the Law* reveals that it consists of four claims about the nature of law. The first two reject, in negative terms, the identification of law with morals and logic; the second two affirmatively describe the nature of legal analysis. These are the four claims:

1. Law is not the same as morals.
2. Law is not logic.

3. Practicing lawyers approach law as a science. They use their knowledge and experience to predict the outcomes of future cases.
4. Judges should approach law in a commonsensical way. Their job is to impartially consider what outcomes most accord with community norms of justice and sound policy.

In this section, I proceed by examining these claims one by one and by placing them in the context of Jamesian moral theory.

1. LAW IS NOT THE SAME AS MORALS. Holmes is often described as a legal positivist, and indeed his insistence on a separation between law and morals seems to fit the very definition of that doctrine. There are, however, many different ways of "separating" the concepts, and the ease with which this particular suggestion is labeled should not prevent us from trying to understand it more precisely. Surely, he did not mean – as many of his harshest critics have taken him to mean – that law and the practice of law are not subject to moral constraint. But it also seems clear that Holmes intended more than just the watered-down versions of positivism that have been suggested by some of his defenders. Presumably, Holmes intended more than the claim that law must be distinct from *conventional* morality or the claim that law should not be based upon an a priori moral system.

To understand Holmes's positivism, we need to keep in mind the Jamesian distinction between the privacy of one's own moral world and the public nature of the questions that are addressed by moral philosophy. In the privacy of one's own moral world, one acts in accordance with a particular set of personal ideals. The resulting conduct may lead others to make critical judgments, but their judgments are of limited force. They come from outside a person's moral world and therefore seem less salient than criticisms mounted from within. Moral philosophy, on the other hand, arises in a shared universe and therefore poses a different kind of moral question. The question is strategic: How can we live together in the same world of limited resources without unduly impeding the moral lives of others? Judgments about this are not private and irreproachable; as community concerns, they are subject to debate and criticism.

Viewed in this context, Holmes's positivism reflects the fact that law is different from private morality. When we make moral judgments about others, they can heed or ignore them at will. Law, however, generates sanctions, and, because of this, it is unduly arbitrary to base legal judgments on the private moral values of any individual person. Thus, law is distinct from morality in two ways: first, it can be forcibly brought to bear on individual conduct; second, it flows not from private feeling but from public debate and community experience.

2. LAW IS NOT LOGIC. We saw in the last paragraph that Holmes rejects the idea of law as a matter of private feeling. So also does he reject the idea that it comes from some kind of universal or abstract truth. Thus, if law must be separated from morals, it must also be distinguished from deductive logic. It is a fallacy, he argues, to think of law as a "given system . . . [that] can be worked out like mathematics from some general axioms of conduct" (180; 998). This does not mean that the law does not use logical forms of reasoning, nor does it mean that the law is irrational. If Holmes – like James – is a pragmatist, then he – like James – must look to experience as the basis for all forms of human knowledge. Logic will not be enough, but it will be a part of the process. Good law – nonarbitrary law – must be the result of an organized community practice that utilizes scientific reasoning and open debate to arrive at a collective understanding of how human conflicts should be resolved.

3. PRACTICING LAWYERS APPROACH LAW AS A SCIENCE. They use their knowledge and experience to predict the outcomes of future cases. The notion of law as a predictive science is meant to describe what it is that lawyers should be doing when they are practicing law. Prediction is the practical task that lawyers are trained (and paid) to do, and as Holmes describes it the process of legal prediction is but a simple application of the pragmatic method:[27] first, lawyers gather data by reading cases relevant to their client's case; second, they place the individual cases into general categories; third, they formulate tentative hypotheses about the reactions of courts when confronted with certain types of conflict; fourth, they test these hypotheses against the actual outcomes of other cases and against their own intuitions about outcomes in hypothetical cases; and finally, they use these hypotheses to make a prediction about the outcome of their client's case.

The predictive theory of law tells us what lawyers ought to do and, by implication, makes it clear that there are certain things that they should not do. Part of the controversy over Holmes's "positivism" is that it seems to rule out the common idea that a lawyer is (or should be) a certain kind of moral counselor. Lawyers, Holmes suggest, should not try to persuade their clients to "do the right thing" – to make safer products, to cause less pollution, or to be nicer to their workers – by misinforming them about the requirements of positive law. While some may feel that the law loses its idealism when lawyers tell their clients that they can do "bad" things without legal consequences, Holmes would say that this feeling is based on a misunderstanding of the particular function that law is supposed to serve. Perspectivism teaches tolerance; it also teaches that the community has an important role in coordinating activities and in resolving private conflicts. When lawyers promote their own ethical concerns, the problem is not just that they are presuming to speak on behalf of the community but that they are engaged in doing something that the law itself is not designed to do. The function of law is not to dispense moral praise and blame; rather it has the more practical function of regulating activities that threaten community life.

4. JUDGES SHOULD APPROACH LAW IN A COMMONSENSICAL WAY. Their job is to impartially consider what outcomes most accord with community norms of justice and sound policy. To understand what Holmes says about the judicial role, we need to distinguish between the science of predicting legal outcomes (the job of the lawyer) and the practice of adjudicating controversies (the task of the judge). Judges do not predict their own decisions. Instead, they must decide each case for themselves, determining which outcome best serves the ongoing life of the community.

There is a lot of confusion about Holmes's conception of the judicial task. How should judges decide cases? How should they unravel the tangled web of policy and precedent? What is the role of legal reasoning? Is there any room for moral considerations or for the judge's personal vision of justice? Understanding Holmes's answers to these questions is complicated by the fact that he rarely addresses them systematically. His comments on judging tend to emphasize that judges should apply someone else's judgment rather than their own. For example, there is this passage from his early work on tort adjudication:

In some cases, [it] . . . is an act of the legislature; . . . and in others it is the custom or course of dealing of those classes most interested; and in others where there is no statute, no clear ground of policy, no practice of a specially interested class, it is the practice of the average member of the community, – what a prudent man would do under the circumstances.[28]

Similarly, we can see this tendency in his well-known dissent in *Lochner v. New York:* "But I do not conceive that to be my duty, because I strongly believe that my agreement or disagreement has nothing to do with the right of a majority to embody their opinions in law."[29]

Like James, Holmes understands that some judgments require detachment; they cannot be made from the narrow perspective of personal morality. The judge and the moral philosopher pursue similar projects; they must adjudicate controversies that arise from the fact that there are many competing agendas and only a limited number of resources. Such decisions should not be the result of simply choosing one individual set of preferences over another. Rather, they should reflect the interests and values of the community as a whole. The right decision in each case is the one that best promotes the welfare of the community. And this is not a simple matter of maximizing wealth; rather it is a question of resolving conflicts in ways that foster accommodation and cooperation.

One hundred years later, Holmes's thoughts about the judicial role may seem neither original nor profound. Nevertheless, in 1897, they were somewhat controversial. Ironically, the controversy at that time was not primarily centered on the notion of the bad man. There were probably few in Holmes's audience who believed that judges should invoke their personal values to decide legal cases. To the contrary, Holmes was more likely to be criticized for deviating from a strict conception of the rule of law. Many of his era believed that legal decisions should be based upon rigorous reasoning from precedent and that it was therefore inappropriate for judges to engage in the kind of freewheeling normative deliberations that Holmes describes. Thus, for his contemporaries, the problem with Holmes's view was not so much that he shunned private morality as that he suggested that legal questions are not narrowly legal. To the contrary, he believed that legal decision making could never be done mechanically on the basis of past practices but rather that it is properly the product of common sense and practical reason. In short, the thing that made Holmes most controversial was the suggestion that legal questions require living and breathing decision makers, who, on the one hand, would not impose their own personal values but, on the other, would shoulder the responsibility of making a real decision.

III. Three Questions about Holmes and the Bad Man

In offering this interpretation of Holmes, I have left unanswered many questions that relate to the correctness of his legal theories. Whether Holmes is right or wrong, my goal is to clarify his views and to provoke some greater interest in pragmatic theories of normative decision making. The deeper questions about the merits of pragmatic decision making must be left to another occasion. I close, instead, by addressing three questions about Holmes that I believe are truly illuminated by the foregoing interpretation.

A. Question 1: Who Is the Bad Man?

As the essays in this volume suggest, there are basically two views about the "bad man" in *The Path of the Law*. On the one hand, there are people who say that Holmes's bad man is a real evildoer. In a recent essay, for example, historian David Siepp suggests that Holmes may have been thinking of a lawyer in a popular work of fiction who advised clients on how to commit evil deeds without suffering legal consequences.[30] The trick was not so much to escape detection as to escape punishment by committing the crime in such a way that legal technicalities would bar its prosecution. Certainly some of Holmes critics understood him to be advocating this kind of practice. Alternatively, his defenders argue that the bad man should not be taken literally, that Holmes used him either as a device to dramatize the predictive theory of law or as a heuristic to clarify a much more narrow point about remedies.

I believe that neither of these alternatives is exactly right. My reading of Holmes suggests that his invocation of the bad man is somewhat ironic. Holmes was a historian of the common law. He knew that there were long periods in its history when the substance of the law was chiefly determined by the movement of armies. Thus, he refers to truth as "the majority vote of the nation that could lick all the others"[31] and describes the requirements of law this way:

I see no *a priori* duty to live with others . . . but simply a statement of what I must do if I wish to remain alive. If I do live with others they tell me that I must do and abstain from doing various things or they will put the screws on to me.³²

Although contemporary law has aspirations of being democratic and just, it is not these qualities that make it law. What makes it law is the organized force of the community. If we take this seriously, it follows that equating the bad man to the lawbreaker means that Holmes's bad man is not necessarily bad. The bad man is simply someone who does not share in the ideals that the law represents. The bad man could, for example, be a feminist, a religious fundamentalist, an abolitionist, a black separatist, a gay activist, or even a Moonie. Of course, he (or she) could also be a psychopath, a murderer, or a bigot. Whoever the bad man is, his opposition to legal values and his consequent violations of law do not by themselves make him truly evil. He is a lawbreaker and nothing more. His violations may include acts that many of us would morally censure, but this is not the point. The law is not about morality; it is about regulating conduct for the benefit of the entire community.

B. Question 2: What Is the Meaning of Holmes's "Big Finish" at the End of the Essay?

Two of the essays in this volume offer new ways of understanding Holmes's "big finish" at the end of *The Path of the Law*. Robert W. Gordon (in Chapter 1) suggests that it should be interpreted in terms of the nineteenth-century style of inspirational speaking. Thomas C. Grey (in Chapter 6) suggests that the dramatic cycle of the speech provides a particular rhetorical context. Although these are both plausible suggestions, they should not lead us to overlook the possibility that the passage conveys a message that, for Holmes, was heartfelt and sincere.

In choosing law, Holmes had worried that the profession was insufficiently philosophical and too far removed from the deeper and more serious questions about life. In the beginning, his own study of the subject seemed tedious and dry as he spent long hours reading cases and analyzing ancient doctrines. With time, however, he saw that his study of law had provided him with a window on the universe. Thus, he writes to Emerson:

It seems to me that I have learned, after a laborious and somewhat painful period of probation, that the law opens a way to philosophy as well as anything else, if pursued far enough, and I hope to prove it before I die.

What Holmes discovered is that in understanding law, we understand a lot about the universe. In a speech at Brown University he said it more explicitly:

[A student learns] that one part of the universe yields the same teaching as any other if only it is mastered, that the difference between the great way of taking things and the small – between philosophy and gossip – is only the difference between realizing the part as a part of a whole and looking at it in its isolation as if it really stood apart.[33]

For Holmes, law is a part of the greater landscape of human nature and its interaction with the wider universe. Knowledge of law imparts knowledge of the political and commercial realities that are a part of community life. From law, we can learn about the requirements of good management and sound policy. More importantly, learning law teaches us about purposive behavior and its results; about its successes and failures, and about the feelings of hope and despair that accompany human conflict. In short, studying law is like reading all of the dials and gizmos in the laboratory – there is a lot of information that can be processed into a deeper and more profound knowledge of truth.

C. Question 3: Is Holmes a Bad Man?

I have argued elsewhere that Holmes has generally been a salutary symbol for American law.[34] There is, however, an edge to Holmes that speaks of arrogance and indifference to human suffering. For example, there is the insensitivity of his dissent in *Buck v. Bell,* with its famous comment "Three generations of imbeciles is enough,"[35] and the tone of callousness that we hear in this comment on war:

> If we want conscripts, we march them up to the front with bayonets in their rear to die for a cause in which perhaps they do not believe. The enemy we treat not even as a means but as an obstacle to be abolished, if so it may be.[36]

Holmes was a complex figure, and it is not easy to make generalized assessments of his character. Keeping this in mind, however, I would like to note one particular aspect of Holmes's character that seems at odds with a pragmatist philosophy.

I have argued that Holmes shared James's pragmatic philosophy and the perspectivism that is its inevitable consequence. Pragmatism is a practical philosophy, in the sense that those who believe in the theory of pragmatism thereby acquire a reason to practice it in their daily lives. Thus, a belief in perspectivism implies the need for practicing humility, tolerance, and compassion. In his own time, James was much beloved for exactly these qualities, and we can hear them resonating in passages such as this, from "The Moral Philosopher and Moral Life":

> [The moral philosopher] knows that he must always vote for the richer universe for the good which seems most organizable, most fit to enter into complex combinations, most apt to be a member of a more inclusive whole; but which particular universe this is, he cannot know for certain in advance. He only knows that if he makes a bad mistake, the cries of the wounded will soon inform him of the fact.[37]

By reminding us that casuistic solutions are always tentative and experimental, James emphasizes that a philosopher's job is never done; that the philosophers must remain on the scene and listen for "the cries of the wounded."

Holmes's own attitude toward these virtues is far more ambivalent. On the one hand, he seems to embrace a sense of his own partial role in the universe. For example, he writes:

[A person must learn] that he cannot set himself over against the universe as a rival god, to criticize it, or to shake his fist at the skies, but that his meaning is its meaning, his only worth is as a part of it, as a humble instrument of its universal power.[38]

But, on the other, Holmes's writing suggests none of James's compassion and vigilance. For example, in talking about his hope for the future, Holmes somewhat casually refers to "our current satisfaction with conventional legal rules."[39] This leaves his reader to wonder exactly whom he means when he says: "our." It may well be that Holmes and his friends were well satisfied with the current state of the law. We could suppose that "society" was satisfied, but only if we take a very restrictive view about who constitutes "society." But certainly in 1915, not everyone was satisfied with the current state of American law. If Holmes had listened for "the cries of the wounded," surely he would have known this and understood the extent of people's discontent. His failure to know this does not necessarily mean that Holmes is the bad man of American law. Rather, it reminds us that pragmatists must be thorough and consistent in their pragmatism and must resist complacency in all of its forms.

Notes

1 Part of the reason why the "legal realist" label is not very helpful is that it is itself an ambiguous term. During the thirties, "realism" was embraced by such disparate writers as Karl Llewellyn, who believed that law should reflect good policy (see, e.g. Karl Llewellyn, "Some Realism – about Realism – Responding to Dean Pound," *Harvard Law Review* 44 [1931]:1222, 1250–56), and Thurman Arnold, who thought of law primarily as ideology (Thurman Arnold, *The Symbols of Government* [New Haven: Yale University Press, 1935]).

2 C. C. Langdell, *Cases on the Law of Contracts, with a Summary of the Topics Covered by the Cases*, 2d ed., 2 vols. (Boston: Little Brown, 1879). Oliver Wendell Holmes, Jr., "Book Notice," *American Law Review* 14 (1880):233, 234.

3 Oliver Wendell Holmes, Jr., "The Path of the Law," in *Collected Legal Papers* (New York: Harcourt, Brace & Howe, 1920), 167, 169–79; "The Path of the Law," *Harvard Law Review* 110 (1997):991, 992–97. Cited hereafter parenthetically in the text by page numbers, separated for the respective sources by semicolons. "The Path" is reprinted in the Appendix to this volume with star paging.

4 See Catharine Wells, "Old Fashioned Post-Modernism and the Legal Theories of Oliver Wendell Holmes, Jr.," *Brooklyn Law Review* 63 (1997):59.

5 William James, "The Moral Philosopher and the Moral Life," in *Essays in Pragmatism* (New York: Hafner, 1948), 65–87 (cited hereafter parenthetically in the text by page number).

6 Sheldon M. Novick, *Henry James: The Young Master* (New York: Random House, 1996), 99. See also Ralph Barton Perry, *The Thought and Character of William James* (Cambridge, Mass.: Harvard University Press, 1948), 89.

7 Charles Sanders Peirce, *Collected Papers,* vol. 5: *Pragmatism and Pragmatism,* ed. Charles Hartshorne and Paul Weiss (Cambridge, Mass.: Harvard University Press, 1934), 402.
8 Thus, pragmatism is a renunciation of Kantian principles of universality. See Immanuel Kant, *Prolegomena to Any Future Metaphysics* (1873).
9 The term "ideal" was commonly used by the pragmatists to mean the actor's own avowed reasons for deciding that an act was worth doing. There are general ideals, e.g., supporting one's family, as well as specific ideals, e.g., working overtime. See, e.g., Peirce, "Every man has certain ideals of the general description of conduct that befits a rational animal in his particular station in life, what most accords with his total nature and relations," *Collected Papers* vol. 1, 591.
10 Indeed, for the pragmatist, normativity is at the heart of every cognitive endeavor. Scientific questions are questions about what one ought to believe, and logic is, according to Peirce, a normative science. See, e.g., Catharine Wells Hantzis, "Peirce's Conception of Philosophy: Its Method and Program," *Transactions of the Charles S. Peirce Society* 23 (1987):289, 294.
11 James insists in "The Moral Philosopher and the Moral Life" that philosophers must reject the idea of an ethical sphere "in which individual minds are the measures of all things, and in which no one 'objective' truth, but only a multitude of 'subjective' opinions, can be found" (71).
12 See Immanuel Kant, *Critique of Pure Reason,* trans. Werner S. Pluhar (Indianapolis: Hackett, 1996), 92–99.
13 See John Locke, *An Essay Concerning Human Understanding* (1689), ed. Peter H. Nidditch (Oxford: Clarendon Press, 1988). See also A. J. Ayer, *Language, Truth and Logic* (New York: Dover, 1952), 33–45.
14 Thus, James begins his essay "The Moral Philosopher and the Moral Life" by saying: "The main purpose of this paper is to show that there is no such thing possible as an ethical philosophy dogmatically made up in advance . . . In other words, there can be no final truth in ethics any more than in physics, until the last man has had his experience and said his say" (65).
15 This analysis is based on the description of pragmatic method in my Holmes article, Catharine Peirce Wells, "Holmes on Legal Method," *Southern Illinois – University Law Journal* 18, p. 1 (1993–94):329, 338 (arguing that Holmes's legal method was the pragmatic method applied to law).
16 A modern pragmatist has put it this way: "Any statement can be held true come what may, if we make drastic enough adjustments elsewhere in the system. Even a statement very close to periphery [sensory experience] can be held true in the face of recalcitrant experience by pleading hallucination or by amending certain statements of the kind called logical laws. Conversely, by the same token, no statement is immune to revision." Willard Van Orman Quine, "Two Dogmas of Empiricism," in *From a Logical Point of View: Nine Logico-Philosophical Essays,* 2d ed. (Cambridge, Mass.: Harvard University Press, 1980), 43.
17 In evaluating an act, consequences count, but they are not the only thing that counts. The act itself has a moral quality that can be assessed – not with reference to certain *a priori* standards but with reference both to the actor's own purposes and to the shared norms of the community.

18 Keep in mind that James does not begin with a restrictive understanding of what constitutes experience.
19 This distinction is meant to be analogous to the distinction between the way in which an object appears in our own private view and the description of an object as it exists in the outside world of public perception.
20 Reprinted in William James, *Talks to Teachers on Psychology: and to Students on Some of Life's Ideals* (Norton: New York, 1958), 149–69, 149–50. Of course, the "blindness" that he is talking about is our inability really to see the private lives of others.
21 Ibid., 129–30.
22 There has been a long philosophical tradition of attempting to reduce or translate all or some of these into a unitary material world. See, e.g., John R. Searle, "Consciousness and the Philosophers," review of David J. Chalmers, *The Conscious Mind: In Search of a Fundamental Theory* (Oxford: Oxford University Press), *New York Review of Books*, 6 March 1997. From a pragmatic perspective, the outcome of such debates makes no difference to the question of viewpoint, because things such as attitude, emotion, etc., have regularities of their own, even if these things can be considered as nothing more than aspects of material phenomena.
23 To the modern ear, these examples sound somewhat unconvincing. E.g., most modern readers would think that reducing anxiety would be a productive way to increase pleasure and decrease pain. One answer to this is to keep in mind that James is talking about bodily pleasures and pains. But I suspect that the main problem is that we understand the cause-and-effect relations of bodily pleasure and pain somewhat differently than James did. This would be an interesting question to think about in reading James's *Principles of Psychology*. In any case, the position he is advancing here – that people act on the basis of some ideals that have nothing to do with bodily pleasure or pain – is less controversial than his examples suggest.
24 As James puts it in "The Moral Philosopher and the Moral Life," "[No] thing can be good or right except so far as some consciousness feels it to be good or thinks it to be right" (71).
25 And indeed in *The Path of the Law* he recognizes these difficulties: "The law is full of phraseology drawn from morals, and by the mere force of language continually invites us to pass from one domain to the other without perceiving it, as we are sure to do unless we have the boundary constantly before our minds" (171–72; 993).
26 Oliver Wendell Holmes, Jr., *The Common Law* (Boston: Little, Brown, 1881). The purpose of *The Common Law* is to show that contemporary legal doctrines can be traced to their practical origins in the life of the people. This, in effect, provides us with a historical account of the ideals and policies that the legal community has pursued.
27 The pragmatic method is described in the text accompanying note 15 in this chapter. For a more detailed argument that this is Holmes's view, see Wells, "Holmes on Legal Method," 329.
28 Oliver Wendell Holmes, Jr., "The Theory of Torts," *American Law Review* (1872–73):652, 658.
29 *Lochner v. New York*, 198 U.S. 45, 74 (1904) (Holmes dissenting).
30 Typescript in author's possession.
31 Oliver Wendell Holmes, Jr., "Natural Law," in Holmes, *Collected Legal Papers*, 310.
32 Ibid., 313.

33 Holmes, "Brown University – Commencement 1897," in Holmes, *Collected Legal Papers,* 166.
34 Wells, "Old-Fashioned Post Modernism," 59.
35 274 U.S. 200, 207 (Holmes dissenting).
36 Holmes, "Ideals and Doubts," in Holmes, *Collected Legal Papers,* 304. The passage concludes: "I feel no pangs of conscience over either step."
37 William James, "The Moral Philosopher and the Moral Life," in *Classical American Philosophy,* ed. John J. Stuhr (Oxford: Oxford University Press, 1987), 143, 152.
38 Holmes, "Brown University," 166.
39 Ibid.

10

Emerson and Holmes

Serene Skeptics

SANFORD LEVINSON*

Like other contributors to this volume, Catharine Peirce Wells takes note of what she calls the "big finish" of *The Path of the Law*, which concludes with the evocation of "an echo of the infinite, a glimpse of its unfathomable process, a hint of the universal law."[1] She argues (in Chapter 9 of this volume) that this powerful statement seems to dissolve the tensions suggested by standard-form positivism, with its sharp separation between law and morals and thus, at the very least, contributes to the difficulty in locating Holmes along any single intellectual spectrum.

Wells's own strategy in overcoming the "seeming inconsistencies"[2] of Holmes's thought is to look at him through what might be called a Jamesian filter. That is, she asks us to interpret Holmes as if he were, in some measure, "really" William James, a contemporary who was also, in fact, a close associate of Holmes during his youth and young adulthood in Boston. We are invited to imagine Holmes and James "drinking whisky, smoking cigars, and discussing philosophy well into the early morning." She argues that such experiences may well account for "a lifelong resonance between the views" of Holmes and James. Appropriately enough, given Jamesian pragmatism, Wells says that "this way of reading Holmes seems to work" by "reconcil[ing] some of the more obvious contradictions" within Holmes's thought, including the relatively few pages of *The Path of the Law* itself, and "makes sense of the inspirational passage at the end of the essay."[3]

There are at least two ways to assess such arguments. One might treat Wells as making a number of causal arguments, rooted in the biographies of both Holmes and James and amenable, therefore, to corroboration (or disproof) by

---

* My deepest thanks to Steven J. Burton for organizing the extraordinary conference "The Path of the Law in the Twentieth Century," held at the University of Iowa College of Law on 24–25 January 1997, at which portions of these remarks were first delivered as a comment on the paper by Catharine Peirce Wells (Chapter 9 of this volume).

careful attention to the details of the lives of these two extraordinary American icons. The second is simply to treat Wells as offering a kind of "rational reconstruction" of Holmes, whose test, as already suggested, is pragmatic helpfulness rather than strictly historical "accuracy."

If one wishes to focus on biography, I note that Holmes and James had a somewhat tenuous relationship after their quite young adulthood. Thus Holmes's best biographer, G. Edward White, says that Holmes "saw less of William James" after 1868 as they went their increasingly separate ways.[4] Indeed, in 1876 James described Holmes as "a powerful battery, formed like a planing machine to gouge a deep self-beneficial groove through life,"[5] and it is clear that this was not meant as a compliment or even a reflection on an otherwise close friend. Nor was Holmes especially well disposed toward James as a philosopher. He wrote to Lewis Einstein in 1908 that James's *Pragmatism* was "amusing humbug," and eight years later he wrote to Harold Laski: "I don't think there is much in either [the pragmatic or pluralistic] part of W. James's philosophy."[6]

Still, I do not read Wells as offering a genuinely causal account of the influences underlying Holmes's thought. Instead, she is arguing that use of the Jamesian filter and the treatment of Holmes *as if* he were a dedicated Jamesian, will enable us to read Holmes more clearly and to make sense of passages that are otherwise incomprehensible.

"Rational reconstruction" is a valuable method of intellectual analysis, and it may even be that the Jamesian filter is an unusually helpful one. I am less interested in disputing the value of that filter than in offering one of my own, based on a quite different figure from Holmes's youth, Ralph Waldo Emerson.[7] It may be the case, of course, that one could join Wells's and my own approaches if Emerson in fact influenced his fellow (and much younger) New Englander James; that question is well beyond the scope of this essay. In any event, I want not so much to question Wells's argument as to complement it by offering a somewhat different perspective.

I

Holmes was, of course, unusually long-lived; born in 1841, he died in 1935, just two days before his ninety-fourth birthday. More to the point, perhaps, he became most truly influential only after his seventieth birthday (though *The Common Law* was written, almost frantically, to meet a self-imposed deadline signaled by his impending fortieth birthday). Given that he became most famous (and influential) at an age when most thinkers have retired, voluntarily or otherwise, from the stage, it has been hard not to view him as a twentieth-century figure (or at least a late nineteenth-century one). Most analysts would perceive Holmes as sharply separated from (perhaps even in revolt against) the "New England summer" identified with Emerson, Thoreau, Melville, and

Hawthorne. We forget at our peril, though, that Holmes was already twenty at the outbreak of the Civil War, and the hothouse intellectual nature of his household made the presence of such figures as Emerson – "Uncle Waldo" – who would reach his widest national audience in the 1840s and 1850s, of more than social importance.

Holmes himself, in 1876, sent the Concord philosopher a note to accompany one of his first legal essays: "Accept this little piece as . . . a slight mark of the gratitude and respect I feel for you who more than anyone else first started the philosophical ferment in my mind."[8] It is harder to dismiss this as mere flattery for the occasion when one discovers that as late as 1930 Holmes could write to Sir Frederick Pollock, one of his oldest correspondents: "[T]he early firebrand of my youth that burns to me as brightly as ever is Emerson."[9] To be sure, it would be foolhardy to attempt to understand Holmes without being attentive to the contexts of his adult years, ranging from the Civil War to the development in the United States of corporate capitalism and the stirrings of a self-conscious labor movement organizing to defend its rights against those who would be its corporate masters. But crucial aspects of Holmes's thought will be missed if one skips too easily over the intellectual milieu presented to Holmes during his early years, even if they represent a relatively small portion of his remarkable (and remarkably lengthy) life.

It is hard to believe, for example, that the adolescent Holmes was not profoundly influenced by the quite feverish arguments of Emerson. Is Holmes not the incarnation of "Man Thinking" presented by Emerson in "The American Scholar"[10] as capturing the highest vocation of life? "Thinking," in the Emersonian universe, was no passive activity, but rather a means of wrestling with the world and, ultimately, attaining what he termed, in his essay "Experience," "the transformation of genius into practical power."[11] To attain such power, Emerson emphasized, the most ruthless self-discipline – a version of the "self-reliance" that Emerson is famous for – is necessary. "Friends, books, pictures, lower duties, talents, flatteries, hopes, – all are distractions" from the duties of the lonely thinker.[12] Indeed, it is just such "self-" (or at least "thinker") centeredness that generated James's caustic critiques of Holmes.

Truly Emersonian thinkers must liberate themselves from the excrescences of the past and from convention. It is as much Emerson as Holmes who speaks when we read that "[t]o an imagination of any scope the most far-reaching form of power is not money, it is the command of ideas."[13] Speaking to Harvard undergraduates in 1886, Holmes addresses forthrightly the meaning of "intellectual ambition" and the "heroic" qualities that it summons forth from those who would make their mark on the world of ideas. But what a thoughtful person might gain as the result of heroic enterprise is "the secret isolated joy of the thinker, who knows that, a hundred years after he is dead and forgotten, men who never heard of him will be moving to the measure of his thought – the subtile rapture of a postponed power, . . . which to his prophetic vision is more real than that which commands an army" ("Path" 405). Holmes would no doubt be delighted to know (and regard as a vindication of his own career ambitions) the fact that in the last decade alone four biographies of him have been published.[14] And the present volume is the record of only one of at least three major symposia that were held in 1997 in honor of the one-hundredth anniversary of *The Path of the Law*. Holmes continues to exert a remarkable degree of intellectual power, certainly more than any other single figure within American law, even a full sixty years after his death.

Holmes finds the task of the thinker heroic because of the monumental self-discipline required. "Only when you have worked alone – when you have felt around you a black gulf of solitude more isolating than that which surrounds the dying man, and in hope and in despair have trusted to your own unshaken will – then only will you have achieved."[15] And consider Holmes's evocation of the Arctic explorer Fridtjof Nansen during an 1897 commencement speech at Brown University entitled "Man and the Universe." Holmes speaks of "many roads" as leading to the "haven" of the "Eternal City" or "City of God" in which abide the enduring "ideals" of our lives.[16] As a commencement speaker, Holmes wishes to give his listeners "a hint of what is to be expected on the way" to the Eternal City, and he notes that his "way has been by the ocean of the law." It is at this point that he self-consciously compares his own quest to that of the explorer.

> Most men of the college-bred type . . . have to go through that experience of sailing for the ice . . . In the first stage one has companions, cold and black though it be . . . But if he is a man of high ambitions he must leave even his fellow-adventurers and go forth into a deeper solitude and greater trials. He must start for the pole. In plain words he must face the loneliness of original work. No one can cut out new paths in company. He does that alone.

Indeed, it is not hard to discern an affinity with Nietzsche in the portrait of the lonely transvaluer whose ultimate reliance is his "unshaken will."[17] Richard Posner goes so far as to label Holmes "the American Nietzsche."[18] This affinity may seem less surprising once one realizes that Nietzsche himself admired Emerson and saw in him a compatriot.

II

Emerson helps us to address another issue that Wells raises, which is how we should understand Holmes's metaphor of the "bad man." In our contribution to a symposium on *The Path of the Law* held at the Boston University Law School, where Holmes delivered his address, J. M. Balkin and I argued that the bad man metaphor is maladroit and that everything that is valuable in the essay could easily have been saved through the use of a quite different metaphor, drawn directly from Emerson, of the "self-reliant" person.[19] Several aspects of Emerson's perhaps most famous essay, "Self-Reliance,"[20] could, suitably paraphrased, be comfortably placed in *The Path of the Law*.

Like Wells in regard to Holmes, we are less concerned to establish the actual influence of Emerson on Holmes, though we obviously believe it is substantial, than to engage in a thought experiment testing the reader's response to an Emersonian–Holmesian account of law emphasizing the "self-reliant individual" rather than the "bad man." We probably cannot determine precisely why Holmes chose the bad man rather than the self-reliant man as his provocative metaphor, though David Seipp has interestingly suggested that the source of the bad man image is a crime novel of the 1880s;[21] this is, at bottom, a question interesting mainly to historians. We can, though, readily ask ourselves how well the terminology of "self-reliance" in fact works analytically, as well as ask if an argument predicated on the self-reliant, rather than the bad, individual, is more attractive.

"Every law which the state enacts, indicates a fact in human nature; that is all."[22] This Emersonian dictum, with its heavily inflected "every" and "all," suggests a positivized notion of law that deprives it of any necessary majesty (and perhaps even legitimacy) supplementing its brute facticity. To be sure, Emerson, like Holmes, would not have questioned the premise that many laws do have moral grandeur, but this is a happy contingency, having nothing to do with the "essence" of law, which is its amoral facticity.

And if moral grandeur is not produced by sheer "enact[ment]," neither is it the product of venerable age. It scarcely seems to require any stretching to see an affinity between Holmes and Emerson in regard to their views of history. Surely one of the keys to understanding the path that law should take is Holmes's "look[ing] forward to a time when the part played by history in the explanation of dogma shall be very small," not to mention the more flamboyant pronouncement that "[i]t is revolting to have no better reason for a rule of law than that so it was laid down in the time of Henry IV" ("Path" 402, 399). One has little doubt that Emerson would have applauded these sentiments and seen in his young friend a worthy successor, for he says in "Self-Reliance": "Whence then this worship of the past? The centuries are conspirators against the sanity and majesty of the soul" (54).

Consider also what is probably the most famous single passage from "Self-Reliance":

Whoso would be a man must be a nonconformist. He who would gather immortal palms must not be hindered by the name of goodness, but must explore if it be goodness. Nothing is at last sacred but the integrity of our own mind. (41)

The fact that these lines have become a cliché of American thought makes it difficult sometimes to grasp their power. Cannot one easily read Emerson as calling for the washing in what his disciple so famously called "cynical acid" of the standard notions of one's society (including, of course, any naive joinder of law and morality), so that one avoids the ultimate primrose path of confusing what society calls good with what is *really* good?

Emerson has little patience with the ordinary language of morality. "Good and bad are but names very readily transferable to that or this; the only right is what is after my constitution, the only wrong what is against it . . . I am ashamed to think how easily we capitulated to badges and names, to large societies and dead institutions" (42). The ultimate message is "What I must do, is all that concerns me, not what people think" (44). The world is full of busybodies "who think they know what is your duty better than you do" (44). Among other things such people do, one might think, is enact laws that ostensibly announce one's duties. To be sure, "It is easy in the world to live after the world's opinion; . . . but the great man is he who in the midst of the crowd keeps with perfect sweetness the independence of solitude" (44).

One must acknowledge that what Emerson finds "sweet" others might denounce as a kind of radical egoism. Apropos of some earlier comments, it is easy enough to imagine Emerson's "great man" as a Nietzschean overman, ever ready to engage in the critique of social pieties and work for "transvaluation." The "transvaluer" is no more necessarily a figure of admiration than is the "conformist" who accepts conventional values; the former might, under some circumstances, be a very "bad man" indeed, whereas we would all express relief for the presence of conformists among us, even if, as conformists, their "goodness" is accidental, because of the contingent fact that the law in that case conformed with independent tests of justice rather than an inherent part of their character. But it is also easy enough to imagine transvaluers as genuinely great, possessing sufficient resources of self-reliance to avoid callow submission to banal notions of duty, including those congealed in law, however defined.

The self-reliant individual, then, rejects all heteronomy; she is the model figure of the autonomous self. It takes relatively little effort to discern Holmes's own idealized self-portrait as just such an autonounous, relentlessly independent, thinker. But choices always are made within a context, including the "facts" that effectively structure the options open to oneself. For most of us these facts certainly include law, precisely as defined by Holmes, that is, as predictions of the incidence of the use of public force. There may come occasions when Emersonian principles require that one defy the law and go to jail or, perhaps, even exhibit comradeship with John Brown's attempt to overthrow the American state insofar as it protected slavery.[23] Perhaps Emerson's failure to join Thoreau behind bars is evidence that Emerson did not think the cost of civil disobedience worth the sacrifice; it is impossible, though, to believe that this devotee of self-reliance would have otherwise castigated Thoreau for daring to question the authority of the state. In any event, the self-reliant, value-choosing (and, ultimately, action-choosing) person would have every incentive to ask about the consequences of certain actions and then to decide accordingly.

Assume that one accepts my general argument. The question still remains:

Does the terminology we choose make a real difference? Not surprisingly, I believe the answer is yes. An almost inevitable consequence of using the "bad man" as a source of jurisprudential wisdom is to discredit what he stands for. Who, after all, generally looks to those who are "bad" for genuine wisdom about social institutions?

It is, of course, possible that Holmes was profoundly serious when he followed his reference to the bad man by stating that "[t]he law is the witness and external deposit of our moral life" and asserting his belief that "[t]he practice of it, in spite of popular jests, tends to make good citizens and good men" ("Path" 392). That is, for all of Holmes's iconoclasm and desire to shock – which Siepp offers as the best way to understand *The Path of the Law* – one might nevertheless discern in Holmes an utterly conventional conformist who would not think, for example, of entitling his own work "Overcoming Law," as did our closest contemporary analogue to Holmes, Judge Richard A. Posner. Anyone familiar with Holmes's life knows that he was a notable statist, and he may have shared the state's worry about the presence of too many self-reliant citizens who question its authority. Even if those who draft legislative statutes must properly weigh the presence of bad men (from their perspective) who view law only as a price system, they obviously do not celebrate the bad man's liberation from a strong sense of legal obligation. From the state's perspective, the "best" citizen is precisely the one who believes that law is self-justifying and who will, sheeplike, do whatever the law requires. Both the Holmesian bad man and the Emersonian self-reliant one understand that law is most certainly *not* self-justifying and that ovine acceptance of the legal status quo may threaten not only one's personal safety (as is literally true of complacent sheep on the way to slaughter), but one's ultimate integrity if one ends up collaborating with an evil regime.

Our students should be taught that there is nothing "bad" about accepting Holmes's basic structure of analysis, though it may well be "bad" to be simply the kind of radical egoist that Holmes seems to identify with the bad man. But the alternative to radical selfishness is not the giving over of one's conscience to the legal sovereign. It is, instead, to adopt a genuine responsibility for our own deeds.

III

It is time now to return to the other theme I want to address, which is Holmes's ability to offer such paragraphs as the conclusion to *The Path of the Law* (and, as we have seen, other essays as well), even as he tosses out his ostensibly "cynical" observations about social reality. Here again it is useful to offer Emerson as a potential template for the Holmesian understanding. Emerson provided far more than a model of the intellectual as man of power, for he was also, of course, one of the most probing analysts of the general cultural situation within which

Holmes had to find his way. In the year that Holmes was born, Emerson delivered an address called "Lecture on the Times" that described "our torment" as "Unbelief, the Uncertainty as to what we ought to do; the distrust of the value of what we do, and the distrust that the Necessity (which we all at last believe in) is fair and beneficent."[24] F. O. Matthiessen was simply incorrect in describing Emerson as without "a trace of skepticism in his being."[25] Indeed, there are few American writers who more emphasize the flux presented by life. "There are many skepticisms," Emerson wrote in his Journal for 1845. "The universe is like an infinite series of planes, each of which is a false bottom, and when we think our feet are planted now at last on the adamant, the slide is drawn out from under us."[26] Later, in his essay "Experience," Emerson emphasized omnipresent uncertainties.[27] "Dream delivers us to dream," he wails, "and there is no end to illusion." Three pages of such illusions follow, capped by the observation, "[G]ladly would we anchor, but the anchorage is quicksand."[28] Just when readers pinch themselves to remember that it is the Sage of Concord they are reading and not some modernist, comes the Emerson on whom Matthiessen relied, who told Thomas Carlyle: "My whole philosophy . . . teaches acquiescence and optimism."[29]

On what was Emerson's "optimism" based? The answer appears in two important essays: "Montaigne: or, the Skeptic," published in *Representative Men* in 1850,[30] and "Fate," which appeared in *The Conduct of Life* in 1860 (when Holmes was 19).[31] Emerson writes in "Montaigne" that a "man of thought" (who, for him, was the best sort of man) "must feel the thought that is parent of the universe." Beneath (or at least beyond) the undulation and flow of experience is an overarching unity to which the skeptic can repair with relief. That recognition that "[t]he world is saturated with deity and with law" makes it possible to be "content with just and unjust, with sots and fools, with the triumph of folly and fraud." Indeed, this sort of thinker "can behold with serenity the yawning gulf between the ambition of man and his power of performance." He ends this essay as follows:

Let a man learn to look for the permanent in the mutable and fleeting; let him learn to bear the disappearance of things he was wont to reverence without losing his reference; let him learn that he is here, not to work but to be worked upon; and that, though abyss open under abyss, and opinion displace opinion, all are at last contained in the Eternal Cause: –

"If my bark sink, 'tis to another sea."[32]

The famous philosopher of self-reliance enjoins his readers to have faith, to be reliant upon the perceptions of their minds at their highest pitch of illumination – that is, to accept joyfully their subservience to Eternal, though mysterious, Law. Stephen Whicher finds the foundation of Emerson's later serenity to be his submission to this Law.[33]

These themes are carried further in the 1860 essay "Fate," which begins with an announcement of disillusionment about the prospect of ordinary social reform, because so much of human life has been "predetermined" (334). Still, "If we must accept Fate, we are not less compelled to affirm liberty, the significance of the individual, the grandeur of duty, the power of character" (331). Even though Fate stands supreme in all aspects of life, from material existence to the moral growth of the race, we suddenly discover that "[i]ntellect annuls Fate. So far as a man thinks, he is free" (340). And freedom is essentially defined in terms of the acceptance of the limits and travails imposed by destiny. "If you please to plant yourself on the side of Fate, and say, Fate is all; then we say, a part of Fate is the freedom of man" (340). Indeed, for Emerson the "instinctive and heroic races" are "proud believers in Destiny. They conspire with it: a loving resignation is with the event" (340). In fact this embrace of the Inevitable builds toward "the day of days, the great day of the feast of life, that in which the inward eye opens to the Unity in things, to the omnipresence of law: – sees that what is must be and ought to be, or is the best" (341). In a familiar doctrine of Idealism, then, we become "lawgivers" insofar as we assent to the Fate above us; freedom is the acceptance of Necessity.

The greatest teaching of life thus becomes "a fatal courage" (340). Should Fate result in apparent harm to an individual, "he is to rally [sic] on his relation to the Universe . . . [H]e is to take sides with the Deity who secures universal benefit by his pain" (351). The essay closes with a plea to his readers to build altars to the Blessed Unity and Beautiful Necessity that resolve the despairing questions of skepticism into an answering vision of reconciliation (351–52). If I am correct that there are, at the very least, affinities between the thought of Emerson and Holmes, this approach may help to answer what otherwise appears to be a central paradox in Holmes, the joinder of a sometimes astonishingly remorseless view of the law with the serenity that was noted both by admirers and by Holmes himself.

It is within this context that we might try to understand Felix Frankfurter's 1929 comment to his fellow Holmes devotee, philosopher Morris Raphael Cohen, that the justice had attained, "by the nature of his temperament, but still more by his achievement, the ultimate serenity and wisdom of life."[34] "Serenity" has become a somewhat unfamiliar notion in the modern world; it is now over a half century since W. H. Auden named this era the "Age of Anxiety," and nothing has happened since Auden wrote to belie his labeling. Holmes was remarkably free from anxiety. As he wrote to a correspondent, "My serenity, such as it is, is based on the conviction that worry is a futile waste of energy and the knowledge that I can do nothing but pay and do my work."[35] Just as Bertolt Brecht once wrote: "[H]e who is happy has not yet heard the news," so might we believe the same about those who are serene. In what world, we might plaintively ask, have they been living their lives?

No doubt the fundamental explanations of Holmes's "serenity" lie in psychological aspects of his life, but there is no reason to doubt that he, like all human beings, had to enact his psychological predispositions within a cultural or intellectual matrix that served to justify them, both to himself and to others. Holmes surely prided himself on his ability to wash the standard approaches to law in a "cynical acid," and from one perspective what remained after the Holmesian bath could well appear a portrait of law that was, in Grant Gilmore's words, "savage, harsh, and cruel."[36] Yet this did not prevent Holmes from approaching life with "serenity" and, indeed, dismissing those who exhibited anxiety or even concern as the appropriate posture. How did he achieve this resolution? One answer lies in Holmes's adoption (and adaptation) of Emersonian tropes.

The Holmesian mode of resolution is seen most vividly, and recurrently, in the many speeches that he delivered on ceremonial occasions. Scholars understandably concentrate on the overt theses and arguments presented in them; I want, instead, to emphasize their last paragraphs, from which I have already drawn many of my quotations. What we observe, over and over again, is that the often jarring content of the main text is neutralized by recourse to Emersonian (some might even say Calvinist) imagery of the transcendental unity that, however much it passeth rational understanding, can be evoked by even the ostensibly most skeptical.

Robert Ferguson, in a study of Holmes's rhetorical depiction of the "judicial figure,"[37] examines Holmes's 1913 essay "Law and the Court,"[38] originally delivered to the Harvard Law School Association of New York as a response to the criticism then being leveled at the judiciary. "I get letters," Holmes cried out, "intimating that we are corrupt. Well, gentlemen, I admit that it makes my heart ache" (505). Such attacks he placed within the context of "the unrest that seems to wonder vaguely whether law and order pay" (506), unrest that could be seen, among other places, in the fact that Eugene V. Debs had won over 1 million votes for the presidency just the year before. We might know now that the United States, for whatever reason, would prove "exceptional" in avoiding the development of a strong socialist or at least labor party that might criticize the capitalist political order, yet nobody could have known that in 1913, when the United States appeared potentially European in its potential for class conflict and rejection of conventional law and order.

One might have expected Holmes to recognize that disillusionment with law as a means of bringing about an unproblematic social order might well have been generated by careful study of his own thought, though I know of no such recognition. Instead, he drew as his moral – and contributed to his heroic status among reformers – by emphasizing the duty of judges to avoid confusing their own sympathies and notions of social justice with the commands of the law. What this meant, in the context of the time, is that judges should become far more tolerant of some of the changes that were being suggested by various legislatures, even if a judge found a particular change abhorrent. "When twenty years ago a vague terror went over the earth and the word socialism began to be heard, I thought and still think that fear was translated into doctrines that had no proper place in the Constitution or the common law" (507). Judges should realize that the political marketplace is full of strife and accept the triumph of those with more social power.

What is most illuminating, though, is the conclusion to Holmes's speech, in which he describes his "glimpse of peace" that lies "beyond the vision of battling races and an impoverished earth" (507). The "glimpse" takes the form of an extended metaphor about the Washington, D.C., landscape, including "the pallid discord of the electric lights," that is transformed by his remembering "the faith that I partly have expressed, faith in the universe not measured by our fears, a universe that has thought and more than thought inside of it, and as I gazed, after the sunset and above the electric lights, there shone the stars" (508).

Who would not be serene if possessing such "faith"? It is, I think, Holmes's last paragraphs that most clearly mark him as a man with a fundamentally different consciousness from our own. Holmes's basic analysis of the law, as well as his relentless skepticism, could make him fully at home in many contemporary salons today, as would also be the case with Emerson. Where Holmes displayed himself as out of synch with our sensibility is his evocation of "faith" and his confidence that all is resolved in an almost mystical notion of "universal law." To the extent that one takes seriously such evocations, and I see no reason not to, it must cause us to challenge those descriptions, like Gilmore's, that emphasize his "pessimism" or, indeed, nihilism.

Concomitantly, to the extent that contemporary speakers cannot themselves make use of such notions – or, a somewhat different point, to the extent that a contemporary audience would find almost incredible the presentation of any such rhetoric – then we are enabled to understand the sea change that occurred at some point in the consciousness of academic intellectuals about their own enterprise. Who among the readers (or authors) of this collection, or of practically any contemporary academic journal, feels the kind of ontological solace – the serenity – that Emerson and Holmes display? If there *are* those among us who no longer feel Audenesque anxiety, it is most likely, for better or worse, because of the adoption of a posture of postmodernist ironic distance from the questions about life's meaningfulness that plagued earlier generations. Such a stance seems similar to Holmes's own sublime indifference to the suffering of his fellow humans and his disdain for the quest for solutions, despite his portrayal of the unafraid, heroic thinker, who would, in his own way, become joined with the Cosmos.

Notes

1 For Wells, see Chapter 9, section III.B, of this volume. For Holmes, see Oliver Wendell Holmes, Jr., "The Path of the Law," in *The Collected Works of Justice Holmes,* ed. Sheldon M. Novick, 3 vols. (Chicago: University of Chicago Press, 1995), vol. 3, 391, 406 (cited

hereafter parenthetically in the text as "Path"). "The Path" is reprinted in the Appendix to this volume with star paging.
2. See text accompanying note 4 in Chapter 9.
3. See text accompanying note 6 in Chapter 9.
4. G. Edward White, *Justice Oliver Wendell Holmes: Law and the Inner Self* (New York: Oxford University Press, 1993), 103.
5. Ibid., 89.
6. Holmes to Lewis Einstein, 17 June 1908, in Oliver Wendell Holmes, *The Essential Holmes,* ed. Richard Posner (Chicago: University of Chicago Press, 1992), 70; Holmes to Harold Laski, 15 September 1916, in ibid., xxiv.
7. My major argument was first formulated in "Skepticism, Democracy, and Judicial Restraint: An Essay on the Thought of Oliver Wendell Holmes and Felix Frankfurter" (Ph.D. diss., Harvard University, 1969).
8. Holmes to Ralph Waldo Emerson, quoted in Mark DeWolfe Howe, *Justice Oliver Wendell Holmes: The Shaping Years* (Cambridge, Mass.: Belknap Press of Harvard University Press, 1957), 203.
9. Holmes to Sir Frederick Pollock, in *Holmes–Pollock Letters: The Correspondence of Mr. Justice Holmes and Sir Frederick Pollock, 1874–1932,* ed. Mark DeWolfe Howe (Cambridge, Mass.: Harvard University Press, 1961), vol. 2, 264. Holmes also reproached Harold Laski for criticizing Emerson: "Emerson, I think, had the gift of imparting a ferment. . . . To my ear some of Emerson's sentences sing, or did so when I read them, enchantingly." Holmes to Laski, in *Holmes–Laski Letters: The Correspondence of Mr. Justice Holmes and Harold J. Laski, 1916–1935,* vol. 1, ed. Mark DeWolfe Howe (Cambridge, Mass.: Harvard University Press, 1953), vol. 1, 471.
10. See Ralph Waldo Emerson, "The American Scholar," in *Selections from Ralph Waldo Emerson: An Organic Anthology,* ed. Stephen E. Whicher (Boston: Houghton Mifflin, 1957), 63, 65.
11. Ralph Waldo Emerson, "Experience," in ibid., 274.
12. Ralph Waldo Emerson, "Power," in *The Conduct of Life* (Boston: Houghton Mifflin, 1887), 74.
13. Oliver Wendell Holmes, Jr., "The Profession of the Law," in Novick, *Collected Works,* 475.
14. See Gary J. Aichele, *Oliver Wendell Holmes, Jr.: Soldier, Scholar, Judge* (Boston: Twayne, 1989); Liva Baker, *The Justice from Beacon Hill: The Life and Times of Oliver Wendell Holmes* (New York: HarperCollins, 1991); Sheldon M. Novick, *Honorable Justice: The Life of Oliver Wendell Holmes* (Boston: Little, Brown, 1989); and G. Edward White, *Justice Oliver Wendell Holmes: Law and the Inner Self* (New York: Oxford University Press, 1992). In addition, John S. Monaghan, *The Grand Panjandrum: The Mellow Years of Justice Holmes* (Lanham, Md.: University Press of America, 1988), is described by White as focusing "on the latter portion of Holmes's life and . . . exclusively directed toward Holmes the person." I note as well such scholarly books as *The Legacy of Oliver Wendell Holmes,* ed. Robert W. Gordon (Stanford: Stanford University Press, 1992), Michael H. Hoffheimer, *Justice Holmes and the Natural Law* (New York: Garland, 1992), and David Rosenberg, *The Hidden Holmes: His Theory of Torts in History* (Cambridge, Mass.: Harvard University Press, 1995). And this does not include collections of Holmes's own writing also published during this past ten years, the most outstanding of which is surely Novick's edition of *The Collected Works* (cited in note 1 to this chapter), as well as the

more accessible collection edited by Richard Posner, *The Essential Holmes* (Chicago: University of Chicago Press, 1992). Finally, see *Holmes and Frankfurter: Their Correspondence, 1912–1934,* ed. Robert M. Memel and Christine L. Compston (Hanover, N.H.: University Press of New England, 1996).

15 Holmes, "Profession of the Law," 472–73.
16 Holmes's address "Man and the Universe" is reprinted in Novick's edition of the *Collected Works* (vol. 3, 517–18), from which all of the quotations from this essay are taken.
17 This Nietzschean element has been especially well developed in David Luban, "Justice Holmes and the Metaphysics of Individual Restraint," *Duke Law Journal* 44 (1994):449.
18 Posner, "Introduction," in *Essential Holmes,* xxviii.
19 See Sanford Levinson and J. M. Balkin, "The 'Bad Man,' the Good, and the Self-Reliant," *Boston University Law Review* (1998).
20 Ralph Waldo Emerson, "Self-Reliance," in *Essays and Essays: Second Series,* ed. Morse Peckham (Columbus, Ohio: Merrill, 1969), 36–73. (Cited hereafter parenthetically in the text by page number.)
21 David Seipp, "Holmes' Path," *Boston University Law Review* 77 (1997):515, 542.
22 Ralph Waldo Emerson, "History," in Peckham, *Essays,* 9.
23 Thus, it has been suggested, Thoreau was an "embodiment of Emerson – not just his Emersonianism, but the process of its representation or 'acting out' . . . While the modern image of Thoreau stresses his autonomy, he was for his contemporaries (both the disconcerted and the appreciative ones) often a sort of 'applied' version of his mentor [Emerson]," nowhere more so than in his decision not only to write "Resistance to Civil Government," better known as "Civil Disobedience," but also to go to jail to register his refusal to collaborate with slavery. See Albert J. Von Frank, *The Trials of Anthony Burns* (Cambridge, Mass.: Harvard University Press, 1998), 104. Emerson himself, however, did not engage in such disobedience. Still, so fervent was his opposition to the Fugitive Slave Act, passed by Congress in 1850, that he seemed in his public statements to embrace civil disobedience. In an 1854 speech, he pronounced the act an "immoral law" and said that "an immoral law cannot be valid." See Ralph Waldo Emerson, "The Fugitive Slave Act," in *Selected Writings of Ralph Waldo Emerson,* ed. Brooks Atkinson (1950), 866. Nevertheless, Emerson had no illusions that the act was not valid law, and he denounced "[t]his filthy enactment" as "the most detestable law that was ever enacted by a civilized state," stating: "I will not obey it[,] by God." See Robert D. Richardson, *Emerson: The Mind on Fire* (Berkeley and Los Angeles: University of California Press, 1995), 498. Emerson scathingly attacked Massachusetts judges for their willingness to support slavery by enforcing the act. "What avails their learning of veneration? At a pinch, they are no more use than idiots" ("Fugitive Slave Act," 881). And he delivered a strong speech on 18 November 1859 on behalf of John Brown, even as Brown stood condemned to death for his raid on Harpers Ferry. See Emerson, "John Brown," in *Selected Writings,* 879–82.
24 Ralph Waldo Emerson, "Lecture on the Times," in *Complete Works* (Boston: Houghton Mifflin, 1984), vol. 1 at 282.
25 F. O. Matthiessen, *American Renaissance: Art and Expression in the Age of Emerson and Whitman* (New York: Oxford University Press, 1941), 65.
26 Ralph Waldo Emerson, *Journals,* ed. Edward Waldo Emerson and Waldo Emerson Forbes (Boston: Houghton Mifflin, 1909), vol. 7, 112.
27 I cannot resist the temptation to point out that Holmes's single most famous comment, at least within the legal community, is almost certainly his injunction that the life of the law

is rooted in experience rather than logic. Oliver Wendell Holmes, Jr., *The Common Law,* ed. M. Howe (Boston: Little, Brown [1881], 1963), 5. The key question then becomes to define what one means by "experience" and to decide how confident one can be in the existence of determinate lessons to be grasped from experience. If one cannot distinguish with any reliability between "illusion" and "reality," then a law ostensibly predicated on the latter may be just as likely to be reflective of the former.

28 Emerson, "Experience," 257, 259.
29 Emerson to Carlyle, in *The Correspondence of Emerson and Carlyle,* ed. Joseph Slater (New York: Columbia University Press, 1964), 394.
30 Emerson, "Montaigne: or, the Skeptic," in Whicher, *Selections from Ralph Waldo Emerson,* 284–301.
31 Emerson, "Fate," in ibid., 330–52. Cited hereafter parenthetically in the text by page number.
32 Emerson, "Montaigne," 300, 301.
33 Stephen E. Whicher, *Freedom and Fate: An Inner Life of Ralph Waldo Emerson* (Philadelphia: University of Pennsylvania Press, 1953), 124.
34 Felix Frankfurter to Morris Ralph Cohen, 14 May 1929, quoted in Lenora Cohen Rosenfield, *Portrait of a Philosopher: Morris R. Cohen in Life and Letters* (New York: Harcourt, Brace & World, 1962), 255.
35 Holmes to Lewis Einstein, 17 September 1917, in Oliver Wendell Holmes, *The Holmes–Einstein Letters: The Correspondence of Mr. Justice Holmes and Lewis Einstein, 1903–1935,* ed. James Bishop Peabody (New York: St. Martin's, 1962), 148.
36 Grant Gilmore, *The Ages of American Law* (New Haven: Yale University Press, 1977), 49.
37 See Robert Ferguson, "Holmes and the Judicial Figure," *University of Chicago Law Review,* 55 (1988):506.
38 Holmes, "Law and the Court" (1913), in Novick, *Collected Works,* vol. 3, 505–8. Cited hereafter parenthetically by page number in the text.

11

The Path Dependence of the Law

CLAYTON P. GILLETTE*

Any legal system that relies on precedent necessarily confronts conflicting objectives. Precedent constrains decision makers (judges and juries) who might otherwise have idiosyncratic preferences and permits the law's subjects to predict the consequences of their conduct.[1] But precedent simultaneously limits the capacity of decision makers to adjust to new conditions and, arguably, discourages detection of those changes by reducing the need for judges to justify their decisions, as long as they discern no novelty in the case they are deciding.[2] This tension between the conflicting characteristics of a precedential system both explains and disputes a major theme of *The Path of the Law*.[3] Much of that essay portrays tradition in the law as worthy of ridicule. While the villain is often legislators rather than judges, the phrases that Holmes employs to critique the use of tradition as a basis for decision ("the pitfall of antiquarianism" by which "tradition . . . overrides rational policy" [474, 472]) suggest that, in the adjudicative context, reliance on precedent does not simply frustrate legal evolution but subjects legal doctrine to misapplication and inappropriate extension (472–73).[4]

This view, however, appears distorted once one considers a broader range of Holmes's writings as commentator and judge. Notwithstanding the strong language in his celebrated essay, his earlier lectures on the common law and his judicial opinions reveal a more measured and more complex role for precedent in the development of legal doctrine. At times, judicial invocation of tradition, embodied in the practice of following precedent without further investigation into the propriety of the preexisting rule, played the role of scoundrel, but at times Holmes himself invoked tradition as a substitute for ad hoc analysis – the very sin against which *The Path of the Law* admonishes others.

---

* Thanks to Gillian Hadfield, Jody Kraus, Daryl Levinson, Liz Magill, and Steven Walt for comments on previous drafts. I am also grateful for comments I received from participants in conferences on *The Path of the Law* at the University of Iowa College of Law and Boston University School of Law.

My objective here is not to chide Holmes for inconsistency, certainly not for drafting opinions at odds with an essay written in the early stage of his judicial career. Taking *The Path of the Law* in isolation seems a dangerous strategy in evaluating Holmes's beliefs over his lifetime. Moreover, if precedential systems generate the conflicting values that I have mentioned, then there may be times when each of the values trumps the other, so that apparent inconsistencies may simply reflect the reality that a factor that dominated in one context was subordinated in another. Indeed, that is precisely the result implicit in Holmes's conception of economic reasoning in the law, which requires balancing the costs of tradition in any case against its benefits. On that understanding, whether precedent is ultimately overutilized or underutilized depends on the ease with which judges distinguish "bad" precedent from "good" and weigh precedents as applied in a given case.

Thus, rather than simply contrasting Holmes's hostile reaction to and hospitable use of precedent, my objective here is to explore the claim implicit in *The Path of the Law* about the hold that tradition has on law's content. A strong reading of Holmes's antipathy toward tradition would be that substantive doctrine, once established, becomes locked in or frozen. Legal doctrines that would have been adopted were decisionmakers writing on a clean slate are instead rejected or simply not considered. Law, on this theory, does not depend on a rational process directed at implementing a particular social, political, or economic view. Instead, it reflects contingencies that arose for reasons unrelated to current needs but that, once established, determine subsequent developments. Critically, Holmes implies, tradition does not simply displace reason but does so "after first having been misunderstood and having been given a new and broader scope than it had when it had a meaning" ("Path" 473).

The claim that law is path dependent, in the sense that prior doctrine determines the content of current doctrine, may be noncontroversial. Holmes's critique goes farther than a positive claim, however, and asserts that legal doctrines rooted solely in tradition are undesirable. At first glance, the Holmesian objection strikes one as odd. First, it seems incongruous in light of Holmes's insistence that the study of law consists of prediction ("Path" 457). One might imagine that binding litigants to previously adopted positions would enhance rather than diminish the predictive character of legal study.[5] What makes prediction possible is the ability to rely on future adherence to rules previously laid down, and that practice implicitly recommends following tradition. (This is not to deny Judge Richard A. Posner's claim that precedents are not the law, under the prediction theory; the law is only the prediction about what courts will say when a case comes before them.[6] Posner's interpretation suggests that a Holmesian legal system could evolve to meet the necessities of the particular time, as long as one trying to discern "the law" could determine when the need for certainty was overridden by the absence of fit between the preexisting rule and current social preferences. But even this understanding of the prediction theory of law admits that precedents, and hence traditions, "are essential inputs into the predictive process,"[7] in part because we expect judges to begin the analysis of current cases with attention to relevant precedents.)

Second, tradition might be thought to have some connection to desirable legal doctrine. Notwithstanding the overused analogy, much favored by Holmes,[8] to evolutionary biology, adaptations within the legal system are generated by human design, not by any external mechanism. Legal actors have the capacity to change law, either by judicial innovation or by overriding legislation. *The Path of the Law* demonstrates Holmes's recognition of exogenous influences on legal developments: most of our laws are "open to reconsideration upon a slight change in the habit of the public mind" ("Path" 466). Appeals to tradition impede change by privileging the status quo. In the face of the human capacity to create legal change when socially desirable but to retain traditions when they are preferable, one might imagine that the preservation of a tradition constituted some evidence that the tradition serves values important within the society (e.g., efficiency, fairness, commitment to community), and that such values override any adverse effects that the tradition might generate.[9]

Notwithstanding these difficulties with Holmes's apparent animosity toward precedent, I believe that *The Path of the Law* hints at a critique of tradition that we are only today reaching sufficient sophistication to use in striking the proper balance among the competing effects of tradition. In this essay, Holmes adopts a crude form of economic analysis that asks us to compare the social "costs" of legal change with the social benefits.[10] His naive economics assumes that those involved in the weighing of gains and losses make their calculations from the perspective of social welfare. His attack on tradition, therefore, initially poses a puzzle, for a proper judge would apply that same calculus to the decision to follow precedent. If decision making subsumes a process of weighing "the ends of legislation, the means of attaining them, and the cost" ("Path" 474), then the survival of tradition after the completion of that process is unproblematic. Thus, for the Holmesian attack to make sense, tradition must be seen either as an impediment to initiating the weighing process or a factor that receives weight disproportionate to actual social preferences. His suspicion of tradition reveals a conviction that judges are committed to prior decisions even when circumstances have changed sufficiently to warrant a modification of the existing legal rule.

In short, Holmes is reacting to what the literature of technology and innovation currently describes as the phenomena of "path dependence" and "lock-in effects."[11] The basic insight of these principles is that once a technology develops along a particular path and produces positive returns, alternatives are ignored. The consequences of following the existing path rather than an alternative, however, may be suboptimal, even if the initial path was optimal at the time that it was selected.[12] Nevertheless, once a choice has been made (and notwithstanding the economist's admonition to ignore sunk costs), exit may be difficult, in large part because others have made similar choices and to act in coordination with others seems superior to casting off on one's own. The result may be to save costs from an individual perspective but to impose significant costs in the form of forgone opportunities on society at large. So it is, Holmes implies, with law. Investment in precedent rewards judges, but only at the social expense of retaining legal rules that have long since failed to reflect the conditions for social progress. Indeed, much of what I want to say may explain Holmes's advocacy for judicial restraint.[13] If judges have incentives to extend traditions beyond their usefulness, so that law is determined largely by the preferences of an earlier time, then we may want to limit the scope of judicial intervention. If, on the other hand, judges have incentives to overcome precedent in situations where its preservation would be socially undesirable, then the stabilizing effects of tradition may be less problematic than the Holmes of *The Path of the Law* indicates.

I begin with a fuller examination of Holmes's views of tradition, in order to demonstrate his awareness of the richness of the subject. Implicitly, this section cautions against inferring too much from Holmes's essay in isolation. I then turn to the claim that allegiance to precedent generates overinvestment in tradition at the expense of social vicissitudes that warrant legal changes. This discussion illustrates that judges have more discretion over the use of precedent than naive conceptions of *stare decisis* suggest. That judges may select among precedents, however, does not mean that they will exercise that discretion. Judges may lack sufficient creativity to escape precedent or may accept precedent of dubious applicability. Either condition would lock us into rules laid down in prior decisions. But path dependence and lock-in are not necessarily cause for dissatisfaction. Where legal precedents simply solve coordination problems or where legal change would create improvements only by generating transition costs not worth incurring, constraints on judicial inventiveness serve a valuable function for the very reason that they lock in an existing legal rule. Thus, judges have significant latitude to use or to ignore precedent. In part IV, I discuss motivational theories to determine whether judges have systemic incentives to overutilize or underutilize precedent. I conclude in part V with the suggestion that Holmes's skeptical view of tradition is warranted, given the mix of judicial incentives.

A final prefatory note is in order. My use of the term "precedent following" does not presume that precedents are given a particular weight. There are substantial discussions of precedent that argue for attaching a range of weights to rules of *stare decisis,* either throughout a legal system or case by case.[14] I assume only that the presence of precedent is not completely determinative, that judges under some circumstances will be able to overturn or avoid precedent, and I ask only whether they have the incentives to interpret that authority broadly or narrowly.

I. Holmes the Traditionalist

The Path of the Law expresses Holmes's antipathy to tradition, which, translated into the judicial forum, constitutes an attack on precedent. Holmes implies that commitment to tradition would cause a judge to apply the rule dictated by a previous decision without exploring any justification for its application to the current case. He speaks of each generation's tendency to "simply obey a law of spontaneous growth," as if legal rules were handed to them with no roots in a reasoning process that might limit their applicability. He criticizes those who act or think unquestioningly because that is what "our fathers have done" ("Path" 470).[15] The concern that tradition will override rational policy (472) or interfere with tradeoffs inherent in legal rules ("the ends of legislation, the means of attaining them, and the cost" [474]) underlies Holmes's strident conclusion that a historical explanation for a rule of law, without more, "is revolting" (469). Indeed, one might infer that giving an historical explanation, even when combined with other explanations, would be cause for Holmes's revulsion. He contends that it would be even "more revolting" if the grounds on which the original rule was laid down had vanished, so that "the rule simply persists from blind imitation of the past" (469). But if that is the case in which following tradition is "more revolting," then presumably it is at least merely "revolting" when the reasons that generated the rule continue to apply. Even in that case, Holmes implies, judges must reconsider the merits of the rule, explore the extent to which its initial justification remains valid, and "recognize their duty of weighing considerations of social advantage" that attach to the rule (467).

It is this language that has led Anthony Kronman to portray Holmes as "contemptuous" of precedent.[16] But fuller consideration of Holmes's views reveals a more complex picture than accusations of "blind imitation" suggest.[17] Judges did not, in Holmes's view, perpetuate precedent without imposing some explanation on the rule they were applying. Rather, in a fashion more complicated than allegations of wooden application imply, judges created a contemporary justification for a rule that had developed previously for reasons that no longer obtained. To illustrate this judicial phenomenon, Holmes explicates the development of the legal principle that a material alteration of a written contract voids the contract against the party making the alteration (472–73).[18] Such *ex post* rationalizations, however, are more fully explored in the first lecture in *The Common Law*.[19] There Holmes demonstrates his understanding, perhaps as advanced for our own age as for his, that evolution is not equivalent to progress, but only to adaptation:

But just as the clavicle in the cat only tells of the existence of some earlier creature to which a collarbone was useful, precedents survive in the law long after the use they once served is at an end and the reason for them has been forgotten. The result of following them must often be failure and confusion from the merely logical point of view.[20]

The Holmes of *The Common Law*, however, seems more tolerant of the phenomenon than the Holmes of "The Path of the Law." In the former work, such logical gaps and *ex post* rationalizations seem inevitable, an intrinsic part of legal development.[21] Indeed, the Holmes of *The Common Law* finds the inconsistencies that result almost charming, so that calls for their abolition are futile insofar as they fail to consider that the law "will become entirely consistent only when it ceases to grow."[22]

The picture becomes more complex as we consider Holmes as judge. Holmes the judge systematically and sympathetically invoked tradition as a preferable constraint on the judicial role. Throughout his judicial career, Holmes suggested that tradition serves social functions, preservation of which warranted deference to previous judicial pronouncements in ways that rival his celebrated deference to legislative judgments.[23] Take, for instance, Holmes's brief opinion in *Stack v. New York, N.H. & H.R. Co.*,[24] a tort suit in which a lower court had refused to order the plaintiff to submit to a physical examination by a doctor to whom the plaintiff objected. In upholding the trial court, Holmes noted that no known precedent authorized judicial intervention. He admitted that recent increases in tort actions arguably represented a change in circumstances that warranted increased judicial involvement. Nevertheless, only a judge "careless or ignorant of precedent" would assume such authority:

> We do not forget the continuous process of developing the law that goes on through the courts, in the form of deduction, or deny that in a clear case it might be possible even to break away from a line of decisions in favor of some rule generally admitted to be based upon a deeper insight into the present wants of society. But the improvements made by the courts are made, almost invariably, by very slow degrees and by very short steps. Their general duty is not to change, but to work out, the principles already sanctioned by the practice of the past.[25]

This seems a remarkable endorsement of tradition just three years after his criticism of reliance on tradition. It may be true that tradition alone does not warrant judicial devotion. But when judges determine what the law should be, Holmes implies, they play an institutional role as well as a substantive one, and the interaction between the two roles cannot be underestimated. Given the absence of any collective forum for judicial decision making and the subsequent capacity for judges to conflict with each other, tradition may play a more important role in adjudication than in legislation.

Or take *Gardiner v. Butler & Co.*,[26] in which Holmes deals tersely with two claims for damages after a lessee had gone into receivership. The first claim was predicated on an explicit damages clause in the lease, while the second, involving the same parties, was predicated on a general contractual claim, the lease being silent as to damages. Holmes recognized the logical similarity of the two cases but held that the first claim was provable in receivership whereas the second was not, on the grounds that "the law as to leases is not a matter of logic in vacuo; it is a matter of history that has not forgotten Lord Coke."[27] Thus, until state law on leases changed, there was no reason for courts, or at least the U.S. Supreme Court, to interfere with "the English tradition" on which that law was based.[28]

Judicial respect for tradition transcended deference to legal precedent. It also meant deference to social traditions, even if legal rules dictated by such traditions were ill suited to contemporary conditions. Take, for instance, *Laurel Hill Cemetery v. City and County of San Francisco*.[29] There Holmes rejected a claim that an ordinance prohibiting burial within the city limits was based on outmoded superstition. Recognizing that contemporary opinion was divided on the safety of cemeteries near residences, Holmes concluded that resolution of the issue could not depend on the reasoning of the justices but was dependent on matters other than "abstract theory."[30] "Tradition and the habits of the community count for more than logic. Since, as before the making of constitutions, regulation of burial and prohibition of it in certain spots"[31] had been a subject of social concern, one contesting such regulations would have to point to a more unified "consensus of civilized opinion"[32] in order for a court to overthrow a law predicated on the traditional position.[33]

Even where some have found Holmes less deferential, as in Constitutional challenges to legislation,[34] he sometimes rejected claims with a simple reference to the shibboleth of tradition. For instance, in *New York Trust Co. v. Eisner*,[35] executors of an estate claimed that a federal estate tax was direct and therefore subject to apportionment. In his brief dismissal of the claim, Holmes revealed an attraction both to precedent and to tradition generally:

But that matter also is disposed of by Knowlton v. Moore, not by an attempt to make some scientific distinction, which would be at least difficult, but on an interpretation of language by its traditional use—on the practical and historical ground that this kind of tax always has been regarded as the antithesis of a direct tax; "has ever been treated as a duty or excise, because of the particular occasion which gives rise to its levy." Upon this point, a page of history is worth a volume of logic.[36]

Again, I use these examples of Holmes's deference to precedent and tradition not to show inconsistency, but to indicate complexity in his thought. Indeed, as I have suggested, the predictive theory of law implies more respect for tradition than a brief reading of *The Path of the Law* suggests. Reflection on Holmes's dual roles reveals him to be not so much an opponent of tradition as he is a proponent of reason. The two may occasionally be juxtaposed to one another. Reason suggests ad hoc analysis, while appeals to tradition suggest unthinking application. But nothing in the appeal to reason requires that every decision be subjected to review from first principles. As Holmes the judge recognized, judicial reexamination is a costly enterprise; and, as Holmes the essayist preached, comprehensive scrutiny of legal rules requires us

to consider and weigh the ends of legislation, the means of attaining them, and the cost. We learn that for everything we have to give up something else, and we are taught to set the advantage we gain against the other advantage we lose, and to know what we are doing when we elect. ("Path" 474)

If Holmes is to follow his own admonition to compare costs and benefits, reconsideration of a traditional rule itself is justified only if the expected value of doing so exceeds the costs of judicial inquiry.[37] If there is a high *ex ante* probability that reconsideration will systematically lead to application of the same rule, then reconsideration seems wasteful in the absence of special circumstances suggesting that the traditional rule is ripe for alteration. Holmes believed that judges who saw similar cases on a routine basis would be better able than juries, which saw only one such case, to discern the content of reasonable conduct in such cases.[38] So might judges who saw similar cases on a regular basis reasonably invoke their prior decisions without rehearsing all of their original justifications. Although this possibility raises the difficult issue of how to calculate the optimal search for changed circumstances, my concern here lies only in noting the possibility that even Holmes's crude cost–benefit analysis suggests that optimal investment may approach zero. If nothing else, such allegiance to precedent serves an economizing function insofar as it reduces judicial investigation. Thus reason and tradition need not be polar opposites, and even blind adherence to precedent may not constitute an "indefensible practice."[39] Indeed, given the admitted benefits that may flow from a precedential system, judges may defer to precedent too little rather than too much.

This conclusion, of course, assumes a probabilistic argument about the initial decision that is perhaps reflected in Holmes's complex mixture of admonitions to reexamine precedent and avoid wooden invocations of precedent. Deference to prior decisions makes sense only if one believes that reconsideration is unlikely to correct an erroneous decision; that is, that the original decision was likely to have been correct in ways that would also properly determine the subsequent decision. If the requirement to follow precedent is not absolute, the survival of a precedent might also suggest that sometimes one *can* infer ought from is, at least where there are forces that would cause shifts where they were appropriate. This explanation is consistent with the presumption that because judicial decisions have been correctly made, there is little reason to relitigate.[40]

But in the absence of a belief that some degree of reexamination is permissible, the probabilistic argument is troublesome. There is no reason to believe that a decision is more likely to be correct simply because it was made first.[41] Indeed, the subsequent decision may be more likely to be correct, because the judge making that decision will have seen the rule applied in a broader range of circumstances. The probabilistic argument is, therefore, troublesome as a defense of precedent and may even be circular. Accordingly, we cannot assume that the initial decision, standing alone, was more likely to be correct than a later, fully considered decision on the same issue. In a system that permits at least some reconsideration of the prior decision (e.g., when the rule of precedent requires only presumptive deference to the prior decision), however, repeat results may indicate correctness and justify reliance on the prior case, as long as there is no affirmative demonstration of changed circumstances. But the very requirement of some degree of precedent following deters thorough reconsideration. Since the possibility of reconsideration suggests that precedents retained for a long period of time are likely to be correct, the deterrent effect undermines the very probabilistic argument on which precedent might be thought to depend. Perversely, the stronger the presumption attached to precedent following (and thus, the less thorough the reconsideration of the rule in subsequent cases), the less we can rely on its survival to support a conclusion that the original decision was "probably" correct.

II. The Scope of Precedent

The claim that I wish to defend in the balance of this essay is that Holmes's critique of precedent reflected a concern about what we would today describe as "lock-in effects." Such effects preclude balancing the economizing and inhibiting effects of precedent. I use the term "reflected" advisedly, since I do not claim that Holmes had in mind the analysis that follows. I suggest only that my argument finds both inspiration and support in his rudimentary statement of an economic view of legal change and his more opaque suggestions about judicial incentives that determine the judicial use of precedent.

Before turning to judicial incentives, we need to recount the nature of precedent and what it means to be "locked in" by a preexisting "path." Examination of incentives reveals only what motivations judges are likely to have. My present concern is less with those abstract motivations than with their manifestation when judges apply legal doctrine. Thus, I examine the range of actions that judges might select when faced with potential precedents. I then turn to an examination of path dependence, in order to disaggregate the array of situations in which judicial discretion determines the application of precedent. My claim is that subsequent cases often depend on precedent either in trivial ways or not at all. Holmes's concerns about precedent, therefore, matter only if there exist nontrivial cases in which prior decisions determine the subsequent path that legal doctrine follows.

A. *Precedent and Judicial Discretion*

Facile explanations of precedent operate on the assumption that a judge, deciding a case today, looks to discover how judges confronted with similar fact situations have decided those cases in the past. The judge in the current case is at least presumptively bound to adhere to these decisions. Although, as I have indicated, a probabilistic argument supports precedent following, the requirement that judges apply prior decisions does not obtain its authority from probability alone. Were that the case, precedent would possess its binding authority by virtue of the continued justification that applied to the prior case. At the very least, a judge in a subsequent case would be warranted in examining whether the justification in the prior case continued to hold. Precedent, however, does not allow *de novo* examination once it is determined that the subsequent case falls within a factual description that is sufficiently similar to the prior case. Even decisions that ultimately reject the precedent must take that precedent into account as the starting point for analysis. To the extent that we believe that precedent has a binding nature, it must lie in the simple fact that it is a precedent rather than in the justification given for the prior case.[42]

Thus, precedent, when first laid down, not only provides reasons for subsequently following the same rule; it also compels rule following.[43] This compulsion both generates the greatest benefits for precedent and maximizes its costs. But this compulsion follows only when the subsequent case is, in fact, governed by the prior case. That is, each of the justifications commonly proffered for a system of precedent – fairness to actors bound by legal rules, efficient decision making, ties to tradition, ensuring certainty and predictability in legal doctrine, or conserving decisional resources[44] – flows from the requirement that the subsequent case be sufficiently "similar" to the prior case that it is appropriate to treat the two cases similarly. This requirement rests on two assumptions that may be either glossed over or ignored entirely in discussions of precedent. The first is that judges can readily discern what counts as precedent for what. The second, and related, assumption is that precedent is primarily a retrospective doctrine.[45]

Take first the notion that judges can determine what counts as precedent for what. The constraining function of precedent is obviously weaker to the extent that judges in the subsequent case have discretion to select what is and what is not properly considered precedent. A judge in such a case, therefore, must determine which facts in the subsequent case are relevant to its outcome. The judge must also discover prior cases in which some of the same facts were present and were relevant to those decisions. The fact that we are dealing with "similar" rather than identical cases means that the current case will not map perfectly with the prior cases but will bear at best the proverbial "family resemblance."[46]

The imperfect mapping of facts permits even a court that wants to portray itself as bound by precedent to foreclose claims of insufficient deference. This may occur in at least three ways. First, the process of determining which precedent governs the current case may be problematic because the current case bears sufficient similarity to multiple precedents that can be classified in conflicting ways. Imagine, for instance, a judge confronted with a case in which during a game of baseball one player intentionally throws a ball at the head of another. The judge is confronted with two lines of precedent that arguably govern the case. Let us assume that the first line involves cases in which ballplayers injured during a consensual game are governed by a rule of no liability. The second involves cases in which individuals who throw rocks and other missiles at each other without provocation face liability for battery. Whether the judge chooses to follow the first or second line of cases may depend on such matters as whether the judge believes that "beanballs" are part of the "game" of baseball, or whether foul play during a game is different from an attack. These decisional points, however, are not settled by a priori principles, but by the judge's decision to emphasize or deemphasize certain circumstances in the case. This is not to say that the decision to distinguish or not is unprincipled or indeterminate. Rather my claim is that principle may justify any of several outcomes. The result is that the reach of any particular rule of law is inherently fuzzy. At least in theory, a judge has significant latitude to break out of a particular line of precedent by following another. In doing so, even a judge who looks retrospectively "creates" precedent rather than "finds" it.

Second, a judge who desires to be perceived as attentive to precedent may seize on factual differences among cases to distinguish the legal rules that apply to them. This process permits not only the selection of a different rule, which might be seen as too radical a departure from precedent, but also the more subtle step of modifying the previous rule to create exceptions that leave the original rule intact in cases that are closer to the prior case. Assume, for instance, that in prior cases, banks that have issued letters of credit had been bound under bank custom to honor drafts drawn against the credit, notwithstanding certain nonconformities in documents accompanying the draft.[47] Such a custom might arise because banks understand that the relevant nonconformities did not threaten the likelihood that conforming goods have been shipped. A custom that arises in this way is likely to be efficient, because the banks that develop it will sometimes be advantaged and sometimes disadvantaged by the custom. Since the parties to the custom internalize both its costs and its benefits, there is reason to believe that it would not have developed unless it generated net benefits. Now assume that a judge, in a case where a bank has refused to pay against nonconforming documents, has observed that the custom arose during peacetime, while the nonconforming documents in the current case were presented during wartime. The judge might conclude that wartime increases the likelihood that the goods would not reach the purchaser. The judge in the case might find that the distinctions between shipment during wartime and peacetime warranted an exception to the prior cases. Conversely, the judge might conclude that nonconformity in documents did not itself indicate any defects in the shipment and that the bank was acting strategically in refusing to comply with custom. The point is not that one of these decisions is clearly correct. To the contrary, the point is that, because cases will not map onto each other perfectly, judges will have substantial leeway in determining whether distinctive facts constitute distinctions with a difference.

In Holmes's view, the frailty of judging often lies in just the opposite flaw – the tendency of judges to make insufficient distinctions. This is one way to understand the story that Holmes tells in *The Path of the Law* about the Vermont justice of the peace asked to adjudicate a suit brought by one farmer against another for breaking a churn. The justice considered the case but determined after perusing the statutes that he could find nothing about churns and gave judgment for the defendant (474–75). Perhaps the most puzzling thing about this story, however, is that it demonstrates the limitations of Holmes's preferred basis of decision making: appeals to reason. The success of those appeals cannot be greater than the judge's capacity to engage in the reasoning process. If his Vermont justice of the peace was incapable of reasoning farther than the story suggests, then economizing on the decision-making process may be perfectly appropriate.

Third, the judge in the subsequent case may seize on the linguistic imprecision of the precedent to conclude that a current case is not covered by the rule previously laid down.[48] Limitations of description and imperfect foresight may preclude a judge in a prior case from characterizing the grounds of decision with sufficient precision that it clearly includes or excludes the subsequent case. After all, the judge in the prior case was presumably attempting to decide that case, not to lay down a rule for hypothetical future cases with similar facts.[49] By "imprecision," I do not mean dicta that can be ignored in a subsequent case, but language that provides insufficient direction about its application to a subsequent case. Thus, the judge in the subsequent case, though attempting to be attentive to his or her obligation to follow precedent, may include facts not intended to be included by the judge in the prior case or may fail to include facts intended to be included. The classic example here is obscenity. But think, more mundanely, of ordinances that preclude "live entertainment" and that are directed at nude dancing. When Chief Justice Burger admonished that such ordinances should be allowed to stand because no one would construe them to "prevent a high school performance of 'The Sound of Music,'"[50] he was essentially saying that a judge in a subsequent case would be able to construe the imprecise scope of a prior case to exclude from the ban situations that the prior judge did not have in mind. There is, however, no reason to believe that the judge in the subsequent case will have the same interpretation of the imprecise phrase as the judge in the prior case. Indeed, if the description in the prior case was "imprecise," different individuals are likely to interpret its scope differently. Hence, there is significant reason to think that a subsequent judge could include such a performance within the ban, even if that is not the kind of performance the judge in the prior case had in mind when upholding the ban against nude dancing.

Each of these mechanisms for deviating from the rules of prior cases is enhanced by the fact that the decision to utilize precedent is made by the judge in the subsequent case.[51] Judges in the prior cases typically decide only the case before them and do not elaborate what variations in the facts would generate different results. Indeed, even if they did so, it is not clear that the judge in the subsequent case would be bound to follow what essentially was dicta in the prior case. By interpreting facts of a previous case as material or not, selecting which line of precedent governs the relevant one, or applying an imprecise locution to a particular set of facts, the judge in the subsequent case has a rather robust set of tools for determining the scope of precedent. That ability provides reasons for us to be less concerned about path dependence, since it permits distinctions that would limit the force of precedent when, in fact, it deserved the public interest. Indeed, where the judgment about when to apply precedent falls to the judge in the subsequent case, these interpretive tools indicate that the judge possesses the same discretion against which the doctrine of precedent was presumably invoked in the first place.

B. Precedent and Prospectivity

At this point, one may wonder why Holmes would be concerned about lock-in effects of tradition. If judges in subsequent cases have the tools to avoid wooden application of precedents, then why would they not use them? The second feature of precedent adds to this puzzle. The standard story of precedent asks why a judge in a subsequent case is bound by a decision in a prior, albeit similar, case.[52] To the extent that the doctrine of precedent imposes a constraint on future decisions, it raises the costs of generating contrary decisions in the future and therefore privileges the status quo. It is this attribute that gives precedent the beneficial characteristic of imposing relative certainty on a legal system. But the function of precedent is not simply to economize retrospectively.[53] Precedent possesses an additional prospective element. Litigants' incentives to overturn inefficient rules suggest that, from their perspective, the prospective element of precedent dominates.[54] A litigant, of course, searches for precedents that allow him to describe his conduct as similar to that of parties who received what was, from that litigant's perspective, a favorable outcome. But where the litigant expects to find himself engaged in the same conduct in the future, the more important value of precedent lies in its prospective effect. Those who can obtain a precedent that favors their view of the law not only obtain victory in the individual case, but also secure the benefits of a favorable decision that is itself privileged and costly to overturn. Thus, parties who enjoys these lock-in effects are willing to incur higher costs in order to obtain a favorable precedent. But this same possibility reduces the lock-in effect itself, since parties to the litigation will spend a greater amount to secure a new precedent, as long as they believe that the expenditure will be amortized over a sufficient period before opposing parties are willing or able to invest in a return to the original rule. Again, lock-in seems to be less of a problem than Holmes suggests, since, as evidenced by litigation campaigns ranging from civil rights issues to tobacco company liability, repeat players will invest in continued litigation until they receive favorable judgments.

III. Path Dependence and Precedent

A. When Path Dependence Matters

Path dependence in common law matters if decisions, once established as precedents, become so locked in that exit from them is too difficult, even though changed conditions would have led us to select a different rule if we were writing on a clean slate. But even if law is path dependent in the sense that former decisions dictate later ones, that result is trivial if the path does not affect the fit between the substantive law and the objective of the legal system. This may be because we are more concerned about having a rule by which to guide conduct than about having a particular rule, or because, although we wish to achieve a particular objective, we are uncertain what rule will accomplish that end. For instance, even if we value efficiency, we may be uncertain whether that objective would be obtained by assigning stolen goods to a good-faith purchaser or to the original owner of those goods, because it is not clear whether the original owner's ability to avoid theft is superior to the purchaser's ability to discern the provenance of the goods.[55] Thus, path dependence dictated by precedent would itself be a trivial problem unless the path determined by prior decisions locked us in to doctrine from which we could not feasibly escape on learning that it disserves the objective of the law. Especially in light of the tools available to resist lock-in effects, the mere existence of path dependence does not necessarily support Holmes's strong assertion that preexisting legal rules not only determine the result of subsequent cases, but do so detrimentally because they inhibit adaptation to changed circumstances.

In speaking of lock-in in this sense, I draw from the literature concerning path dependence in the development of technological standards.[56] Path dependence in this area describes the adoption of a standard based on technology available at the time of adoption that determines subsequent technological developments. Traditional examples are the size of light-bulb bases, the QWERTY typewriter, the narrow-gauge railroad, and VHS recording systems.[57] Such a standard becomes self-perpetuating, or locked in, when a critical mass of potential users must accept an improvement in order to amortize the substantial investment in its creation. The very function of the existing standard, however, impedes its acceptance. Standards solve coordination problems, allowing parties within an industry or users of a technology to interact with each other in ways that would not be possible if actors used variants of the standard. They are useful in industries that have the characteristics of network externalities, where cooperation and coordination among potential beneficiaries of the technology is facilitated if all accept the same standard for the technology. Once such a standard has been widely adopted and it generates positive returns, there is little incentive to use alternative technologies, even those that would have been selected in the absence of the existing standard. Any deviation from what others are doing frustrates participation in the network and will succeed only if a sufficient number of others also adopt the new standard. If others fail to accept the improved standard, the party who does switch outside the relevant network will be less able to coordinate with others in the industry. As long as all light bulb receptacles accept the same-sized light bulb, users of light bulbs can shift among light bulb manufacturers, who can increase their markets. A manufacturer who could make a bulb last twice as long by changing the size of the bulb's base would still face the difficulty of ensuring that enough other bulb and bulb-receptacle manufacturers would adopt the new standard to make the new product marketable and the costs of shifting to the new technology recoverable. Similarly, development of a superior alternative to VHS recording will be rejected unless potential users are confident that recordings will be available in the new format; alternatives to narrow-gauge railroads will be rejected if potential operators of those railroads fear that their trains will be unable to connect with others that fail to make the transition.

In the legal literature, Marcel Kahan and Michael Klausner have suggested that contract terms and transactional forms in corporate documents are path dependent in this way.[58] Once a term attains a meaning through customary use and potential ambiguities are resolved through litigation, attorneys have incentives to use those terms or transactional forms rather than to introduce new and potentially superior ones. The existing ones are well understood in the industry. Thus, those who might create or adopt improved standards will do so only if they can capture sufficient private benefits to offset the private costs of retraining, retooling, and purchasing the new standard. Add to this difficulty the incentives that managers have to eschew innovation, and the possibility of inertia in the face of potential social improvement is complete.[59] The result is that lock-in can generate what appears ex post to be inefficient results.

As I have implied, however, path dependence does not necessarily generate inefficiencies. As applied to legal rules, we should distinguish path dependence that impedes adoption of superior rules from path dependence in the trivial sense that a prior rule either (1) determines the selection of a particular rule among equally plausible candidates, or (2) causes selection of a legal rule that actually satisfies an accepted social objective. In either of these cases, the fact that one rule was selected over another rule in the past does not impose significant costs on the current legal regime; in addition, preservation of the existing rule avoids the costs that would accompany subsequent selection of an alternative legal rule (e.g., the costs of informing target actors and their legal advisers of the new rule).[60] Take, as an example of path dependence among equally plausible legal rules, any rule that is implemented to solve a coordination problem or that selects among a series of equally preferred possibilities, such as the proper period for filing an appeal from a final judgment. We may be indifferent as to whether that period is thirty days, forty-five days, or sixty days. We are not indifferent, however, as to the existence of a well-publicized and commonly accepted rule. Thus, once we select one rule from the set of plausible alternatives, that rule may stick, even if some of the reasons for its original choice (such as the need to ensure sufficient time for proofreading and getting documents from printers) are rendered obsolete by technological advances (such as the advent of overnight delivery and desktop publishing). The disappearance of the reasons that may have favored the initial selection does not necessarily warrant a shift to some alternative, because no justification for an alternative establishes that it would be superior to the existing rule. Thus, even if the extant legal rule is path dependent, that path dependency does not privilege a suboptimal rule.[61] In this situation, it may be perfectly appropriate to select among plausible rules solely on the basis that the selected rule "was laid down in the time of Henry IV."

Indeed, appeals to tradition may generate substantial benefits in this situation. Assuming that we are speaking of situations in which there is no clear social advantage to any particular alternative, any selection is likely to be based on grounds such as the preferences of the parties to the litigation in which the rule was initially established. This phenomenon suggests that cycling may occur because a rule that was not preferred in that litigation may be out of contention in subsequent litigation in which a third rule is adopted, even though the rule initially rejected would have been preferable to the third rule that was adopted.[62] Where multiple possible rules simply reflect equally plausible alternatives, the use of precedent may be a useful mechanism to avoid cycling among personally, as opposed to socially, favored alternatives.

Alternatively, tradition may favor extant legal rules even if they would not be selected today were we writing on a clean slate, because the change is not worth the cost of publication and implementation. Even if we regret our prior selection, the earlier choice may have been based on imperfect foresight rather than erroneous calculation of the net benefits of the rule at that time. Certainly tradition dictates the rule in such a case, but again, we should hesitate to criticize the rule on that basis. Think, for example, of the Uniform Commercial Code rule that treats separate branches of the same bank as separate banks for the purpose of deadlines for taking action with respect to the payment of checks.[63] The rule may have made substantial sense when it was first formulated. At that time, branches of the same bank may still have had difficulty making prompt exchange of documents relevant to the decision whether to pay a check. For instance, drawers whose signature cards are located at one branch of a bank could issue checks that are presented at other branches of the same bank. Because the decision whether or not to pay the check might have to await comparison of the signature on the check to the signature on the card, additional time might be required to send the check to the bank that possessed the relevant document. We can now foresee technological changes that would allow one branch to call up computerized facsimiles of signature cards that are physically held at another branch. That capability might justify a new legal rule treating all bank branches as part of the same institution for the purpose of the timing deadlines. Nevertheless, the costs related to passing the legislation in fifty states (or of having a period of time in which different rules exist in different states) might be sufficiently great to negate the marginal gains available from transition. In this case as well, it is difficult to imagine that Holmes would object to following tradition.[64]

The cases in which reliance on traditional legal rules is detrimental, then, must be cases in which the conditions that justified a preexisting rule have changed so much that (1) some alternative rule is now desirable, and (2) it would be worth incurring the transition costs, but (3) the existence of the current rule prevents the transition to the more desirable rule. For instance, the requirement to follow precedent would be considered both path dependent and locked in, in this strong and negative sense, if we believed that common law processes, devoid of precedent-following, would lead to the evolution of efficient legal rules (assuming, for the moment, that we valued efficiency in legal rules).[65]

There are independent reasons to believe that there are substantial constraints on efficient evolution in the common law.[66] And no one claims that the common law contains no inefficient rules. To the extent that precedent following does lock in those rules, tradition may saddle us with greater (or at least different) inefficiencies than would exist if courts were not required to follow precedent. Before concluding that lock-in is a significant problem in such cases, however, it is necessary to consider the mechanisms of path dependence. Even where following a previously established path would be problematic, lock-in should be avoidable if the path can be avoided when a superior alternative arises. Thus, our reactions to precedent should depend on whether application of legal rules is susceptible to the mechanisms that avert lock-in.

B. Inertia and the Conditions of Path Dependence

As I have indicated, the path-dependence literature suggests that standards may be locked in where a critical mass of potential users must accept an improvement in order to amortize the substantial investment in the creation of the improvement. Contrivances for solving the problem of inertia do exist, however. If the potential private gains from an improvement are sufficiently great, the creator or entrepreneur of the new standard can subsidize transition costs (e.g., by giving away free software, new light bulbs, or cellular phones) to increase the expected return from adopting the new standard. The entrepreneur may also subsidize or disseminate information that suggests that a large number of potential adopters will ultimately accept the standard, with the promise of high rewards for early adopters.[67] Risk-taking managers who are attracted to new standards may also counteract risk aversion in some cases.[68] Thus, even in an environment that might be thought most susceptible to lock-in effects, path dependence does not necessarily maintain inferior standards.

The evolution of legal rules may be even less susceptible to inertia than technological standards. Think of the conditions under which common law develops. One might initially believe that the public-good nature of law will frustrate legal change, since beneficiaries of the change will realize those same benefits without making any expenditure, if others incur the costs of creating the new law. But the public-good nature of law may simultaneously reduce the likelihood that inertia will dominate where a new legal doctrine would be an improvement. The possibility that an insufficient number of potential adopters would accept the improvement does not exist, because where law binds it binds all within its jurisdiction. Thus, those who might otherwise adopt a change in legal standards will not fail to do so out of fear that insufficient numbers of others will concur. Because no one shifts to the new legal rule unless all do, the prisoner's dilemma paradigm that is often applied to explain inertia in technological standards[69] is transformed into an Assurance Game. Potential litigants will have less concern that initiating litigation will cause the law they create to be inconsistent with laws created by others. When potential litigants do fear that legal change will detract from their ability to join networks, they may elect to litigate in multiple jurisdictions or to select a more centralized jurisdiction that can lay down a single law for a larger number of those in the relevant network. Additionally, some entrepreneurs in law, such as law professors and reform groups, may invest in urging legal change. Unlike manufacturers who might otherwise propose new standards, they do not have to bear any of the costs related to transition. At the same time, they obtain significant benefits (tenure, professional reputation) simply by advocating the reform.[70] As the discussion of the prospective role of precedent demonstrates, some repeat players will have substantial incentives to overcome precedent because they are personally disfavored by the existing rule of law and will benefit if they can convince lawmakers to adopt an alternative.

The incentives of litigants and others will not overcome tradition, however, if precedent is not institutionally susceptible to change, that is, if judges have neither the tools nor the inclination to overcome precedent. I have demonstrated earlier that judges possess the tools needed to break out of precedent by selecting among competing precedents, distinguishing cases on the basis of factual differences, and construing linguistic imprecision in a manner that makes precedent inapplicable to the current case. But the availability of these tools indicates only that judges are not locked in to a path created by prior decisions. It remains possible that they could be so constrained. Holmes's antipathy toward precedent is warranted if judges are motivated by incentives that systematically favor inappropriate following of precedent.

I am not suggesting that motivations for precedent following are always inappropriate. Judges may properly be driven to inertia by concerns for the network externalities of their decisions. In a limited jurisdiction, where members must interact with members of other jurisdictions, a judge may worry that deviation from widely accepted precedent will cause adverse network effects similar to those that exist when one party uses a variant of an industry standard. Assume, for instance, that a judge must decide under state law a case involving the liability of a company that manufactures a product that is sold throughout the country. Assume further that arguable precedents within the jurisdiction have laid down a rule of no liability and that similar rules govern in other jurisdictions. Even a judge who otherwise believed that there was a basis for distinguishing the precedent might be concerned that the effects of distinguishing could cause substantial dislocations for parties in the local jurisdiction when dealing with parties in other jurisdictions. This argument, of course, is an argument about the desirability of uniformity rather than one strictly of precedent. But a judge might believe that the desirability of maintaining uniformity warrants subordination of the arguments for breaking from precedent. Although cases in one jurisdiction do not serve as binding precedent elsewhere, they may be used as examples of persuasive decisions from other jurisdictions. Thus, we frequently see uniformity among jurisdictions in areas such as tort or contract law because a decision in any jurisdiction serves as a salient coordination point for the others. (Of course, this may manifest a trivial example of trivial path dependence. The costs of deviating from the standard simply may not be worth the benefits of carving out occasional exceptions.)

The fact remains, however, that the judge in such a case has discretion to follow precedent or not. The mechanisms for applying or rejecting arguable precedent, discussed earlier, indicate the breadth of that discretion. Hence, the scope of path dependence and the extent to which it will generate inferior legal rules depend on the incentives that judges possess either to favor or disfavor narrow application of precedent. I turn next to an investigation of those incentives.

IV. The Incentives of Judges

Our discussion to this point suggests that judges have tools to narrow the adverse effects of following precedent. In addition, given the possibility of nontrivial path dependence, they also have opportunities to avoid following an inefficient precedent. But discretion also means that judges may fail to select these tools and thus remain locked in to existing standards. That, of course, is Holmes's fear. But once we admit the possibility that judges will not perfectly apply Holmes's crude cost–benefit analysis, so that application of tradition varies from the ideal, it is equally plausible – contra Holmes – that the tools for distinguishing precedents will be overutilized, and that judges will be insufficiently deferential toward precedent.

Our final inquiry, therefore, is whether judges have incentives to take advantage of those tools when, but only when, deviation from precedent would be useful. As Gillian Hadfield has indicated,[71] motivational theories of the evolution of common law have not been well developed, at least in the literature concerning efficient evolution. The theories that have emerged assume either that judges pursue efficiency or that litigants, acting out of self-interest, tend toward efficiency. A more recent literature focuses on the incentives of judges and allows us to consider those incentives that have systemic effects on judges' use of precedent. I am concerned here only with systemic effects, not with incentives that judges may have in individual cases. Incentives that judges may have include bribes, personal interest in the outcome of a case, or, to use Holmes's example, irritability caused by gout. None of those incentives systematically favors a narrow or broad interpretation of precedent. A judge susceptible to bribery is as susceptible to a litigant who wants a particular line of precedent followed as to one who wants that line disregarded. Similarly, judges may be susceptible to other forms of personal gain, such as increasing their own future employment opportunities by making certain decisions. We may believe that judges are less susceptible than legislators to the entreaties of interest groups, perhaps because life tenure or high return rates for elected judges makes them less needful of those groups, perhaps because judges have fewer opportunities for logrolling (because they either vote singly or in panels that frequently change composition), perhaps because judges must give reasons for their decisions. But prospective employment opportunities do not systematically affect attitudes toward precedent, other than as a by-product of other objectives, such as reputation or fame. Finally, lower-court judges may be thought to have an incentive to avoid reversal, in part to avoid criticism from peers and in part to avoid investment of time in an enterprise (creating the judge's own precedent) that is easily undone.[72] But (and perhaps counterintuitively) this desire does not inexorably favor adherence to precedent. Although precedent following might be seen as the safer course, its effect depends on the incentives of the reviewing court. If that court favors precedent creation rather than precedent following, then a lower-court judge who departs from prior law is less likely to suffer reversal than one who adheres to existing doctrine. Thus, aversion to reversal does not systematically favor broad conceptions of precedent apart from an understanding of the incentives of judges generally. Nonetheless, given that appeals courts infrequently overrule prior opinions, concern for reversal will tend to generate adherence to precedent in lower courts.

Judges, of course, decide only cases that litigants bring before them. Even the judge who seeks to distinguish among cases or otherwise to break from tradition cannot do so until offered an opportunity by litigants. We have identified a variety of constraints that prevent even judges faced with real litigants from reaching too far to overturn precedent, since judges are limited as to what disputes they can hear (case or controversy requirements), the circumstances under which they can make decisions (mootness and jurisdictional requirements), and the breadth of the decisions they can lay down (pronouncements characterized as obiter dicta will not be binding). These doctrines may be mechanisms that insulate judges from interest groups and thus increase the probability that decisions reflect the public interest. But these doctrines similarly have implications for our conception of judicial incentives. If we believe that judges are insufficiently motivated to depart from precedent, then we might want to construe narrowly the limitations on judicial jurisdiction to make those departures. On the other hand, if we believe that judges have incentive to depart from precedent too frequently, then we might want to construe those doctrines more broadly.

Assume, then, that a legal rule established by precedent disserves society. Our earlier discussion suggests that judges (1) have the tools to distinguish the precedent and thus (2) are not locked in by the constraints that cause inertia in other settings. Certainly we would believe that publicly interested judges – those whose interests align perfectly with those of the society that the judges represent – would strive mightily to determine a precedent's appropriate application. Recall that this objective function would not necessarily mean full reexamination of the established rule in each case. Even Holmes's crude cost–benefit analysis suggests that the economizing functions of precedent following could override the desire for reexamination. It might be that judges suffer from intellectual limitations in discerning proper from improper application of precedent. But that characteristic would provide insufficient reason for railing against precedent, since those intellectual limitations would likely affect the same judges in their ability to decide cases from first principles without the guidance of precedent.

But then, some richer analysis is necessary to understand what might cause judges to ignore the conditions that require a change in path. Here again, it is useful to begin with Holmes. But this is not the Holmes of facile social cost–benefit analysis. Rather it is a Holmes more sympathetic to the possibility that individual actors who perform the necessary calculus may have incentives to deviate from the socially beneficial, and that those motivations may be manifest in attitudes toward precedent. In an 1872 "Book Notice," reviewing an article by Frederick Pollock on John Austin's definition of law, Holmes offered an early insight into the basis for predicting how judges would define the law. Judges were not simply purveyors of legal science but persons inspired by complex and flexible tools that could be used to reach a variety of results, given any set of facts. His response to the Austinian assertion of law as the command of the sovereign will manifested by judicial adoption was to demonstrate how custom and trade usage have the same compulsory power as formal law, and, more importantly, how judicial expression of that will constitutes little more than a "motive for decision" in future cases. For "[a] precedent may not be followed; a statute may be emptied of its contents by construction . . . It must be remembered . . . that in a civilized state it is not the will of the sovereign that makes the lawyers' law, even when that is its source, but what a body of subjects, namely, the judges, by whom it is enforced, *say* is his will."[73] The motives of judges serve as sources of law, but only insofar as they allow prediction of what the judge will say.[74]

This early view of Holmes is remarkable in two respects. First, it suggests a more activist capacity for judges than the locked-in judge of *The Path of the Law*. To predict the law is to predict what judges will say, but that prediction requires knowledge of far more than what other judges have said on previous occasions. When Holmes states that a precedent "may not be followed," he allows for the possibility not only of overrulings, but of refinements and exceptions. Second, Holmes, in discounting the role of arbitrary will as a predictor of law, still recognizes that the "singular" may affect what judges do, even if those singularities are not appropriate sources of law. Yet once we grant the capacity of judges to make fine distinctions, to ignore precedent, to be moved as much by "the political aspirations of the judge, or his gout"[75] as by statute or constitution, we have the rudiments of a more complete explanation of the significance of precedent.

Judges, like entrepreneurs, may have incentives to leave an accepted standard in place, notwithstanding its inferiority to an alternative. Or, judges may enjoy personal benefits that induce insufficient reliance on precedent. If judges overcome path dependence in trivial cases, then they impose the costs of disseminating information and implementing the new standard without generating sufficient offsetting benefits. If tradition privileges the status quo, it privileges the good along with the bad. But if judges distinguish precedent only in nontrivial cases of path dependence, then Holmes's objection to precedent following seems misplaced.

That leaves open, of course, the issue of what personal benefits and costs would influence judicial attitudes toward precedent. Judges, at least those at high levels of the state or federal judiciary, typically receive monetary rewards less than those they could receive in other uses of their talents, such as in the private practice of law. Thus, the economic assumption is that judges seek their offices in pursuit of nonmonetized benefits, the value of which exceeds the value of the monetized rewards that they have forgone. Our current, but crude, understanding of those benefits includes the possibility of leisure, of being involved in the process of making law, and of enhanced reputation.

These incentives cut in very different directions from the perspective of precedent following. Judges who seek leisure should want to invest as little time as possible in the decision-making process. The hypothesis that judges place value on leisure is reinforced by many of the characteristics of judging at both the federal and the state level: fixed pay, life tenure (or a high rate of return to office), inability to secure a residuum of their efforts,[76] and the limited ability to achieve fame (within either an expanding federal judiciary or a state judiciary that has less visibility and prestige than its federal counterpart). These characteristics all tend toward circumventing the rigorous analysis inherent in the effort of the Holmesian judge "to consider more definitely and explicitly the social advantage on which the rule they lay down must be justified" ("Path" 468). Tradition reinforces these tendencies, insofar as adherence to precedent reduces the need for creative effort and justifies the practice of simply citing cases deemed similar and following the rule laid down in them.

The result is that judges may underinvest in making fine distinctions by satisficing or settling on satisfactory, rather than optimal, legal rules.[77] Judges may select the first line of available precedent without determining whether a competing line of precedent has equal application. Although judges who follow precedent must still invest in the discovery of precedent,[78] the research necessary for that function may be less than the research necessary for full consideration of each case. Were that not so, the economizing justification for following precedent would have no weight. Here, Holmes's Vermont justice of the peace offers the caricature that contains a ring of truth. Although that justice purported to have examined the statutes, he found nothing about churns that would dictate his decision, thus revealing insufficient investment in decision making. Had he found a decision involving the theft of a churn in which the plaintiff had won, he might have given a decision for the plaintiff in his case involving the breaking of a churn on the rationale that the first churn case was binding precedent for the second, notwithstanding the dissimilarities between stealing and breaking. There is no reason that leisure-seeking judges will invest in distinguishing between cases in which the lock-in effects of precedent are trivial or nontrivial. Thus, Holmes seems rightly concerned that a doctrine of precedent following induces inappropriate lock-in if leisure maximization is judges' primary incentive.

The press of judicial reports, the lengthiness of opinions, and the increased number of dissents and concurrences in multijudge courts, however, indicate that a preference for sloth alone cannot explain judicial behavior. Rather, at least some judges write long and often (or have their clerks do so), because they wish to maximize some alternative objective, such as fame or reputation,[79] or participation in a law-making process. Reputation for excellence in judging may increase the availability of certain types of postjudicial employment (e.g., positions in high-paying law firms, teaching posts), opportunities for enhanced earning power (lecture invitations), emblems of professional respect (membership in professional associations, assignment of highly qualified law clerks), or opportunities for advancement within the ranks of judges.[80]

A concern for reputation generates a complicated set of actions. The same act that enhances reputation with one group may diminish it with another. Judges who wish to increase their reputation with their peers may simply want to clear their dockets quickly, so that they are not seen as imposing a heavy caseload on their colleagues. Judges with these incentives may spend little time rethinking established rules or questioning arguably applicable precedents. For others, however, enhancing reputation may require emergence from the pack of judges. These objectives might be thought to generate insufficient respect for precedent. Judges are less likely to develop reputations if their opinions fail to develop the law but only restate and apply the law laid down by others. If constrained by the past, therefore, judges will be less able to demonstrate subtlety in making distinctions, finding conflicts among competing lines of precedent, or adding refinements to previously imprecise locutions. To the extent that judicial reputation is generated by both practitioner and academic commentary, those commentaries are likely to focus on the novel and the extraordinary rather than on the wooden and mundane. One need not posit the extreme position that judges seek to create inefficient precedents in order to maximize citations by generating additional litigation;[81] a less heroic claim that judges seek professional acclaim is sufficient to contend that judges overinvest in distinguishing precedent.

These incentives are amplified by the prospective function of precedent. My account of prospectivity focused on its utility to litigants to bind future decision makers. The prospective function of a precedent also enhances the value of a decision to the judge who makes it. The force of tradition means that a judge able to write an opinion that survives the appellate process has created a rule that others will follow presumptively. If judges in subsequent cases take a retrospective view of precedent, they are likely to follow the rule laid down by the judge in the prior case, increasing his or her visibility and reputation.[82] Thus, a judge who uses precedent prospectively may see tradition as a tool for personal advancement rather than as a constraint. While there is, of course, a likelihood that judges in subsequent cases will be equally creative and thus distinguish the prior case, merely following the established rule deprives the judge in the prior case of reputational enhancement by subsequent citation. Even if subsequent judges choose to distinguish the precedent created by the prior case, they must at least discuss the case being distinguished, thus providing greater notoriety for the judge in that prior case.

These objectives suggest that there will be some judges, call them "rogue judges," who are likely to overinvest in creating new law; that is, they are likely to overutilize the tools of distinction that are available to them. I mean by this that they are likely to avoid path dependence in trivial cases as well as nontrivial ones. Recall that avoiding tradition in such cases imposes excessive costs by changing rules under circumstances that do not produce social advances. Rogue judges may make such overinvestments because they obtain personal benefits from the new decision but do not suffer the costs of rule changes. A requirement of adhering to precedent may be perceived as an effort to constrain rogue judges by causing them to internalize more of these costs, as by requiring them to justify deviations from precedent with more rigor than is necessary when a court simply follows an established rule.[83] But for at least some rogues, this requirement has a perverse effect. Judges who seek reputational advantage, or who benefit from participating in the lawmaking process, may treat opinion writing as a consumption good rather than a cost.[84] To the extent that this is true, complex opinions filled with fine distinctions will return greater benefits than opinions that simply cite preexisting law favorably. Thus, the very effort to constrain rogue opinions risks producing more of them.

Rogue judges may favor deviation from precedent for additional reasons. Judges may seek approval outside of their professional rank and within a broader political forum, perhaps motivated by the possibility of advancement in the political arena. Political recognition, however, is more likely to come from departure with precedent than from following it. Political support is likely to form because a group seeks to alter the status quo. Judges inclined to make such changes may be more attractive to those groups. While politically ambitious judges who preserve the status quo may be able to blame earlier decision makers for unpopular decisions and offer their own fidelity to law as a characteristic worthy of political support, they are unlikely to generate the same political enthusiasm as judges who demonstrate independence and commitment to a political agenda. Thus, political rogues may care more that their decisions are popular than that they are consistent with a preexisting body of law.

It is in this context that Holmes's appeal for flexibility in legal doctrine leads him into direct confrontation with tradition. When he insists that legal doctrine does not flow from "exact logical conclusions," so that determinations about preferable rules are not "good for all time" but are "open to reconsideration upon a slight change in the habit of the public mind" ("Path" 466), Holmes recognizes that resort to tradition suppresses the adaptation of legal rules to vicissitudes in public opinion. But this appears to be a virtue of precedent. Notwithstanding his epigrammatic description of his role as judge as helping his fellow citizens "go to Hell" if that is their desire,[85] little in Holmes's judicial writings indicates a willingness to follow popular movements uncritically. Perhaps one reason for favoring precedent is that tradition may itself be one of the institutional constraints that leads us to believe that courts can resist inconstancy in popular views.[86] In short, of the two functions of precedent with which I began this essay, constraining the scope of reconsideration may be more important.

Finally, tradition may serve as a constraint on the capacity of judges to receive entreaties of limited interests. To the extent that it limits opportunities for variation, the doctrine of precedent complements doctrines such as standing and ripeness, and restraints on advisory opinions (case or controversy requirements and limitations on declaratory judgments) that repress opportunities for judges to serve the idiosyncratic interests of particular groups. Situations in which parties are willing to bear the costs of litigation even though they are not directly interested in the specific facts that give rise to the litigation (standing and ripeness), or are unwilling to invest in the underlying activity that gives rise to litigation (advisory opinions) may suggest that those parties have idiosyncratic interests and are poor representatives of the social interests that we want the legal rule to reflect. Judges, of course, may use the same tools of interpretation that apply to precedent to circumvent these doctrines, such as by finding standing or ripeness in dubious circumstances. These doctrines, therefore, cannot fully restrain judges from hearing special pleas if they are otherwise inclined. But just as these doctrines limit such parties from coming before courts in the first place, so the doctrine of precedent inhibits judges who hear those appeals from making substantive decisions based on those interests. Combined with a requirement that judges explain their rationales, a requirement of precedent following serves as a signaling mechanism to indicate that deviations from established law have occurred. The requirement thus facilitates monitoring of potential rogue judges. Again, however, the existence of a monitoring device suggests that, in the absence of a precedent-following rule, judges will defer too little, rather than too much, to tradition.

V. Conclusion: Striking the Balance

Restraints and signaling mechanisms, of course, are not costless. Tradition is underinclusive insofar as it is drawn with fuzzy lines that make its content indistinct. It is overinclusive insofar as it locks in practices developed for an earlier time, perhaps for reasons long forgotten, and that would not have been adopted if considered afresh today. Precedent, as an embodiment of tradition, suffers from both these defects. Entrepreneurial judges who are capable of manipulating legal doctrine can easily escape; judges who substitute history for the rational study of law, or who recharacterize justifications for existing doctrine that evolved from different circumstances rather than ask whether the doctrine makes sense in the first place will find escape more difficult ("Path" 469).

Tradition, then, may be a mechanism for lock-in, as Holmes suggests. But lock-in effects in adjudication are not necessarily evil. The issue that remains is whether precedent is overutilized by judges who maximize interests unrelated to their assumed roles or underutilized by rogues. One might fear that rogue judges are the real villains. If exercise of judicial discretion can overcome the constraints of precedent as easily as I have suggested, then it may be that Holmes's concern was misplaced, because we should be more concerned with the effect of precedent as a constraint on rogues than as a tool for sloth. And if path dependence typically arises in cases where the rule dictated by the path is trivial, the fact that precedent binds judges may be untroublesome because the doctrine's economizing features outweigh any harm of overreliance on tradition.

But maybe Holmes was right after all. Given the capacity of the judge in the subsequent case to define and distinguish what he or she deems to be controlling precedent, there may be precious little we can do about rogue judges, once a case properly appears before them. Even if underinvestment in precedent by rogues threatens more damage than underinvestment by slothful judges, the ease with which precedent can be circumvented limits our capacity to use that doctrine to address the issue. Our controls on rogue judges must instead be directed at the variety of jurisdictional doctrines that prevent too many cases, especially those in which we think the parties' interests are idiosyncratic, from reaching courts in the first place. Accordingly, those cases in which precedent has a significant effect may, systematically, be those cases in which the greater threat is lazy judges rather than rogues. By signaling that mere citation to prior authority is an acceptable judicial practice, precedent may underwrite more judicial leisure than is acceptable. Absent more judges who (perhaps like Holmes) are able to strike the crude balance from a social perspective and to distinguish the trivial from the nontrivial cases of path dependence, maybe such rough judgments about the general tendency of judicial incentives is the most we can accomplish.

Notes

1 See Richard A. Wasserstrom, *The Judicial Decision* (Stanford: Stanford University Press, 1961). On the value of precedent for predictability, see Benjamin Klein, "Comment," *Journal of Law and Economics* 19 (1976):309.
2 On the willingness of at least some judges to underinvest in their decision making, see Richard A. Posner, "What Do Judges and Justices Maximize? (The Same Thing Everybody Else Does)," *Supreme Court Economics Review* 3 (1993):1.
3 Oliver W. Holmes, Jr., "The Path of the Law," *Harvard Law Review* 10 (1897):457 (cited hereafter parenthetically in the text as "Path"). "The Path" is reprinted in the Appendix to this volume with star paging.
4 In his judicial opinions, Holmes occasionally issued the same complaint about the arbitrary survival of legal doctrine. See E. Donald Elliott, "Holmes and Evolution: Legal Process as Artificial Intelligence," *Journal of Legal Studies* 13 (1984):113, 133–34.
5 See Klein, "Comment." A predictive view of the law does not necessarily require binding precedent. Prediction, for instance would include the capacity to foretell when courts would deviate from prior decisions. Nevertheless, one imagines that deviations would be infrequent, so that reliance on precedent would strengthen predictive capacities.
6 Richard A. Posner, *The Problems of Jurisprudence* (Cambridge, Mass.: Harvard University Press, 1990), 227.
7 Ibid.
8 Mark DeWolfe Howe, *Justice Oliver Wendell Holmes: The Proving Years, 1870–1882* (Cambridge, Mass.: Belknap Press of Harvard University Press, 1963), 43–50.
9 Holmes takes just this position at one point in *The Common Law*. See Oliver Wendell Holmes, *The Common Law* (Boston: Little, Brown, 1881), 26 (if a legal doctrine "were not supported by the appearance of good sense, it would not survive"). Note also Thomas Grey's conclusion that Holmes was "slow to depart from precedent," in large part because of his doubt that legal reforms would generate social progress. Thomas C. Grey, "Holmes and Legal Pragmatism," *Stanford Law Review* 41 (1989):787, 812.

I do not deny that there are powerful forces that allow legal rules to remain intact even when they disserve social values. Interest groups that obtain favorable legislation or judicial decisions may also maintain that legislation. Unless we believe that much of the lawmaking enterprise is dominated by special-interest groups whose conduct disserves the society, or that social conditions outstrip prevailing law, some presumption that existing law fits underlying social conditions seems appropriate.

10 "We learn that for everything we have to give up something else, and we are taught to set the advantage we gain against the other advantage we lose, and to know what we are doing when we elect" (474).
11 See, e.g., Lars Magnusson and Jan Ottosson, *Evolutionary Economics and Path Dependence* (Brookfield: Ed Elger, 1997); W. Brian Arthur, *Increasing Returns and Path Dependence in the Economy* (Ann Arbor: University of Michigan Press, 1994).
12 See Douglass C. North, *Institutional Change and Economic Performance* (Cambridge: Cambridge University Press, 1990), 76.
13 See, e.g., David Luban, "Justice Holmes and the Metaphysics of Judicial Restraint," *Duke Law Journal* 44 (1994):449, 489–501; Thomas C. Grey, "Molecular Motions: The Holmesian Judge in Theory and Practice," *William and Mary Law Review* 37 (1995):19.
14 See e.g., Steven J. Burton, *Judging in Good Faith* (Cambridge: Cambridge University Press, 1992), chapter 2, sections 3–4; Lewis A. Kornhauser, "An Economic Perspective on *Stare Decisis*," *Chicago–Kent Law Review* 65 (1989):63; Jonathan R. Macey, "The Internal and External Costs and Benefits of *Stare Decisis*," *Chicago–Kent Law Review* 65 (1989):93.
15 Two years later, Holmes continued this attack on tradition. Contending that the "true science of the law" depends on establishing postulates based on "accurately measured social desires instead of tradition," he demonstrated how a series of legal rules was based on historical artifacts that no longer justified their application. See Oliver Wendell Holmes, Jr., "Law in Science and Science in Law," *Harvard Law Review* 112 (1899):443, 452–55.
16 See Anthony Kronman, "Precedent and Tradition," *Yale Law Journal* 99 (1990):1029, 1035.
17 For the proposition that Holmes's epigrammatic style has led to oversimplified interpretations of his thought, see Grey, "Molecular Motions," 24.
18 See also Holmes, "Law in Science," 455 (discussing "the danger of inventing reasons offhand for whatever we find established in law").
19 Holmes, *Common Law,* 5–33.
20 Ibid., 31.
21 Here is Holmes's general account of the phenomenon:
    The customs, beliefs, or needs of a primitive time establish a rule or a formula. In the course of centuries, the custom, belief, or necessity disappears, but the rule remains. The reason which gave rise to the rule has been forgotten, and ingenious minds set themselves to inquire how it is to be accounted for. Some ground of policy is thought of, which seems to explain it and to reconcile it with the present state of things; and then the rule adapts itself to the new reasons which have been found for it, and enters on a new career. The old form receives a new content, and in time even the form modifies itself to fit the meaning which it has received. (Ibid., 8)
22 Ibid., 32.
23 On Holmes's deference to legislatures, see Luban, "Metaphysics of Judicial Restraint," 491.
24 *Stack v. New York, N. H. & H. R. Co.*, 58 N.E. 686 (Mass. 1900).
25 Ibid., 687.
26 245 U.S. 603 (1918).
27 Ibid.
28 Elliott also notes that Holmes, despite his appeal to reason, could sometimes be found on the side of "arbitrary historical rules." See Elliott, "Holmes and Evolution," 133. My claim is that there may be no necessary conflict between reason and appeal to arbitrary rules.

29 216 U.S. 358 (1910).
30 Ibid., 366.
31 Ibid.
32 Ibid.
33 See also *Lewin v. Folsom,* 171 Mass. 188 (1898), in which Holmes justified the grant of simple rather than compound interest on a judgment, "reasoning" that the law had demonstrated an "ancient unwillingness to allow compound interest."
34 See, e.g., Grey, "Molecular Motions," 37–38.
35 256 U.S. 506 (1921).
36 256 U.S. at 507 (citation omitted).
37 This is a form of the more general question "When should a rational individual 'stop considering the pros and cons of an issue and reach a decision'?" James M. Buchanan and Gordon Tollock, *The Calculus of Consent* (Ann Arbor: University of Michigan Press, 1962), 97.
38 See *Pokora v. Wabash Ry.,* 292 U.S. 98 (1934); Holmes, *Common Law,* 97–99.
39 Holmes, *Common Law,* 97–99.
40 Wasserstrom, *Judicial Decision,* 43.
41 See ibid., 76 ("There is no reason to suppose – certainly none has ever been suggested – that the court which is first forced to decide a question of a certain kind will inevitably formulate the best rule for that kind of case").
42 See Frederick Schauer, "Precedent," *Stanford Law Review* 39 (1987):571, 575–76; Kenneth J. Kress, "Legal Reasoning and Coherence Theories: Dworkin's Rights Thesis, Retroactivity, and the Linear Order of Decisions," *California Law Review* 72 (1984):369, 400–1. It may be that even on this understanding an economizing explanation could justify precedent. If we believe not only that prior decisions were likely to be correct, and that conditions that would warrant changing the justification for similar cases evolve slowly, then a decision reached today about a case similar to one decided yesterday is likely to be similarly decided. Following the prior decision without investigating the current applicability of its underlying justification, therefore, may simply be a rough but cost-saving surrogate for fuller examination of the current case.
43 One may, of course, create a weaker form of precedent in which prior decisions are presumptively correct but subject to review. For defenses of weaker forms of precedent, see Kornhauser, "Economic Perspective," 78–92; Macey, "Costs and Benefits," 93–113.
44 These are the traditional justifications for the doctrine. See Frank H. Easterbrook, "Stability and Reliability in Judicial Decisions," *Cornell Law Review* 73 (1988):422; Wasserstrom, *Judicial Decision,* 56–83; Schauer, "Precedent," 595–605; Kronman, "Precedent and Tradition," 1036–47; Kornhauser, "Economic Perspective," 71–78.
45 For discussions that rely exclusively on the retrospective nature of precedent, see Kronman, "Economic Perspective"; Gerald J. Postema, "On the Moral Presence of the Past," *McGill Law Journal* 36 (1991):1153. For exceptions that confront both assumptions, see Schauer, "Precedent"; Kenneth I. Winston, "On Treating Like Cases Alike," *California Law Review* 62 (1974):1, 4.
46 See Bruce Chapman, "The Rational and the Reasonable: Social Choice Theory and Adjudication," *University of Chicago Law Review* 61 (1994):41, 78–79.
47 The hypothetical example is drawn from the facts of *Dixon, Iramos & Cia v. Chase National Bank,* 144 F2d 759 (2d Cir. 1944), cert. denied 324 U.S. 850 (1945).
48 See Frederick Schauer, "Slippery Slopes," *Harvard Law Review* 99 (1985):361, 370–73.

49 See "The Rule of Precedent," by Theodore M. Benditt, in *Precedent in Law*, ed. Laurence Goldstein (New York: Oxford University Press, 1987), 104–6; A. W. B. Simpson, "The *Ration Decidendi* of a Case and the Doctrine of Binding Precedent," in *Oxford Essays in Jurisprudence*, ed. A. G. Guest (London: Oxford University Press, 1961), 148.
50 *Schad v. Borough of Mount Ephraim*, 452 U.S. 61 (1981) (Burger dissenting).
51 As Edward H. Levi wrote,
   [T]he judge in the present case may find irrelevant the existence or absence of facts which prior judges thought important. It is not what the prior judge intended that is of any importance; rather it is what the present judge, attempting to see the law as a fairly consistent whole, thinks should be the determining classification.
   Edward H. Levi, *An Introduction to Legal Reasoning* (Chicago: University of Chicago Press, 1968), 2–3.
52 See, e.g., the statement by Wasserstrom of the doctrine of *stare decisis:* "The rule of stare decisis requires that cases which are similar to earlier cases be decided in the same way in which those earlier cases were adjudicated," *Judicial Decision*, 54.
53 See, e.g., Ronald A. Cass, "Judging: Norms and Incentives of Retrospective Decision-Making," *Boston University Law Review* 41 (1995):75.
54 See Paul Rubin, "Common Law and Statute Law," *Journal of Legal Studies* 11 (1982):205.
55 See Saul Levmore, "Rethinking Comparative Law: Variety and Uniformity in Ancient and Modern Tort Law," *Tulane Law Review* 61 (1986):235.
56 See, e.g., Stan J. Liebowitz and Stephen E. Margolis, "Path Dependence, Lock-Ins, and History," *Journal of Law, Economics, and Organizations* 11 (1995):205–7; Paul A. David, "Why Are Institutions the 'Carriers of History'?: Path Dependence and the Evolution of Conventions, Organizations and Institutions," *Structural Change and Economic Dynamics* 5 (1994):205–20.
57 See, e.g., W. Brian Arthur, "Competing Technologies, Increasing Returns, and Lock-In by Historical Events," *Economics Journal* 99 (1989):116.
58 See Marcel Kahan and Michael Klausner, "Path Dependence in Corporate Contracting: Increasing Returns, Herd Behavior and Cognitive Biases," *Washington University Law Quarterly* 74 (1996):347; Michael Klausner, "Corporations, Corporate Law, and Networks of Contracts," *Virginia Law Review* 81 (1995):757. See also Mark Roe, "Chaos and Evolution in Law Economics," *Harvard Law Review* 109 (1996):641.
59 I discuss the problem at greater length in Clayton P. Gillette, "Rules, Standards, and Precautions in Payment Systems," *Virginia Law Review* 82 (1996):181, 214–16.
60 See Louis Kaplow, "An Economic Analysis of Legal Transitions," *Harvard Law Review* 99 (1986):509.
61 This set of path-dependent examples may come closest to what Liebowitz and Margolis term "second-degree path dependence." In that set of cases, a standard that was previously selected on the basis of the best information then available turns out to be inferior to a rule that would have been selected had all of the relevant information been known. Once investment is made in the standard adopted under the information then available, it may make sense to stay with that standard. Given that imperfect information is simply part of the human condition, decisions made with proper use of the then-best available information cannot be said to be inefficient. Liebowitz and Margolis, "Path Dependence," 206–7.
62 Explored by Frank H. Easterbrook, "Ways of Criticizing the Court," *Harvard Law Review* 95 (1982):802, 818; Maxwell L. Stearns, "Standing Back from the Forest: Justiciability and Social Choice," *California Law Review* 83 (1995):1309, 1356–59.

63 U.C.C. § 4–107.
64 This example corresponds to what Liebowitz and Margolis call "first-degree path dependence" ("Path Dependence," 207). In that set of cases, a standard that was previously selected could subsequently be superseded by a "better" standard. Nevertheless, it is retained, because it is costly to shift to the new standard. The fact that the present value of continuing the old technology exceeds the present value of adopting the new indicates that no inefficiency results from the decision to reject the new standard.
65 Initially we might believe that adherence to tradition serves evolution toward efficiency because, once entrenched, precedent ensures that efficient rules will be difficult to undo, and this, in turn, ensures that longstanding rules are likely to be efficient. But the argument from efficient evolution in the common law assumes that inefficient rules are more likely than efficient rules to be relitigated. See George L. Priest, "The Common Law Process and the Selection of Efficient Rules," *Journal of Legal Studies* 6 (1977):65; Paul H. Rubin, "Why Is the Common Law Efficient?", *Journal of Legal Studies* 6 (1977):51. Rubin argues that because the deadweight losses imposed by inefficient rules will always be higher than the losses imposed by efficient rules, the parties' incentives to litigate are greater for inefficient than efficient rules. This is particularly true where parties are repeat players and have incentives to create precedents that will serve their interests in future transactions (53–55). Thus, although longstanding rules may be efficient, they are not the rules that are the subject of litigation and thus are not susceptible to the judicial invocation of precedent. Rather, and consistent with Holmes's concern, precedent will be invoked primarily in litigated cases that tend to involve inefficient rules, and the effect of precedent will be to lock in the inefficiencies.

  Indeed, even to the extent that courts have authority to reverse a precedent, the incentive of potential litigants to induce courts to exercise that authority is reduced by a norm of precedent following. The evolutionary model assumes that precedent is not always conclusive, because inefficient decisions are relitigated until a court recognizes the need to break from precedent. Potential litigants who have high stakes in the outcome of litigation will incur the costs of litigation to secure a precedent. Those high stakes, however, may be offset by a low probability of obtaining a favorable decision. Because tradition privileges the status quo, it raises the costs to litigants who seek to overturn precedent. Of course, where the rule embodied in precedent is efficient, this privilege is beneficial, insofar as it deters relitigation by persons who would favor a socially inefficient rule. But if the rule embodied in precedent is inefficient and the probability of overturning it is reduced by a requirement of precedent following, then even large stakes will not induce parties to incur the costs of relitigation, because the expected value of the litigation remains small.
66 Where repeat players litigate against non–repeat players, they will have different incentives to invest in the production of a favorable rule, so that any deviation between the socially efficient rule and the rule favored by repeat players will be exacerbated. In addition, selection biases in instituting litigation will preclude even efficiency-minded courts from formulating a rule with a representative sample of cases before them. See Gillian Hadfield, "Bias in the Evolution of Legal Rules," *Georgetown Law Journal* 80 (1992):583. For other critiques of the efficient-evolution thesis, see, e.g., Martin J. Bailey and Paul H. Rubin, "A Positive Theory of Legal Change," *International Review of Law and Economics* 14 (1994):467; John C. Goodman, "An Economic Theory of the Evolution of the Common Law," *Journal of Legal Studies* 7 (1977):235; Robert Cooter and

Lewis Kornhauser, "Can Litigation Improve the Law without the Help of Judges?", *Journal of Legal Studies* 9 (1980):139.
67 See Liebowitz and Margolis, "Path Dependence," 215–16.
68 See Zur Shapira, *Risk Taking: A Managerial Perspective* (New York: Russell Sage Foundation, 1995), 45–46; Zur Shapira, "Ambiguity and Risk Taking in Organizations," *Journal of Risk and Uncertainty* 7 (1993):89, 92.
69 See Michael I. Krauss, "Regulation vs. Markets in the Development of Standards," *Southern California Interdisciplinary Law Journal* 13 (1994):781.
70 I discuss the role of law reform–minded entrepreneurs at greater length in Gillette, "Rules, Standards," 216–20.
71 Hadfield, "Bias," 584.
72 See Cass, "Judging," 984; William M. Landes and Richard A. Posner, "Legal Precedent: A Theoretical and Legal Analysis," *Journal of Law and Economics* 19 (1976):249, 273.
73 Oliver Wendell Holmes, Jr., "Book Notice," *American Law Review* 6 (1972):723, 724. Holmes continues:
> The judges have other motives for decision, outside their own arbitrary will, beside the commands of their sovereign. And whether those motives are, or are not, equally compulsory, is immaterial, if they are sufficiently likely to prevail to afford a ground for prediction. The only question for the lawyer is, how will the judges act? Any motive for their action, be it constitution, statute, custom, or precedent, which can be relied upon as likely in the generality of cases to prevail, is worthy of consideration as one of the sources of law, in a treatise on jurisprudence. Singular motives, like the blandishments of the emperor's wife, are not a ground of prediction, and are therefore not considered.

74 Here Holmes recognizes that judges may have illicit motives, such as arbitrary will or "the blandishments of the emperor's wife," but they are not properly considered the basis for prediction because they are "singular," that is, they apply only to a particular judge, while the constitution, statutes, customs, and precedents are systemic and thus explain how the judiciary as an institution decides what the law is (ibid.).
75 Ibid.
76 The inability to obtain the residual profits from their efforts limits the willingness of managers in governmental or nonprofit positions to foster efficient practices. See, e.g., Henry B. Hansmann, "Unfair Competition and the Unrelated Business Income Tax," *Virginia Law Review* 75 (1989):605.
77 On satisficing, see Herbert A. Simon, *Models of Man* (New York: Wiley, 1957), 200; Herbert A. Simon, "A Behavioral Model of Rational Choice," *Quarterly Journal of Economics* 69 (1955):99.
78 See Posner, "What Do Judges and Justices Maximize?", 22.
79 See Cass, "Judging," 971–72; Posner, "What Do Judges and Justices Maximize?", 5–6.
80 See Mark A. Cohen, "The Motives of Judges: Empirical Evidence from Antitrust Sentencing," *International Review of Law and Economics* 12 (1992):13.
81 See Bruce H. Kobayashi and John R. Lott, Jr., "Judicial Reputation and the Efficiency of the Common Law," in Richard A. Posner, *Overcoming Law* (Cambridge, Mass.: Harvard University Press, 1995), 113.
82 See, e.g., Wasserstrom, *Judicial Decision,* 78–79; Posner, "What Do Judges and Justices Maximize?", 18; Landes and Posner, "Legal Precedent," 273; Richard S. Higgins and Paul H. Rubin, "Judicial Discretion," *Journal of Legal Studies* 9 (1980):129.
83 This explanation of precedent following obviously assumes that it is imposed on an unwilling judiciary that would prefer to maximize selfish interests. The doctrine may also

solve a prisoner's dilemma among judges who desire to be bound as long as all other judges are bound. See Erin O'Hara, "Social Constraint or Implicit Collusion? Toward a Game Theoretic Analysis of *Stare Decisis*," *Seton Hall Law Review* 24 (1993):736; Macey, "Costs and Benefits," 11. While my explanation differs from O'Hara's elaborate recitation of the prisoner's dilemma explanation, hers has the advantage of explaining the origins of a doctrine that judges impose on themselves. It is, of course, possible that judges are not all of the same mind, and that judges who prefer leisure impose *stare decisis* on others.

84 Posner has suggested that voting may be a consumption good for judges. Posner, "What Do Judges and Justices Maximize?", 15–23. See also Albert O. Hirschman, *Shifting Involvements: Private Interest and Public Action* (Princeton: Princeton University Press, 1982). But voting is less the measure of participation than opinion writing, which may vary in quantity and quality. Whereas Posner suggests that preferences for voting may explain why judges "adhere to stare decisis but not rigidly" (21), my argument suggests that the consumption value of opinion writing pursuant to the voting function will lead to underinvestment in *stare decisis.*

85 Holmes to Harold Laski, 4 March 1920, quoted in Posner, *Problems of Jurisprudence,* 222.

86 William Landes and Richard A. Posner, "The Independent Judiciary in an Interest-Group Perspective," *Journal of Law and Economics* 18 (1975):875.

12

Changing the Path of the Law

GILLIAN K. HADFIELD

Holmes is an irresistible figure for those of us with economics in our quiver, uttering as he does such sweet nothings as these: "For the rational study of law the black-letter man may be the man of the present but the man of the future is the man of statistics and the master of economics."[1] Holmes was remarkably prescient in forecasting the ever-widening use of economic analysis in the study of the law, a phenomenon that has been well entrenched now for a quarter of the century that has passed since *The Path of the Law* was published.[2] In his thoughtful essay, "The Path Dependence of the Law" (Chapter 11 of this volume), Clayton Gillette brings Holmes's prediction home, perhaps to the surprise (but undoubtedly to the posthumous delight) of the master himself, turning to economics to study the vision of the law that Holmes put forth. From this we get a sharp picture of what a Holmes with access to modern neoclassical economic analysis of law could have said about optimal degrees of deference to precedent.

My claim in this essay is that even if Holmes could have said these things that Gillette sets out in modern terms, he did not. Not because Gillette is in error about the economic approach to the question of optimality and precedent, but because Holmes was not engaged in an analytical project in *The Path of the Law*. Rather, he was engaged in a rhetorical project, an appeal to law students and the legal profession: he was not merely analyzing the optimal choice for judges to make between fresh reasoning and deference to precedent; he was seeking to change the very way in which judges perceived the choices they make. Hence in the same way that economics misses some important truths about the nature of choice by focusing on monistic theories of value and consequential choice, we miss important truths in and about *The Path of the Law* if we interpret Holmes's claims in the work as the claims of a modern neoclassical economist.

Let me begin by offering my interpretation of what Gillette suggests was Holmes's implicit analytical claim in *The Path of the Law*. Boiled down for inspection, it seems to be this: the law, the practice of judges, displays an excessive deference to precedent which causes the actual substance of the law to depart from the optimal substance of the law. With modern economics in hand, Gillette can present this as a claim about path dependence, a divergence from optimal social choice that occurs because history plays too great a role.

To fix these ideas more concretely, here are two examples, drawing on divergences between the legal regimes of Canada and the United States. First, promissory estoppel. Both the United States and Canada began at a common point in English common law with respect to the doctrine of promissory estoppel, a doctrine which states that, in contrast to standard rules of contract, a promise can be binding without consideration if the promise was intended to be relied upon and is in fact relied upon. The original English doctrine limited the operation of promissory estoppel to cases in which the promise was a promise to modify existing legal relations, and this is the state of the modern Canadian doctrine. U.S. doctrine, however, has developed on a different path; from the common origin, U.S. doctrine now extends the realm of promissory estoppel to promises that do not merely modify existing legal relations but that create such relations. Given the commonalities in both socioeconomic conditions and the principles of justice between Canada and the United States, it is hard to see the differential application of promissory estoppel as something other than purely historical. Similarly, as a second example, it is hard to see more than history in the fact that U.S. tort law establishes a strict liability standard for products liability, whereas Canada adheres to a negligence standard.

Gillette, reading *The Path of the Law* as a work of (implicit) economic analysis, says Holmes's claim is that judges' reliance on precedent is excessive; hence the scornful picture of judges who needed a law about butter churns in order to adjudicate the theft of one. Gillette then proceeds to ask the modern economist's two questions, normative and positive: (1) What is the optimal extent of reliance on precedent? (2) Does the legal system in practice deviate from the optimum? In answer to the first question, Gillette's economic analysis conceptualizes precedent as a means of economizing on decision-making costs, both the decision-making costs of judges and the decision-making costs of those who must determine what the law is and then determine their conduct. The "optimum" reliance on precedent is then defined by the tradeoff between resolving a case by recapitulating a precedent and resolving it by the costly process of determining anew the "correct" result according to some criterion, such as the standard of efficiency or corrective justice. The optimal degree of deference to precedent is reached when the social welfare gains of abandoning a precedent in favor of a fresh result are equal to the increase in decision-making costs imposed on the judge and the judged.

In answer to the second (positive) question – Does the actual path of the law deviate from this optimal path? – Gillette's analysis rests on economic behavioral theory, which inquires into judges' incentives to engage in decision making. Gillette proposes two types of judges: the slothful judge, whose private valuation of leisure causes him or her to overutilize the less taxing precedential approach to decision making; and the rogue judge, whose private valuation on the returns from judicial innovation and fame causes him or her to underutilize precedent. Assessing the validity of Holmes's claim, then, is a matter of determining the empirical facts: Which type of judge predominates in the legal system, and what is the marginal effect of precedent on either type?

As Gillette is aware, this is complex territory. The literature on the economic analysis of judicial incentives and the production of law is fairly unsatisfactory. Applying the self-interest model to judges, and hence focusing on whether judges are more likely to be lazy or ambitious, seems to leave a lot of judicial behavior unexplained. Moreover, judicial incentives alone are inadequate as a basis for predicting the evolution of the law, as I have explored elsewhere. For example, even judges with infinite sophistication and perfectly socially aligned incentives to pursue the development of efficient rules will fail to produce such rules, because of the structure of the legal system and because of rules such as the rule of precedent and case-or-controversy requirements.[3]

Both the difficulty of capturing judicial incentives and the constraints of the legal system just mentioned imply that Gillette's modern interpretation of Holmes, if it were to succeed in rehabilitating the economic claim Gillette attributes to Holmes about optimal path dependence in the law, would require a great deal of machinery, certainly more than we can imagine Holmes bringing to bear. It would have to address, for example, the broader functions of precedent, functions which go beyond economizing on decision-making costs. The value of precedent is not merely instrumental: within the common law, in particular, the application of precedent is of constitutive importance to a system of "governance by law not men." Precedent is the source of what is "lawlike" about judge-made law; unfettered discretion to decide is the antithesis of what we understand law to be in Anglo-American legal systems. This is not to say that law can function, or should function without fresh reasoning and insight. But an analysis of precedent has to account for the value of precedent, not merely as a response to the high cost of reasoning but also as a means of structuring a set of constraints on the exercise of discretion. Precedent also has a role to play in coordinating legal argument. Again, in the common law, the *stare decisis* value of cases is what permits litigating parties to determine what issues are pertinent to the court's determination in the event of a trial. Without precedent, this determination becomes unmoored. A complete economic analysis of the value of deference to precedent would have to include these considerations as well.

There are also structural reasons for the persistence of precedent. The literature on the evolution of the common law has explored how incentives to sue or to settle a case affect the substance and persistence of legal rules;[4] the observed resilience of precedent is also a function of the pattern of decision. Perhaps of even more importance is the fact that legal rules influence how people behave in the first place. This behavior determines the cases that develop, and hence the opportunities that judges have to make a decision regarding the application of precedent. Focusing exclusively on judges' incentives, without taking into account the systematic and structural features of a system based on precedent, cannot give us the complete picture. An economist might put this in terms of "partial" versus "general" equilibrium analysis. Gillette's reinterpretation of Holmes focuses on judicial incentives, and yet path dependence, like the path dependence in the technology literature he draws on, is at least as much a consequence of structural features as it is of incentive problems. Indeed, one of the principal sources of path dependence in other settings – network externalities – is precisely about the structural obstacles (in the form of coordination difficulties) facing actors who nonetheless face perfect incentives to choose the appropriate industry standard. In the legal system, excessive reliance on precedent may arise even in a world in which judges have perfect incentives.

But Gillette's focus on judicial incentives – the slothful judge, the rogue judge – comes because he is attempting to be true to Holmes, and it is clear that Holmes in *The Path of the Law* is talking about judges – individual judges – and not about systematic or structural tendencies to unintended results. My question is, given that Holmes is talking about judges, and given that an economic analysis of claims about the optimal degree of precedent requires attention also to a wide array of other considerations, should we read something else from what Holmes has to say? I believe the answer is yes. Holmes is focusing on judges, not because he is grasping, almost a century too early, for the idea of path dependence and distortions in optimal judicial decision-making economy, but because he wants to change judges. Holmes version of path dependence is precisely about judges getting it wrong, about judges pursuing the wrong path.

But Holmes's diatribe about rigid or unimaginative judges is *not* about those judges miscalculating when they weigh the social benefits of fresh reasoning against the application of precedent; one doubts that Holmes would have become so agitated about such an analytical approach to the question. If this were the problem Holmes perceived, *The Path of the Law* would likely have been more collegial, more of an effort to move judges already on side closer to their true aim. No, the rhetoric in Holmes's article is directed at shaking judges up, changing the way they see what it is they do. Indeed, it is about getting them to conceive that there is a judgment to be made about when to rely on precedent and when to reason anew.

This takes us off the economist's traditional terrain in both a superficial and a deep sense. In a superficial sense, *The Path of the Law* is engaged in the project of trying to change judges' preferences for goods such as leisure or fame, preferences economists generally treat as given and terra incognita. In a deeper sense, *The Path of the Law* is engaged in a project that economists do not imagine: the publicly mediated process of framing and conceptualizing choice. Holmes is not merely trying to correct the placement of a marker on a given metric of social welfare and private utility. Holmes was working from a point prior to the conceptualization of choice; his project was to urge judges to conceptualize choice differently from the way they had thought of it. The economist, because he or she starts after this point and assumes a particular conceptualization of choice, misses this.

Economists are not particularly aware that there are multiple ways of framing choice. This insight is the product of the philosophical literature on incommensurability, a literature that emphasizes that values are plural, not reducible to a single metric: love is not just respect or admiration times ten. When the plurality of value is acknowledged, it becomes clear that much decision making is about *how* to value something, in what terms to value something, and not just about *how much* to value something.[5] When Holmes spoke to judges in *The Path of the Law*, he addressed himself to *how* they value precedent, not *how much*. His was a project of persuasion, not prediction.

The Path of the Law urged judges to hold up a mirror to themselves and see that they were not playing a noble role in implementing the given wisdom of a complete doctrinal system and passively discovering external and fixed laws; rather, they were blindly following a possibly random or empty past and, sometimes, masking the exercise of unarticulated and unjustifiable judgments. Holmes wanted judges to value precedent differently: not as an expression of a noble past, but as the product of a sometimes haphazard and error prone, even prejudice prone, process. He wanted judges to value their role differently: not as passive expositors of received wisdom, but as active judges of human conduct and shapers of human society. Holmes is scornful of hidebound judges – not because they are lazy, but because they have misunderstood what precedent and judging is all about.

Consider Gillette's slothful judge, who must decide whether to reach for an easy precedent and then knock off early to play golf or to struggle with a difficult case and stay late. The economist's conception of this choice is that the judge faces a tradeoff between the value he or she places on playing golf and the value he or she places on the product of struggling with the case. But this way of seeing the choice, this consequentialist framing of the choice as the selection of a point on a continuum, is not the only approach. We – more precisely the judge – could see the problem as a matter of self-respect – or as a matter of determining what fidelity to the judge's oath requires – or a matter of signaling to fellow judges disgust, despair, or solidarity. Perhaps for the economist all of these things amount to the same thing; perhaps we can come up with a way to value self-respect or fidelity or signaling solidarity in our utility or welfare metric. But even if this will do for the economist, after the fact, it will not do for the judge who must decide. For the very struggle the judge faces is the struggle to know *whether* this is a case of self-respect or fidelity or signaling solidarity, and therefore what rational choosing requires. Different forms of valuation will matter for how the judge chooses.

Indeed, the passion with which *The Path of the Law* is delivered is attributable precisely to the fact that the understanding of what a choice is *about* is of great importance to the making of a choice. Holmes was afire with the need, as he saw it, to get judges to see that taking the precedential route in deciding a case was not fidelity to the judge's role or cause for self-respect or self-congratulation or self-esteem. Holmes's audience saw deference to precedent as an expression of being a good judge. Holmes saw differently, and *The Path of the Law* was his effort to get other judges to see differently, too.

One supposes that Holmes believed that, having seen differently, his fellow judges could not help but judge differently. For to understand that precedent is a tool and not a god is to begin thinking, as one has never thought before, about how to use precedent, and when to use precedent. A judge committed to justice will choose differently when precedent is understood differently. A judge whose prejudices have found expression through the application of precedent will be forced (if not on his own accord, then by the enlightened lawyers graduating from Boston University) to acknowledge this use of precedent, or at least to work harder and more overtly to express his prejudices. Even the rogue judge will have to choose differently, if his brilliance and wisdom are being assessed on the basis of how he makes use of precedent.

And so I do not see what Gillette sees in *The Path of the Law*, namely an analytical claim that judges are deviating from the optimal degree of reliance on precedent and so constructing excessively path-dependent law. Rather I see an impassioned effort to change the way judges, and lawyers, understand the project of law. As Gillette indicates, throughout his career Holmes showed humility in the face of this project; his recognition of the importance of precedent in moderating the pace of legal evolution suggests that Holmes was not prepared to stake a claim regarding the optimal degree of reliance on precedent. But he was prepared to stake a claim regarding the proper way to understand the meaning of precedent and the obligation of judicial choice.

In the end, I conclude that Holmes's appeal to the "man of the future" as against the "man of the past" is not merely felicitous language to make the point that law is about economics, nor is it a clue that Holmes was the forefather of the modern economic analysis of law. Holmes was speaking to, literally speaking to, the "black-letter man" and urging him to see himself differently; to see himself, like the "man of statistics and the master of economics" of his time, as one who has choices to make about what the law requires, not merely about what it says.

Notes

1 Oliver Wendell Holmes, Jr., "The Path of the Law," *Harvard Law Review* 10 (1897):457. "The Path" is reprinted in the Appendix to this volume with star paging.
2 Holmes was less prescient about matters of gender.

3 Gillian K. Hadfield, "Bias in the Evolution of Legal Rules," *Georgetown Law Journal* 80 (1992):583.
4 See, e.g., George L. Priest, "The Common Law Process and the Selection of Efficient Rules," *Journal of Legal Studies* 6 (1977):65; Paul H. Rubin, "Why Is the Common Law Efficient?", *Journal of Legal Studies* 6 (1997):51; Robert Cooter and Lewis Kornhauser, "Can Litigation Improve the Law without the Help of Judges?", *Journal of Legal Studies* 9 (1980):139.
5 I discuss this literature and the idea of pluralistic choice in the context of contract law in Gillian Hadfield, "An Expressive Theory of Contract: From Feminist Dilemmas to a Reconceptualization of Rational Choice in Contract Law," *University of Pennsylvania Law Review* 146(5) (1998):1235–85.

13

Holmes, Economics, and Classical Realism

BRIAN LEITER*

Oliver Wendell Holmes, Jr., and Friedrich Nietzsche might seem unlikely bedfellows, but Richard A. Posner's striking suggestion that Holmes is "the American Nietzsche"[1] contains more than a grain of truth. Posner, for example, identifies several affinities between the two thinkers, including their putative proto-existentialism (their "taking seriously the definite possibility that man is the puny product of an unplanned series of natural shocks having no tincture of the divine" [*Essential Holmes* xviii]) and their alleged view that force and the "will to power" are the determining features of human existence, so that, in Holmes's words, morality is "only a check for varying intensity upon force, which seems to me likely to remain the ultimate" factor in human affairs (Holmes to Laski, 23 July 1925, quoted in *Essential Holmes* 140).

Although these views clearly resonate with certain widespread (if superficial) images of Nietzsche, the overall picture is deeply flawed. The proto-existentialism, for example, sits uneasily with Nietzsche's more clearly expressed fatalism and naturalism.[2] Similarly, the emphasis on the centrality of the "will to power" to Nietzsche's thought – an emphasis laid by both Posner and David Luban, as well as many Nietzsche scholars[3] – is not supported by recent scholarship, which establishes a less prominent role for both the concept of "will to power" and the text *The Will to Power* in a proper understanding of Nietzsche's philosophy.[4]

---

* Thanks to Sheila Sokolowski for comments on an early draft, to Paul Woodruff for helpful discussion about Thucydides and Nietzsche, and to the participants in the conference "The Path of the Law in the Twentieth Century" (University of Iowa College of Law, 24–25 January 1997) for their useful suggestions on a later draft. Special thanks to my commentator Jody Kraus, as well as to conference participants David Luban (for written comments) and Clayton Gillette and Gillian Hadfield (for their insights regarding economics). Stefan Sciaraffa provided valuable research assistance at several points. For comments on the penultimate draft, I am grateful to Steven Burton, William Forbath, Mark Gergen, Douglas Laycock, Neil Netanel, David Rabban, Jordan Steiker, and, especially, Maurice Leiter. A special word of thanks to Steve Burton for his unusually conscientious and judicious editing.

Yet there remains something essentially right about Posner's intuition concerning the great American judge and the great German philosopher, and it is this point of genuine thematic (and temperamental) affinity that is my main concern in this essay. For both Holmes and Nietzsche are proponents of a more general, but neglected, perspective on questions of moral, political, and legal theory. I call this perspective "classical realism." This perspective is clearly visible in Holmes's seminal paper "The Path of the Law,"[5] just as it is in Nietzsche's mature writings. Significantly, the classical realism of Holmes and Nietzsche places them in a long tradition of theories of morals, politics, and society that we find in writers like Thucydides, Machiavelli, Freud and (to a lesser extent) Marx, among others. It is the most general aim of this essay to revive the doctrine of classical realism as a serious – albeit debunking – position in normative theory.

While I doubt either Posner or Luban would disagree with the characterization of Holmes as a classical realist – indeed, both say things that lend support to this reading[6] – both writers claim to find other affinities between Nietzsche and Holmes that go beyond classical realism. As approximate contemporaries, it should hardly be surprising that Holmes and Nietzsche would share many typical late nineteenth-century views and concerns.[7] Luban's more detailed reading makes the case for deeper connections, though evaluating their plausibility would take me too far afield from my concerns in this essay.[8] I hope simply to show that, whatever other connections there are between Holmes and Nietzsche, one significant one is their participation in the long tradition of classical realism.

I proceed as follows. In part I, I describe the basic doctrine of classical realism, its distinctive position in normative theory. I then briefly illustrate some variations on the basic doctrine over the history of Western thought from antiquity to the modern era, with particular attention to Nietzsche and Holmes. I turn in part II to the question of what classical realism means for law, emphasizing Holmes's suggestion in *The Path of the Law* that "the man of the future is . . . the master of economics" (469). Later writers like Posner plainly find this suggestion attractive. I argue that, although Holmes could not have known it in 1897, "economics" has proved an unlikely torchbearer for classical realism. Ultimately, Holmes's realism may have to be severed from his faith in economics.

I. Classical Realism

A. *Definitions*

By using the label "classical realism" I wish to reclaim for the term "realism" a meaning both older than and different from that current in academic debates, especially in philosophy.[9] In contemporary philosophy, "realism" names either of two views. *Semantic realism* is the view that (a) the statements in some discourse are cognitive (i.e., apt for evaluation in terms of truth or falsity), (b) the meaning of any particular statement is given by its truth conditions, and (c) these truth conditions can, in principle, transcend our capacity to verify or detect them. *Metaphysical realism* is the view that some class of entities has a real existence and character apart from whatever we humans may happen to think about it. Often, "realism" encompasses both positions. Thus, for example, the "realist" about moral discourse typically holds that (a) moral statements are cognitive, that is, they are apt for evaluation in terms of their truth or falsity, and so the meaning of moral statements is a matter of their truth conditions; (b) whether or not any moral statement is true is not dependent on what we humans happen to think about the matter; and (c) at least some moral statements are true (i.e., there are some moral facts).[10]

Classical realism, by contrast, is a very different doctrine; indeed, it entails no particular semantic and metaphysical views at all. Classical realism denotes a certain hard-headed, unromantic, uncompromising attitude, which manifests itself in a brutal honesty and candor in the assessment of human motives and the portrayal of human affairs.[11] More precisely, a classical realist accepts the following three theses:

> *The naturalistic thesis.* There exist certain (largely) incorrigible (and generally unattractive) facts about human beings and human nature.
> *The quietistic thesis.* Any normative theorizing that fails to respect the limits imposed by these facts about human nature is idle and pointless; it is better to "keep quiet" about normative matters than to theorize in ways that make no difference to practice.
> *The realistic thesis.* The aim of theory construction is to depict the incorrigible facts as they really are, without illusion or romance; theory aims for descriptive and explanatory adequacy rather than normative edification or rationalization.

A consequence of the conjunction of the quietistic and realistic theses is that classical realists tend not to pursue the sort of justificatory or normative projects that characterize contemporary moral and political theory (in writers like John Rawls, Jürgen Habermas, Ronald Dworkin, and many others). Realists want to understand and explain the way things are rather than engage in idle talk about how they "ought" to be. To the extent that they take theory construction to have a significant normative dimension, as, for example, in Machiavelli (see section I.C of this chapter), realists view this normative advice as circumscribed by the naturalistic thesis.

Classical realism, then, stands in opposition to the dominant tradition in the modern academy, which maintains an optimistic view about the potential for normative theory to "make a difference." The realist view is deeply skeptical, in much the way Charles Lindblom has recently expressed:

> [T]here is no clear, unmistakable, demonstrated connection between . . . the distinguished contributions of a whole history of political philosophy and any of society's ma-

jor ventures . . . We have to face, at one extreme, the *possibility* that the world of the 1940s and 1950s – and today's world, too – would look pretty much as it does had there never been a Plato or Aristotle or their equivalents; never a Hobbes, a Locke, a Weber, or their equivalents.[12]

What could motivate such skepticism? One possibility is that it is grounded in a certain materialist view of the world, according to which only material facts (suitably defined) make a causal difference. Ideas, on this view, are merely epiphenomenal. Some classical realists (perhaps Marx) seem to be moved by this consideration. But the more common motive among realists is the naturalistic thesis. Indeed, this latter thesis is in many ways the crux of classical realism, since it underpins normative quietism and the conception of theory construction as essentially descriptive and explanatory rather than normative. How, then, do classical realists conceive of human nature or the "incorrigible facts" about human beings? Two themes run through their writings.

First, classical realists view human beings as essentially selfish (or self-interested), and their actions as essentially immoral or amoral. Human beings are "selfish" in the precise sense that in acting, their primary (though perhaps not their exclusive) motivation is that they expect an action to (a) constitute their well-being; or (b) contribute (as a means) to their well-being. Many classical realists have substantive views about what agents typically take to constitute their well-being: for example, power, fame, wealth, and sexual gratification. But we can also speak generally about the classical realist idea that in acting an agent's primary motivation is his own well-being, however exactly well-being is construed.

Of course, this egocentric view of human nature can be strengthened or weakened by placing constraints upon the notion of an agent's "well-being." For example, to what extent can an agent's well-being depend on the satisfaction of other people's desires? At a minimum, though, the realist must claim that agents are characterized by a certain "self-regardingness."[13] An agent's motivations *may* take into account other people's well-being, but the more others' well-being is to the agent's own advantage, then the stronger the agent's motivation will be. "[P]eople's self-regarding desires," in a nutshell, "are generally stronger than their other-regarding desires."[14]

Secondly, classical realists, though thinking human beings are basically selfish, also have a fairly dim view of human intelligence and capacities. Most people, on the classical realist view, are frequently susceptible to the force of irrational wishes and desires; they are essentially gullible, naive, and perhaps even foolish; and they are easily manipulated. Humankind constitutes, in large part, of what Nietzsche called the "herd," with all the bovine (or sheepish) connotations of that label. This makes for a rather unhappy combination of traits. People are largely self-serving in their behavior yet are prone to irrational behavior and are simple-minded, easily fooled, and susceptible to being controlled and used. As a result, while people are generally motivated by selfish concerns, they cannot be expected to do particularly well in satisfying even their perceived self-interest, let alone what is really in their interest (should that be different). Another upshot of this rather dim view of human capacities and intelligence is that classical realists tend to view human conduct in large measure as necessary or determined: the capacity for autonomous choice is largely beyond the reach of creatures like us, or at least the vast majority of us.

In the following pages, I propose to make a rather whirlwind tour through classical realist themes in a variety of thinkers. The treatment is, necessarily, superficial in certain ways, though not, I believe, in ways that bear on the basic contention that all of these thinkers exemplify classical realism.

B. Thucydides versus Plato (According to Nietzsche)

For Nietzsche, the story of ancient philosophy is the unhappy story of how Plato and Socratic rationalism triumphed over the Presocratics and, especially, the culture of the Sophists of the fifth century B.C.[15] For Nietzsche, Thucydides represents the high point of this period in Greek culture. In Thucydides, he says,

> that *culture of the most impartial knowledge of the world* finds its last glorious flower: that culture which had in Sophocles its poet, in Pericles its statesman, in Hippocrates its physician, in Democritus its natural philosopher; which deserves to be baptised with the name of its teachers, the Sophists.[16] (D, 168)

In Thucydides, in other words, "the culture of the Sophists, by which I mean the culture of the realists [*die Realisten-Cultur*], reaches its perfect expression" (TI, X, 2). The essence of Sophistic culture, for Nietzsche, is precisely its classical realism: "The Sophists are no more than realists . . . [T]hey possess the courage of all strong spirits to *know* their own immorality" (WP, 429). It is, in turn, Thucydides, in his great *History of the Peloponnesian War*,[17] who displays this courage more completely than anyone else. Thus, Nietzsche calls Thucydides

> the great sum, the last revelation of that strong, severe, hard factuality which was instinctive with the older Hellenes. In the end, it is *courage* in the face of reality that distinguishes a man like Thucydides from Plato: Plato is a coward before reality, consequently he flees into the ideal; Thucydides has control of *himself,* consequently he also maintains control of things. (TI, X, 2)

In what, precisely, does the "courage" or "realism" of Thucydides consist? The most useful illustration is the dialogue between the Athenians and the vanquished Melians recounted in Thucydides' *History* – a dialogue that one distinguished commentator has called "the most famous example of amoral realism."[18] Negotiating over the terms of surrender, the Athenians address the Melians, in relevant part, as follows:

> For our part, we will not make a long speech no one would believe, full of fine moral arguments – that our empire is justified because we defeated the Persians, or that we are coming against you for an injustice you have done to us . . . Instead, let's work out what

we can do on the basis of what both sides truly accept: we both know that decisions about justice are made in human discussions only when both sides are under equal compulsion [i.e., only among equals does right prevail over might]; but when one side is stronger, it gets as much as it can, and the weak must accept that.

Nature always compels gods (we believe) and men (we are certain) to rule over anyone they can control. We did not make this law, and we were not the first to follow it; but we will take it as we found it and leave it to posterity forever, because we know that you would do the same if you had our power, and so would anyone else. (Woodruff, 103, 106, pars. 89, 105)

Nietzsche's own commentary on this particular dialogue highlights some of the key themes of classical realism:

Do you suppose perchance that these little Greek free cities, which from rage and envy would have liked to devour each other, were guided by philanthropic and righteous principles? Does one reproach Thucydides for the words he puts into the mouths of the Athenian ambassadors when they negotiated with the Melians on the question of destruction or submission?

Only complete Tartuffes [i.e., Socrates and Plato] could possibly have talked of virtue in the midst of this terrible tension – or men living apart, hermits, refugees, and emigrants from reality – people who negated in order to be able to live themselves –

The Sophists were Greeks: when Socrates and Plato took up the cause of virtue and justice, they were *Jews* [i.e., promulgators of Judeo-Christian, or slave, morality] or I know not what – Grote's tactics in defense of the Sophists are false: he wants to raise them to the rank of men of honor and ensigns of morality – but it was precisely their honor not to indulge in any swindle with big words and virtues. (WP, 429)

Thucydides "the realist" recognizes quite clearly that the Athenians are not moved by "philanthropic and righteous principles," that they are driven, instead, by selfish and self-aggrandizing concerns, restrained only by the limits of their power. Socrates and Plato, by contrast, chatter irrelevantly about "virtue and justice," even though, as Thucydides makes plain, virtue and justice play no role in human affairs.

Of course, the speeches Thucydides recorded are his own creations; in many cases (as with the Melian dialogue) he could not even have been present to hear them. Yet this is precisely why Thucydides is a realist, in Nietzsche's view: how he chooses to reconstruct events marks Thucydides as a realist. As Paul Woodruff aptly observes,

a frequent purpose of the speeches [in Thucydides' *History*] is to reveal the [true] motives of the speakers. The speeches are part of Thucydides' larger project of bringing submerged realities to the surface . . . Thucydides wants to bring the darker side of human nature to light by revealing motives such as fear that speakers would want to conceal in real life . . . Thucydides' speakers are made to say what Thucydides thinks they actually believe, whether they would have said those things in public or not . . . He shows us their speeches refracted through a lens of honesty. (Woodruff, xxiii)

Thucydides, in other words, puts into the speakers' mouths their true, amoral motives, reflecting Thucydides' realistic view of human nature and human affairs, by contrast with the idealistic fantasies of a Socrates or Plato.[19] Thus, Nietzsche declares:

> my *cure* from all Platonism has always been *Thucydides*. Thucydides and, perhaps Machiavelli's *Principe* are most closely related to myself by the unconditional will not to gull oneself and to see reason in *reality* – not in "reason," still less in "morality." (TI, X, 2)

It bears noting that Holmes admired exactly the same features in Thucydides as did Nietzsche:

> I am struck [in the dialogues of Thucydides] . . . by the absence of our notion of manners. They say what they think with no polite veils . . . I like the absence of the hypocritic Christian unction. They say outright that of course the crowd that has the force means to have the top – and everybody understands it. (*Essential Holmes,* 60)

Thucydides the classical realist views humans as essentially motivated by selfish concerns – power, fear, wealth – and as creatures for whom morality is at best window dressing, rather than a reason for action.[20] The *History of the Peloponnesian War* is a microcosm for what happens when the perennial dark facts about human nature encounter the recurring circumstances of human existence. Nietzsche the classical realist, in turn, views Socrates and Plato as violating the quietistic thesis by promulgating theories about justice and virtue even though, as Thucydides so vividly demonstrates, such norms play little or no role in human affairs.

Of course, as Nietzsche's earlier comments suggest, Thucydides is not alone as a spokesman for classical realism in antiquity. The Sophist Gorgias, as well as Glaucon and Thrasymachus in Plato's *Republic,* are also realists in large measure. As W. K. C. Guthrie puts it, they share "an attitude of hard-headed realism or fact-facing which without passing judgment declares that the more powerful will always take advantage of the weaker, and will give the name of law and justice to whatever they lay down in their own interests" (*Sophists* 60). The realists, according to Guthrie, all agree with Glaucon in the *Republic* that "[s]elf-interest . . . is what every nature [*physis*] naturally pursues as good" (99).

C. *Machiavelli versus Cicero*

The views just described obviously resonate at many points with those of Machiavelli. Indeed, as we have seen, Nietzsche thinks Machiavelli shared with Thucydides (and we might add, all other classical realists in antiquity and since) "the unconditional will not to gull oneself" about reality. This, in Machiavelli's view, is precisely the failing of earlier writers who offered advice to princes. "[I]t seems to me," he declares, "better to concentrate on what really happens rather than on theories or speculations."[21] Accordingly, Machiavelli will "set aside fantasies about rulers . . . and consider what happens in fact" (XV). He follows with a point-by-point refutation of the utterly unrealistic "wisdom" of antiquity, especially in the person of Cicero.[22] Thus, Machiavelli denies that generosity is a virtue (XVI); he says that "because men are excessively self-interested," it is better to be feared than loved, since fear appeals more directly to the self-interest of the subjects (XVII); he argues that a ruler should feel bound by his promises only "if all men were upright; but because they are treacherous and would not keep their promises to you, you should not consider yourself bound to keep your promises to them" (XVIII). Much of Machiavelli's advice is predicated on the supposition that "men are so naive, and so much dominated by immediate needs" that deception is both quite possible and profitable. "The common people," he says, "are impressed by appearances and results" (XVIII).

The Prince, in sum, "is passionately driven forward by a sense of what must realistically be said and done if political success is to be achieved" (Skinner, "Introduction," xxiv). Machiavelli thinks this normative advice is constrained by the permanent facts about human nature. In his view, men are self-interested, "the end which everyone aims at . . . [is] glory and riches" (XXV). These facts make the idealistic advice of a Cicero or Seneca – the spokesmen for "classical humanism" – irrelevant at best and pernicious at worst.

D. Marx versus Habermas

Marx may, at first, seem an unlikely candidate for membership in the pantheon of classical realists. How could Marx, for example, embrace any claim about human nature, since he seems to deny that there is such a thing? For example, in the *Theses on Feuerbach* he sounds a familiar theme when he asserts that "men are products of circumstances and upbringing,"[23] while in *The Communist Manifesto* he derides the German socialists for claiming to speak for "the interests of Human Nature, of Man in general, who belongs to no class, has no reality, who exists only in the misty realm of philosophical fantasy" (494).

Remarks like these, however, are somewhat misleading. Marx does want to argue, to be sure, that many features of human behavior that are chalked up to an invariant human nature by the forces of reaction are rather the product of socioeconomic circumstances and so are malleable. Yet one can think conservatives are wrong about certain facts about human nature, while still thinking, as Marx does, that there is an essential, unchanging human nature.[24]

Yet this may not help in the present context. For Marx held, famously, that the putatively "selfish" nature of human beings is a socioeconomic artifact, not an enduring feature of the human condition. Thus, in a typical passage from *The Communist Manifesto,* Marx writes that

> The bourgeoisie, wherever it has got the upper hand, has put an end to all feudal, patriarchal, idyllic relations. It has pitilessly torn asunder the motley feudal ties that bound

man to his "natural superiors," and has left remaining no other nexus between man and man than naked self-interest, than callous "cash payment." It has drowned the most heavenly ecstasies of religious fervour, of chivalrous enthusiasm, of philistine sentimentalism, in the icy water of egotistical calculation. (475)

There are two possible responses to this Marxist skepticism about whether the "ugly" features of human beings are deep facts about human nature or mere artifacts of the reign of the bourgeoisie. One response sides with Freud against Marx on the question of what is "natural" and what is mere "social construct" when it comes to the familiar, unattractive features of human social existence.[25] But a second, more modest response will suffice here: even if selfishness is not a permanent feature of human nature, it remains a permanent feature of human beings in capitalist society. Since capitalism remains dominant – indeed, will, by Marx's own theory, remain dominant for the foreseeable future[26] – Marx can agree with the classical realist appraisal of human beings in every respect except one: human beings must necessarily and always be this way.

Indeed, beyond this one issue, the points of affinity between Marx and classical realism are manifold. The standard Marxist refrains that "[t]he ideas of the ruling class are in every epoch the ruling ideas" (*German Ideology,* 172) and that "[l]aw, morality, religion are to [the proletariat] so many bourgeois prejudices, behind which lurk in ambush just as many bourgeois interests" (*Communist Manifesto,* 482) are not far removed from the Sophistic view that "the more powerful will always take advantage of the weaker, and will give the name of law and justice to whatever they lay down in their own interests" (Guthrie, *Sophists,* 60). Like Thucydides, Marx is also skeptical of self-serving explanations that agents proffer for their behavior. In fact, he endlessly derides nonrealistic historians for taking actors and events at face value:

Whilst in ordinary life every shopkeeper is very well able to distinguish between what somebody professes to be and what he really is, our historians have not yet won even this trivial insight. They take every epoch at its word and believe that everything it says and imagines about itself is true. (*German Ideology,* 175)

But in fact what people profess is a mere ideology, behind which lurks the real selfish interests of a particular class:

For each new class which puts itself in the place of one ruling before it, is compelled, merely in order to carry through its aim, to represent its interest as the common interest of all the members of society, that is, expressed in ideal form: it has to give its ideas the form of universality, and represent them as the only rational, universally valid ones. (*German Ideology,* 174)

This is the essence of "ideology," on Marx's view – to present the (selfish) interests of a particular class as really being in the general interest.[27] Like a classical realist, Marx forces us to see through this ideological illusion to the truth of the situation.[28]

Perhaps the most striking affinity between Marx and classical realism concerns the quietistic and realistic theses. For Marx's theoretical efforts are not spent in justifying communism (as, e.g., morally desirable or just). Rather, he tries to construct an adequate descriptive and explanatory account of human society and history that will have practical payoffs in political organizing and revolutionary activity. (In this sense, Marx is the quintessential pragmatist: the value of any theory is measured by the difference it makes to practice.)[29] Making arguments about the "injustice" or "immorality" of capitalism has no practical value for Marx. The ruling classes will not give up their privileges because philosophers show them that they are violating some putatively timeless moral precept, whether it be the difference principle, the categorical imperative or the principle of utility.[30] On normative matters, then, Marx keeps quiet; to have a normative philosophical theory would be pointless. Thus, in *The Communist Manifesto,* Marx does not reject the suggestion of a hypothetical critic who says: "Communism abolishes eternal truths, it abolishes all religion, and all morality, instead of constituting them on a new basis" (489). In effect, he says, this is exactly what communism does! Similarly, in *The German Ideology* Marx says that "real, positive science begins" with

the representation of the practical activity, of the practical process of development of men. Empty talk about consciousness [including, e.g., moral consciousness] ceases, and real knowledge has to take its place. When reality is depicted, philosophy as an independent branch of knowledge loses its medium of existence. (155)

For Marx, like the modern Quinean naturalist,[31] philosophy collapses into a certain sort of descriptive/explanatory theory. As such, it is continuous with the empirical sciences. "Empty talk" about moral duties or injustice plays no role in theory construction so understood.[32]

Marx's classical realism is most vivid when contrasted with the views of the currently most influential member of the quasi-Marxist Frankfurt school, Jürgen Habermas. I say "quasi-Marxist" not only because of the familiar fact that the early Frankfurt school breaks with Marx over a variety of issues (e.g., the revolutionary potential of the working classes).[33] In the work of Habermas, we reach what can only be fairly called the total collapse of the Marxist tradition in European social theory. For at the heart of Habermas's writings, there has been precisely a set of normative and "purely scholastic"[34] questions, indistinguishable in kind from the questions that have occupied all of the great bourgeois moral philosophers from Kant to Rawls. Through "the ideal speech situation" (in his early work) and "communicative ethics" (in his later work), Habermas tries to justify a particular normative perspective on questions of right action and just social ordering.[35] One can well imagine what Marx, the classical realist, would have thought of such efforts. Recall, for example, Marx's complaint about the German socialists presenting themselves as advancing "the requirements of truth; not the interests of the proletariat, but the interests of Human Nature, of Man in general, who belongs to no class, has no reality, who exists only in the misty realm of philosophical fantasy" (*Communist Manifesto,* 494). Marx might just as well have been referring to the Habermas who thinks that "truth" in moral and social matters would be fixed by consensus in a situation of open and rational argument among free and equal persons. The revival of normative theory within critical theory marks a decisive turn away from the whole (realistic) spirit of Marx's own work.

E. Nietzsche versus Kant and Schopenhauer

Two broad images of Nietzsche figure in his reception over the course of the twentieth century. In the "naturalistic" picture, Nietzsche is a thinker, like Hume or Freud, who believes there are certain deep facts about human nature that he aims to identify and then employ in explaining human beliefs and actions. In another "postmodern" image, associated, for example, with Foucault, Nietzsche is precisely the philosopher who denies that there are any deep facts about human nature, that there is any human essence. All such facts, says the postmodern Nietzsche, are mere social constructs.

It is the naturalistic Nietzsche – the *real* Nietzsche[36] – who embraces classical realism. This Nietzsche constructs an explanatory theory to account for various human phenomena, especially the prevalence among human beings of "ascetic" moralities and religions. This explanation, in turn, is organized around a certain egoistic thesis about human nature, namely that

> Every animal . . . instinctively strives for an optimum of favourable conditions in which fully to release his power and achieve his maximum of power-sensation; every animal abhors equally instinctively, with an acute sense of smell which is "higher than all reason," any kind of disturbance and hindrance which blocks or could block his path to the optimum. (GM, III, 7)

Our morality, then, is explicable by reference to the need of the weak, the sick, and the oppressed to make prevail a system of values favorable to the "conditions in which" they may "fully . . . release [their] power."[37]

This explanatory approach constitutes what we might call Nietzsche's "Callicleanism." It has now become something of a commonplace for commentators to note (correctly) that Nietzsche did not accept one sort of Calliclean view – the view that "anyone who is to live aright should suffer his appetites to grow to the greatest extent and not check them" (*Gorgias* 419e).[38] To the contrary, Nietzsche seems to have well appreciated the value of self-restraint and self-denial, especially for productive, creative work (e.g., BGE, 188).

At the same time, the genuine need to correct this one (and, at one time, widespread) misperception about Nietzsche's relation to Callicles has obscured a much more important point of similarity. For Nietzsche embraces the Calliclean doctrine that the inferior employ morality to make "slaves of those who are naturally better" (*Gorgias* 491e–92a), that "the weaker folk, the majority ... frame the laws [and, we might add, the morals] for their own advantage" in order to "frighten [the strong] by saying that to overreach others is shameful and evil" (483b–d). In short, Callicles' view is that morality is simply the prudence of the weak, who, unable to do what the strong can do, opt instead to put the actions of the strong under the ban of morality. This, of course, is Nietzsche's view as well.[39]

For example, in the *Genealogy*, he describes slave morality as simply "the prudence of the lowest order" (I, 13), adding that

When the oppressed, downtrodden, outraged exhort one another with the vengeful cunning of impotence: "let us be different from the evil, namely good! And he is good who does not outrage, who harms nobody, who does not attack, who does not requite . . ." – this listened to calmly and without previous bias really amounts to no more than: "we weak ones are, after all, weak; it would be good if we did nothing *for which we are not strong enough.* . . ."

We hear echoes of the same Calliclean/realistic view when Nietzsche observes that "everything that elevates an individual above the herd and intimidates the neighbor is . . . called *evil*" (BGE, 201); when he suggests that "[m]oral judgments and condemnations constitute the favorite revenge of the spiritually limited against those less limited" (BGE, 219); finally, when he claims that the "chief means" by which the "weak and mediocre . . . weaken and pull down the stronger" is "the moral judgment" (WP, 345). In short, like a classical realist, Nietzsche thinks morality is a mask behind which hides the prudence or self-interest of particular classes of people. Unlike, say, Marx, however, Nietzsche has a rather different view about whose "interests" morality really serves.

By contrast, moral philosophers like Kant and Schopenhauer violate the quietistic thesis in offering their utterly "unrealistic" normative guidance. Commenting on Schopenhauer's promotion of a morality of pity or compassion, Nietzsche notes "how insipidly false and sentimental this [morality] is in a world whose essence is will to power" (BGE, 186). He later asserts that we must "resist all sentimental weakness" and recognize that

life itself is *essentially* appropriation, injury, overpowering of what is alien and weaker; suppression, hardness, imposition of one's own forms, incorporation and at least, at its mildest, exploitation . . . "Exploitation" does not belong to a corrupt or imperfect and primitive society: it belongs to the *essence* of what lives, as a basic organic function; it is a consequence of the will to power, which is after all the will of life. (BGE, 259)[40]

Nietzsche is no more charitable to Kant, in whom he says he detects that "theologians' instinct" (A, 10) after noting that the theologian's "instinct of self-preservation forbids him to respect reality at any point" (A, 9). Accordingly, Kant "invented a special kind of reason [i.e., "practical reason"] for cases in which one need not bother about reason – that is, when morality . . . raises its voice" (A, 12). Like Schopenhauer's morality of pity, Kant's notion of grounding moral duty in respect for the moral law contradicts the fundamental demands of life:

> [V]irtue that is prompted solely by a feeling of respect . . . , as Kant would have it, is harmful . . . The fundamental laws of self-preservation and growth demand the opposite – that everyone invent *his own* virtue, *his own* categorical imperative. A people perishes when it confuses *its* duty with duty in general . . . How could one fail to feel how Kant's categorical imperative endangered life itself! The theologians' instinct alone protected it!
>
> An action demanded by the instinct of life is proved to be *right* by the pleasure that accompanies it; yet this nihilist with his Christian dogmatic entrails considered pleasure an *objection*. What could destroy us more quickly than working, thinking, and feeling without any inner necessity, without any deeply personal choice, without *pleasure* – as an automaton of "duty"? This is the very recipe for decadence, even for idiocy. Kant became an idiot. (A, 11)

Nietzsche's posture may appear to be complicated by the fact that he thinks there are naturalistic explanations for the choice that some people make to embrace the moral philosophies of Kant and Schopenhauer, or at least their commonsense ethico-religious surrogates (see esp. GM, III). The real objection to the moral philosophies of Kant and Schopenhauer may seem to be that they are pernicious – rather than simply idle – prescriptions. But this appearance is somewhat misleading. While Nietzsche thinks that many people do believe in these moral philosophies, in the sense of paying lip service to them, he also thinks that, in reality, the vast majority of human behaviors does not conform to them at all. In that sense, they really are idle.[41]

F. Holmes (and the Legal Realists) versus Dworkin

Among the features that make *The Path of the Law* one of the seminal documents in American legal thought, the most outstanding is its vivid articulation of what would become, thirty years later, the dominant attitude toward law and legal theory characteristic of "legal realism."[42] Holmes, the proto-realist, wastes no time telling his audience that the object of legal study is not moral truth or justice, nor abstract principles or logical systems, but rather "the prediction of the incidence of the public force through the instrumentality of the courts" ("Path" 457). The student of the law must know "what the courts will do in fact" (461), which requires that one "look straight through all the dramatic incidents [in order] to discern the true basis for prophecy" (475). This "true basis" demands no understanding of morality, for law is one thing and morality another, nor even much of legal logic ("You can give any conclusion a logical form" [466]). Instead, it requires recognizing that every decision represents a "half conscious battle on the question of legislative policy" (467). For Holmes, "the man of the future" will be "the master of economics" (469), in part because economics will anchor prediction in the way Holmes's realistic perspective demands. Economics, in Posner's words, provides "the key to an accurate description of what the judges are up to" (PJ, 360). Of course, Holmes says, "such a mode of looking at the matter [may] stink in the nostrils of those who think it advantageous to get as much ethics into the law as they can" (462). But this is of no concern to Holmes the hard-headed realist. We can imagine Holmes agreeing with Nietzsche in ridiculing those who "indulge in any swindle with big [moral] words and virtues" (WP, 429), when all that is required is a willingness to confront the facts squarely. For Holmes, that meant the facts about what the courts really do.[43]

Holmes similarly anticipates the legal realists in his approach to normative theorizing about courts.[44] Although he speaks of the judge's "duty of weighing considerations of social advantage" ("Path" 467), he quickly makes clear that as normative advice it does not amount to much, for this is what courts do anyway! "The duty is inevitable" (467), says Holmes, so telling judges that they "ought" to weigh social advantage only amounts to the modest suggestion that they do openly what they do anyway, albeit "inarticulate[ly], and often unconscious[ly]" (467). Normative theory, at least in *The Path of the Law*, takes a back seat to the practical task of making a systematic, empirical study of the real grounds of decision. We need to explain and describe judicial decision making, rather than tell judges what they "ought" to do.

This type of normative quietism is prominent in the later legal realists. Jerome Frank, for example, commenting on what he called "Cadi justice" (essentially, justice by personal predilection), remarks that "[t]he true question . . . is not whether we should 'revert' to [it], but whether (a) we have ever abandoned it and (b) we can ever pass beyond it."[45] Advocating a "'reversion to Cadi justice' . . . is as meaningless as [advocating] a 'reversion to mortality' or a 'return to breathing'" (31), because, according to Frank, "the personal element is unavoidable in judicial decisions" (25).

A more interesting example of normative quietism in legal realism is Karl Llewellyn's work on Article 2 of the Uniform Commercial Code. For drafting a code is, of course, an explicitly normative enterprise, one a realist, on my construal, should not be able to undertake. In fact, though, Llewellyn uses Article 2 to tell judges that what they ought to do in commercial disputes is precisely what his descriptive theory claims they do already, namely enforce the norms of the prevailing commercial culture (or mercantile practice) in which the dispute arose.[46] Thus, for example, the code imposes an obligation of "good faith" in all contractual dealings (sections 1–203), which means "the observance of reasonable commercial standards of fair dealing in the trade" (sections 2–103). But for a court, then, to enforce the rule requiring "good faith" is just for that court to enforce the relevant norms of commercial culture! The reliance of Article 2 throughout on norms of "good faith" and "reasonableness" is a constant invitation to the judge to do what he would, on the realist theory, do anyway.

The quietism of Holmes and the legal realists contrasts markedly with the normative ambitions of contemporary jurisprudents like Ronald Dworkin. Dworkin, of course, claims descriptive adequacy for his theory, at least with respect to the underlying logic of what it is that judges are doing.[47] But it is not always clear that lawyers or judges find Dworkin's "description" of what they are doing recognizable.[48] And when Dworkin himself comes to actually discuss substantive legal issues – abortion, affirmative action, and the like – he seems to be doing something quite different from what lawyers do.[49] Certainly, Dworkin's most famous claim, that even "hard cases" have right answers, has won little acceptance among either academics or judges. Indeed, Judge Posner's recent observations would surely have been congenial to Justice Cardozo or any of the legal realists more than a half century earlier:

> It is precisely to resolve the most difficult, the most uncertain, disputes that we have judges. Compelled to decide such cases, many judges pretend – sometimes to themselves as well as to the world – that what they have done is added two and two and gotten four, so that anyone who disagrees with their decision is crazy, or that what they have done is chosen Right over Wrong, so that anyone who disagrees with the decision is morally obtuse. In fact they are more likely to have engaged in the same kind of inconclusive practical reasoning, heavily influenced by personal experiences and by temperament, that jurors and politicians and civil servants use to make judgments. The distinctive things about the judges are that their incentives are a bit "purer" than those of most other officials, that their experiences are those of a lawyer, that their reading is dominated by legal materials largely unknown and incomprehensible to the lay public, and that convention requires of them . . . a written justification of their important rulings. (PJ, 233)[50]

If Posner is right, then Dworkin's repeated claims about the greater descriptive adequacy of his theory over others seem dubious at best. Rather than merely advising judges to do explicitly what they already do – as Holmes does – Dworkin would reform their practice in line with a philosophically superior theory of adjudication and political legitimacy. But such an undertaking, according to realism, is an irrelevant undertaking.

Indeed, quietist complaints about Dworkin are not merely speculative. There are empirical reasons for thinking his normative theory of how judges should decide cases really has been an idle exercise. Although Dworkin has been perhaps the leading figure in Anglo-American jurisprudence for more than a quarter century, he has been cited only *six* times in U.S. Supreme Court opinions during this time – and only *once,* remarkably, in the majority (and even then, on a quite minor point).[51] This is surely striking, if defeasible, evidence that thirty years of telling courts how they *ought* to decide cases has made little difference to the practice of the courts.

It is possible, of course, that even without citing Dworkin, the Court may have adopted his distinctive way of thinking about legal problems. But even this seems manifestly not to have been the case. Over the quarter century that Dworkin has been one of the leading defenders of "noninterpretivist" approaches to the Constitution – those approaches that defend the propriety of finding Constitutional rights beyond the history, structure, and text of the document itself[52] – the Court has gradually repudiated this entire approach to reading the Constitution, culminating with its 1986 decision in *Bowers v. Hardwick*.[53] Dworkin's rise to academic prominence, in short, has coincided exactly with the decline of his favored approach to Constitutional interpretation. Surely this fact supports the quietist suspicion that certain types of normative theorizing are idle exercises, that "styles" of Constitutional interpretation (and the political consequences that flow from them) rise and fall for reasons that have *nothing* to do with the arguments of philosophers.

Perhaps, though, this whole critique presupposes an unrealistic time frame in which to register influence or impact.[54] Perhaps it is not thirty years, but a century that we must look at; perhaps it is not particular citations, but the gradual shaping of an enabling ethos that becomes the historical consciousness of a later period and, in turn, affects decisions and actions. Understood this way, of course, the claim of normative theorizing to have "made a difference" gets much harder to assess.[55] The fact that we speak of an "idea whose time has come" does not mean that its time has come because of the labor of moral philosophers. How are we, over the course of a century or two, to disentangle the causal mechanisms at work? If Marx or Braudel is right, can we expect anything more from normative theory than that it should make a difference only in virtue of favorable material circumstances making the time ripe? I cannot hope to resolve these difficult questions here, though their intelligibility – and the obvious plausibility of skeptical answers to them – should suffice here to undergird classical realism's skepticism about normative theory.

Let me also emphasize, at this point, that much of Holmes's own affinity with classical realism must be sought beyond his theory of adjudication as developed in *The Path of the Law*. For example, the naturalistic thesis does not appear to undergird Holmes's quietism and realism in this essay. A hard-headed look at what judges really do shows that they make half-conscious judgments of policy, not that they are essentially self-interested.[56] Like the classical realist, however, Holmes thinks certain incorrigible facts about adjudication constitute a profound constraint on what would count as sensible thinking about law and legal processes.

The Holmes of his letters and other essays is an even more thoroughgoing realist. There, Holmes praises Thucydides' realism (see section I.B of this chapter) and writes to Harold Laski as follows:

You think more nobly of man than I do – and of course, you may be right. But I look at men through Malthus's glasses – as like flies – here swept away by pestilence – there multiplying unduly and paying for it. I think your morals (I am struck by the delicacy of your feeling) are not the last word but only a check for varying intensity upon force, which seems to me likely to remain the ultimate as far as I can look ahead. (*Essential Holmes*, 140)[57]

We should not, as Posner advises, "go overboard in comparing Holmes to Nietzsche" (PJ, 241).[58] I suggest, however, that we do not "go overboard" in recognizing that Holmes and Nietzsche both belong to a long tradition of quite various thinkers all of whom are classical realists. Perhaps it may help to conclude this section by briefly reviewing the classical realist themes in the two thinkers with whom we began.

In keeping with the naturalistic thesis, both Holmes and Nietzsche think there are certain permanent features of human nature, including that people are basically selfish. In accordance with the quietistic thesis, both Holmes and Nietzsche resist normative theorizing that contravenes the incorrigible facts definitive of the respective domains with which they are each concerned. Holmes would simply tell judges that they "ought" to do what it is they do already, while Nietzsche refrains from telling people how they "ought" to live, since "[t]he single human being is a piece of *fatum* from the front and from the rear, one law more, one necessity more for all that is yet to come and to be" (TI, V, 6). Thus, to talk about "[a] man as he *ought* to be . . . sounds to us as insipid as 'a tree as it ought to be'" (WP, 332).[59]

Finally, in line with the realistic thesis, both Holmes and Nietzsche aim for theories that are descriptively and explanatorily adequate to their respective subject matters: Holmes proposes we look to economics to understand what courts do in fact, while Nietzsche, like Freud after him, constructs a naturalistic account to explain morality and human behavior generally.

II. Realism, Economics, and Legal Theory

It should now be clear why Holmes's famous prophecy that in the law "the man of the future is . . . the master of economics" ("Path" 469) is of a piece with his classical realism. The economist, like the realist, takes a hard-headed look at what is really going on, without sentimental or romantic assumptions (or so it seems). In this section, I want to pose the question, however, whether Holmes was right. Is economics an adequate torchbearer for classical realism in law? I shall argue that it probably is not.

At the start, however, a word of historical caution. Turn-of-the-century "economics" was not the same discipline that looms so large on the academic horizon today.[60] In particular, Herbert Hovenkamp's influential work on what he calls the "first great law and economics movement" has taught us that these early lawyer-economists (unlike their present-day heirs) "were generally dubious about markets and about the common law as a welfare-enhancing device."[61] These views could not have been what Holmes had in mind in proposing to turn law's future over to economists, and not simply because the reactionary Holmes would not have shared such views. Rather, and more importantly, as Hovenkamp has also noted, "[t]he dominant political economy in America in the 1880's and 1890's" was still largely committed to laissez-faire.[62] When Holmes lectured in 1897, the real attack on the market as a utility-maximizing device was yet to come.

What Holmes did mean may be appreciated by recalling his complete statement: "the man of the future is the man of statistics and the master of economics" ("Path" 469). What is it that statistics *and* economics make possible? It is nothing other than reliable prediction of the consequences of differing legal rules. Rather than relying on age-old custom and habit, we may rationally (i.e., instrumentally) assess rules in virtue of being able to predict scientifically (via economics and statistics) their effects in practice.[63]

This conception of economics (and of statistics) as the source of scientific predictions was current in the late nineteenth century and must surely be what Holmes had in mind. For example, the well-known economist A. T. Hadley wrote in 1896 as follows:

In the majority of cases, the economist is primarily occupied with establishing and investigating natural laws, or observed sequences of cause and effect. In spite of individual variations, it is now recognized that the average or typical conduct of masses of men operate with a high degree of regularity. The modern science of statistics is based on the existence of such regularity, and concerns itself exclusively with natural laws of this kind.[64]

Like Holmes, then, we are concerned here primarily with economics as a descriptive/explanatory (or as economists like to say, "positive") theory. Thus, in the discussion that follows, I take no position on the value of "efficiency" as a goal of the legal system.[65] Nor does much of what I have to say in the following pages bear directly on economics as a normative theory – the use to which economic theory has been increasingly put in recent years.[66] Even if economics is not a science, it may still be adequate for some modest normative purposes (i.e., those that make modest demands on its modest predictive capacities).

As a descriptive/explanatory theory, economics might have two domains of legal explananda: on the one hand, we might want an explanation for "why a rule of law has taken its particular shape" ("Path" 469) (or, if we are drafting rules, a prediction of their likely effects); on the other hand, we might want a tool for predicting "what the courts will do in fact" ("Path" 461). (The two explanations may, of course, coincide – e.g., in the case of certain common law doctrines.) Should the classical realist embrace economics as the core of his explanatory theory?

There is much about economics that should make it attractive to the classical realist. Economics has seemed to many legal academics the right tool (as Posner puts it) for "a skeptic ... tough-minded, no-nonsense antisentimentalist" ("Introduction," xxi). For one thing, economics, at its explanatory core, relies on the naturalistic thesis. As Posner explains, "The basic assumption of economics . . . is that people are rational maximizers of their satisfactions – *all* people . . . in *all* of their activities . . . that involve choice" (PJ, 353). From such a starting point, the economist proposes "to explain judicial decision-making and place it on an objective basis" (PJ, 353). It is, however, more than just judicial decision making that falls within the explanatory purview of economics, since it is "*all* people . . . in *all* of their activities . . . that involve choice" who are rational maximizers of their satisfactions. Thus, for example,

[L]egislators are rational maximizers of their satisfactions, just like everyone else. Thus nothing they do is motivated by the public interest as such. But they want to be elected and reelected, and they need money to wage an effective campaign. This money is more likely to be forthcoming from well-organized groups than from unorganized individuals . . . Only an organized group of individuals . . . will be able to overcome the informational and free-rider problems that plague collective action. But such a group will not organize and act effectively unless its members have much to gain or much to lose from specific policies . . . The basic tactic of an interest group is to trade the votes of its members and its financial support to candidates in exchange for an implied promise of favorable legislation. Such legislation will normally take the form of a statute transferring wealth from unorganized taxpayers (for example, consumers) to the interest group . . . The unorganized are unlikely to mount effective opposition, and it is their wealth, therefore, that typically is transferred to interest groups. (PJ, 354–55)

Although decidedly unrealistic in one crucial respect (to which I return subsequently), this picture is surely far more realistic, more "hard-headed" and "unsentimental" than, for example, the civic republican fantasies that enjoyed their "fifteen minutes of fame" among the legal professoriate not that many years ago.[67] So economics not only provides "the key to an accurate description of what the judges are up to" (PJ, 360), but also the key to what legislators and all other actors "are up to" as well. As Posner observes,

Economists pride themselves on being engaged in a scientific endeavor. From the basic premise that people are rational maximizers of their satisfactions the economist deduces a variety of hypotheses, of which the best known is the "law of demand" – a rise in the relative price of a product will, other things held constant, cause a reduction in the quantity of the product demanded. These hypotheses are confirmed or refuted by studies of actual economic behavior. (PJ, 362–63)

In passages like these, we see how the economist conceives of himself as continuing that tradition of "strong, severe, hard factuality" (TI, X, 2) that Nietzsche found in Thucydides. With realistic assumptions in hand, the economist now realizes the classical realist tradition in the form of modern science.

It is important to remember that the credibility of economics depends precisely on its claim to be a science, in the precise sense of generating successful predictions.[68] As Morton Horwitz has remarked, "[O]nly the prestige of the sciences could have brought law-and-economics such prominence during the past two decades."[69] Indeed, many economists and lawyer-economists have emphasized the putatively "scientific" character of economic theory. Friedman's classic paper "The Methodology of Positive Economics" is predicated on the idea that economics is "a positive science [whose] generalizations about economic phenomena . . . can be used to predict the consequences of changes in circumstances."[70] This, of course, is also Posner's view.[71] In his Nobel lecture, laureate George Stigler puts it this way: "The central task of an empirical science *such as economics* is to provide general understanding of events in the real world, and ultimately all of its theories and techniques must be instrumental to that task" (emphasis added).[72] Indeed, most economists would probably agree with Mark Blaug that "no time [should] be wasted defending the assertion that economics is a science."[73]

All of these realistic (and scientific) sentiments about economics coexist, of course, with a very different picture of the discipline as essentially a pseudo science. It is better, perhaps, than astrology, but not much more predictively successful than commonsense psychology. It parlays a set of implausible and utterly unrealistic assumptions into tidy, mathematically expressible theories that have little or no connection to reality. A recent article in the *New Yorker* captures this sentiment well: "[A] good deal of modern economic theory," says the author, "even the kind that wins Nobel Prizes, simply doesn't matter much."[74] The article continues:

If economics had made the same intellectual progress as physics or chemistry, it wouldn't matter that it often appears baffling and impenetrable to the layman . . . [But] it is gradually becoming clear that the attempt to convert economics into an exact science has failed. (52)

The *New Yorker* uses the example of Nobel laureate Robert Lucas's anti-Keynesian theories attacking the ability of the Federal Reserve Bank to affect the economy, theories that exerted a profound effect on public policy for some time. "[A] number of [subsequent] empirical studies" (55) disconfirmed them. So also, two Princeton economists attacked, "in a novel and powerful way," the prevailing "wisdom" that minimum-wage laws destroy jobs. "Instead of concocting a mathematical model and 'testing' it with advanced statistical techniques, which is what most economists call research, they decided to test the theory in the real world." They found that employment actually "*expanded* with the increase in the minimum wage" (60).[75]

This debunking view of economics is not merely the stuff of popular culture. A recent study by the American Economic Association found that top economics graduate students were better trained in "formal modeling techniques than" in solving "real world problems" and that nonacademic employers "registered disquiet about the ability of the profession's recruits to conduct empirical research."[76] Legal academics who actually do empirical work confirm this worry.

They have routinely found economic treatments of their subject matters to be fanciful and irrelevant.[77] Often, modern economic analyses of law turn out to be remarkably indifferent to the empirical facts. Even predictions generated from the Coase theorem – the cornerstone of modern law-and-economics – have been empirically falsified![78]

Philosophers, too, have recently launched a devastating attack on the scientific and cognitive credentials of economics, starting from the observation that "[e]conomic theory [is] one of the more dismal empirical failures in the history of science."[79] This is widely conceded about the laughably unsuccessful predictions of macroeconomics, but it is only somewhat less true of microeconomics, which "has made no advances in the management of economic processes since its current formalism was first elaborated in the nineteenth century."[80] This last point bears elaboration.

Like Newtonian mechanics and Darwinian evolution, microeconomics pursues what philosophers of science call an "extremal strategy" of explanation. Such an approach views the phenomena to be explained "as reflecting forces which always move towards stable equilibria that maximize or minimize some theoretically crucial variable. In the case of microeconomics this crucial variable is utility (or its latter day surrogates)" (Rosenberg II, 378). Such a strategy entails that the theory be preserved in the face of any putatively falsifying data by revising the auxiliary hypotheses that inform any empirical test of the theory.[81] This, of course, permits economic theory to persist in the face of a dismal record of empirical failure. But if Newtonian mechanics or Darwinian evolution is none the worse for pursuing such a strategy, why should we worry about economics? Because, as Alexander Rosenberg notes, economics cannot

> boast even a small part of the startling successes that other extremal research programs have achieved. . . . [T]wo hundred years of work in the same direction have produced nothing comparable to the physicists' discovery of new planets, or of new technologies by which to control the mechanical phenomena that Newton's laws systemized. Economists have attained no independently substantiated insight into their domain to rival the biologists' understanding of macroevolution and its underlying mechanism of adaptation and heredity. There has been no signal success of economic theory akin to these advances of extremal theory. (Rosenberg II, 380)[82]

In other words, economics is a *failed* extremal research program, one whose own resistance to falsification belies the empiricist and Popperian rhetoric of which economists are so enamored.[83] That Holmes, in 1897, should have felt so much fervent optimism about economics is understandable. It is a bit harder to fathom Posner's faith in the discipline after one hundred years of minimal empirical progress. Such, one might say, is the nature of "faith."

Of course, economists have generated an extensive literature of apologetics to account for the fact that their discipline has met with so little empirical success. Two typical responses bear consideration here.

First, and most simply, is the frequent assertion that economics has met with predictive success. Thus, Posner writes:

> Here is a random sample of economic predictions that have empirical support: a price ceiling will cause queues, black markets, and quality problems; deregulation results in lower prices and more product variety; communist economies are less productive than capitalist; ... dirty or dangerous jobs pay more (ceteris paribus) than clean or safe ones; ... an increase in the severity of punishment will (ceteris paribus) reduce the amount of crime.... I could go on for hours.[84]

Even a sharp critic of economics' pretension to scientific status like Alexander Rosenberg concedes that "for all its infirmities, economic theory does at least sometimes *seem* to be insightful. Occasionally, [its] qualitative predictions are borne out, and even more frequently, retrospective economic explanations of events that were unexpected ... can be given" (Rosenberg II, 384).

Even if we were to concede these predictive/empirical successes to economics, the force of the preceding argument would not be vitiated. The crux of this argument has not been that economics generates no successful predictions, but only that (a) the quality of its predictions (their precision and reliability) and (b) the growth of its predictive power over time are not of scientific quality. They do not live up to the standards that economists themselves claim for them. Generating true generic predictions is not the hallmark of science. All of us, drawing on commonsense psychological assumptions, do that all of the time. Genuinely scientific theories must anticipate the future with a degree of precision and consistency greater than that realized by common sense.[85]

I predict, for example, that a movie that receives a rave review in Friday's *New York Times* will produce queues at the New York City movie theaters on Friday and Saturday nights – ceteris paribus, of course (e.g., as long as there is no strike that Friday by the newspaper delivery drivers). I predict that ignoring the curve and giving A's to all my students will increase enrollment in my courses. I predict that covering a class for an absent colleague will make it more likely that that colleague will give me detailed comments on a manuscript I have given him to read. All of this is the stuff of common sense, but no one would think of characterizing the commonsense psychology that undergirds such predictions as the core of a scientific research program. The question is, does economics really do any better, in predictive precision and reliability?

The sort of mundane predictions Posner proffers hardly give one confidence in an affirmative answer.[86] That price ceilings will generate queues, for example, seems a simple enough conclusion to draw from a set of plausible psychological assumptions. Unable to charge the real price that the market will bear, merchants and producers (selfishly seeking the highest price) will withhold goods from the marketplace, thus producing lines for the limited stock actually made available, in order to divert some of their product to the black market where it can command a higher price. But what is the precise relationship between price ceilings and queues? What (quantifiable) changes in ceilings will produce what (quantifiable) changes in lines? What antecedent conditions must obtain for price ceilings to produce lines? What additional penalties or incentives will block the queuing effect? Economics simply has no answers to these questions.

The banality of economic "predictions" is especially vivid in Posner's claim that "an increase in the severity of punishment will (ceteris paribus) reduce the amount of crime." But surely we do not need economics – or any putative social science – to draw that conclusion![87] As to the precise correlation between severity of punishment and crime reduction, or the causally relevant parameters of the *ceteris paribus* condition, economics is largely silent. As one commentator on Gary Becker's recent work puts it, economics "abounds in pronouncements of such transparent banality that they would seem to spring more from common sense or ordinary introspection than from sophisticated science."[88]

In fact, most theoretically self-conscious defenders of economics concede that economics does no better than "generic" predictions[89] – that is, "predictions of the existence of a phenomenon, process, or entity, as opposed to specific predictions about its detailed character" (Rosenberg I, 69). In this sense, economics is largely indistinguishable from the predictions generated all the time by the (admittedly nonscientific) applications of commonsense psychology that are a feature of ordinary coping in daily life. But, the economist might point out, generic predictions are also a feature of parts of evolutionary theory and even thermodynamics.[90]

Once again, however, Rosenberg identifies a significant difference:

[I]n other disciplines, generic theories have been either supplemented or improved in order to make specific predictions. Thus, if we add theories about heredity, physiology, development, behavior, and environment to evolution's mechanism of variation and natural selection, we can hope to increase the specificity of generic predictions. In thermodynamics, if we provide a measure of entropy and a description of the mechanical and thermal properties of a system, we can make specific predictions about the amount of entropy increase it will manifest. (Rosenberg I, 70)

The difficulty for putative economic "laws" and predictions is, as Rosenberg puts it, that

we cannot sharpen their applicability beyond the most qualitative or generic levels, or quantify the values of their parameters like elasticity, or improve our foresight or hindsight in the employment of these principles. Now the fact that we can usefully employ false or vacuous general statements, up to certain limits, is no mystery in the philosophy of science at all. The clearest instance of such restrictedly useful though false or vacuous general statements is Euclidean geometry . . . [I]nterpreted as a theory of actual spatial relations, Euclidean geometry is false, and interpreted as a body of *a priori* truths implicitly defining the terms that figure in it, Euclidean geometry is vacuous. More important, . . . it was shown to be useless and inapplicable as a body of conventions, beyond certain values of distance and mass in space. (Rosenberg II, 386)

So the fact that some generic economic predictions work is hardly reason to give us confidence in the cognitive content of economic theory, for, unlike real sciences, economics does not seem to be able to move beyond the purely qualitative level in its predictions.[91]

Rosenberg's comments do suggest, however, a second line of defense for economics. The demand for quantitative precision is really, the economist might say, a demand that all of the *ceteris paribus* clauses he purged from economic laws. But perhaps economic laws simply contain irremediably vague *ceteris paribus* clauses. This would not preclude their being genuine laws, assuming certain other conditions are satisfied.[92] So the "law of demand" – that "a rise in the relative price of a product will, other things held constant, cause a reduction in the quantity of the product demanded" (PJ, 363) – can be a genuine law, even though we can never specify all of the causally relevant parameters picked out by the "other things held constant" clause. As a result the predictions generated by this law will be irremediably generic.[93]

In fairness to economics, it should be noted that all experimentally confirmed laws of physics and chemistry involve *ceteris paribus* clauses, often in the form of ad hoc "phenomenological" factors. It is only in the rarefied atmosphere of pure theoretical physics that one encounters universal, exceptionless laws.[94] That economic laws include *ceteris paribus* clauses is not then, per se, worrisome.

What is worrisome, however, is that in economics *ceteris paribus* does not serve as a placeholder for, for example, phenomenological factors that simply do not admit of quantification. Rather, it serves primarily as an excuse for predictive weakness. The details on what constitute "normal conditions" and the like (i.e., the *cetera*) never seem to be forthcoming. Scientific laws, to repeat, need not be "strict" in the Davidsonian sense of specifying with precision all of the parameters of the boundary conditions that fall under the *ceteris paribus* clauses. But over time, genuine scientific research programs are distinguished by their ability to at least approximate or approach strictness, even if they never realize it. The "progress" of economics over the twentieth century gives little reason for thinking it is moving in this direction. Even with the "law" of demand, for example, a price increase can actually trigger an increase in demand, since "consumers often take prices as an index of quality and often are warranted in doing so" (PJ, 364). But this, of course, means – as Posner recognizes – that "it is distressingly easy to explain away empirical findings that appear to conflict with the basic theoretical assumptions and propositions of economics" (PJ, 364).[95] Add to this problem the purely generic character of the predictions generated in the first place, and it becomes sorely tempting to look for some explanation other than its supposed high cognitive content as the reason why the "science" of economics has exerted such a profound influence on social policy in recent decades. Perhaps, a classical realist might say, the ascendancy of economics as a force in public policy has much more to do with its ability to rationalize policies that tangibly benefit ruling groups in American society than with its empirical and cognitive credentials.

Defenders of economics are fond of saying, as Posner does, that while "economics is weak in comparison with the natural sciences . . . , it is the strongest of the human sciences" (PJ, 366). Yet while economics is certainly the most pretentious and formalized of the human sciences, it clearly has none of the successes of, say, empirical cognitive psychology over the past quarter century.[96] And even calling economics the most predictively successful of the human sciences may be to damn economics with faint praise. Perhaps the real question to ask is why economics has performed so poorly. Daniel Hausman, in an otherwise sympathetic philosophical account of economic methodology, concludes with the following observation, which bears quoting at length:

> [T]he justification for a particular paradigm or research program, like the justification for the commitment to economics as a separate science, is success and progress, including especially empirical success and progress. Since economics has not been very successful and has not made much empirical progress, economists should be exploring alternatives . . . [U]nless equilibrium theory [the core of what makes economics a distinct science, according to Hausman] has captured the major causes of economic phenomena, the separate science of economics can never be successful. If, as seems likely to me, there are systematic failings of human rationality, and economic behavior is significantly influenced by many motive forces, apart from consumerism and diminishing marginal rates of substitution, then equilibrium theory is not a very good theory, whether or not there is anything better.[97]

Although economists like Gary Becker have tried to bring "irrational" behavior within the framework of neoclassical economic theory, it is far from clear that they have been successful.[98] But this, perhaps, is where a genuine classical realist would have an advantage. For recall that it is characteristic of classical realism to think that people are both selfish and foolish, perhaps to the point of "irrationality." A classical realist would hardly be surprised if the "herd" were characterized by "systematic failings of human rationality." Indeed, much of classical realism – in Machiavelli, in Marx, in Nietzsche, in Freud – is built around the notion that to understand human behavior and human societies one must understand them as largely irrational, as susceptible to the influence of irrational wishes and desires.

Of course, to abandon rationality in this way has costs for the normative program of economics. As Hausman notes, economics is committed

> not only [to] the heuristic power of microeconomics but also the rational prescriptive force of utility theory and the moral argument for perfectly competitive equilibrium. Any step away from microeconomics weakens these links between purported facts, rational oughts, and moral oughts and surrenders the grand vision of a unified theory of all economic phenomena.[99]

But given the empirical failure of economics, if the best economics can do is to offer up its normative prejudices, then a commitment to economics starts to look more and more like a political position, and less like the cognitive one it so often purports to be.

Even with Holmes, it is clear that his attraction to economic ways of thinking is strongly driven by his undefended (and largely indefensible) moral and political commitments. We could not imagine, for example, a full-blooded classical realist saying, as Holmes does, that "[i]f a man makes a great fortune by selling some patent medicine to the crowd, that shows that in those circumstances the crowd wants it – and I can see no justification in a government's undertaking to rectify social desires – except upon an aristocratic assumption that you know what is good for them better than they" (*Essential Holmes*, 141). But empirical investigation in economics hardly rules out this last "aristocratic assumption."[100] Indeed, given that the classical realist will agree with Machiavelli that "men are . . . naive, and . . . much dominated by immediate needs" and that they "are impressed by appearances and results" (*The Prince*, XVIII), surely the realist might have doubts about the value of respecting what "the crowd wants."[101]

III. Concluding Thoughts

Even if the argument of the preceding section were correct on all counts, this would still leave unanswered the question of how the classical realist should view economics.[102] All I have shown is that economic "science" is a failed empirical research program. That means economics could still turn out to be, comparatively speaking, the best theory (warts and all!) for a realist interested in law. After all, a quantitatively precise science of human affairs does not seem to be on the horizon from any source, whether Gary Becker or Karl Marx or Sigmund Freud. So even if Holmes knew what we know today about the limitations of economics, he might still stand by his slogan.

The sorry empirical record of economics – a point all too rarely acknowledged by economists or legal scholars – does, nonetheless, contain an important lesson for the genuine classical realist. The crux of the problem with economics, as Hausman suggests, appears to be its inattention to systematic failings of human rationality.[103] This accounts for its systematic predictive weakness. The realist, then, might ask if a research program more sensitive to this problem would fare better, even if only at the qualitative level.

I have argued that the major American legal realists are proponents of what I call "naturalized jurisprudence."[104] Naturalized jurisprudence, like naturalized epistemology on the Quinean model, replaces the conventional jurisprudent's normative question "How ought judges to decide cases?" with the descriptive/explanatory question "How do judges actually decide cases, and what causes them to do so?" Naturalized jurisprudence abandons the normative question because of the perceived failure of traditional normative jurisprudence to produce the desired foundational account of judicial decision making.[105] But naturalized jurisprudence is also animated by the classical realist's quietistic thesis, by the sense that normative theories of adjudication are idle exercises, that the real explanation for patterns of judicial decision may bypass normative jurisprudence altogether and yet come up with more fruitful accounts of what courts do.

So far, of course, lawyer-economists like Posner should feel right at home. Economics, he will say, provides the desired descriptive/explanatory theory of a naturalized jurisprudence. But a naturalized jurisprudence, unlike economics, need not be committed to rational-choice theory as the core of its explanatory strategy. A naturalized jurisprudence, in short, will be attuned to "systematic failings of human rationality" and will look for causal patterns beyond those that track patterns of (instrumentally) rational desire satisfaction. The difference between classical realism and the economic approach may be illustrated by revisiting Posner's economic analysis of the legislative (rather than judicial) process. Recall that on Posner's analysis, "legislators are rational maximizers of their satisfactions, just like everyone else." Legislators want to be reelected, and they respond, accordingly, to powerful interest groups that finance their ambitions, enacting, for example, legislation "transferring wealth from unorganized taxpayers (for example, consumers) to the interest group" (PJ, 345–55).

What is oddly missing in this story – indeed, what renders it, in the end, unrealistic and uninformative – is any recognition that structural and ideological factors circumscribe the causes around which interest groups form in the first place. The interest groups we actually find – say, the insurance industry, the airline industry, the elderly, labor unions – already define their interests against an entrenched and unquestioned background of the relative inviolability of the free market and the existing distribution of wealth. After all, if people really were rational maximizers of their satisfactions, then it would be puzzling indeed (would it not?) that 1 percent of the U.S. population should control 40 percent of the wealth, or that the top 20 percent should control 80 percent of the wealth.[106] Surely 99 percent of the population might get some desire satisfaction in having at least part of 40 percent of the wealth! But no such interest group is to be found, and no elected official to take up the cause of the vast majority, for reasons that any realist should acknowledge. The Republocrats (or is it the Demublicans?) – "[T]here ain't a dime's worth of difference," George Wallace aptly commented in 1968 – represent the same monied interests, who, in turn, own the major means of communication and information dissemination.[107] And since "the common people are impressed by appearances and results" and are, in any event, "so naive, and so much dominated by immediate needs" (*The Prince*, XVIII), it should hardly be surprising that they come to conceive of their "interests" in terms that take for granted the essential features of the status quo.

This much should be obvious, given the determined tough-mindedness of the classical realist. For the realist tells us that we must have "*courage* in the face of reality" (TI, X, 2), and that it is "better to concentrate on what really happens rather than on theories or speculations" (*The Prince*, XV). We speak as "a skeptic, a tough-minded, no-nonsense, antisentimentalist" (*Essential*

Holmes, xxi) not when we speak of government in Posner's inadequate public-choice-theory language, but when we speak, as one German philosopher did, of the "executive [and legislative branches] of the modern State . . . [as] but a committee for managing the common affairs of the whole bourgeoisie."[108]

None of the foregoing explains, of course, how a classical realist should view adjudication itself. Here, as I have argued elsewhere,[109] the Holmesian proto–legal realist perspective will fare better – though even in this case I think we need to take more seriously Jerome Frank's notorious (but not at all that foolish) admonition that "the personality of the judge is the pivotal factor in law administration."[110] Judicial personality, moreover, cannot be understood at all adequately through the lens of rational desire satisfaction (as Posner himself seems at times to recognize), but requires rather a richer picture of the essential irrationality or arationality of human personality and character, a picture of the sort we find in writers like Nietzsche and Freud.[111] To gesture at a position is one thing, of course, and to actually articulate and defend it another. It does remain, then, an open question whether naturalized jurisprudence, in my sense, should supplant the economic theory of judicial decision making favored by Posner. *What is clearer is that the poor empirical record of economics demands that we seek alternatives to the dismal science.*

Even if it does turn out that Holmes's attachment to economics is misplaced, this does not undermine his deep and lasting significance as the first classical realist in legal theory. For what Machiavelli did for politics, or Nietzsche for morality, or Marx and Freud for society, Holmes did for law – by challenging the primacy of normative theory, by calling on us to take a hard-headed look at the phenomena in question, by appreciating, in short, as all classical realists do, that "philosophical theories are in peril if they are constructed in disregard of the nature of the empirical world to which they are supposed to apply."[112]

Notes

1. Richard Posner, "Introduction," in *The Essential Holmes,* ed. Posner (Chicago: University Chicago Press, 1992), xxviii (cited hereafter as "*Essential Holmes*"). See also, Richard Posner, *The Problems of Jurisprudence* (Cambridge, Mass.: Harvard University Press, 1990), 239–44 (cited hereafter as "PJ"). For another important recent discussion of Holmes and Nietzsche, see David Luban, "Justice Holmes and the Metaphysics of Judicial Restraint," *Duke Law Journal* 44 (1994):449–523 (cited hereafter by page number only in the text). See also, J. W. Burrow, "Holmes in His Intellectual Milieu," in *The Legacy of Oliver Wendell Holmes, Jr.,* ed. R. W. Gordon (Stanford: Stanford University Press, 1992), esp. 29.
2. See Brian Leiter, "The Paradox of Fatalism and Self-Creation in Nietzsche," in *Willing and Nothingness: Schopenhauer as Nietzsche's Educator,* ed. C. Janaway (Oxford: Oxford University Press, 1998).
3. See, e.g., Karl Jaspers, *Nietzsche: An Introduction to the Understanding of His Philosophical Activity,* trans. C. Wallraff and F. Schmitz (South Bend, Ind.: Regnery/Gateway, 1965), 287. For similar views, see Wolfgang Müller-Lauter, "Nietzsche Lehre vom Willen

zur Macht," *Nietzsche-Studien* 3 (1971):1–61; Martin Heidegger, *Nietzsche, vol. 4: Nihilism,* trans. D. Krell (San Francisco: Harper & Row, 1982); Richard Schacht, *Nietzsche* (London: Routledge, 1983). The most sophisticated account of the centrality of the will to power to Nietzsche's thought is presented in John Richardson, *Nietzsche's System* (Oxford: Oxford University Press, 1996), though Richardson never quite comes to terms with the problems raised in the recent literature. For further discussion, see my review of Richardson in *Mind* (forthcoming).

4 See, e.g., Mazzino Montinari, "Nietzsches Nachlass von 1885 bis 1888 oder Textkritik und Wille zur Macht," in his *Nietzsche Lesen* (Berlin: de Gruyter, 1982); Maudemarie Clark, *Nietzsche on Truth and Philosophy* (Cambridge: Cambridge University Press, 1990), 212–27; R. J. Hollingdale, *Nietzsche: The Man and His Philosophy* (London: Ark, 1985), 166–72, 182–86; Bernd Magnus, "The Use and Abuse of *The Will to Power*," in *Reading Nietzsche,* ed. R. C. Solomon and K. M. Higgins (New York: Oxford University Press, 1988); Brian Leiter, "Nietzsche and the Critique of Morality: Philosophical Naturalism in Nietzsche's Theory of Value" (Ph.D. diss., University of Michigan, 1995), chapter IV. Of course, some of the themes broached in *The Will to Power* are clearly continuous with themes developed in the works Nietzsche chose to publish. But it is less clear that this is the case for the theme in which Posner and Luban are interested.

A note on citations format to Nietzsche: I cite Nietzsche's texts by their standard English-language acronyms: *Dawn* (D), *The Gay Science* (GS), *Thus Spoke Zarathustra* (TSZ), *Beyond Good and Evil* (BGE), *On the Genealogy of Morality* (GM), *Twilight of the Idols* (TI), *The Antichrist* (A), *Ecce Homo* (EH), *The Will to Power* (WP). Translations, with minor emendations, are by Walter Kaufmann and/or R. J. Hollingdale; for emendations I rely on *Sämtliche Werke: Kritische Studienausgabe in 15 Bänden,* ed. G. Colli and M. Montinari (Berlin: de Gruyter, 1980). Roman numerals refer to major chapters or divisions in Nietzsche's works; Arabic numerals refer to sections, not pages.

5 Oliver Wendell Holmes, "The Path of the Law," *Harvard Law Review* 10 (1897):457–78 (cited hereafter by page number only in the text). "The Path" is reprinted in the Appendix to this volume with star paging. It is not, I hasten to add, the only perspective visible in Holmes's essay, as many others have noted. See, e.g., William W. Fisher III, "Interpreting Holmes," *Harvard Law Review* 110 (1997):1010, 1010–12.

6 Thus, Posner characterizes one of the strongest influences on Holmes, James Fitzjames Stephen, as "a skeptic, a tough-minded, no-nonsense antisentimentalist" ("Introduction," xxi), which might serve as a pithy statement of the classical realist mind set. Similarly, Luban notes that Nietzsche "shared with Holmes a debunking attitude towards moralizing" (464, note 41). This, too, evokes the classical realists' "quietistic thesis," though Luban adds (more problematically) that they also shared "a profound reverence for force." This claim strikes me as too ambiguous to be analyzed. Luban also quotes Holmes writing to Wigmore: "Doesn't this squashy sentimentality of a big minority of our people about human life make you puke? . . . [O]f people . . . who think that . . . the universe is no longer predatory. Oh bring in a basin" (469). This, too, evokes Nietzsche in BGE 259.

7 As Posner aptly observes, in Holmes

[o]ne can find pragmatism, atheism, (nineteenth-century) liberalism, materialism, aestheticism, utilitarianism, militarism, biological, social, and historical Darwinism, skepticism, nihilism, Nietzschean vitalism and "will to power," Calvinism, logical positivism, stoicism, behaviorism, and existentialism, together with the explicit rejection of most of these "isms" and a sheer zest for living that may be the central plank in the Holmesian platform. Whether the elements of his thought coalesce to form a coherent philosophy of life I doubt.

8 Let me just briefly state my doubts about Luban's interpretation. According to Luban, for the proto-existentialist Nietzsche the "root problem [is], How in a godless world filled up with senseless destruction, can one find meaning and avoid sinking into nihilism?" (464). "Nietzsche's solution," says Luban, "lies in the affirmation of the very contingency and goallessness of the universe that provokes us to nihilism in the first place" (466). "To Holmes as well as to Nietzsche, we overcome nihilism and despair by joyfully affirming the greatness of the universe" (485), a notion captured by Nietzsche's notion of the "will to power" (467) and "infusion of 'vital force'" that can "transfigure us and lift us out of the etiolated half-experience of daily life" (479).

As a preliminary matter, I worry that this interpretation makes Nietzsche sound a bit too much like a late-night self-help infomercial. More seriously, it is striking that Luban's discussion of Nietzsche's solution to the problem of nihilism makes no reference to Nietzsche's major philosophical project, the revaluation of values. Yet surely Nietzsche's main strategy for resisting Schopenhauer's pessimism and nihilism is to challenge the evaluative perspective from which the world appears to lack value: hence the centrality of the revaluation of all values. As Nietzsche summarizes the strategy in *Dawn,* in challenging the Kantian and Schopenhaurian view that egoistic actions are immoral,

[O]ur counter-reckoning is that we shall restore to men their goodwill towards the actions decried as egoistic and restore to these actions their *value – we shall deprive them of their bad conscience!* And since they have hitherto been by far the most frequent actions, and will continue to be so for all future time, we thus remove from the entire aspect of action and life its *evil appearance!* This is a very significant result! (Section 148)

A result, he might have added, that makes it possible to resist nihilistic despair, brought on by a sense that, judged by the standards of our existing morality, this world is corrupt, depraved, and reprehensible.

I also find problematic Luban's assertion that "Nietzsche . . . dismissed the thing-in-itself and fell into idealist hallucinations" (488). I take Nietzsche's point to be precisely that the force of the idealist–realist distinction makes no sense once one repudiates the intelligibility of the thing-in-itself as a conceptual category. Like the later Wittgenstein, Quine, and perhaps John McDowell, Nietzsche accepts the Kantian insight that the human mind structures the world but rejects both (a) the Kantian claim that such structuring takes a universal and necessary form, and, importantly, (b) the Kantian dualism contrasting the world as it appears to us with the world as it really is in itself. It seems highly misleading, at best, to call this view "idealism." For an attempt to work out this interpretation of Nietzsche, see my "Perspectivism in Nietzsche's *Genealogy of Morals,*" in *Nietzsche, Genealogy, Morality: Essays on Nietzsche's "On the Genealogy of Morals,"* ed. R. Schacht (Berkeley and Los Angeles: University of California Press, 1994). (Luban tells me [personal communication] that he really meant something more like "solipsistic" rather than "idealist" here; in context, I do not think this meaning is obvious.)

9 For a representative treatment of "realism" in current philosophy, notable for the clarity and precision with which the position is characterized, see Peter Railton, "Moral Realism: Prospects and Problems," in *Moral Knowledge? New Readings in Moral Epistemology,* ed. W. Sinnott-Armstrong and M. Timmons (Oxford: Oxford University Press, 1996). For somewhat different (though related) approaches to "realism," see Philip Pettit, "Embracing Objectivity in Ethics," in *Objectivity in Law and Morals,* ed. B. Leiter (Cambridge: Cambridge University Press, 1998), and Crispin Wright, "Introduction" to *Realism, Meaning and Truth* (Oxford: Blackwell, 1987).

10 Point (c) distinguishes the "realist" from an error theorist like John Mackie, who can ac-

cept (a) and (b). For a more refined account of these basic criteria, see Railton, "Moral Realism," and Pettit, "Embracing Objectivity."

11 One area in which the "realist" label has retained this meaning is international affairs. See, e.g., Hans J. Morgenthau, *Politics among Nations,* 4th ed. (New York: Knopf, 1967) esp. 4–8; Steven Forde, "International Realism and the Science of Politics: Thucydides, Machiavelli, and Neorealism," *International Studies Quarterly* 141 (1995):141–60.

12 Charles E. Lindblom, "Political Sciences in the 1940s and 1950s" *Daedalus* 126 (1997):225, 241–42. I am grateful to Calvin Johnson for calling this article to my attention.

13 I take the term from Philip Pettit's illuminating discussion in "The Virtual Reality of *Homo Economicus,*" *Monist* 78 (1995):308, 310–12.

14 Ibid., at 312.

15 E.g., "The real philosophers of Greece are those before Socrates" (WP 437); "for the whole phenomenon Plato I would sooner use the harsh phrase 'higher swindle'" (T1, X, 2).

16 Cf. WP, 428 (a note of 1888): "The Greek culture of the Sophists had developed out of all the Greek instincts; it belongs to the culture of the Periclean age as necessarily as Plato does *not;* it has its predecessors in Heraclitus, Democritus, in the scientific types of the old philosophy; it finds its expression in, e.g., the high culture of Thucydides."

17 I rely on the translations by Paul Woodruff in his invaluable critical edition, *Thucydides on Justice, Power and Human Nature* (Indianapolis: Hackett, 1993) (cited hereafter as "Woodruff").

18 W. K. C. Guthrie, *The Sophists* (Cambridge: Cambridge University Press, 1971), 85. Further citations are cited as *Sophists.*

19 Of course, on one prevalent understanding of Plato, he too accepts that humans are self-interested and tries to show them simply that "justice" and "virtue" are in their self-interest. The realist might object that this identification of morality with self-interest is so implausible as to be no different from preaching justice and virtue, quite apart from any appeal to self-interest.

20 Cf. Guthrie, *Sophists,* 85: "[I]t is remarkable how seldom even [Thucydides's] orators, aiming at persuasion, see any point in appealing to considerations of right, justice or other normally accepted moral standards: it is taken for granted that only an appeal to self-interest is likely to succeed."

21 Niccolò Machiavelli, *The Prince,* ed. Q. Skinner and R. Price (Cambridge: Cambridge University Press, 1988), chapter XV. All further citations, by chapter number, are cited parenthetically in the text, except for citations to Skinner's introduction, which are cited as "Skinner, 'Introduction.'" I take no position in this essay on the difficult interpretive question of whether the later Machiavelli of *The Discourses* is also a classical realist in my sense.

22 See Skinner, "Introduction," xvii–xx.

23 In Karl Marx, *Theses on Feuerbach,* in *The Marx–Engels Reader,* ed. R. C. Tucker, 2d edition (New York: Norton, 1978), 144. (Cited hereafter parenthetically in the text by page number.)

24 See the discussion in G. A. Cohen, *Karl Marx's Theory of History: A Defence* (Princeton: Princeton University Press, 1978), 151; Allen Wood, *Karl Marx* (London: Routledge & Kegan Paul, 1981), 17–24.

25 The classic expression of this view is Sigmund Freud, *Civilization and Its Discontents,* ed. and trans. J. Strachey (New York: Norton, 1961). Freud's embrace of the classical realist's quietistic thesis is strikingly explicit in the concluding pages of this seminal work:

[I]t is very far from my intention to express an opinion upon the value of human civilization ... One thing only do I know for certain and that is that man's judgments of value follow directly his wishes for happiness — that, accordingly, they are an attempt to support his illusions with arguments ... I have not the courage to rise up before my fellow-men as a prophet, and I bow to their reproach that I can offer them no consolation: for at bottom that is what they are all demanding — the wildest revolutionaries no less passionately than the most virtuous believers. (103–4)

26 The party line of the capitalist media in recent years has been that the collapse of the Soviet Union constitutes a "refutation" of Marx, assigning him to the "dustbin of history." But this is obviously silly. It is quite clear that the conditions for communist revolution that Marx explicitly sets out — that capitalism has produced the maximal development of the forces of production, reduced the great mass of humanity to a condition of poverty, destroyed all of the hitherto-existing national, ethnic, and religious identities, and exhausted all of the potential markets for goods (see *The Communist Manifesto,* 475–83, 488) — were not satisfied in 1917, nor have they been satisfied even today. Nonetheless, it seems equally clear that current global economic tendencies and trends point precisely toward the conditions that Marx wrongly thought were around the corner in the mid-nineteenth century. (Even the seemingly resilient national, ethnic, and religious chauvinisms that have captured the headlines from Bosnia, Iran, and Rwanda (among other places) must be set against a backdrop of the gradual triumph of American pop culture over much of the globe, and the resulting homogenization of attitudes and values; no doubt the market will have similar effects in the aforementioned retrograde countries in due course.) In this regard, Marx was quite prescient in his understanding of the logic of capitalism, though his timing was badly off. It remains, in turn, an open empirical question whether the realization of these conditions will bring about the triumph of communism and an open empirical question whether selfishness will turn out to be a permanent feature of human nature or a mere socioeconomic artifact of a particular era.

27 On the different possible senses of "ideology," see Raymond Geuss, *The Idea of a Critical Theory: Habermas and the Frankfurt School* (Cambridge: Cambridge University Press, 1981), 13–14. Marx's usage is what Geuss calls an ideology in the "epistemic" sense.

28 One might also argue that Marx shares the classical realists' view that human beings are naive, gullible, and easily misled insofar as he thinks that the vast majority of people who embrace bourgeois morals, law, and religion have been badly duped about their own interests. But this aspect of classical realism is probably more vivid in the early writers of the Frankfurt school — e.g., Theodor Adorno and Herbert Marcuse — who no longer share Marx's optimism about the revolutionary potential of the working classes and have a far more contemptuous view of the intelligence and revolutionary capacities of ordinary persons.

29 This, in a nutshell, is one of the principal theses of Marx's *Theses on Feuerbach,* esp. theses II, VIII, and XI. For a related understanding of pragmatism, in a more contemporary idiom, see Mark Johnston's important essay, "Objectivity Refigured: Pragmatism without Verificationism," in *Reality, Representation, and Projection,* ed. J. Haldane and C. Wright (Oxford: Oxford University Press, 1993).

30 Thus, Marx derides the Young Hegelians and Geuerback for wanting "merely to produce a correct [philosophical] consciousness about an existing fact; whereas for the real communist it is a question of overthrowing the existing state of things" (*German Ideology,* 167–68). This Marxist criticism is, ironically, apt with respect to parts of the critical le-

gal studies literature. See the discussion in my essay, "Is there an 'American' Jurisprudence?", *Oxford Journal of Legal Studies* 17 (1997):367, 383–84.

The irrelevance of the arguments of moral and political philosophers to social change has sometimes been noted by such philosophers. See, e.g., Thomas Nagel, *Mortal Questions* (Cambridge: Cambridge University Press, 1979), xii ("Moral judgment and moral theory certainly apply to public questions, but they are notably ineffective"). The classical realist explanation for this is straightforward: the great "herd" of humanity is too driven by selfish concerns and too uninterested in grasping (or unable to understand) moral argument for the labor of moral philosophers to make any difference.

Indeed, the often breathtaking moral illiteracy and self-serving pettiness of people is made vivid in the newspapers every day. Thus, the *New York Times* for 8 January 1997 – an example chosen at random – reports that wealthy whites in a suburb of Johannesburg, South Africa, are refusing to pay their new, higher property taxes. The *Times* explains:

[M]any of the whites here feel blameless for apartheid. They say that they never voted for the National Party, which devised and carried out South Africa's repressive racial policies when it headed a white minority government, and that they were active in various charities. For instance, [one wealthy white woman] says that she used to make peanut butter cookies for poor black children in Pretoria and that her husband's firm sponsors an adult illiteracy course for domestic servants. (A4)

Everything in my own experience suggests that these (no doubt) "educated" South Africans are the norm, not the exception, in the quality of their moral calculus.

31 On Quinean naturalism, see my "Rethinking Legal Realism: Toward a Naturalized Jurisprudence," *Texas Law Review* 76 (1997):267, and, more generally, my "Naturalism and Naturalized Jurisprudence," in *Analyzing Law: New Essays in Legal Theory,* ed. B. Bix (Oxford: Oxford University Press, 1998). For a useful characterization of Quine for my purposes here, see especially, Jaegwon Kim, "What Is Naturalized Epistemology?", in *Naturalizing Epistemology,* ed. H. Kornblith, 2d ed. (Cambridge, Mass.: MIT, 1994).

32 Notice that this interpretation is compatible with the possibility that Marx is, say, a tacit (sophisticated) utilitarian, a view favored by contemporary analytical Marxists like Richard Boyd and Peter Railton. My point is not that Marx did not have what might fairly be called "moral" views, but rather that he did not see the construction of a moral theory as a worthwhile or necessary undertaking.

33 For a useful but somewhat polemical account of the differences, see Leszek Kolakowski, *Main Currents of Marxism,* vol. 3: *The Breakdown,* trans. P. S. Fallo (Oxford: Clarendon Press, 1978), 341–43.

34 Marx, *Theses on Feuerbach,* 144.

35 For description and criticism of the earlier versions of the normative argument, see Geuss, *Idea,* 55–75, and Steven Lukes, "Of Gods and Demons: Habermas and Practical Reason," in *Habermas: Critical Debates,* ed. J. B. Thompson and D. Held (London: Macmillan, 1982). Contrary to some defenders of Habermas, it does not seem to me that these critiques are deflected by the shifts in thinking of the later Habermas.

36 For a sustained defense, see my *Nietzsche on Morality* (London: Routledge, forthcoming).

37 I am oversimplifying greatly. For more detailed discussion, see my essays "Beyond Good and Evil," *History of Philosophy Quarterly,* 10 (1993):261; "Morality in the Pejorative Sense: On the Logic of Nietzsche's Critique of Morality," *British Journal for the History of Philosophy* 13 (1995):113; and "Nietzsche and the Morality Critics," *Ethics* 107 (1997):255–90. For discussion of Nietzsche's critique of Schopenhauer's ethics in par-

ticular, see Maudemarie Clark and Brian Leiter, "Introduction," in Friedrich Nietzsche, *Daybreak: Thoughts on the Prejudices of Morality,* trans. R. J. Hollingdale (Cambridge: Cambridge University Press, 1997), esp. xv–xxxiv.

38 See, e.g., Alexander Nehamas, *Nietzsche: Life as Literature* (Cambridge, Mass.: Harvard University Press, 1985), 202–3; Philippa Foot, "Nietzsche's Immoralism," *New York Review of Books,* 13 June 1991, 19. The mistaken view of Nietzsche's relation to Callicles is usually attributed to E. R. Dodds in "Socrates, Callicles, and Nietzsche," an appendix to his edition of *Plato's Gorgias* (Oxford: Clarendon Press, 1959). This is actually unfair, since Dodds's treatment is much better than that. For example, Dodds only remarks in passing on a possible affinity between Nietzsche and Calliclean hedonism (390); the bulk of the discussion focuses, instead, on the very affinities I emphasize in the text (Dodds 389–90). Dodds even concludes by observing – again quite rightly – that, "Callicles ... would certainly not have understood [Nietzschean] concepts like 'sublimation' and 'self-transcendence," while Nietzsche would have rejected with contempt the crude hedonism" of Callicles (*Gorgias* 494a) (Dodds, 391).

A much better example of the crude misreading of Nietzsche's relation to Callicles is found in Guthrie, *Sophists.* Guthrie depicts Callicles as holding that "the strong man should live to the utmost of his powers and give free play to his desires" and then abruptly concludes that Nietzsche "was blood-brother to Callicles" (106, 107). Guthrie's dismissive reference to Nietzsche here is a fine example of how otherwise impeccable scholarly standards collapse in the vicinity of Nietzsche. Here again, though, Dodds strikes the right note when he suggests that what Nietzsche admired was Callicles' "realism," his "saying plainly what others think but do not care to say" (389). This observation suggests that in Guthrie's tripartite division of "Sophistic" themes – upholders of human convention (e.g., Protagoras), realists (e.g., Thucydides), and upholders of nature (e.g., Callicles [not a Sophist], Antiphon) – Nietzsche is, as I have been arguing, closer to the second rather than the third group.

39 See especially my discussion of the "prudence thesis" in "Morality in the Pejorative Sense," 120–21.

40 On how to reconcile these passages with the general deemphasis on the concept of will to power advocated earlier, see my *Nietzsche on Morality,* esp. chapter 5.

41 For discussion and citations, see my "Nietzsche and the Morality Critics," 280–83.

42 "The Path of the Law," *Harvard Law Review* 10 (1897):457–78, is cited hereafter as "Path" with page number. The essay is reprinted in the Appendix to this volume with star paging. For a brief overview of the main themes of the legal-realist movement see my "Legal Realism," in *The Philosophy of Law: An Encyclopedia,* ed. C. B. Gray (New York: Garland, forthcoming).

43 I confess it is not clear to me how this aspect of Holmes's classical realism is to be squared with the concluding pages of "The Path of the Law." Holmes may simply have shared another feature with the later legal realists: a tendency to say inconsistent things.

44 On this issue, see in particular my "Legal Realism," in *A Companion to the Philosophy of Law and Legal Theory,* ed. D. M. Patterson (Oxford: Blackwell, 1996), esp. 276–78 (cited hereafter as "Legal Realism").

45 Jerome Frank, "Are Judges Human? Part I," *University of Pennsylvania Law Review* 80 (1931):31. (Cited hereafter parenthetically in the text by page number.)

46 For the descriptive theory of the "Sociological Wing" of realism, see my "Legal Realism," 272–75. For a more detailed discussion – one consistent with the quietism I emphasize

here – see James J. White, "The Influence of American Legal Realism on Article 2 of the Uniform Commercial Code," in *Prescriptive Formality and Normative Rationality in Modern Legal Systems,* ed. W. Krawietz et al. (Berlin: Duncker & Humboldt, 1994).
47 Ronald Dworkin, *Law's Empire* (Cambridge, Mass.: Belknap Press, 1986), 265. See the discussion in my "Heidegger and the Theory of Adjudication," *Yale Law Journal* 106 (1996):253, 255–58.
48 See, e.g., John Noonan, "Hercules and the Snail Darter," *New York Times Book Review,* 25 May 1986, 12. See also John Hart Ely, *Democracy and Distrust* (Cambridge, Mass.: Harvard University Press, 1980), 56–60.
49 All of this is, admittedly, defeasible evidence as to the descriptive adequacy of Dworkin's theory.
50 Cf. Karl Llewellyn's discussion of the "steadying factors" in appellate decision making in *The Common Law Tradition* (Boston: Little, Brown, 1960), 19–51.
51 The citation count is as of 20 December 1996. The majority citation comes in *Board of Pardons v. Allen,* 482 U.S. 369, 375 (1987). The other citations, all in dissent, appear in *Hewitt v. Helms,* 459 U.S. 460, 485 (1983); *Delaware v. Van Arsdall,* 475 U.S. 673, 698 (1986); *Young v. Community Nutrition Institute,* 476 U.S. 974, 988 (1986); *Webster v. Reproductive Health Services,* 492 U.S. 490, 541 (1989); *Planned Parenthood v. Casey,* 505 U.S. 833, 914 (1992). The citations to Dworkin in the dissents in *Casey, Webster,* and *Van Arsdall* are all a bit more substantive than in *Allen.* But in none of these cases could the Court, by any stretch of the imagination, be described as embracing Dworkin's theory of adjudication.
52 Dworkin has, rightly it seems to me, criticized the "noninterpretivist" label as question begging. See "The Forum of Principle," reprinted in Ronald Dworkin, *A Matter of Principle* (Cambridge, Mass.: Harvard University Press, 1985). This does not alter the fact that Dworkin's interpretive methodology is quite different from that of John Hart Ely or Antonin Scalia or Henry Monaghan.
53 478 U.S. 186 (1986).
54 I am grateful to Maurice Leiter for a forceful articulation of this point, from which I borrow in the text.
55 Understood this way, the point is also of no help to Dworkin, who clearly expresses but one aspect of an enabling ethos created by others, e.g., Kant and Locke and Rousseau. And perhaps even these latter writers are mere expressions of an "ethos" whose sources are not at all philosophical, as, e.g., Nietzsche argues in the *Genealogy.*
56 By contrast, the "bad man" perspective on law seems rooted in the conjunction of the view that people are essentially self-interested (all they care about are what legal officials will do to them or for them) and Holmes's pragmatism (the view that any theory of law must have practical cash value).
57 This letter continues in a strangely unrealist fashion, with Holmes drawing all sorts of non sequitur moral conclusions from this basic picture of the human condition. For example, "As to the *right* of citizens to support and education I don't see it. It may be a desirable ideal to aim at, but I see no right in my neighbor to share my bread [i.e., to infringe upon my property rights]." *Essential Holmes,* 141.
58 Luban expresses similar notes of caution, though I am less confident that he has really heeded Posner's or his own advice on this score.
59 For further discussion of these themes in Nietzsche, see Leiter, "Paradox of Fatalism."
60 I am indebted to Michael Saks for calling this potential confusion to my attention.

61 Herbert Hovenkamp, "The First Great Law and Economics Movement," *Stanford Law Review* 42 (1990):993, 995.
62 Herbert Hovenkamp, *Enterprise and American Law, 1836–1937* (Cambridge, Mass.: Harvard University Press, 1991), 192.
63 Obviously, Holmes did not have in mind neoclassical economic theory as the "predictive" science of law, nor is he likely to have endorsed all of the scientistic rhetoric favored by Posner and other contemporaries of ours.
64 A. T. Hadley, *Economics: An Account of the Relations between Private Property and Public Welfare* (New York: Knickerbocker Press, 1896), 13.
65 For what remain the seminal discussions of this issue, see the essays by Ronald Dworkin, Jules Coleman, and Duncan Kennedy with Frank Michelman in "Symposium on Efficiency as a Legal Concern," *Hofstra Law Review* 81 (1980):485.
66 See, e.g., Jon D. Hanson and Melissa R. Hart, "Law and Economics," in Patterson, *A Companion to Philosophy of Law and Legal Theory,* 325 (despite the failure of its descriptive program, "law and economics continues to thrive, largely because of the work of legions of normativists, who accept efficiency as the relevant goal of law and employ the tools of law and economics to identify how the law can best serve that goal").
67 See, e.g., Frank Michelman, "Law's Republic," *Yale Law Journal* 97 (1988):1493; Cass Sunstein, "Beyond the Republican Revival," *Yale Law Journal* 97 (1988):1539. For, broadly speaking, "realistic" critiques of civic republicanism, see Richard Epstein, "Modern Republicanism – or the Flight from Substance," *Yale Law Journal* 97 (1988):1633; J. M. Balkin, "Populism and Progressivism as Constitutional Categories," *Yale Law Journal* 104 (1995):1935.
68 Predictive power may be neither a necessary nor sufficient condition for science, but economists generally view it as what makes their discipline "scientific."
69 "Law and Economics: Science or Politics?", *Hofstra Law Review* 8 (1980):905. Horwitz, of course, proved spectacularly wrong in his prediction that "the economic analysis of law has 'peaked out' as the latest fad in legal scholarship" and in his claim "that the scientific pretensions of the economic analysis of the law are rapidly crumbling."
70 Milton Friedman, "The Methodology of Positive Economics," in *Essays in Positive Economics* (Chicago: University of Chicago Press, 1953), 39.
71 See, e.g., Richard Posner, "The Economic Approach to Law," *Texas Law Review* 53 (1975):757, 769. See also PJ, chapter 15.
72 "The Process and Progress of Economics," *Journal of Political Economy* 91 (1983):529, 533.
73 *The Methodology of Economics, or, How Economists Explain,* 2d ed. (Cambridge: Cambridge University Press, 1992), xxv. That most writers think that economics aspires to the status of a natural science is also suggested by Robert Solow's recently felt need to chide his fellow economists for being too "enamored of the physics style." "How Did Economics Get That Way, and What Way Did It Get?", *Daedalus* 126 (1997):39, 53.
74 John Cassidy, "The Decline of Economics," *New Yorker,* 2 December 1996, 50. (Cited hereafter parenthetically by page number in the text.)
75 See David Card and Alan B. Krueger, *Myth and Measurement: The New Economics of the Minimum Wage* (Princeton: Princeton University Press, 1995).
76 William J. Barber, "Reconfigurations in American Academic Economics: A General Practitioner's Perspective," *Daedalus* 126 (1997):87, 96–98.
77 See, e.g., the work of the "Texas empiricists," including Julius Getman and Thomas

Kohler, "The Common Law, Labor Law, and Reality: A Response to Professor Epstein," *Yale Law Journal* 92 (1983):1415; Julius Getman and F. Ray Marshall, "Industrial Relations in Transition: The Paper Industry Example," *Yale Law Journal* 102 (1993):1803; Ronald J. Mann, "Explaining the Pattern of Secured Credit," *Harvard Law Review* 110 (1997):625; Thomas O. McGarity, "The Expanded Debate over the Future of the Regulatory State," *University of Chicago Law Review* 63 (1996):1463; Teresa Sullivan, Elizabeth Warren, and Jay Lawrence Westbrook, *As We Forgive Our Debtors: Bankruptcy and Consumer Credit in America* (Oxford: Oxford University Press, 1989); Elizabeth Warren and Jay Lawrence Westbrook, "Searching for Reorganization Realities," *Washington University Law Quarterly* 72 (1994):1257.

78 See Robert Ellickson, *Order Without Law: How Neighbors Settle Disputes* (Cambridge, Mass.: Harvard University Press, 1991). The Coase theorem says that "if there are no transaction costs to impede bargaining, legal rights will be allocated efficiently through private exchanges, regardless of the underlying rule of law." Robert Cooter, "Against Legal Centrism," *California Law Review* 81 (1993):417, 419, note 6. As Cooter explains:
> Liability rules can be structured in different ways. With cattle, for example, the law can make owners of cows responsible for fencing them in ("closed range") or non-owners responsible for fencing them out ("open range"). Coase reasoned that owners will fence cows in or non-owners will fence them out, whichever is cheaper, regardless of the law . . . Ranchers need only bargain together . . . The law simply tilts bargaining against the party who is legally liable. Thus the law affects who pays for the fence ("*distribution* prediction"), but not its extent or location ("*efficiency* prediction"). (419)

What Ellickson found is that neither prediction was borne out among real ranchers that Ellickson studied in northern California. Cooter notes: "Not only does the Coase Theorem fare poorly in empirical tests, but theorists who have tried to prove it mathematically usually conclude that it is either false or a tautology" (422). None of this, remarkably, has undermined its importance for the "science" of economics!

79 John Dupré, review of Philip Kitcher, *The Advancement of Science, Philosophical Review* 104 (1995):147, 151. See especially Alexander Rosenberg, *Economics – Mathematical Politics or Science of Diminishing Returns?* (Chicago: University of Chicago Press, 1992), 56–86 (cited hereafter as "Rosenberg I"). See also Alan Nelson's review of Rosenberg I in *Ethics* 104 (1994):637. ("Many consider it a truism that economics miserably fails at showing improvements in predictive power; others, mostly economists, consider it certainly and utterly false").

80 Alexander Rosenberg, "If Economics Isn't Science, What Is It?", reprinted in *The Philosophy of Economics: An Anthology*, 2d ed., ed. D. Hausman (Cambridge: Cambridge University Press, 1994), 377 (cited hereafter parenthetically in the text by page number only as "Rosenberg I"). See also, Wassily Leontief, "Input–Output Economics," *Scientific American* 185 (1951):15–21.

81 The so-called Duhem–Quine thesis about the underdetermination of theories by evidence claims that for any test result inconsistent with a theory's prediction, there is neither empirical nor logical reason to give up the theory rather than give up the assumptions that informed the test of the theory. Here is a helpful example (originally suggested to me by Gila Sher). Recall the biblical story of King Solomon, in which Solomon must decide which of two women is the real mother of a particular child. Suppose Solomon hypothesizes that woman A is the real mother of the child, while woman B is not. Solomon tests the hypothesis by proposing that the women each get half of the child. If his hypothesis is correct, then he predicts that A will decline to "split" the child and will let woman B

keep the whole child. But notice that this prediction and test depend on an auxiliary hypothesis that the biblical story never mentions: namely, that a real mother's concern for the well-being of her child is always stronger than her jealousy that another should have her child. Suppose, now, that, contrary to the prediction, A is eager to split the child rather than let B just have the child. Logically, this is compatible with the hypothesis that A is the real mother, if we reject the auxiliary hypothesis. If we remain committed, however, to the auxiliary hypothesis, then experience falsifies the original hypothesis. Yet neither logic nor experience gives us any basis for choosing between these two options.

82 Even Posner concedes that while "economic theory can take credit for some new trading strategies in securities markets, some new methods of pricing, and some new public policies, such as the deregulation of transportation and banking — these interventions are less dramatic, and more ambiguous in their results and interpretations, than the interventions of natural science in such areas as weaponry and medicine" (PJ, 365). For some related criticisms of Posner's version of economic analysis, see David Luban, "The Posner Variations (Twenty-Seven Variations on a Theme by Holmes)," *Stanford Law Review* 48 (1996):1001, 1020–25.

83 The classic statements are T. W. Hutchison, *The Significance and Basic Postulates of Economic Theory* (London: Macmillan, 1938), and Milton Friedman, "The Methodology of Positive Economics," reprinted in Hausman, *Philosophy of Economics*. Recognizing that economists, in fact, preserve their theories in the face of falsifying data all of the time, some writers have suggested that the philosophy of science at the core of economics is not Popperian falsificationism. See, e.g., E. Roy Weintraub, *General Equilibrium Analysis: Studies in Appraisal* (Cambridge: Cambridge University Press, 1985); Daniel Hausman, *The Inexact and Separate Science of Economics* (Cambridge: Cambridge University Press, 1992). For criticism of attempts, like Weintraub's, to characterize equilibrium analysis in economics as the "core" of a Lakatosian research programme, see Kevin Hoover, "Scientific Research Programme or Tribe? A Joint Appraisal of Lakatos and the New Classical Macroeconomics," in *Applying Economic Theories: Studies in the Methodology of Research Programmes,* ed. M. Blaug and N. DeMarchi (Aldershot, UK: Edward Elgar, 1991); Deborah A. Redman, *Economics and the Philosophy of Science* (Oxford: Oxford University Press, 1991).

84 Personal communication, 22 July 1996.

85 See generally, Rosenberg I.

86 This is not simply a peculiarity of Posner's examples. Many of the predictive claims put forward in the economics literature traffic in, at best, the generic and, at worst, the banal or mundane. Thus, to take just one example, a group of lawyers and economists conducted experiments to establish the proposition that "When people estimate quantities that are relevant to their own self-image ... their estimates tend to be biased in a self-serving fashion." George Loewenstein et al., "Self-Serving Assessments of Fairness and Pretrial Bargaining," *Journal of Legal Studies* 22 (1993):135, 138. Contrary, then, to the influential Priest–Klein model that it is imperfect information that leads parties to go to trial, the authors argue that "predictions of the value of the claim and judgments of what settlement would be fair are both biased in a self-serving manner" (139), and that it is this that prevents settlements and leads to (inefficient) trials. (Notice that these economists had to conduct experiments to establish the obvious, because other economic theories failed to recognize it!) For other examples, see Robert E. Thomas, "The Trial Selection Hypothesis without the 50 Percent Rule: Some Experimental Evidence," *Journal of Legal Studies* 24

(1995):209 (showing that "the most significant determinants of dispute disposition" are "the two sides' estimates [as to fault] as well as the closeness of the dispute"); R. Beck et al., "Rent Extraction through Political Extortion: An Empirical Examination," *Journal of Legal Studies* 21 (1992):217 (showing, among other things, that political threats against particular firms "will decrease the firm's stock price" [218]).

87 One worries here that the *ceteris paribus* clause may swallow the law. Crime, for example, often seems more strongly correlated with economic conditions (e.g., recessions), than with severity of punishment.

88 David Throsby, reviewing Gary Becker's *Accounting for Tastes, New York Times Book Review,* 24 January 1997, 31. Surely it is worrisome, too, that Posner's short list of putative predictive successes should contain not only the generic and the banal, but also the false, empty, and (at best) controversial. It is at least empty, and perhaps false, for example, that dirty or dangerous jobs pay more than clean or safe ones. One need only think, for example, of the garbageman, the maid, or the coal miner, versus the bond trader, the law professor, or the CEO. (The *ceteris paribus* clause here must, one suspects, swallow the "law.") That deregulation yields lower prices will come as a surprise to consumers of retail banking, telephone, or cable television services. And while Marx would no doubt agree with Posner that communist societies are "less productive" than capitalist, the point is not obvious on the most frequently adduced evidence, namely the twentieth century. Prior to World War II, for example, the USSR was more productive than the capitalist West, in part because the Soviet Union withstood the worldwide Great Depression that felled the capitalist economies in the 1930s. See, e.g., Eric Hobsbawm, *The Age of Extremes: A History of the World, 1914–1991* (New York: Vintage, 1994), 48, 377. In the decades after World War II, the only fair thing to say is that we are comparing apples and oranges – a society which lost tens of millions of people and much of its infrastructure to war, while still maintaining commitments to, e.g., full employment and universal medical care, was "less productive" than a country (i.e., the United States) laboring under none of these burdens. The "apples and oranges" problem holds even for a comparison of East and West Germany. East Germany provided far more social services than the West, at the same time that it did not enjoy the benefit of the Marshall Plan's economic "jump-start." That West Germany was more "productive," under these conditions, is not surprising.

89 See, e.g., Allan Gibbard and Hal Varian, "Economic Models," *Journal of Philosophy* 75 (1978):664.

90 Yet most scientists share the view that, as the Nobel laureate in physics Steven Weinberg puts it, "[W]hat a successful scientific explanation would have to accomplish . . . [is] the *quantitative* understanding of phenomena" (*Dreams of a Final Theory* [New York: Pantheon, 1992], 7). "[T]he capacity for quantitative prediction" is so essential to science that Weinberg says he views it as his "most important task [in teaching undergraduates] . . . to give the students a taste of the power of being able to calculate in detail what happens under various circumstances in various physical systems" (7, 8).

91 In some cases, of course, this level of predictive success may be quite adequate for economics to discharge its normative role of helping us shape legal rules.

92 See Hausman, *Inexact and Separate Science,* 139–42.

93 Even Posner notes the obstacles presented by "the large, sometimes indefinite number of omitted independent variables that may be correlated with the independent variables the researcher is trying to test for" (PJ, 346–65).

94 See, e.g., Nancy Cartwright, *How the Laws of Physics Lie* (Oxford: Clarendon Press,

1983). Even the fundamental laws of Newtonian mechanics involve *ceteris paribus* conditions. See Richard Montague, "Determinism," in *Formal Philosophy: Selected Papers of Richard Montague,* ed. R. H. Thomason (New Haven: Yale University Press, 1994). (I am grateful to Robert C. Koons for guidance on this subject.)

95 Another quite astonishing example of this problem is the theory of rational choice, on which modern economics rests. According to this theory, the preferences of agents are consistent and (usually) transitive. Yet the phenomenon of "preference reversal" has been well established by empirical psychologists, thus undermining the core of rational-choice theory. See Hausman, *Inexact and Separate Science,* 227–41.

96 See, e.g., the three-volume series edited by Daniel Osherson, *An Invitation to Cognitive Science,* 2d ed. (Cambridge, Mass.: MIT, 1995) (with volumes on language, visual cognition, and thinking). The second edition contains valuable empirical case studies.

97 Ibid., 279–80.

98 This bald assertion will have to suffice for my purposes here, as a discussion of Becker's work would take me too far afield. For relevant critical discussion of Becker in particular, and the wide-ranging application of rational-choice theory that he pioneered, see Jon Elster, *Ulysses and the Sirens: Studies in Rationality and Irrationality* (Cambridge: Cambridge University Press, 1979), sections I.4 and III.7; Jon Elster, "Some Unresolved Problems in the Theory of Rational Choice," *Acta Sociologica* 36 (1993):179, 184–89; Donald P. Green and Ian Shapiro, *Pathologies of Rational Choice Theory: A Critique of Applications in Political Science* (New Haven: Yale University Press, 1994), 186–87.

99 Hausman, *Inexact and Separate Science,* 280.

100 Less controversially, Holmes's assumption here is that an objective theory of well-being is false and a subjective theory is true. A subjective theory of well-being fixes an agent's well-being, at some level, by reference to desire satisfaction (real or hypothetical); thus, the popular full-information accounts of well-being are subjective accounts (what is good for a person is what the person would desire under conditions of full information). By contrast, objective theories of well-being fix a person's interests without reference to desires, real or imagined. Hegel and Marx, of course, both held objective theories of well-being, as did Aristotle and other thinkers in antiquity.

101 I can imagine counterarguments, but the point is that they are nowhere in Holmes's remarks.

102 I am indebted to Steven J. Burton and Jody Kraus here.

103 A point that some economists, especially neo-institutionalists, have noted. See, e.g., Herbert Simon, "Rationality in Psychology and Economics," in *Rational Choice: The Contrast between Economics and Psychology,* ed. R. M. Hogarth and M. W. Reder (Chicago: University of Chicago Press, 1987), esp. 33–40; Oliver E. Williamson, *The Economic Institutions of Capitalism* (New York: Free Press, 1985), esp. 45. (I am grateful to Neil Netanel for guidance on this subject.)

104 See my "Rethinking Legal Realism" and my "Naturalism and Naturalized Jurisprudence."

105 By a "foundational account," I mean one that tries to demonstrate the uniquely correct outcome for some or all legal controversies.

106 See Edward Wolff, *Top Heavy: A Study of the Increasing Inequality of Wealth in America* (New York: Twentieth Century Fund, 1995). The facile appeal to alleged "collective-action" problems is beside the point here. The history of the world is the history of collective actions; the "problem" arises only in accounting for the fact of collective actions

within the a priori constraints placed by rational-choice theory on explanations of human behavior. For a penetrating critique, see Robert Paul Wolff, "Methodological Individualism and Marx: Some Remarks on Jon Elster, Game Theory, and Other Things," *Canadian Journal of Philosophy* 20 (1990):469.
107 See, e.g., the data and analysis in Edward S. Herman and Noam Chomsky, *Manufacturing Consent: The Political Economy of the Mass Media* (New York: Pantheon, 1988). The situation has grown worse since then, as indicated in the special issue of *The Nation* devoted to the media (vol. 262, no. 22, 3 June 1996).
108 The quotation, of course, is from *The Communist Manifesto*. Marx's famous observation is usefully compared with that of former congressman Dan Hamburg (D-California): "The real government of our country is economic, dominated by large corporations that charter the state to do their bidding." "Inside the Money Chase," *Nation* (5 May 1997), 25.
109 See my "Rethinking Legal Realism" and my "Legal Realism."
110 Jerome Frank, *Law and the Modern Mind* (New York: Brentano, 1930), 111.
111 I try to make this case in an essay I am now writing on the jurisprudence of Justice Antonin Scalia.
112 This is Jeffrie Murphy's apt summary of one of Marx's central insights. See Jeffrie Murphy, "Marxism and Retribution," reprinted in *Marx, Justice, and History,* ed. M. Cohen et al. (Princeton: Princeton University Press, 1980), 173.

14

Comment on Brian Leiter's "Holmes, Economics, and Classical Realism"

JODY S. KRAUS

In "Holmes, Economics, and Classical Realism" (Chapter 13 of this volume), Brian Leiter[1] takes recent comparisons between Holmes and Nietzsche as an occasion to excavate the remarkably well-preserved remains of a view he calls *classical realism*. That view asserts three formal theses: (1) the *naturalistic thesis*, which claims that there exist certain "incorrigible . . . facts about human beings and human nature"; (2) the *quietistic thesis*, which holds that "any normative theorizing which fails to respect the limits imposed by these facts about human nature is idle and pointless; it is better to 'keep quiet' about normative matters than to theorize in ways that make no difference to practice"; and (3) the *realistic thesis*, which claims that the "aim of theory construction is to depict the incorrigible facts as they really are, without illusion or romance; theory aims for descriptive and explanatory accuracy rather than normative edification or rationalization." The substantive theory of classical realism is that (1) human beings are essentially selfish, and (2) that human beings are consistently irrational, "simple-minded, easily fooled, and susceptible to being controlled and used." A good deal of Leiter's essay is devoted to vindicating the claim that classical realism is not a figment of his imagination, but instead enjoys a rather distinguished intellectual history, traceable in its general form from Thucydides through Nietzsche and Marx and finding its jurisprudential expression in the work of Jerome Frank, Karl Llewellyn, and, not incidentally, Oliver Wendell Holmes, Jr. Leiter's analysis is designed for the Holmes and Nietzsche scholar, carefully marshaling the resources necessary to uncover the essence of classical realism in the work of both figures and forcefully arguing against the alternative reading of their common ground offered by Richard Posner and David Luban.

I trust that Holmes and Nietzsche scholars will judge for themselves the merits of Leiter's claim that classical realism finds a home in Nietzsche and Holmes. For those readers who are not Nietzsche scholars, I feel your pain. I, like you, am no Nietzsche scholar. Although I read his discussion with great interest and care, I am prepared to stipulate to Leiter's claim, for purposes of this comment. I therefore spare you my thoughts on whether Nietzsche's notebook material, unpublished at the time of his mental collapse but subsequently published under the title *The Will to Power* (due to the efforts of third parties who acted despite Nietzsche's evident intent to destroy the material), should be disqualified as a bona fide source for interpreting the role of the will to power in Nietzsche's mature views. Instead, I confine my remarks to themes of section II of Leiter's essay. In section II, Leiter takes seriously Holmes's claim that "the man of the future is . . . the master of economics."[2] Since Leiter argues that Holmes is a classical realist, the question Leiter asks here is whether "economics [is] an adequate torchbearer for classical realism in law." Leiter thinks not.

The nub of Leiter's argument is that classical realism is wedded both to the *naturalistic thesis,* which claims that there exist "incorrigible facts . . . about human beings and human nature," and to the *realistic thesis,* which requires theories to aim "for descriptive and explanatory accuracy rather than normative edification or rationalization." According to Leiter, in order to bear the torch for classical realism, economics would have to provide a descriptively and explanatorily accurate account of the incorrigible facts about human beings and human nature. Leiter's critique of this claim is plain: in his view, economics does not pass the laugh-aloud test. Leiter relies on economists, social scientists, and philosophers to support his claim that economics is a "pseudo science" – "better, perhaps, than astrology, but not much more predictively successful than commonsense psychology" – one that "parlays a set of implausible and utterly unrealistic assumptions into tidy, mathematically expressible theories that have little or no connection to reality" (section II). Leiter's claim is not merely that economics does not accurately describe or explain all incorrigible facts about human beings and human nature. Economics, of course, makes no such pretensions. Leiter's claim is that economics does not accurately describe or explain *economic* phenomena. It either fails to yield definite predictions, or its predictions are inaccurate. Beyond this, Leiter's claim is that economic theory's psychological assumptions about human motivation are demonstrably false: people are neither rational nor utility maximizers.

I have three objections to Leiter's argument.[3] The first is that he misunderstands the requirements of classical realism's realistic thesis, as he himself defines it. The critique of economics he rehearses is supposed to demonstrate why economics, *pace* Holmes, is unsuitable for classical realism. But a demonstration of the predictive shortcomings of economics, compared to other sciences, would suffice to disqualify it for classical realism only if classical realism required predictive accuracy. But classical realism, and in particular, the realistic thesis Leiter ascribes to it, requires no such thing. To use Leiter's own word, classical realism's realistic thesis only *aims* for a theory that provides a descriptively and explanatorily accurate account of the incorrigible facts about human beings and human nature. It does not require of theories that they in fact *attain* descriptive and explanatory accuracy. No empirical theory provides an absolutely accurate account of the facts, incorrigible or not, about human beings and human nature – not even the so-called hard sciences, such as physics or chemistry. All empirical theories have their descriptive and predictive limits, and few would argue that even the predictively most impressive theories are completely and entirely accurate. Our empirical theories are our best currently available theories. So if classical realism must reject economics, as Leiter argues, then it is not simply because economics is inaccurate, or less accurate than other currently available empirical theories of noneconomic phenomena. The suitability of economics for classical realism does not turn on whether economics – in spite of Leiter, and no doubt over his dead body – should be accorded the dignity and respect of a "real science." Instead, it turns on whether economics is the best currently available theory of economic phenomena, irrespective of whether it has earned the rank of "real" or "hard" science.[4]

Leiter's claim, then, must be that economics is not the best available theory for describing, explaining, and predicting economic phenomena. He can show that only by comparing economics to a competitor theory. Leiter comes closest to providing such an argument when he responds to Posner's list of examples of the predictive success of economics – for example, the prediction that a price ceiling will cause queues, black markets, and quality problems, or that deregulation will result in lower prices and more product variety (section II). Leiter writes:

Genuinely scientific theories must anticipate the future with a degree of precision and consistency greater than that realized by common sense . . . All of [Posner's predictions are] the stuff of common sense, but no one would think of characterizing the common-sense psychology that undergirds such predictions as the core of a scientific research program. The question is, Does economics really do any better, in predictive precision and reliability? (section II)

Here, in the midst of the recurring red-herring argument against the elevation of economics to the status of a science, Leiter locates for the first time at least the right kind of question: is economic theory better than alternative theories of the same phenomena? But then he answers it with the wrong kind of answer. Instead of offering up a superior competitor theory, he merely denies the claim that economics is superior to the nonscientific, pseudo theory of folk psychology. The implicit concession is that there is no "real" scientific competitor to economics. Again, Leiter's only complaint reduces to the claim that, to paraphrase Lloyd Benson, Leiter knows hard science; hard science is a good friend of his; Economics is no hard science. It may not be hard, but it is all we have. More to the point, it is all classical realism has. Leiter insists that we call it by the name it deserves: common sense. This is fine, but the question of whether economics adds value over and above folk psychology is of no moment to classical realism. Classical realism aims for the best theory it can find to describe, explain, and predict economic phenomena. Whether we call it "real science" or "dressed-up folk psychology masquerading as real science," economics is the only game in town.

Perhaps, in Leiter's view, economics performs so miserably that any classical realist worth his salt would sooner have no theory at all. But given its aim of finding a descriptively accurate theory, classical realism is unable, under its own mandate, to choose agnosticism over the best available theory. Thus, when Leiter argues that genuine classical realists want the best possible descriptive and explanatory theory, and that economics, as a failed empirical research program, cannot be that theory, his conclusion is a non sequitur. If economics is the best possible descriptive, explanatory, and predictive theory available, classical realists should want it.

Nor should the fact that economics contains demonstrably false postulates about human motivation, by itself, dissuade the classical realist from embracing economics. In most empirical theories, increased predictive power can be purchased only by trading off descriptive accuracy. Empirical theories intentionally forgo descriptive accuracy in order to render empirical problems tractable. Tractability requires simplification that entails inaccuracy, at least in basic assumptions. The success of such theories depends on whether use of these intentionally simplifying assumptions reveals more than it obscures.

Finally, the predictive failures of economics do not, by themselves, justify the wholesale rejection of economics by anyone, including classical realists. Economics lacks the kind of predictive precision that hard science requires because of the complexity of the phenomena it seeks to describe, explain, and predict. Meteorology, for example, arguably lacks the predictive success necessary to qualify it as one of Leiter's hard sciences, even though it relies on concededly hard sciences within its descriptions, explanations, and predictions. The problem is not the integrity of the kind of accounts it seeks to provide, but the complexity of the real-world macrophenomena it seeks to explain. The predictive success of both meteorology and economics requires both an increase in the theories' complexity and an increase in our ability to detect and measure the causal factors the theories identify. The simplifying assumptions are, over time, tailored and revised to increase predictive power. We increase the predictive success of meteorology and economics by building on them, not by abandoning them. The growing research in experimental economics and behavioral decision theory, for example, reflects the efforts of theoretical economists to improve the descriptive, explanatory, and predictive power of economics. It is possible that economics is building the internal credentials of a hard science. In spite of its past performance, once economic theory and its measurement techniques become more sophisticated, it may well begin to achieve the corresponding predictive success of a hard science.

My second objection to Leiter's claim is that the economic analysis of law, if not economics generally, has, in fact, enjoyed at least limited descriptive, explanatory, and predictive success. I have so far followed Leiter in focusing on the question of whether classical realism should embrace economics. But the only question he needs to answer is the narrower one of whether economics is an adequate torchbearer for classical realism in law. Economic theory may explain, describe, and predict legal phenomena better than it does economic phenomena generally. And just as classical realism cannot reject economics merely because it fails to compare in predictive power to other empirical theories, it certainly cannot reject economics as a theory of law on that same ground. Again, classical realists must ask whether economics fares better or worse than other, currently available theories of law. And again, the mere fact that law-and-economics has demonstrably false motivational assumptions need not prevent the classical realist from accepting it. These assumptions may be justified abstractions that reveal more than they obscure. The abiding question is whether the economic analysis of law increases our understanding of legal phenomena even though it postulates simplifying, and therefore inaccurate, assumptions. I would argue that it does – at least within certain areas of the law.

The assumption of rational profit maximization, for example, has significant power in explaining and predicting the outcome in corporate and commercial-law cases. By engaging in an analysis of, for example, what contracting practices are likely to be efficient, and what legal decision would facilitate these practices at least cost, commercial-law scholars have successfully explained past decisions and predicted future cases. To be sure, classical realists may view explanations of past decisions simply as *ex post* rationalizations, and the evidence of actual predictive success (rather than *ex post* accounts) is largely anecdotal. But the challenge from law-and-economics is to find a theory that accounts for the vast majority of the outcomes in corporate and commercial law cases with the same consistency that this theory does. In my judgment, there are no close contenders. Economics provides an invaluable tool for organizing statutory and case law materials in commercial law and for predicting the likely outcome of cases in this area. The same can be said of much, though of course not all, tort law. Of course, the farther law-and-economics strays from the province of contract, commercial, and corporate law, the less plausible its simplifying assumptions, and the less accurate its explanations, descriptions, and predictions (notwithstanding Judge Posner's penchant for extrapolating law-and-economics far beyond self-evidently commercial contexts). Nonetheless, we should not lose sight of the fact that economic analysis enjoys considerable success in the context of corporate and commercial law.

This brings me to my final objection to Leiter's claim. The case for making economics the torchbearer for classical realism in the law rests not only on its descriptive power, but on its normative power as well. Leiter seems to believe that classical realists could not endorse any normative theory, let alone a normative version of the economic analysis of law. But classical realism does not logically proscribe the use of normative theory. Indeed, the realistic thesis, which describes theory as aiming for descriptive and explanatory adequacy rather than for normative edification or rationalization, simply does not follow from the quietistic thesis. The quietistic thesis requires only that "any normative theorizing which fails to respect the limits imposed by . . . facts about human nature is idle and pointless" (section I). Far from proscribing normative theorizing, the quietistic thesis simply constrains it. The quietistic thesis asserts no more than the moral maxim of "ought" implies "can." According to the quietistic thesis, then, the realistic thesis need not be true: theory can aim for normative edification, as long as its reach does not exceed our grasp.

Normative economic theory, then, would be congenial to classical realism in law if economic analysis, as a normative theory, does not require more of humans than they are capable of delivering. The substantive classical realism Leiter ascribes to Holmes posits that human beings are primarily selfish and regularly irrational (section I). Must a Holmesian classical realist reject the normative aspirations of the economic analysis of law because it violates the quietistic thesis? Surely not. As long as people are capable of acting rationally, even if not consistently, a normative theory that requires or presupposes that individuals act rationally is not futile and thus pointless. If we look again to corporate and commercial law, where the rationality and profit-maximizing assumptions of economics are most at home, the normative force of economic analysis is considerable. Nothing, therefore, would prevent Holmes, the classical realist about law, from embracing economic analysis as a normative theory.[5]

Leiter would have us believe that Holmes's interest in the young economics of his day was a schoolboy crush. Economics did not, in Leiter's view, mature into a suitable bride for classical realism. But given its lack of competition in the empirical sciences, and its descriptive and normative success in at least some areas of the law, classical realism has no choice but to engage economics. And Leiter has given us no reason to object to the marriage.

Notes

1 Cited hereafter parenthetically in the text by section number. The quotations in my first paragraph are from section I.
2 Oliver Wendell Holmes, Jr., "The Path of the Law," *Harvard Law Review* 10 (1897), 469. "The Path" is reprinted in the Appendix to this volume with star paging.
3 In the confines of this brief essay, I cannot debate Leiter's central claim that economics – and thus the field of law-and-economics – is a failed enterprise. But before listening to Leiter's eulogy for law-and-economics, it is worth pausing to inspect his basis for issuing its death certificate: namely, the articles he cites in his note 77. Leiter's reliance on this literature is, to say the least, troubling. It is troubling because it naively assumes both that these critics have properly construed the positions they attack (an assumption many would resist), and that the methodology of the critique it presents meets the standard for "real science" to which Leiter holds economics. The fact that law-and-economics dominates the fields of corporate and commercial law at least ought to signal that these six articles (two

pairs of which are coauthored by the same two authors) have yet to ring the death knell for law-and-economics.
4 Leiter concedes that "economics could still turn out to be, comparatively speaking, the best theory (warts and all!) for a realist interested in law. After all, a quantitatively precise science of human affairs does not seem to be on the horizon from any source . . . So even if Holmes knew what we know today about the limitation of economics, he might still stand by his slogan" (section III).
5 Leiter concedes that "[e]ven if economics is not a science, it may still be adequate for some modest normative purposes (i.e., those that make modest demands on its modest predictive capacities) (section II).

APPENDIX

The Path of the Law

OLIVER WENDELL HOLMES, JR.*

✦457, ✦✦991, ✦✦✦167, ✦✦✦✦391 When we study law we are not studying a mystery but a well known profession. We are studying what we shall want in order to appear before judges, or to advise people in such a way as to keep them out of court. The reason why it is a profession, why people will pay lawyers to argue for them or to advise them, is that in societies like ours the command of the public force is intrusted to the judges in certain cases, and the whole power of the state will be put forth, if necessary, to carry out their judgments and decrees. People want to know under what circumstances and how far they will run the risk of coming against what is so much stronger than themselves, and hence it becomes a business to find out when this danger is to be feared. The object of our study, then, is prediction, the prediction of the incidence of the public force through the instrumentality of the courts.

The means of the study are a body of reports, of treatises, and of statutes, in this country and in England, extending back for six hundred years, and now increasing annually by hundreds. In these ✦✦✦**168** sibylline leaves are gathered the scattered prophecies of the past upon the cases in which the axe will fall. These are what properly have been called the oracles of the law. Far the most important and pretty nearly the whole meaning of every new effort of legal thought is to make these prophecies more precise, and to ✦**458** generalize them into a thoroughly connected system. The process is one, from a lawyer's statement of a case, eliminating as it does all the dramatic elements with which his client's story has clothed it, and retaining only the facts of legal import, up to the final analyses and abstract universals of theoretic jurisprudence. The reason

---

* An Address delivered by Mr. Justice Holmes, of the Supreme Judicial Court of Massachusetts, at the dedication of the new hall of the Boston University School of Law, on January 8, 1897. Copyrighted by O. W. Holmes, 1897. [The star paging refers to previous publications of this speech: ✦*Harvard Law Review* 10 (1897) 457–78; ✦✦*Harvard Law Review* 110 (1997) 991–1009; ✦✦✦ Oliver Wendell Holmes, Jr., *Collected Legal Papers* (New York: Harcourt Brace & Howe, 1920), 167–202; ✦✦✦✦ *The Collected Works of Justice Holmes,* ed. Sheldon M. Novick (Chicago: University of Chicago Press, 1995–) vol. 3, 391–406.]

why a lawyer does not mention that his client wore a white hat when he made a contract, while Mrs. Quickly would be sure to dwell upon it along with the parcel gilt goblet and the sea-coal fire, is that he foresees that the public force will act in the same way whatever his client had upon his head. It is to make the prophecies easier to be remembered and to be understood that the teachings of the decisions of the past are put into general propositions and gathered into textbooks, or that statutes are passed in a general form. The primary rights and duties with which jurisprudence busies itself again are nothing but prophecies. One of the many evil effects of the confusion between legal and moral ideas, about which I shall have ✦✦992 something to say in a moment, is that theory is apt to get the cart before the horse, and to consider the right or the duty as something existing apart from and independent of the consequences ✦✦✦169 of its breach, to which certain sanctions are added afterward. But, as I shall try to show, a legal duty so called is nothing but a prediction that if a man does or omits certain things he will be made to suffer in this or that way by judgment of the court; – and so of a legal right.

The number of our predictions when generalized and reduced to a system is not unmanageably large. They present themselves as a finite body of dogma which may be mastered within a reasonable time. It is a great mistake to be frightened by the ✦✦✦✦392 ever increasing number of reports. The reports of a given jurisdiction in the course of a generation take up pretty much the whole body of the law, and restate it from the present point of view. We could reconstruct the corpus from them if all that went before were burned. The use of the earlier reports is mainly historical, a use about which I shall have something to say before I have finished.

I wish, if I can, to lay down some first principles for the study of this body of dogma or systematized prediction which we call the law, for men who want to use it as the instrument of their business to enable them to prophesy in their turn, and, as bearing upon the study, I wish to point out an ideal which as yet our law has not attained.

✦459 The first thing for a business-like understanding of the matter is to understand its limits, and therefore I think it desirable at once to point out and dispel a confusion between morality and law, which sometimes rises to the height of conscious theory, ✦✦✦170 and more often and indeed constantly is making trouble in detail without reaching the point of consciousness. You can see very plainly that a bad man has as much reason as a good one for wishing to avoid an encounter with the public force, and therefore you can see the practical importance of the distinction between morality and law. A man who cares nothing for an ethical rule which is believed and practised by his neighbors is likely nevertheless to care a good deal to avoid being made to pay money, and will want to keep out of jail if he can.

I take it for granted that no hearer of mine will misinterpret what I have to say as the language of cynicism. The law is the witness and external deposit of our moral life. Its history is the history of the moral development of the race. The practice of it, in spite of popular jests, tends to make good citizens and good men. When I emphasize the difference between law and morals I do so with reference to a single end, that of learning and understanding the law. For that purpose you must definitely master its specific marks, and it is for that that I ask you for the moment to imagine yourselves indifferent to other and greater things.

I do not say that there is not a wider point of view from which the distinction between law and morals becomes of secondary or no importance, as all mathematical distinctions vanish in presence of the infinite. But I do say that that distinction is of the first importance for the object which we are here to consider, – a right study and mastery of the law as a business with well understood limits, a body of dogma enclosed within definite lines. I have just shown the practical reason for saying so. If you want to know the law and nothing else, you must look at it as a bad man, who cares only for the material consequences which such knowledge enables him to predict, not as a good one, who finds his reasons for conduct, whether inside the law or outside of it, in the vaguer sanctions of conscience. The theoretical importance of the distinction is no less, if you would reason on your subject aright. The law is full of phraseology drawn from morals, and by the mere force of language continually invites us to pass from one domain to the other without perceiving it, as we are sure to do unless we have the boundary constantly before our minds. The law talks about rights, and duties, and malice, and intent, and negligence, and so forth, and nothing is easier, or, I may say, more common in legal reasoning, than to take these words in their moral sense, at some stage of the argument, and so to drop into fallacy. For instance, when we speak of the rights of man in a moral sense, we mean to mark the limits of interference with individual freedom which we think are prescribed by conscience, or by our ideal, however reached. Yet it is certain that many laws have been enforced in the past, and it is likely that some are enforced now, which are condemned by the most enlightened opinion of the time, or which at all events pass the limit of interference as many consciences would draw it. Manifestly, therefore, nothing but confusion of thought can result from assuming that the rights of man in a moral sense are equally rights in the sense of the Constitution and the law. No doubt simple and extreme cases can be put of imaginable laws which the statute-making power would not dare to enact, even in the absence of written constitutional prohibitions, because the community would rise in rebellion and fight; and this gives some plausibility to the proposition that the law, if not a part of morality, is limited by it. But this limit of power is not coextensive with any system of morals. For the most part it falls far within the lines of any such system, and in some cases may extend beyond them, for reasons drawn from the habits of a particular people at a particular time. I once heard the late Professor Agassiz say that a German population would rise if you added two cents to the price of a glass of beer. A statute in such a case would be empty words, not because it was wrong, but because it could not be enforced. No one will deny that wrong statutes can be and are enforced, and we should not all agree as to which were the wrong ones.

✣✣**994** The confusion with which I am dealing besets confessedly legal conceptions. Take the fundamental question, What constitutes the law? You will find some text writers telling you that it is something different from what is decided by the courts of Massachusetts or England, that it is a system of reason, that it is a deduction from principles of ethics or admitted axioms or what not, which may or may not coincide with the decisions. But if we ✣✣✣**173** take the view of our friend the bad man we shall find that he does not care two straws for the axioms or deductions, but that ✣**461** he does want to know what the Massachusetts or English courts are likely to do in fact. I am much of his mind. The prophecies of what the courts will do in fact, and nothing more pretentious, are what I mean by the law.

Take again a notion which as popularly understood is the widest conception which the law contains; – the notion of legal duty, to which already I have referred. We fill the word with all the content which we draw from morals. But what does it mean to a bad man? Mainly, and in the first place, a prophecy that if he does certain things he will be subjected to disagreeable consequences by way of imprisonment or compulsory payment of money. But from his point of view, what is the difference between being fined and being taxed a certain sum for doing a certain thing? That his point of view is the test of legal principles is shown by the many discussions which have arisen in the courts on the very question whether a given statutory liability is a penalty or a tax. On the answer to this question depends the decision whether conduct is legally wrong or right, and also whether a man is under compulsion or free. Leaving the criminal law on one side, what is the difference between the liability under the mill acts or statutes authorizing a taking by eminent domain and the liability for what we call a wrongful conversion of property where restoration is out of the question. In both ✣✣✣**174** cases the party taking another man's property has to pay its fair value as assessed by a jury, and no more. What significance is there in calling one taking right and another wrong from the point of view of the law? ✣✣✣✣**394** It does not matter, so far as the given consequence, the compulsory payment, is concerned, whether the act to which it is attached is described in terms of praise or in terms of blame, or whether the law purports to prohibit it or to allow it. If it matters at all, still speaking from the bad man's point of view, it must be because in one case and not in the other some further disadvantages, or at least some further consequences, are attached to the act by the law. The only other disadvantages thus attached to it which I ever have been able to think of are to be found in two somewhat insignificant legal doctrines, both of which might be abolished without much disturbance. One is, that a contract to do a prohibited act is unlawful, and the other, that, if one of two or more joint wrongdoers has to pay all the damages, he cannot recover contribution from his ✦✦995 fellows. And that I believe is all. You see ✦462 how the vague circumference of the notion of duty shrinks and at the same time grows more precise when we wash it with cynical acid and expel everything except the object of our study, the operations of the law.

Nowhere is the confusion between legal and moral ideas more manifest than in the law of contract. Among other things, here again the so called primary rights and duties are invested with a mystic significance beyond what can be assigned and explained. ✦✦✦175 The duty to keep a contract at common law means a prediction that you must pay damages if you do not keep it, – and nothing else. If you commit a tort, you are liable to pay a compensatory sum. If you commit a contract, you are liable to pay a compensatory sum unless the promised event comes to pass, and that is all the difference. But such a mode of looking at the matter stinks in the nostrils of those who think it advantageous to get as much ethics into the law as they can. It was good enough for Lord Coke, however, and here, as in many other cases, I am content to abide with him. In *Bromage v. Genning*,[1] a prohibition was sought in the King's Bench against a suit in the marches of Wales for the specific performance of a covenant to grant a lease, and Coke said that it would subvert the intention of the covenantor, since he intends it to be at his election either to lose the damages or to make the lease. Sergeant Harris for the plaintiff confessed that he moved the matter against his conscience, and a prohibition was granted. This goes further than we should go now, but it shows what I venture to say has been the common law point of view from the beginning, although Mr. Harriman, in his very able little book upon Contracts has been misled, as I humbly think, to a different conclusion.

I have spoken only of the common law, because there are some cases in which a logical justification can be found for speaking of civil liabilities as imposing duties in an intelligible sense. These are ✦✦✦176 the relatively few in which equity will grant an injunction, and will enforce it by putting the defendant in prison or otherwise punishing him unless he complies with the order of the court. But I hardly think it advisable to shape general theory from the exception, and I think it would be better to cease troubling ourselves about primary rights and sanctions altogether, than to ✦463 describe our prophecies concerning the liabilities commonly imposed by the law in those inappropriate terms.

✦✦✦✦395 I mentioned, as other examples of the use by the law of words drawn from morals, malice, intent, and negligence. It is enough to take malice as it is used in the law of civil liability for wrongs, – what we lawyers call the law of torts, – to show you that it means something different in law from what it means in morals, and also to ✦✦996 show how the difference has been obscured by giving to principles which have little or nothing to do with each other

---

[1] 1 Roll. Rep. 368.

the same name. Three hundred years ago a parson preached a sermon and told a story out of Fox's Book of Martyrs of a man who had assisted at the torture of one of the saints, and afterward died, suffering compensatory inward torment. It happened that Fox was wrong. The man was alive and chanced to hear the sermon, and thereupon he sued the parson. Chief Justice Wray instructed the jury that the defendant was not liable, because the story was told innocently, without malice. He took malice in the moral sense, as importing a malevolent motive. But nowadays no one doubts that a man may be liable, without any malevolent motive at all, for false statements manifestly calculated to inflict temporal damage. In stating the case in pleading, we still should call the defendant's conduct malicious; but, in my opinion at least, the word means nothing about motives, or even about the defendant's attitude toward the future, but only signifies that the tendency of his conduct under the known circumstances was very plainly to cause the plaintiff temporal harm.[1]

In the law of contract the use of moral phraseology has led to equal confusion, as I have shown in part already, but only in part. Morals deal with the actual internal state of the individual's mind, what he actually intends. From the time of the Romans down to now, this mode of dealing has affected the language of the law as to contract, and the language used has reacted upon the thought. We talk about a contract as a meeting of the minds of the parties, and thence it is inferred in various cases that there is no contract because their minds have not met; that is, because they have intended different things or because one party has not known of the assent of the other. Yet nothing is more certain than that parties may be bound by a contract to things which neither of them intended, and when one does not know of the other's assent. Suppose a contract is executed in due form and in writing to deliver a lecture, mentioning no time. One of the parties thinks that the promise will be construed to mean at once, within a week. The other thinks that it means when he is ready. The court says that it means within a reasonable time. The parties are bound by the contract as it is interpreted by the court, yet neither of them meant what the court declares that they have said. In my opinion no one will understand the true theory of contract or be able even to discuss some fundamental questions intelligently until he has understood that all contracts are formal, that the making of a contract depends not on the agreement of two minds in one intention, but on the agreement of two sets of external signs, – not on the parties' having meant the same thing but on their having said the same thing. Furthermore, as the signs may be addressed to one sense or another, – to sight or to hearing, – on the nature of the sign will depend the moment when the contract is made. If the sign is tangible, for instance, a letter, the contract is made when the letter of acceptance is delivered. If it is necessary that the minds of the parties meet, there will be no contract until the acceptance can be read, – none,

---

[1] See *Hanson v. Globe Newspaper Co.,* 159 Mass. 293, 302.

for example, if the acceptance be snatched from the hand of the offerer by a third person.

This is not the time to work out a theory in detail, or to answer many obvious doubts and questions which are suggested by these general views. I know of none which are not easy to answer, but what I am trying to do now is only by a series of hints to throw some light on the narrow path of legal doctrine, and upon two pitfalls which, as it seems to me, lie perilously near to it. Of the first of these ✦✦✦**179** I have said enough. I hope that my illustrations have shown the danger, both to speculation and to practice, of confounding morality with law, and the trap which legal language lays for us on that side of our way. For my own part, I often doubt whether it would not be a gain if every word of moral significance could be banished from the law altogether, and other words adopted which should convey legal ideas uncolored by anything outside the law. We should lose the fossil records of a good deal of history and the majesty got from ethical associations, but by ridding ourselves of an unnecessary confusion we should gain very much in the clearness of our thought.

So much for the limits of the law. The next thing which I wish to consider is what are the forces which determine its content ✦**465** and its growth. You may assume, with Hobbes and Bentham and Austin, that all law emanates from the sovereign, even when the first human beings to enunciate it are the judges, or you may think that law is the voice of the Zeitgeist, or what you like. It is all one to my present purpose. Even if every decision required the sanction of an emperor with despotic power and a whimsical turn of mind, we should be interested none the less, still with a view to prediction, in discovering some order, some rational explanation, and some principle of growth for the rules which he laid down. In every system there are such explanations and principles to be found. It is with regard to them that a second fallacy comes in, which I think it important to expose.

✦✦✦**180** The fallacy to which I refer is the notion that the only force at work in the development of the law is logic. In the broadest sense, indeed, that notion would be true. The postulate on which we think about the universe is that there is a fixed quantitative relation between every phenomenon and its antecedents and consequents. If there is such a thing as a phenomenon without these fixed quantitative relations, it is a miracle. It is outside the law of cause and effect, and as such transcends our power of thought, or at least is something to or from which we cannot reason. The condition of our thinking about the universe is that it is capable of being thought about rationally, or, ✦✦**998** in other words, that every part of it is effect and cause in the same sense in which those parts are with which we are most familiar. So in the broadest sense it is true that the law is a logical development, like everything else. The danger of which I speak is not the admission that the principles governing other phenomena also govern the law, but the notion that a given system, ours, for instance, can be worked out like mathematics from some general axioms of conduct. This is the natural error of the schools, but it is not confined to them. I once heard a very eminent judge say that he never let a decision go until he was absolutely sure that it was right. So judicial dissent often is blamed, as if it meant simply that one side or the other were not doing their sums right, and, if they would take more trouble, agreement inevitably would come.

✦✦✦181 ✦✦✦✦397 This mode of thinking is entirely natural. The training of lawyers is a training in logic. The processes of analogy, discrimination, and deduction are those in which they are most at home. The language of judicial decision is mainly the language of logic. ✦466 The logical method and form flatter that longing for certainty and for repose which is in every human mind. But certainty generally is illusion, and repose is not the destiny of man. Behind the logical form lies a judgment as to the relative worth and importance of competing legislative grounds, often an inarticulate and unconscious judgment, it is true, and yet the very root and nerve of the whole proceeding. You can give any conclusion a logical form. You always can imply a condition in a contract. But why do you imply it? It is because of some belief as to the practice of the community or of a class, or because of some opinion as to policy, or, in short, because of some attitude of yours upon a matter not capable of exact quantitative measurement, and therefore not capable of founding exact logical conclusions. Such matters really are battle grounds where the means do not exist for determinations that shall be good for all time, and where the decision can do no more than embody the preference of a given body in a given time and place. We do not realize how large a part of our law is open to reconsideration upon a slight change in the habit of the public mind. No concrete proposition is self-evident, no matter how ready we may be to accept it, not even Mr. Herbert Spencer's. ✦✦✦182 Every man has a right to do what he wills, provided he interferes not with a like right on the part of his neighbors.

Why is a false and injurious statement privileged, if it is made honestly in giving information about a servant? It is because it has been thought more important that information should be given freely, than that a man should be protected from what under other circumstances would be an actionable wrong. Why is a man at liberty to set up a business which he knows will ruin his neighbor? It is because the public good is supposed to be best subserved by free competition. ✦✦999 Obviously such judgments of relative importance may vary in different times and places. Why does a judge instruct a jury that an employer is not liable to an employee for an injury received in the course of his employment unless he is negligent, and why do the jury generally find for the plaintiff if the case is allowed to go to them? It is because the traditional policy of our law is to confine liability to cases where a prudent man might have foreseen the injury, or at least the danger, while the inclination of a very large part of the community is to make certain classes of persons insure the safety of those with whom they deal. Since the last words were written, I have seen the requirement of such insur- ✦467 ance put forth as part of the programme of one of the best known labor organizations. There is a concealed, half conscious battle on the question of legislative policy, and if any one thinks that it can be settled deductively, or once for all, I only ♦♦♦183 can say that I think he is theoretically wrong, and that I am certain that his conclusion will not be accepted in *practice semper ubique et ab omnibus.*

Indeed, I think that even now our theory upon this matter is open to reconsideration, although I am not prepared to say how I should decide if a reconsideration were proposed. Our law of torts comes from the old days of isolated, ungeneralized wrongs, assaults, slanders, and the like, where the damages might be taken to lie where they fell by legal judgment. But the torts with which our courts are kept busy ♦♦♦♦398 to-day are mainly the incidents of certain well known businesses. They are injuries to person or property by railroads, factories, and the like. The liability for them is estimated, and sooner or later goes into the price paid by the public. The public really pays the damages, and the question of liability, if pressed far enough, is really the question how far it is desirable that the public should insure the safety of those whose work it uses. It might be said that in such cases the chance of a jury finding for the defendant is merely a chance, once in a while rather arbitrarily interrupting the regular course of recovery, most likely in the case of an unusually conscientious plaintiff, and therefore better done away with. On the other hand, the economic value even of a life to the community can be estimated, and no recovery, it may be said, ought to go beyond that amount. It is conceivable that some day in certain cases we may find ourselves imitating, ♦♦♦184 on a higher plane, the tariff for life and limb which we see in the Leges Barbarorum.

I think that the judges themselves have failed adequately to recognize their duty of weighing considerations of social advantage. The duty is inevitable, and the result of the often proclaimed judicial aversion to deal with such considerations is simply to leave the very ground and foundation of judgments inarticulate, and often unconscious, as I have said. When socialism first began to be talked about, ♦♦1000 the comfortable classes of the community were a good deal frightened. I suspect that this fear has influenced judicial action both here and in England, yet it is certain that it is not a conscious factor in the decisions to which I refer. I think that something similar has led people who no longer hope to control the legislatures to look to the courts as expounders of the Consti-♦468 tutions, and that in some courts new principles have been discovered outside the bodies of those instruments, which may be generalized into acceptance of the economic doctrines which prevailed about fifty years ago, and a wholesale prohibition of what a tribunal of lawyers does not think about right. I cannot but believe that if the training of lawyers led them habitually to consider more definitely and explicitly the social advantage on which the rule they lay down must be justified, they sometimes would hesitate where now they are confident, and see that really they were taking sides upon debatable and often burning questions.

So much for the fallacy of logical form. Now let ✦✦✦**185** us consider the present condition of the law as a subject for study, and the ideal toward which it tends. We still are far from the point of view which I desire to see reached. No one has reached it or can reach it as yet. We are only at the beginning of a philosophical reaction, and of a reconsideration of the worth of doctrines which for the most part still are taken for granted without any deliberate, conscious, and systematic questioning of their grounds. The development of our law has gone on for nearly a thousand years, like the development of a plant, each generation taking the inevitable next step, mind, like matter, simply obeying a law of spontaneous growth. It is perfectly natural and right that it should have been so. Imitation is a necessity of human nature, as has been illustrated by a remarkable French writer, M. Tarde, in an admirable book, "Les Lois de l'Imitation." Most of the things we do, we do for no better reason than that our fathers have done them or that our neighbors do them, and the same is true of a larger part than we suspect of what we think. The reason is a good one, because our short life gives us no time for a better, but it is not the best. It does not ✦✦✦✦**399** follow, because we all are compelled to take on faith at second hand most of the rules on which we base our action and our thought, that each of us may not try to set some corner of his world in the order of reason, or that all of us collectively should not aspire to carry reason as far as it will go throughout the whole domain. In regard to the law, it is true, no doubt, that an evo- ✦✦✦**186** lutionist will hesitate to affirm universal validity for his social ideals, or for the principles which he thinks should be embodied in legislation. He is content if he can prove them best for here and now. He may be ready to admit that he knows nothing about an absolute best in the cosmos, and even that he knows next to nothing ✦**469** about a permanent best for men. Still it is true that a body of law is more rational and more civilized when every rule ✦✦**1001** it contains is referred articulately and definitely to an end which it subserves, and when the grounds for desiring that end are stated or are ready to be stated in words.

At present, in very many cases, if we want to know why a rule of law has taken its particular shape, and more or less if we want to know why it exists at all, we go to tradition. We follow it into the Year Books, and perhaps beyond them to the customs of the Salian Franks, and somewhere in the past, in the German forests, in the needs of Norman kings, in the assumptions of a dominant class, in the absence of generalized ideas, we find out the practical motive for what now best is justified by the mere fact of its acceptance and that men are accustomed to it. The rational study of law is still to a large extent the study of history. History must be a part of the study, because without it we cannot know the precise scope of rules which it is our business to know. It is a part of the rational study, because it is the first step toward an enlightened scepticism, that is, toward a deliberate reconsidera- ✦✦✦**187** tion of the worth of those rules. When you get the dragon out of his cave on to the plain and in the daylight, you can count his teeth and claws, and see just what is his strength. But to get him out is only the first step. The next is either to kill him, or to tame him and make him a useful animal. For the rational study of the law the black-letter man may be the man of the present, but the man of the future is the man of statistics and the master of economics. It is revolting to have no better reason for a rule of law than that so it was laid down in the time of Henry IV. It is still more revolting if the grounds upon which it was laid down have vanished long since, and the rule simply persists from blind imitation of the past. I am thinking of the technical rule as to trespass *ab initio,* as it is called, which I attempted to explain in a recent Massachusetts case.[1]

Let me take an illustration, which can be stated in a few words, to show how the social end which is aimed at by a rule of law is obscured and only partially attained in consequence of the fact that the rule owes its form to a gradual historical development, instead of being reshaped as a whole, with conscious articulate reference to the end in view. We think it desirable to prevent one man's property being misappropriated by another, and so we make larceny a crime. The evil is the same whether the misappropriation is made by a man into whose hands the owner has put the property, or by one who wrongfully takes it away. But primitive law in its weakness did not get much beyond an effort to prevent violence, and very naturally made a wrongful taking, a trespass, part of its definition of the crime. In modern times the judges enlarged the definition a little by holding that, if the wrongdoer gets possession by a trick or device, the crime is committed. This really was giving up the requirement of a trespass, and it would have been more logical, as well as truer to the present object of the law, to abandon the requirement altogether. That, however, would have seemed too bold, and was left to statute. Statutes were passed making embezzlement a crime. But the force of tradition caused the crime of embezzlement to be regarded as so far distinct from larceny that to this day, in some jurisdictions at least, a slip corner is kept open for thieves to contend, if indicted for larceny, that they should have been indicted for embezzlement, and if indicted for embezzlement, that they should have been indicted for larceny, and to escape on that ground.

Far more fundamental questions still await a better answer than that we do as our fathers have done. What have we better than a blind guess to show that the criminal law in its present form does more good than harm? I do not stop to refer to the effect which it has had in degrading prisoners and in plunging them further into crime, or to the question whether fine and imprisonment do not fall more heavily on a criminal's wife and children than on himself. I have in mind more far-reaching questions. Does punishment deter? Do we deal with criminals on proper principles? A modern school of Continental criminalists plumes itself on the formula, first suggested, it is said, by Gall, that we must consider the criminal rather than the crime. The formula does not carry us very

---

[1] *Commonwealth v. Rubin,* a 165 Mass. 453.

far, but the inquiries which have been started look toward an answer of my questions based on science for the first time. If the typical criminal is a degenerate, bound to swindle or to murder by as deep seated an organic necessity as that which makes the rattlesnake bite, it is idle to talk of deterring him by the classical method of imprisonment. He must be got rid of; he cannot be improved, or frightened out of his structural reaction. If, on the other hand, crime, like normal human conduct, is mainly a matter of imitation, punishment fairly may be ✦471 expected to help to keep it out of fashion. The study of criminals has been thought by some well known men of science to sustain the former hypothesis. The statistics of the relative increase of crime in crowded places like large cities, where example has the greatest chance to work, and in less populated parts, where the contagion spreads more slowly, have been used with great force in favor of the latter view. But there is weighty authority for the belief that, however this may be, "not the nature of the crime, but the dangerousness of the criminal, constitutes the only reasonable legal criterion to guide the inevitable social reaction against the criminal."[1]

✦✦✦190 The impediments to rational generalization, which I illustrated from the law of larceny, are shown in the other branches of the law, as well as in that of crime. Take the law of tort or civil liability for damages apart from contract and the like. Is there any general theory ✦✦1003 of such liability, or are the cases in which it exists simply to be enumerated, and to be explained each on its special ground, as is easy to believe from the fact that the right of action for certain well known classes of wrongs like ✦✦✦✦401 trespass or slander has its special history for each class? I think that there is a general theory to be discovered, although resting in tendency rather than established and accepted. I think that the law regards the infliction of temporal damage by a responsible person as actionable, if under the circumstances known to him the danger of his act is manifest according to common experience, or according to his own experience if it is more than common, except in cases where upon special grounds of policy the law refuses to protect the plaintiff or grants a privilege to the defendant.[2] I think that commonly malice, intent, and negligence mean only that the danger was manifest to a greater or less degree, under the circumstances known to the actor, although in some cases of privilege malice may mean an actual malevolent motive, ✦✦✦191 and such a motive may take away a permission knowingly to inflict harm, which otherwise would be granted on this or that ground of dominant public good. But when I stated my view to a very eminent English judge the other ✦472 day, he said: "You are discussing what the law ought to be; as

---

[1] Havelock Ellis, "The Criminal," 41, citing Garofalo. See also Ferri, "Sociologie Criminelle," passim. Compare Tarde, "La Philosophie Penale."

[2] An example of the law's refusing to protect the plaintiff is when he is interrupted by a stranger in the use of a valuable way, which he has travelled adversely for a week less than the period of prescription. A week later he will have gained a right, but now he is only a trespasser. Examples of privilege I have given already. One of the best is competition in business.

the law is, you must show a right. A man is not liable for negligence unless he is subject to a duty." If our difference was more than a difference in words, or with regard to the proportion between the exceptions and the rule, then, in his opinion, liability for an act cannot be referred to the manifest tendency of the act to cause temporal damage in general as a sufficient explanation, but must be referred to the special nature of the damage, or must be derived from some special circumstances outside of the tendency of the act, for which no generalized explanation exists. I think that such a view is wrong, but it is familiar, and I dare say generally is accepted in England.

Everywhere the basis of principle is tradition, to such an extent that we even are in danger of making the role of history more important than it is. The other day Professor Ames wrote a learned article to show, among other things, that the common law did not recognize the defence of fraud in actions upon specialties, and the moral might seem to be that the personal character of that defence is due to its equitable origin. But if, as I have said, all contracts are formal, the difference is not merely historical, but theoretic, between defects of form ✦✦✦**192** which prevent a contract from being made, and mistaken motives which manifestly could not be considered in any system that we should call rational except against one who was privy to those mo- ✦✦**1004** tives. It is not confined to specialties, but is of universal application. I ought to add that I do not suppose that Mr. Ames would disagree with what I suggest.

However, if we consider the law of contract, we find it full of history. The distinctions between debt, covenant, and assumpsit are merely historical. The classification of certain obligations to pay money, imposed by the law irrespective of any bargain as quasi contracts, is merely historical. The doctrine of consideration is merely historical. The effect given to a seal is to be explained by history alone. – Consideration is a mere form. Is it a useful form? If so, why should it not be required in all contracts? A seal is a mere form, and is vanishing in the scroll and in enactments that a consideration must be given, seal or no seal. – Why should any merely historical distinction be allowed to affect the rights and obligations of business men?

✦✦✦✦**402** Since I wrote this discourse I have come on a very good example of the way in which tradition not only overrides rational policy, but ✦**473** overrides it after first having been misunderstood and having been given a new and broader scope than it had when it had a meaning. It is the settled law of England that a material alteration of a written contract by a party avoids it as against him. The doctrine is contrary to the general tendency of the law. ✦✦✦**193** We do not tell a jury that if a man ever has lied in one particular he is to be presumed to lie in all. Even if a man has tried to defraud, it seems no sufficient reason for preventing him from proving the truth. Objections of like nature in general go to the weight, not to the admissibility, of evidence. Moreover, this rule is irrespective of fraud, and is not confined to evidence. It is not merely that you cannot use the writing, but that the contract is at an end. What does this mean? The existence of a written contract depends on the fact that the offerer and offeree have interchanged their written expressions, not on the continued existence of those expressions. But in the case of a bond the primitive notion was different. The contract was inseparable from the parchment. If a stranger destroyed it, or tore off the seal, or altered it, the obligee could not recover, however free from fault, because the defendant's contract, that is, the actual tangible bond which he had sealed, could not be produced in the form in which it bound him. About a hundred years ago Lord Kenyon undertook to use his reason on this tradition, as he sometimes did to the detriment of the law, and, not understanding it, said he could see no reason why what was true of a bond should not be true of other contracts. His decision happened to be right, as it concerned a promissory note, where again the common law regarded the contract as inseparable from the paper on which it was written, but the reasoning was general, and soon was extended to other written contracts, and various ab- 194 surd and unreal grounds of policy were invented to account for the enlarged rule.

1005 I trust that no one will understand me to be speaking with disrespect of the law, because I criticise it so freely. I venerate the law, and especially our system of law, as one of the vastest products of the human mind. No one knows better than I do the countless number of great intellects that have spent themselves in making some addition or improvement, the greatest of which is trifling when compared with the mighty whole. It has the final title to respect that it exists, that it is not a Hegelian dream, but a part of the lives of men. But one may criticise even what one reveres. Law is the business to which my life is devoted, and I should 474 show less than devotion if I did not do what in me lies to improve it, and, when I perceive what seems to me the ideal of its future, if I hesitated to point it out and to press toward it with all my heart.

Perhaps I have said enough to show the part which the study of history necessarily plays in the intelligent study of the law as it is to-day. In the teaching of this school and at Cambridge it is in no danger of being undervalued. Mr. Bigelow here and Mr. Ames and Mr. Thayer there have made important contributions which will not be forgotten, and in England the recent history of early English law by Sir Frederick Pollock and Mr. Maitland has lent the subject an almost deceptive charm. We must beware of the pitfall of antiquarianism, and must remember that for our purposes our only interest in 195 the past is for the light it throws upon the present. I look forward to a time when the part played by history in the explanation of dogma 403 shall be very small, and instead of ingenious research we shall spend our energy on a study of the ends sought to be attained and the reasons for desiring them. As a step toward that ideal it seems to me that every lawyer ought to seek an understanding of economics. The present divorce between the schools of political economy and law seems to me an evidence of how much progress in philosophical study still remains to be made. In the present state of political economy, indeed, we come again upon history on a larger scale, but there we are called on to consider and weigh the ends of legislation, the means of attaining them, and the cost. We learn that for everything we have to give up something else, and we are taught to set the advantage we gain against the other advantage we lose, and to know what we are doing when we elect.

There is another study which sometimes is undervalued by the practical minded, for which I wish to say a good word, although I think a good deal of pretty poor stuff goes under that name. I mean the study of what is called jurisprudence. Jurisprudence, as I look at it, is simply law in its most generalized part. Every effort to reduce a case to a rule is an effort of jurisprudence, although the name as used in English is confined to the broadest rules and most fundamental conceptions. One mark of a great lawyer is that he sees the application of the broadest rules. There is a story of a Vermont justice of the peace before whom a suit was brought by one farmer against another for breaking a churn. The justice took time to consider, and then said that he had looked through the statutes and could find nothing about churns, and gave judgment for the defendant. The same state of mind is shown in all our common digests and text-books. Applications of rudimentary rules of contract or tort are tucked away under the head of Railroads or Telegraphs or go to swell treatises on historical subdivisions, such as Shipping or Equity, or are gathered under an arbitrary title which is thought likely to appeal to the practical mind, such as Mercantile Law. If a man goes into law it pays to be a master of it, and to be a master of it means to look straight through all the dramatic incidents and to discern the true basis for prophecy. Therefore, it is well to have an accurate notion of what you mean by law, by a right, by a duty, by malice, intent, and negligence, by ownership, by possession, and so forth. I have in my mind cases in which the highest courts seem to me to have floundered because they had no clear ideas on some of these themes. I have illustrated their importance already. If a further illustration is wished, it may be found by reading the Appendix to Sir James Stephen's Criminal Law on the subject of possession, and then turning to Pollock and Wright's enlightened book. Sir James Stephen is not the only writer whose attempts to analyze legal ideas have been confused by striving for a useless quintessence of all systems, instead of an accurate anatomy of one. The trouble with Austin was that he did not know enough English law. But still it is a practical advantage to master Austin, and his predecessors, Hobbes and Bentham, and his worthy successors, Holland and Pollock. Sir Frederick Pollock's recent little book is touched with the felicity which marks all his works, and is wholly free from the perverting influence of Roman models.

The advice of the elders to young men is very apt to be as unreal as a list of the hundred best books. At least in my day I had my share of such counsels, and high among the unrealities I place the recommendation to study the Roman law. I assume that such advice means more than collecting a few Latin maxims with which to ornament the discourse, – the purpose for which Lord Coke recommended Bracton. If that is all that is wanted, the title "De Regulis

Juris Antiqui" can be read in an hour. I assume that, if it is well to study the Roman law, it is well to study it as a working system. That means mastering a set of technicalities more difficult and less understood than our own, and studying another course of history by which even more than our own the Roman law must be explained. If any one doubts me, let him read Keller's "Der Römische Civil Process und die Actionen," a treatise on the praetor's edict, Muirhead's most interesting "Historical Introduction to the Private Law of Rome," and, to give him the best chance possible, Sohm's admirable Institutes. No. The way to gain a liberal view of your subject is not to read something else, but to get to the bottom of the subject itself. The means of doing that are, in the first place, to follow the existing body of dogma into its highest generalizations by the help of jurisprudence; next, to discover from history how it has come to be what it is; and, finally, so far as you can, to consider the ends which the several rules seek to accomplish, the reasons why those ends are desired, what is given up to gain them, and whether they are worth the price.

We have too little theory in the law rather than too much, especially on this final branch of study. When I was speaking of history, I mentioned larceny as an example to show how the law suffered from not having embodied in a clear form a rule which will accomplish its manifest purpose. In that case the trouble was due to the survival of forms coming from a time when a more limited purpose was entertained. Let me now give an example to show the practical importance, for the decision of actual cases, of understanding the reasons of the law, by taking an example from rules which, so far as I know, never have been explained or theorized about in any adequate way. I refer to statutes of limitation and the law of prescription. The end of such rules is obvious, but what is the justification for depriving a man of his rights, a pure evil as far as it goes, in consequence of the lapse of time? Sometimes the loss of evidence is referred to, but that is a secondary matter. Sometimes the desirability of peace, but why is peace more desirable after twenty years than before? It is increasingly likely to come without the aid of legislation. Sometimes it is said that, if a man neglects to enforce his rights, he cannot complain if, after a while, the law follows his example. Now if this is all that can be said about it, you probably will decide a case I am going to put, for the plaintiff; if you take the view which I shall suggest, you possibly will decide it for the defendant. A man is sued for trespass upon land, and justifies under a right of way. He proves that he has used the way openly and adversely for twenty years, but it turns out that the plaintiff had granted a license to a person whom he reasonably supposed to be the defendant's agent, although not so in fact, and therefore had assumed that the use of the way was permissive, in which case no right would be gained. Has the defendant gained a right or not? If his gaining it stands on the fault and neglect of the landowner in the ordinary sense, as seems commonly to be supposed, there has been no such neglect, and the right of way has not been acquired. But if I were the defendant's counsel, I should suggest that the foundation of the acquisition of rights by lapse of time is to be looked for in the position of the person who gains them, not in that of the loser. Sir Henry Maine has made it fashionable to connect the archaic notion of property with prescription. But the connection is further back than the first recorded history. It is in the nature of man's mind. A thing which you have enjoyed and used as your own for a long time, whether property or an opinion, takes root in your being and cannot be torn away without your resenting the act and trying to defend yourself, however you came by it. The law can ask no better justification than the deepest instincts of man. It is only by way of reply to the suggestion that you are disappointing the former owner, that you refer to his neglect having allowed the gradual dissociation between himself and what he claims, and the gradual association of it with another. If he knows that another is doing acts which on their face show that he is on the way toward establishing such an association, I should argue that in justice to that other he was bound at his peril to find out whether the other was acting under his permission, to see that he was warned, and, if necessary, stopped.

I have been speaking about the study of the law, and I have said next to nothing of what commonly is talked about in that connection, – text-books and the case system, and all the machinery with which a student comes most immediately in contact. Nor shall I say anything about them. Theory is my subject, not practical details. The modes of teaching have been improved since my time, no doubt, but ability and industry will master the raw material with any mode. Theory is the most important part of the dogma of the law, as the architect is the most important man who takes part in the building of a house. The most important improvements of the last twenty-five years are improvements in theory. It is not to be feared as unpractical, for, to the competent, it simply means going to the bottom of the subject. For the incompetent, it sometimes is true, as has been said, that an interest in general ideas means an absence of particular knowledge. I remember in army days reading of a youth who, being examined for the lowest grade and being asked a question about squadron drill, answered that he never had considered the evolutions of less than ten thousand men. But the weak and foolish must be left to their folly. The danger is that the able and practical minded should look with indifference or distrust upon ideas the connection of which with their business is remote. I heard a story, the other day, of a man who had a valet to whom he paid high wages, subject to deduction for faults. One of his deductions was, "For lack of imagination, five dollars." The lack is not confined to valets. The object of ambition, power, generally presents itself nowadays in the form of money alone. Money is the most immediate form, and is a proper object of desire. "The fortune," said Rachel, "is the measure of the intelligence." That is a good text to waken people out of a fool's paradise. But, as Hegel says,[1] "It is in the end not the appetite, but the

---

[1] Phil. des Rechts, § 190.

opinion, which has to be satisfied." To an imagination of any scope the most far-reaching form of power is not money, it is the command of ideas. If you want great examples read Mr. Leslie Stephen's "History of English Thought in the Eighteenth Century," and see how a hundred years after his death the abstract speculations of Descartes had become a practical force controlling the conduct of men. Read the works of the great German jurists, and see how much more the world is governed to-day by Kant than by Bonaparte. We cannot all be Descartes or Kant, but we all want happiness. And happiness, I am sure from having known many successful men, cannot be won simply by being counsel for great corporations and having an income of fifty thousand dollars. An intellect great enough to win the prize needs other food beside success. The remoter and more general aspects of the law are those which give it universal interest. It is through them that you not only become a great master in your calling, but connect your subject with the universe and catch an echo of the infinite, a glimpse of its unfathomable process, a hint of the universal law.

Index

Adams, Charles Francis, Jr., 25
Adams, Henry, 27
adjudication, *see* judging
Alcott, Louisa May, 7
Aquinas, Thomas, 51, 56
Aristotle, 54, 56, 60, 65, 66, 75
Auden, W. H., 239
Aurelius, Marcus, 51
Austin, John, 137, 160, 178, 183–184, 190, 265, 347

bad man, the, 3, 14, 36–44, 46, 159, 160, 161–168, 168–176, 178–179, 197 *et seq.*, 211 *et seq.*, 224–227, 234–237
   see also prediction theory of law
Baier, Annette, 52, 56, 65, 68
Balkin, J. M., 234
Becker, Gary, 307, 309, 310
Beerbohm, Max, 28
Benson, Lloyd, 328
Bentham, Jeremy, 20, 56, 65, 89, 160, 218
   see also utilitarianism
Bierce, Ambrose, 44
Blackstone, Sir William, 137, 144
Blaug, Mark, 304
Brandeis, Louis D., 25–26, 44
Brecht, Bertold, 239
Bromage v. Genning, 337
Brougham, Lord, 9
Brunner, Heinrich, 19
Burger, Warren, 256

Cahill, Robert, 88–91
character, 8–11
Choate, Rufus, 10
Cicero, 60, 61–62, 66–67, 71, 77–78, 291–292
coercion, 333
Cohen, Morris R., 239
Constitution, U.S., 12, 23, 335, 341
contract, 3, 26, 337, 338–339, 345, 346
crimes, 343, 344
critical legal studies, 2
"cynical acid," 3, 337

Darwin, Charles, 17
Debs, Eugene V., 240
Descartes, René, 27
Dewey, John, 52
Diamond, Cora, 52–53, 56, 65, 68, 70, 75
duty, legal, 3, 37, 39–40, 158–159, 181–185, 334, 336, 344–345
Dworkin, Ronald, 53, 123, 160, 188, 191, 287, 297–301

economics, 24, 278 *et seq.*, 285 *et seq.*, 343, 327 *et seq.*
   law and, 2, 20, 42, 246, 298, 301–310
education, legal, *see* law, study of
Einstein, Lewis, 232
Elster, Jon, 175
Emerson, Ralph Waldo, 225, 231 *et seq.*
ethical theory
   attacks on, 51–55, 63

ethical theory *(continued)*
  concrete judgments and, 53
  emotions and, 88, 144
  general criteria for, 53, 55–59
  Holmes and, 53–54, 87
  law and, 53–54
  need for, 53, 69–79
  objections to, 64–69
  particularism and, *see* legal reasoning, particularism and
  pragmatism and, 213–220
  rules and, 53, 59, 60–64
  social norms and, 87–91
ethics, *see* law, morality and *and* profession, legal

Ferguson, Robert, 240
Foucault, Michel, 295
Frank, Jerome, 298, 312, 326
Frankfurter, Felix, 36, 151, 239
Freud, Sigmund, 295, 301, 309, 310, 312
Friedman, Milton, 304
Fuller, Lon, 123

Gentili, Alberico, 62
Gilmore, Grant, 240
Gray, John Chipman, 184, 189
Greenleaf, Simon, 9
Grotius, Hugo de, 51, 55, 62, 71, 77–78
Guthrie, W. K. C., 291

Habermas, Jürgen, 287, 292–295
Hadley, A.T., 302
Hale, Sir Matthew, 70–71
Hampton, Jack, 87–91
happiness, 350
Hart, H. L. A., 38, 89, 135, 160 *et seq.*, 197 *et seq.*
Hausman, Daniel, 309, 310
Hegel, G. W. F., 16, 66
Herbert, George, 16
history, 12, 19–20, 342–343, 345, 346
  see also tradition
Hobbes, Thomas, 160, 172–173, 175–176, 191–192
Hohfield, Wesley N., 151
Horwitz, Morton, 303–304

Hovenkamp, Herbert, 301
Hume, David, 51, 56, 66, 295
Hypatia, 51

ideas, 350
imagination, 6, 349–350
internal point of view, 161 *et seq.*, 197 *et seq.*

Jackson, Joseph, 9
James, Henry, 25, 64, 70
James, William, 160, 211 *et seq.*, 231
judging, 17–18, 185–190, 263–270
  see also precedent
judgment, 340
jurisprudence, 158–161, 170–171, 191, 346–350
  see also theory of law

Kahan, Marcel, 259
Kant, Immanuel, 27, 50, 51, 53, 55, 56, 60, 61, 62, 65, 66, 70, 70–71, 73–77, 294, 295–297
Kelsen, Hans, 197, 204–205, 206, 207
Kent, James, 144
King, Martin Luther, Jr., 90
Klausner, Michael, 259
Kronman, Anthony, 249

Langdell, Cristopher Columbus, 2, 19, 94, 133, 137, 139, 146, 148, 187, 211
language, legal, 40–42, 137
Laski, Harold, 232, 300
law
  causes of, 247, 339–41
  determinacy and, 137, 139–140
  development of, 339–341, 342
  functions of, 168–177
  growth of, 2, 3–4, 339–341, 342
  limits of, 334–339
  morality and, 2–3, 11, 19, 37–43, 95, 96–97, 185–190, 221, 334–339
    (*see also* law, normativity of)
  normativity of, 2–3, 5, 168–176, 187, 204–207 (*see also* law, morality and)

practice of, *see* law, vocation of *and* profession, legal
as predictions, *see* prediction theory of law
preferences and, 136–138
sanctions and, 197, 208–209
skepticism about, 2–4, 124
sources of, 339–41, 347–48
study of, 5–6, 33, 333, 335, 336, 341, 342–347, 349
theory of, *see* theory of law
universal, 35–36, 350
veneration of, 346
vocation of, 5, 7–32, 33–34, 45–46
legal feminism, 87
legal formalism, 138–140
legal orthodoxy, *see* legal formalism
legal positivism, 168–176, 181, 186, 199, 211–212, 221, 235
legal pragmatism, 87, 136–138, 188, 220–224
  see also ethical theory, pragmatism and
legal realism, 2, 4, 20, 144, 180, 211, 297–301
legal reasoning
  particularism and, 87–91, 144–147
  pretheory, and, 89–90
  theory and, 88–91, 170–171 (*see also* ethical theory)
  see also logic
legislation, judicial, 141–144, 149, 187–189
Lindblom, Charles, 287–288
Llewelyn, Karl N., 87, 298–299, 326
logic, 2, 4, 11–12, 94–126, 133–134, 159, 221–222, 339–42
  abduction, 109–116
  analogy, 116–120, 147–150
  anti-logic thesis, 94–98
  conceptual analysis and, 135–136, 148
  deduction, 120–123
  easy cases and, 140–144
  enthememe, 105–106,
  five senses of, 99–103
  induction, 106–109
  inference, logical, 105
  justification, in, 123–124
  see also legal formalism
logical positivism, 199–200, 202
Lucas, Robert, 304

Machiavelli, Nicoló, 286, 287, 291–292, 309, 312
MacIntyre, Alisdair, 52, 68
MacKinnon, Catharine, 55, 78
Maitland, F. W., 19
Marx, Karl, 288, 292–295, 300, 309, 310, 326
Matthiessen, F. O., 238
Mill, John Stuart, 20, 50, 56, 66, 70, 72, 75, 78–79, 123, 218
  see also utilitarianism
Miller, Perry, 10
morality, *see* ethical theory *and* law, morality and

Nansen, Fridtjof, 234
Nero, 51
Nietzsche, Friedrich, 18, 234, 285, 289–291, 292, 309, 312, 326

Obligation, 163
  see also duty, legal

Parmenides, 63
path of legal doctrine, 245 *et seq.*, 339
Peirce, Charles Sanders, 110, 150, 160, 213, 214
perspectivism, 217–218, 226
Plato, 289–291
policy, 13, 17–24, 34, 340–341, 348–349
Pollock, Frederick, 172, 178, 184, 265
positivism, legal, 13, 37–42
Posner, Richard, 218, 237, 246–247, 285–286, 299, 301, 302–303, 305–307, 309, 311, 312, 326, 328, 330
pragmatism, *see* ethical theory, pragmatism and *and* legal pragmatism
precedent, 245 *et seq.*
  judicial discretion and, 253–257

precedent *(continued)*
  path dependence and, 258–263, 261–263
  prospectivity and, 257
  scope of, 253–258
  see also judging
prediction theory of law, 5, 13–14, 95–96, 161–168, 177–185, 202–203, 222, 246, 333–35, 347
  see also bad man
principle, 345
profession, legal, 14–16, 16–24, 34–35, 44
prudence, 165–166, 171–174, 201, 334
punishment, 343–344

Quine, W. V. O., 294, 310

Rawls, John, 54–55, 56, 75, 123, 287, 294
Raz, Joseph, 123, 160, 171, 186, 187, 191–192
realism, classical, 285 *et seq.*
  defined, 286–289, 326
reason, 339, 164, 167
  see also legal reasoning
reform, legal, 21, 95, 97–98
rights, legal, 3, 16, 158–159, 182–185, 334, 344–345
Roman law, 8, 347–348
Rosenberg, Alexander, 306, 307–308
Ross, Alf, 197, 202–203
Rousseau, Jean-Jacques, 51
rule of recognition, 163, 164, 171, 188
rules, 206
  see also ethical theory, rules and *and* social rules
Russell, Bertrand, 52

Santayana, George, 27
Santayana, James, 27
Schopenhauer, Arthur, 295–297
science, 8, 15–16, 18–24, 27, 285 *et seq.*, 327 *et seq.*

Seneca, 50, 53, 59, 60–61, 64, 71, 79, 292
Shattuck, George Otis, 35
Sidgwick, Henry, 56, 59, 65, 66
  see also utilitarianism
Siepp, David, 224, 335
Simon, William, 34
Smith, Adam, 56, 66, 75
social advantage, *see* policy
social rules, 163
Socrates, 51, 63, 75, 76
Spencer, Herbert, 13, 23, 146
Stevens, Wallace, 13
Stigler, George, 304
Stoics, the, 53, 56, 63, 66, 72
Storey, Moorfield, 25, 26, 44
Sumner, Charles, 25

theory, 344, 345, 348–50
  see also ethical theory
theory of law, 13, 159–161, 164–165, 180, 190, 197–200, 208–209
Thornburgh, Richard, 37, 39
Thucydides, 286, 289–291, 292, 293, 300, 326
Toqueville, Alexis de, 24
torts, 341
tradition, 5, 12, 16, 246 *et seq.*, 342–345
  see also history

utilitarianism, 20–21, 54, 59, 65, 136, 141

vocation of law, *see* law, vocation of *and* profession, legal
vocational address, 7–11, 12, 33, 37
Voltaire, 51

Whicher, Stephen, 238
White, G. Edward, 1, 18, 232
Williams, Bernard, 52, 54–55, 56, 65, 68, 69–70, 77, 79

Zane, John M., 2